HOUSING, COMMUNITY AND CONFLICT:
UNDERSTANDING RESIDENT 'INVOLVEMENT'

Housing, Community and Conflict:

Understanding resident 'involvement'

Edited by Charlie Cooper and Murray Hawtin

arena

Published by
Arena
Ashgate Publishing Limited
Gower House
Croft Road
Aldershot
Hants GU11 3HR
England

Ashgate Publishing Company
Old Post Road
Brookfield
Vermont 05036
USA

British Library Cataloguing in Publication Data
Housing, community and conflict: understanding resident 'involvement'
  1. Public housing – Citizen participation
  I. Cooper, Charlie II. Hawtin, Murray
  363.5'85

Library of Congress Cataloging-in-Publication Data
Housing community and conflict : understanding resident 'involvement' / edited by
  Charlie Cooper and Murray Hawtin.
    p.   cm.
  Includes index.
  ISBN 1–85742–341–0 (cloth)
  1. Self-help housing– Great Britain. 2. Shared housing–Great Britain.
  3. Housing management–Great Britain. I. Cooper, Charlie, 1952–   . II. Hawtin,
  Murray, 1953–   .
  HD7333.A3H683   1997
  363.5—DC21   97–12472
                                                                        CIP

ISBN 1–85742–341–0

Typeset in Palatino by Bournemouth Colour Press, Poole and printed and bound in Great Britain by MPG Books Ltd, Bodmin, Cornwall

Contents

List of figures and tables

Figures

Tables

Notes on contributors

Bo Bengtsson is Senior Lecturer in Political Science and Housing Policy at the Institute for Housing Research at Uppsala University in Gävle, Sweden. He has done research on housing policy, housing organizations, tenant participation and co-operative housing, and has published several books and articles on these subjects.

Johnston Birchall is Lecturer in Public Policy at Brunel University. He has experience as a community worker and housing association manager putting tenant participation into practice. He originated and helped set up the National Certificate in Tenant Participation. His publications include *What Makes People Co-operate?, Building Communities: The Co-operative Way* and an edited book *Housing Policy in the 1990s*.

David Clapham is Professor of Housing and Director of the Centre for Housing Management and Development at the University of Wales, Cardiff. He has undertaken research on tenant participation in housing management in Britain and is the co-author of *Housing Co-operatives in Britain* (with Keith Kintrea) and *Housing Management, Consumers and Citizens* (with Liz Cairncross and Robina Goodlad).

Charlie Cooper writes and teaches on a range of housing, social policy and tenant involvement themes at the University of Lincolnshire and Humberside. He has experience as a social worker and housing practitioner with community-based housing collectives. He was involved in developing the National Certificate in Tenant Participation at South Bank University and in Humberside.

Rob Furbey teaches Urban Sociology and Politics at Sheffield Hallam

University. His publications include *The Eclipse of Council Housing*, written with Ian Cole. He has undertaken research for the Joseph Rowntree Foundation on training for tenant participation and contributed to the development of the National Certificate in Tenant Participation in South Yorkshire.

John Grayson teaches Social and Labour History at the Northern College, near Barnsley, and has written teaching material for the National Certificate in Tenant Participation. He has worked for the Workers Education Association, was a councillor for ten years and chaired a housing committee from 1978 to 1980. He has published in the fields of training, adult education and social history, including *Solid Labour*, a history of the Labour Party in Yorkshire.

Murray Hawtin is Senior Policy Analyst in the Policy Research Institute at Leeds Metropolitan University. He is a qualified social worker and practised as a community worker for many years, working mainly with tenants' groups. Working with a large housing authority he helped to develop one of the first estate management boards in the country. He now researches, writes and teaches on a range of housing and tenant participation issues.

Stuart Lowe is Lecturer in Social Policy at the University of York. He has published many books, chapters and articles, most recently *Social Housing Law and Policy* with Professor David Hughes. He is interested in the interface between housing and social policy, housing needs, and housing and social theory. For many years he has studied the development of housing in east and central European societies.

Paul Lusk has worked with tenants' organizations since 1977. He is co-author of *Helping Ourselves* and has written for various housing-related journals. He currently teaches a regular course in 'Housing Futures' at Liverpool John Moores University and is also a consultant working with tenant-controlled housing.

Charles Ritchie is Director of the Community Operational Research Unit at the Northern College. Before joining the Unit he worked for ten years in Operational Research in a number of organizations, including British Coal and the then Department of Health and Social Security. Since moving to the Northern College he has, through the activities of the Unit, worked with a variety of community and housing groups looking to find solutions to organizational, management and financial problems.

Jerry Smith is the Northern Regional Director of the Tenant Participation

Advisory Service. He has worked in the housing and community development field since 1970 and has written extensively on tenant participation, community organizational development and community government. He co-edited *Community and Public Policy* and was a member of the advisory group for the Joseph Rowntree Foundation's 'Action on Estates' programme.

Benita Wishart is Lecturer in Housing at the University of Central England in Birmingham where she teaches on a range of housing courses. She was previously Course Co-ordinator for the National Certificate in Tenant Participation at Sheffield Hallam University. She has been actively involved in tenant participation research and has facilitated a number of workshops for the Tenant Participation Advisory Service. She has also worked with tenants and officers to help establish an Estate Management Board.

1 An introduction to community development and housing

Charlie Cooper and Murray Hawtin

Community involvement has re-emerged in the 1990s as a central component of social and economic renewal strategies in a variety of contexts, from international aid programmes to neighbourhood regeneration schemes (Craig and Mayo 1995). At the same time, more and more people appear to be becoming increasingly disillusioned with the traditional institutions of western liberal democracies and new forms of political action are appearing. Two days before the 1996/97 Global Partnership[1] festival, John Vidal proclaimed that:

> something is happening. There is a feeling – it cannot be measured – that what is fundamental to individual, community and planetary survival is being ignored by the economic forces shaping our societies; that our priorities are awry; and that people everywhere are being denied democracy, commonsense and generosity of spirit. There is a sense that politicians are not listening or are unable to act and that remote, unaccountable, globalized corporations are value-free ... As governments absent themselves from social leadership and the power of the unaccountable increases, so civil society emerges from the bottom, hungry for global justice and radical social change. (Vidal 1996 p.1)

In industrialized countries, political and economic change has resulted in the withdrawal of state responsibility for a number of welfare and economic development programmes. Obligations once perceived to be public liabilities have increasingly become the concern of individuals, their families, the voluntary sector or community action. In Britain, central government, local authorities and 'quangos' are increasingly adopting community-oriented policies in urban regeneration strategies.

[1] Global Partnership is an attempt to influence the political agenda of world states and promote a wider understanding of global issues through co-ordinating the activities of world charities and promoting world music, food and fashion festivals.

1

While the idea of community participation goes back a long way, it only emerged as a 'profession' in Britain in the 1970s – partly in response to concerns about poor practices in state bureaucracies. 'The idea that the poor and oppressed should be mobilized by external agents and encouraged to participate in decision-making for social development at the local level has been formalized and popularized only during the last ten or fifteen years' (Midgley 1986 p.13). In British housing policy, official government support for tenant participation has only been evident since 1980 (see Richardson 1984, Hague 1990, Birchall 1992). Previously, council tenants had gained few legal rights while landlords held powers to impose a range of restrictions on how people lived in their home (Kay *et al.* 1986). Under the first Thatcher administration, tenants were given a number of rights, albeit individual rights, to be involved more in decisions made about their homes and neighbourhoods.

Indeed, as we approach the new millennium, it would seem that we are all communitarians now, 'for community and communitarian are the political buzzwords of the moment: uttered comfortably by David Willetts on the right and Tony Blair on the left' (*The Guardian* 18 February 1995 p.29). The notion of community involvement sits comfortably with the ideology of the libertarian right, with its emphasis on the values of individual responsibility and freedom from the state, as well as the social theory of the libertarian left, which emphasizes the need for collective responsibility and freedom from the state. The fact that community participation can be embraced by such diverse political positions illustrates the flexibility of the concept and its very different meanings, values and conditions. For instance, in housing the concept might anticipate the involvement of tenants as individual consumers *or* as collective citizens, as well as different degrees and levels of decision-making. It may involve state agencies simply informing or consulting residents, or empowering them to control their neighbourhoods. As Arnstein suggests, the concept of community participation remains problematic as its purpose holds different and sometimes contradictory meanings and objectives (Arnstein 1969). Additionally, as McArthur argues, a 'theoretical rationale is developing around community partnership but a number of political, conceptual and practical issues require to be explored before full appreciation of the potential contribution of local residents can be reached' (McArthur 1995 p.61).

Contemporary community-development policies and practices have been largely founded on a weak conceptualization of both the nature of urban problems and the meaning of 'community' itself, as well as a lack of realization (or will) to see the potential of *genuine* community empowerment. Furthermore, much of the current research on community involvement in housing tends to conclude with a shopping list of simple 'ingredients of success'. For instance, the fundamental assumption behind most of the Joseph Rowntree Foundation (JRF) studies on estate regeneration schemes is that action targeted through small-area-based programmes and focused on locally defined needs will generate broader social and economic benefits (see Taylor 1995). However, this assumption ignores (and even disguises) the wider structural context of social, political and economic disempowerment experienced by many inner-city communities. As McArthur suggests, such programmes are being implemented within areas of 'economic decline, persistently high and often rising unemployment, and slack labour market conditions. In this context there are major limitations to what any area regeneration strategy could have achieved in reducing disadvantage without massive expenditure on social measures' (McArthur 1995 p.64). Such 'massive expenditure' will not be forthcoming within the present context of an urban policy agenda dominated by the hegemony of neo-liberal political economy. Furthermore, as Croft and Beresford observe, the current renewed interest in participation has come at a time when the fundamental problems associated with western market economies remain unresolved, including:

> gross inequalities, the concentration of political and economic power, and the failure to reconcile profit and the accumulation of capital with the meeting of need and guaranteeing of people's rights. The market success and rising poverty and material inequality that have been synonymous with Britain in the 1980s are symbolic of this unresolved issue. (Croft and Beresford 1996 p.176)

In addition to the refusal to recognize these structural constraints, urban renewal strategies and research studies have also failed to adopt an adequate conceptualization of 'community'. It is taken as almost axiomatic by urban policy-makers and the JRF studies that 'community' is a homogenous spatial concentration of neighbours. However, as Vernon Clarke's research for the Federation of Black Housing Organizations suggests, neighbourhoods are more likely to be made up of groupings of different interests. In particular, he argues that black households are not participating in mainstream community-development structures, and that this lack of involvement:

> is not a result of apathy amongst black tenants but is due mainly to the exclusion of black households from participation. Exclusion takes the form of blatant refusal to allow black tenants to use community facilities or to gain access to other available resources such as funding, the non-existence of black workers on tenants federations, activities organized from the perception of white tenants which had little appeal to black tenants, and the absence of issues of importance to black households on tenants associations' agendas. (see Cooper 1991 p.4)

What has largely been absent from mainstream debates on community participation in the 1990s has been a rigorous attention to the processes of marginalization structured around 'race', class, gender, disability, age and sexuality. This can be explained largely in terms of the patriarchal and ethnocentric consensus which has dominated the British policy debate on citizenship and community participation. This is perhaps not surprising, as state-sponsored community work in Britain has its 'origins in community development approaches used by the West in the developing world, first to integrate colonial territories and subsequently to support western political and economic objectives there' (Croft and Beresford 1996 p.183).

Recent debates about community participation have rarely attempted to contest the social exclusion of marginalized groups, while participatory schemes in practice have largely 'mirrored rather than challenged broader oppressions and discriminations. The average participant of traditional public participation in planning exercises has been typified as a middle class, middle-aged, able-bodied white man' (Croft and Beresford 1996 p.187). There can be little surprise, therefore, that community participation as a process has been attacked from various sources as a tokenistic means of controlling, placating, treating, manipulating and/or incorporating discontented groups while achieving the legitimation of the state (Arnstein 1969, Croft and Beresford 1990, Dowson 1990). However, despite these limitations and ambiguities, there are strong arguments for supporting the notion of community development as a liberating tool. In addition to the practical benefits of achieving greater efficiencies through synergy, community development does have the potential to achieve greater accountability and democracy in the way people's life experiences are determined. How this might be achieved is the main purpose of this book.

While the emphasis is on community development in housing and, more specifically, tenant involvement, we recognize that issues common to this theme are mirrored throughout the social policy field. Therefore, issues common to tenant involvement are directly applicable to other areas – for instance welfare, urban regeneration, town planning, education, health and leisure are notable fields which are concerned with user participation. However, it is within *housing* that participation structures and methods are arguably most developed and, subsequently, from which meaningful lessons can be drawn for other social policy disciplines.

Before outlining the scope of this book we take a look at what is meant by 'community development'. The Association of Metropolitan Authorities (AMA) defines community development as 'a way in which a local authority deliberately stimulates and encourages groups of people to express their needs, supports them in their collective action and helps with their projects and schemes as part of an authority's overall objectives' (AMA 1993 p.10). These objectives should include giving people the opportunity to influence and assert control over social, economic and political issues affecting them, encouraging people to take initiatives in responding to problems, and confronting attitudes and practices which discriminate against particular sections of the community (AMA 1993). A similar definition is offered by the Association of District Councils (ADC), which sees community development as central to the 'enabling vision' of district councils (ADC 1994).

The Association of Community Workers (ACW) adopts a more radical view of community development which is founded on the belief that the 'organization and structure of society cause problems of powerlessness, alienation and inequality' (Harris 1994, Section 3 p.1). It defines community development as:

> crucially concerned with the issues of powerlessness and disadvantage: as such it should involve all members of society, and offers a practice that is part of a process of social change. Community Development is about the active involvement of people in the issues which affect their lives. It is a process based on the sharing of power, skills, knowledge, and experience. (Harris 1994, Section 3 p.3)

Twelvetrees (1991) categorizes a number of different approaches to working with communities. He identifies *radical community work*, where the accent is on tackling local problems by changing social relationships with the aid of *community development*, emphasizing 'bottom-up' non-directive approaches to problem solving where the paid 'professional' is seen as an advocate or facilitator, while the unpaid activists in the 'community' determine the direction of community action. This is the approach advocated by the ACW, which argues that community development should seek to 'enable individuals and communities to grow and change according to their own needs and priorities, and at their own pace, provided this does not oppress other groups and communities, or damage the environment' (Harris 1994, Section 3 p.3). Twelvetrees contrasts radical community work with *professional community work*, where the emphasis is on *social planning* and usually involves the community worker adopting a 'top-down' directive approach, working largely to an agenda set by the service provider. The existing social structures and balance of power remain unchallenged. Professional community work is perhaps the most widespread, particularly in housing departments, but it is an approach which the ACW opposes. It argues that the community worker must avoid imposing 'their own or their employing agencies' concealed ideologies or methods of work' so that people can 'develop their own leadership and ability to speak for themselves' (Harris 1994, Section 3 p.2).

Community work can also involve different strategic approaches. Twelvetrees identifies *self-help strategies*, which aim to utilize existing resources within the 'community' (such as local skills, knowledge, labour or finance) to tackle local problems, which he contrasts with *influence strategies*, where the focus is more on campaigning to change government policy or to attract inward investment. These strategies might usefully be combined. The ACW suggests that the aims and objectives of community work should include both 'seeking to influence statutory, voluntary and private organizations and make them more responsive to … the needs and demands of community groups' and 'supporting community groups to run mutual aid projects' (Harris 1994, Section 3 p.1). The role of the community worker within these strategic approaches might either be *generic*, where the worker is able to address a wide range of community issues, or *specialist*, where the worker is tied to a specific agency usually concerned with a single issue (such as a housing department or social services). The causes of disadvantage in communities are multifarious (see Jerry Smith in Chapter 7); as such, community groups will be concerned with a wide range of social, political, economic and environmental issues. Community development therefore needs to adopt a holistic approach to regeneration, requiring the community worker to take on a generic role.

Twelvetrees distinguishes between community work as a *process*, where the emphasis is on developing people's confidence and abilities, and community work as a *product*, where the focus is more on achieving concrete changes in a locality, such as improvements in the physical environment or a reduction in crime. The ACW stresses that 'the experience of the process enhances the integrity, skills, knowledge and experience, as well as the equality of power, for each individual who is involved' (Harris 1994, Section 3 p.3). In practice, Twelvetrees suggests that both foci might operate simultaneously.

Twelvetrees also states that community work can be perceived as an *attitude* or an *approach*. As an attitude, community workers hold on to the belief that communities themselves need to be empowered to overcome local problems. This is the conviction held by the ACW, which suggests:

> Where Community Development takes place, there are certain principles central to it. The first priority of the Community Development process is the empowering and enabling of those who are traditionally deprived of power and control over their common affairs. It claims as important the ability of people to act together to influence the social, economic, political and environmental issues which affect them. Community Development aims to encourage sharing, and to create structures which give genuine participation and involvement. (Harris 1994, Section 3 p.3)

Perceived as an approach, community work is viewed as merely a mechanism for treating a problem; as such it can be adopted by a wide range of professionals – community architects, community social workers, community health workers, tenant participation workers and so on.

Twelvetrees contrasts the concept of community as a neighbourhood or *locality* with that of community as *social* (that is, 'communities of interest' based on, for example, 'race', class, gender or disability). As the ACW states, community development 'takes place both in neighbourhoods and within communities of interest' (Harris 1994, Section 3 p.3). Consequently, if community development is to achieve the wider objectives of tackling social exclusion and confronting oppression, it is crucial to establish the nature of the community concerned and the issues that it sees as important. This can be done through the development of a *community profile* which allows the necessary information to be gathered to identify the characteristics and needs of different interest groups in an area (Hawtin *et al.* 1994). While hard data will be available from official statistics, this can be supplemented with the views of the community obtained through consultation exercises. Once the issues have been identified an analysis of possible courses of action can be made. In practice this analysis will usually be influenced by various factors, including the needs assessment, the community work agency's expectations and objectives, the ideological values of the community worker, the likelihood of success and the motivation of the community.

Having carried out the community profile analysis, and if the potential for community development seems positive, then the community worker will usually look to develop a *steering group* to take the project forward (although some commentators recommend establishing a steering group before the community profile – see Hawtin *et al.* 1994). Initially, forming a steering group may involve some time spent teasing out the concerns of particular individuals, perhaps involving only two or three people, and motivating them to think about what might be done. From these initial contacts the worker can then seek to identify how many other people might share the same concerns. The community worker might encourage the two or three 'initiators' to arrange a first meeting themselves to allow some autonomy from the start. The community worker could then take a back seat role, concentrating on maintaining momentum and focus in group discussions. While the membership of the group may well expand in this way, it is also advisable for the community worker to approach new people to avoid the emergence of an unrepresentative clique.

After a steering group has been established, ideally about six motivated people, the community worker's role can be directed towards facilitating the development of key objectives. This will initially involve getting the group to progress, perhaps from feelings of discontent, to the development of clear aims, identifying tasks and resource needs and allocating roles and responsibilities. Simultaneously, there will be a need to develop a training strategy, aimed at building up the confidence, knowledge and skills base of the group. Twelvetrees suggests two types of skill which are essential for effective community development – *organizational skills* (including analytical and planning skills) and *interactional skills*.

The organizational skills required will include the ability to:

- develop convincing arguments in support of a campaign;
- identify the practicalities of a proposal and the evidence needed to support it;
- understand the best way of presenting an argument or case;
- identify possible support networks;
- predict the likely opposition to the case presented;
- identify the best organizational structure needed to achieve the aims of the campaign;
- identify the necessary resources to achieve a task; and
- organize effective meetings.

The interactional skills needed include the ability to:

- get on with other people and gain their support;
- communicate clearly and simply, avoiding jargon and abstract language;
- be effective at meetings;
- speak at public meetings; and
- be assertive.

At some stage early on in the process, a group will need to legitimize itself by adopting a constitution that is acceptable to the 'community' at large and by establishing a democratic mechanism of accountability. This will involve publicizing the activities of the group through newsletters, personal contact, videos, media coverage and, perhaps, holding public meetings. Once an acceptable constituency has been formed the group will be in a legitimate position to approach and negotiate with 'power-holders'.

In British urban policy, community involvement and tenant participation have mainly been approached in a 'top-down', directive way, largely serving to meet the more limited objectives of the professionals and sponsoring organizations involved. The 'product' has overridden the 'process', while the 'approach' has taken priority over the 'attitude'. Furthermore, the social dimension of 'community' has largely been subordinated to the neighbourhood concept. The more substantive issues of power, self-determination, democratic accountability and equal opportunity – issues of concern to local communities – have largely been neglected. It is our belief that this represents a lost opportunity. Consequently, we would argue that tenant-participation strategies are currently failing to address the wider problems of social, economic and political exclusion faced by many communities in Britain's run-down neighbourhoods. We also suggest that this is because the broader objectives of the community-development approach – that is, to strengthen political and economic representation and to promote equal opportunities through a shift in the balance of power – have been absent from mainstream tenant-participation schemes. This leads us to advocate a broader definition of tenant participation, one that incorporates the principles and values of community development where the notion of 'empowerment' is placed at the centre of the tenant-participation process. We argue that policy-makers and practitioners need to begin to view the term 'tenant participation' as synonymous with 'community development', where community development is:

> about developing the power, skills, knowledge and experience of people as individuals and in groups, thus enabling them to undertake initiatives of their own to combat social, economic, political and environmental problems, and enabling them to fully participate in a truly democratic process. (Harris 1994, Section 3 p.3)

Only then might tenant-participation initiatives begin to remove the barriers to people's personal and collective social and economic development. At certain junctures in the book, therefore, the two terms – 'tenant participation' and 'community development' – are perceived as synonymous and used interchangeably.

The themes of the book

The starting point for our discussion locates tenant participation within its historical context. John Grayson's overview of tenant involvement in Chapter 2 traces the social history of developmental trends in tenant involvement in Britain from 1800 to 1979. The influence of tenant campaigns on housing policy developments has remained largely invisible in accounts of the social history of housing. Grayson redresses this neglect by exploring the hidden history of working-class housing movements organized around wage and rent campaigns. He highlights the link between the origins and development of tenant involvement and the wider social, political and economic struggle between the capitalist class and the working class. He shows how tenant involvement has held different meanings for different people, depending on their relative position in relation to power and wealth. Initially, tenant organizations developed as autonomous working-class movements, struggling to gain reasonable living standards. Since the 1970s we have seen tenant involvement appropriated by the state and professionals as a mechanism for achieving broader social policy aims. Grayson identifies 1979 as a watershed in the history of tenant participation as the Conservatives began to dismantle the central pillar around which many tenant campaigns had been conducted – council housing itself.

In Chapter 3, Paul Lusk takes up the story after 1979. He shows how the early attempts of the Thatcher administrations to include tenant-led stock transfers in their privatization plans were eventually superseded in the 1990s by a more rationed approach to the transfer of control, one that was largely being initiated by local authority landlords themselves. Local authorities had begun to see voluntary stock transfer as the preferred option for escaping the ever-tightening strait-jacket of public expenditure controls. The change to a more rationed approach by central government was mainly in response to the significant financial burden on the Treasury from tenant-controlled transfers. Lusk concludes that any future development of tenant-controlled ownership through stock transfer would be required to demonstrate less financial commitment from the state.

As the historical account of tenant participation in Britain has shown, the aims and objectives have been different for the various constituencies involved. Consequently, the concept of community involvement in housing has remained ambiguous and problematic. In Chapter 4, therefore, we seek to develop a more systematic understanding of community involvement by examining the concept from a range of different theoretical positions, drawn largely from the political sciences and sociology. While community involvement and tenant participation cannot be characterized by any single theory, we conclude that central to any understanding is an explanation of the exercise of 'power' and the processes of social exclusion. In particular, we argue that housing policy-makers and practitioners need to give greater currency to perceptions articulated by those subjectified through power techniques – such as the 'residualized poor'.

In Chapter 5, Bo Bengtsson and David Clapham widen the lens through which tenant participation can be examined by offering a cross-national comparative perspective on resident involvement in Britain and Sweden. Participation practices in Sweden would appear to give residents far greater influence over decisions relating to their living environment, reflecting the existence of a more diverse policy-making community in that country. The Swedish tenants' movement would appear to have achieved a stronger position within the political arena of decision-making than in Britain where the market discipline has been predominant. While opportunities for transferring policies, institutional arrangements and systems from one country to another will be checked by historical, cultural and political factors unique to each nation, Bengtsson and Clapham's cross-national comparative approach does offer a useful framework for examining the landlord–tenant relationship in different contexts and in different arenas, as well as the factors shaping actions and the likely outcomes of this interaction.

In Chapter 6, Stuart Lowe explores the current legal context in which tenant participation occurs in Britain. The landlord–tenant relationship is largely acted out within boundaries defined by statute which, as Lowe demonstrates, restricts it to essentially individualistic terms, permitting tenants to quit council housing and to enter the uncertain domain of home ownership or an assured tenancy. In contrast, collective rights remain largely undeveloped. Lowe argues that if the cleavage between the rights of the public and private housing sectors is to be bridged, more comprehensive legislation is needed, extending tenants' rights to representation in joint decision-making and harmonizing the legal terms, conditions and subsidies between the different sectors (as is the case in Sweden).

In Chapter 7, Jerry Smith examines how the focus of community involvement in estate regeneration in Britain has changed over time, from concern about the 'inner-city problem' in the 1970s; to achieving management efficiencies and 'value for money' in the early 1980s; to addressing crime, social conflict and employment creation in the mid-1980s; to stimulating tenure restructuring from the late 1980s; and to tackling neighbourhood nuisance in the 1990s. Smith suggests that all these approaches have failed to tackle the broader structural causes of neighbourhood decline and therefore represent a missed opportunity. He calls for a broader inter-disciplinary approach developed within a more comprehensive national, regional and local framework. This would require holistic approaches linking capital investment in physical improvements to job creation, training and community development; a commitment by professionals to genuine power-sharing with communities; a willingness on the part of organizations to rethink their culture and to build genuine partnership structures with communities; the development of the skills base, knowledge and competence of community groups; and building sustainability into estate regeneration programmes by giving communities a long-term stake or psychological sense of ownership in the continued social, economic and environmental upkeep of their neighbourhood.

The psychology of participation is considered further in Chapter 8 by Johnston Birchall, although here the focus is on the motivations behind participation from the position of tenants themselves. Understanding these motivations is essential if tenant-participation strategies are to be developed in an effective way. Therefore, drawing on ideas from social psychology and organization theory, Birchall suggests a number of important lines of enquiry for tenant-participation promoters and activists seeking to determine which types of structure are likely to succeed in a given situation and how these might be maintained. For instance, such enquiries might explore the rewards likely to motivate people to become involved, the emotional ties people hold to their community and the attitudes to participation among a community's membership.

However, even if there is evidence of a strong motivation to become involved, it is unreasonable to expect people to engage in tenant-involvement schemes without a sufficient understanding of the processes, issues and skills entailed. In Chapter 9, therefore, Benita Wishart and Rob Furbey show that effective training is a vital prerequisite for successful tenant participation. Drawing on recent research exploring both tenants' and trainers' views, Wishart and Furbey identify a wide range of organizations involved in tenant-training programmes and the different degrees of satisfaction achieved from these. They conclude that no single training organization has the ability to offer a comprehensive training service to tenants. Therefore, they suggest that the way ahead may lie in the development of local 'tenant-training forums' (composed of tenants, landlord bodies and a range of local trainers) which would be responsible for assessing local training needs and priorities, reviewing the content and quality of existing provision, identifying funding sources and commissioning the delivery of training programmes.

In Chapter 10, Charles Ritchie explores some of the more practical issues surrounding the empowerment of local communities by drawing on his own long-term involvement with two established community housing groups. While both groups faced very different situations, they both placed a high priority on empowering their members through involvement in housing management decision-making. Ritchie describes how the use of community operational research (COR), a technique drawn from the disciplines of mathematics and management studies, could, if developed alongside other community-development practices, offer tenants a structured approach to community planning and decision-making. COR offers a process through which communities can, for example, identify their information needs; conduct financial appraisals; understand and handle complex technical data; structure their deliberations; analyse strategic options and make strategic choices (the SWOT analysis) and so on. COR also offers a method for identifying the stakeholders in any community and consequently those people who should be involved in the decision-making process.

The 'stakeholders' theme is explored further in Chapter 11 where we argue that if community participation is to have any real meaning it must involve everyone who has a stake in the decisions made. Recent research has shown that certain interests are excluded from tenant-participation practices, an exclusion that has been particularly forged along the lines of 'race', gender and disability. We therefore examine the barriers to effective participation for all and offer a number of practical recommendations on how these might be removed.

Finally, in Chapter 12 we pull together the threads of the arguments and ideas presented throughout the book to offer an analytical framework for understanding tenant participation. We have constructed a model for conceptualizing the complex aims and objectives of community involvement in housing within a range of settings. Consequently, we have endeavoured to enhance the possibility of adopting a more rigorous approach to evaluating tenant-participation policies, processes, practices and outcomes in the future.

References

Arnstein, S. (1969), 'A ladder of citizen participation', *Journal of the American Institute of Planners*, **35**(4), pp.216–224.

Association of District Councils (ADC) (1994), *Harnessing Community Energies*, London: ADC.

Association of Metropolitan Authorities (AMA) (1993), *Local Authorities and Community Development: A Strategic Opportunity for the 1990s*, London: AMA.

Birchall, J. (1992), 'Council tenants: sovereign consumers or pawns in the game?' in Birchall, J. (ed.), *Housing Policy in the 1990s*, London: Routledge, pp.163–189.

Cooper, C. (1991), 'Tenant participation in the 1990's', *Black Housing*, **7**(11), pp.4–5.

Craig, G. and Mayo, M. (eds) (1995), *Community Empowerment: A Reader in Participation and Development*, London: Zed Books.

Croft, S. and Beresford, P. (1990), *From Paternalism to Participation: Involving People in Social Services*, London: Open Services Project/Joseph Rowntree Foundation.

Croft, S. and Beresford, P. (1996), 'The politics of participation' in Taylor, D. (ed.), *Critical Social Policy: A Reader*, London: Sage, pp.175–198.

Dowson, S. (1990), *Keeping It Safe: Self-advocacy by People with Learning Difficulties and the Professional Response*, London: Values into Action.

Hague, C. (1990), 'The development and politics of tenant participation in British council housing', *Housing Studies*, **5**(4), pp.242–256.

Harris, V. (ed.) (1994), *Community Work Skills Manual*, Newcastle: Association of Community Workers.

Hawtin, M., Hughes, G. and Percy-Smith, J. (1994), *Community Profiling – Auditing Social Needs*, Buckingham: Open University Press.

Kay, A., Legg, C. and Foot, J. (1986), *The 1980 Tenants Rights in Practice*, London: City University.

McArthur, A. (1995), 'The active involvement of local residents in strategic community partnerships', *Policy and Politics*, **23**(1), pp.61–71.

Midgley, J. (1986), *Community Participation, Social Development and the State*, London: Methuen.

Richardson, A. (1984), *Participation*, London: Routledge.

Taylor, M. (1995), *Unleashing the Potential – Bringing Residents to the Centre of Regeneration*, York: Joseph Rowntree Foundation.

Twelvetrees, A. (1991), *Community Work*, 2nd edn, Basingstoke: Macmillan.

Vidal, J. (1996), 'Links' supplement, *The Guardian*, 20 Nov.

2 Campaigning tenants: a pre-history of tenant involvement to 1979

John Grayson

Historians have found it extremely difficult to come to terms with a history of social movements of the poor in Britain. There is a cultural chasm which even in the 1990s seems unbridgeable, as academics, journalists and politicians once again seize on the dubious notion of an 'underclass'. This seething mass of humanity is seen to inhabit the council estates of urban Britain and the 'black' inner city. The conceptualization of working-class communities as 'idle, thieving bastards' (Bagguley and Mann 1992) is, however, simply a continuation of traditional middle-class responses characterized by Englander as 'little more than a register of revulsion suffused with a Hogarthian grotesqueness and characterized by a fixation upon the pathological, a fascination for the curious' (Englander 1983 p.xv). To the Victorians the poor lived in 'warrens' and 'rookeries' and poverty was often synonymous with crime, as illustrated in the novels of Charles Dickens. Jack London wrote of travels 'into the Abyss' of the East End of London. General Booth wrote of travels in 'Darkest England' – a rather crude link between missionary work in Africa and working-class neighbourhoods. These attitudes to working-class housing distanced commentators from the reality of the working-class experience. 'It is a curious fact that, notwithstanding the voluminous literature on the housing question, it was not until shortly before the Second World War that any systematic survey was made of working-class opinion' (Englander 1983 p.xiii).

The true history of working-class housing movements has, until relatively recently, been well and truly 'hidden' – distorted by cultural and class barriers and, alongside 'Labour' history generally, firmly rooted in a crude worker/employer, capital/labour framework. It has also been largely a 'male' history of social movements, with associations and campaigns dominated by women seen as less important than the work-related

15

organizations of men. Whatever the reasons for this neglect, the effects have been profound. Tenant organizations in the 1990s have no perceived 'roots' – they have no history in which to situate themselves. Tenant participation is seen as something 'given' by local authority and housing association landlords. But the reality is somewhat different.

The effective organization of tenants largely depends on self-organized campaigning groups, 'empowered' by experience and struggle. As Jordan argues, power can never be given – it can only be *taken* (Jordan 1989). An archaeology of the history of tenant campaigns adds support to this view, illustrating how working-class movements have been generated in response to the inequalities and inadequacies of housing provision in Britain from around 1800. The aim of this chapter is to reflect on this long history of tenant campaigns for better living standards up to 1979. A more recent experience of tenant participation after 1979 is examined in Chapter 3.

'Spec' building, rents and riots – the early nineteenth century

In the early nineteenth century British towns and cities were expanding rapidly. Housing conditions in most of the new industrial cities were appalling. James Smith, describing in characteristic Victorian style the courtyards of Leeds before the 1845 Royal Commission on the Health of Towns, observed that:

> . . . by far the most unhealthy localities of Leeds are close squares of houses, or yards, as they are called, which have been erected for the accommodation of working people. Some of these, though situated in comparatively high ground, are airless from the enclosed structure, and, being wholly unprovided with any form of under-drainage or convenience, or arrangements for cleansing, are one mass of damp and filth . . . The ashes, garbage, and filth of all kinds are thrown from the doors and windows of the houses upon the surface of the streets and courts . . . The privies, as usual in such situations, are few, in proportion to the number of inhabitants; they are open to view both in front and rear, are invariably in a filthy condition, and often remain without the removal of any portion of the filth for six months. (cited in Merrett 1979 pp.5–6)

In many working-class areas mortality and morbidity were at levels associated with contemporary shanty towns in developing countries. Infant mortality rates of 250 per 1000 live births were standard up to the First World War.

Housing provision from the early nineteenth century was dominated by the private landlord and 'spec'-built housing – unplanned and of dubious quality – was often the experience for working-class tenants. A local builder would build properties 'speculatively' and local traders and business people would buy properties for investment. Housing was a characteristic investment of members of the petty bourgeoisie who, by 1834, were generally retired tradesmen and small property owners (Daunton 1990). This form of landlordism could be flexible, with tenants moving regularly, trading up or down in accordance with the level of casual earnings. The song 'My old man said "follow the van"' tells of the reality of 'flitting' between tenancies, in many cases with rent owing. Middle-class observers often commented on the 'nomadic' nature of the poor. Charles Booth noted that people were always on the move, shifting from one place to another. These moves were often forced on families because of slum clearance, employment or variations in income. But this did not prevent a Walworth clergyman in 1894 seeing such movements as threatening, equating the poor with wanderers like the Arabs of old, living in tenements instead of tents and forming no attachment to any locality (quoted in Davin 1996).

Rents were generally high and consequently a greater risk of default meant the poor frequently paid rents which were quite out of proportion to their income (Tebbutt 1983). Tenants, particularly women, were forced into developing credit networks and using local pawnshops to pay the regular Monday rent. They seemed to be constantly in conflict with landlords and there is evidence of tenant organizing and rent strikes (Englander 1983). Working-class people often had to resort to the 'moral economy' of the riot (see Thompson 1993). Riots were relatively common in British towns in the first half of the nineteenth century. By the 1830s the frequent communal rent riots, and assaults on landlords collecting rents or attempting evictions, resulted in draconian legislation (Englander 1983). The Small Tenements Recovery Act 1838 gave landlords of properties of a rental value up to £20 per annum possession on a simple application to a magistrate – grounds being irrelevant and magistrates simply a mere cipher. The Act seemed to satisfy the landlord lobby in the short term, but there was little evidence that it reduced conflicts between tenant and landlord:

> Widespread rent evasion represented a necessary form of income redistribution practised informally and sometimes collectively amongst the poor . . . Tenants, however, found it even more difficult than their landlords to engage in continuous organization. Nevertheless the *ad hoc* movements that emerged, however fragmentary and ephemeral, are not without significance. (Englander 1983 p.85)

Tenants, rates and socialism – the first tenants' movements 1867–1900

Tenant organizing and activity in the tenements, courtyards and estates were closely linked to wider social and political disaffection and rebellion. Between 1800 and 1848 there had been a series of social movements – Luddism, Captain Swing riots and Chartism – which challenged the state with varying degrees of success. Protests on rents and housing conditions were certainly part of the general social unrest of this period. By the 1850s the 'Age of Equipoise' had arrived, a high point of Victorian imperialism and prosperity, reflected in the growth of the 'labour aristocracy', leading to the emergence of building societies and an interest in home-ownership (but only for a very small number of skilled workers). However, with the revival of political movements demanding suffrage reform in the 1860s (see Finn 1993), organizations based on tenant issues again emerged. The Reform League, formed by 'respectable' artisans, trade unionists and a number of intellectuals, championed the rights of working-class voters.

The Reform Act 1867 virtually established complete household suffrage as the basis of the borough franchise in England and Wales – while also causing havoc between landlord and tenant. The franchise raised the question of who should be responsible for payment of the rates, the property owner or the tenant. 'Compounding' had become the general rule, with 500 000 tenants paying the rates with the weekly rent to their landlord who had become responsible for rates collection on behalf of some local councils. The 1867 Act, however, encouraged the direct rating of occupiers, and tenants were forced into paying their rates directly to the local council. Consequently, rents were expected to fall. However, they actually rose and tenants protested.

A Tenants' Mutual Protection Association was formed after a rally in Victoria Park, Hackney, attended by around 2000 people. Similar organizing occurred in Birmingham, Salford and Hulme. The Reform League postponed celebration of the 1867 Act and started to campaign for tenants. There was widespread resistance when local authorities attempted to collect rates directly from tenants. In Norwich, the overseers received threats of personal violence. In Bethnal Green, wholesale prosecution followed refusals to pay the rates and the higher rents. By the end of 1867, 137 000 summonses had been taken out and 29 000 distress warrants issued. However, as a result of the tenants' campaigns, the Rate Assessment and Collection Act 1869 was hurriedly passed and compounding was restored, with a rebate for property owners to cover collection costs. This was perhaps the first major victory for collective tenant action.

The question of rates and rents was to become a major issue again during the late-Victorian 'housing crisis'. The building of houses slowed in economic downturns during the 1880s and 1890s, leading to insufficient numbers of affordable, convenient houses for the low paid (Rodger 1989). City-centre demolition exacerbated the shortage, leading to increased overcrowding and rent rises of 47 per cent in real terms between 1875 and 1900. Revenue from rates also increased by 200 per cent. Improvements in municipal services and utilities – sewage, water, gas, roads, clearance and so on – increased the expenditure burden on the rates by a massive 316 per cent between 1870 and 1910. Property taxes increased, property values dropped, and investment in housing therefore fell. The net effect was increased tenant activity in response to landlords squeezing out profits from their homes.

In the latter part of the nineteenth century the emerging socialist and labour organizations campaigned alongside tenants and the 'housing question' became an increasingly important political issue. Campaigns by journalists, such as Mearns's *Bitter Cry of Outcast London*, were to have some influence on policy-makers, resulting for example in the enactment of the Housing of the Working Classes Act 1890. However, before 1914 both the Liberals and Conservatives avoided the central issue of housing supply and rents. In 1881 the Democratic Federation announced that it had taken up the question of fair rents in London (Englander 1983). This federation comprised those class-conscious militants who had continued the Chartist tradition. They became the backbone of the Social Democratic Federation (SDF) – the first Marxist group in England – and claimed that the Royal Commission on Housing 1887 (leading to the 1890 Act) had been a response to their threats of rent strikes in the East End, although this 'stump oratory' was rarely matched by action. However, 'the idea of the rent strike as an instrument of mass radicalization lingered' (Englander 1983 p.104).

In the 1890s the Bermondsey Labour League had also campaigned on behalf of tenants on a range of issues – against church rates, against the biscuit manufacturer Peak Frean's attempts to pass on water rates to tenants, and against the railway companies' clearance schemes. It co-operated with the emerging Workmen's National Housing Council (WNHC) to campaign for municipal housing through a co-ordinated series of rent strikes aimed at forcing Parliament to concede legislation. The WNHC had been founded in 1898 by three compositors, all members of the SDF, following continuing problems with high rents. The SDF newspaper *Justice* had been agitating for non-profit-making municipal housing since 1885. Its campaigns meant that by the outbreak of the First World War every liberal and left-wing group in the country, including trades councils, had the municipalization of housing as a central political issue (Damer 1980). Fred Knee, the Secretary of the WNHC, summed up the general mood of the campaigns:

It is not the housing of the poor, but the housing of the people by the people themselves, that we must work for – not the herding into slums for the benefit of private enterprise, not the crowding into barracks in order to provide interest for municipal bondholders, but by a feasible honest system and plan. (Knee 1977 p.105)

But the question of rents remained a more pressing concern than municipal ownership and in 1899 a number of Tenant Defence Leagues were formed, including the Tottenham Working Men's Housing League:

> The Tottenham Working Men's Housing League was formed to bring the protection of the law to the harassed occupants of the area. Membership reached 800 following an early victory on the Coleraine Park Estate which resulted in a negotiated reduction . . . A spokesman for the nearly 500-strong Cheshunt Working Men's Housing League told an early meeting he would 'like to see bigger joints to carve in the houses of the working classes and more room to carve them in'. The campaign was also taken up by the 450 members of the newly formed Edmonton Housing League. (Englander 1983 p.123)

The rent-strike weapon, suggested by Knee, was rarely supported by solid trade unionists. As the Independent Labour Party (ILP) *Labour Leader* put it:

> This law of rent . . . which takes to itself automatically every rise in wages, every municipal improvement, though that may also involve an increase in rates, every social betterment of whatever description, is the modern Frankenstein. It is far more of an iron law than ever Ricardo's law of wages was. For you can strike against industrial conditions; but a rent strike at once involves a thousand laws which safeguard private property. (*Labour Leader* 24 June 1904, quoted in Englander 1983 p.125)

Employers as landlords, workers as tenants

Although the private landlord dominated working-class housing, workers in a range of industries were housed by their employers. Housing was an integral part of factory discipline and labour supply (Rodger 1989). The 1833 Factory Commission reported that 168 of 881 large firms provided housing and 19 per cent of all firms provided some. One of the questions the commissioners asked was aimed at employers who monitored their workers beyond the factory wall:

> Do the workpeople live in the houses of their employers; and if so, is any control or superintendence exercised for their moral and social improvement, or are any arrangements made to enforce domestic cleanliness? (quoted in Daunton 1990 p.220)

The Ashworths of Hyde responded that:

> The state and cleanliness of their rooms, their bedding and furniture are very minutely examined, and the condition of their children, their income and habits of life, are carefully enquired into, and remarks thereon are entered in books which are kept for the purpose. (quoted in Daunton 1990 p.221)

The employer-landlord was an ever-present figure in the lives of their worker-tenants. Joyce argues that in the Northern textile towns 'the factory itself rather than direct control of housing acted as the principal focus of workplace influence [but that] in the out-districts of towns and in the semi-rural industrial colonies such ownership continued to be of great significance throughout the period' (Joyce 1980 p.121). As late as 1859 employers were still building a significant number of houses, with about 10 per cent of housing in Yorkshire and Lancashire towns owned by employer-landlords.

> But the effect of the employer's holdings should not be minimized, whether they were used as punishment or reward . . . The moral, reformative use of housing, seen especially in the early industrial revolution, continued to be practised in the remote colonies as well as in the more rigorous of the urban 'villages'. Aside from house provision for key groups of workers, the employer's need of a loyal and stable workforce meant that housing was a bond tying the entire workforce to the neighbourhood.
>   The employers might forgo rents in bad times, or charge low rents in good . . . the remission of rent could act as a form of dole for the old. There are numerous instances of employers enforcing particular work practices through housing, such as the labour of family groups. (Joyce 1980 p.123)

In some cases skilled workers, foremen and lower management were housed in 'model' housing. Villages and estates were developed by a range of philanthropic or progressive employers such as Salt at Saltaire (1853), Ackroyd at Ackroydon (1801), Pim at Harold's Cross, Dublin (1853), Cadbury at Bournville (1879), Lever at Port Sunlight (1888) and Rowntree at New Earswick (1902). But most housing was not of this standard. Employees had 'tied' housing, linking their tenancies to their jobs. When industrial conflicts erupted employers would routinely evict strikers – a practice common in the coal industry. Coal companies became notorious for the poor quality of housing they provided. Miners called 'Sinkers', who developed the mine, were faced with appalling conditions. In one Welsh valley:

> To house these and other workers the company built rows of corrugated iron huts near the pit head: low, one-storey buildings with a single window and a door at the front and tall chimney stacks rising above their squat frames . . . Other workers

lived in accommodation of tarred canvas stretched over wooden frames. (Lieven 1994 p.14)

According to the *Morning Chronicle* in the 1840s, 'pit rows' in Durham were like 'nothing whatever in . . . England . . . neither like a country village nor a section the meaner part of a manufacturing town' (quoted in Beynon and Austrin 1994 p.22). Housing was part of the almost feudal annual 'bond' which miners were forced to sign each year until the middle of the nineteenth century. The Hetton Coal Company's bond of 1829–30 had a clause stating that 'it is also distinctly understood and agreed that the dwelling house, provided for any of the persons hereby hired or engaged. . . [forms] part of the wages of such persons' (quoted in Beynon and Austrin 1994 p.32). But when miners challenged the bond and tried to establish trade unions they were evicted:

> In 1832 . . . the miners of Friar's Goose colliery in South Tyneside were threatened with eviction. They drove off the bailiffs and on 4th May faced a party of special constables armed with firearms and cutlasses. After a fracas in which five miners were shot and wounded, the soldiers arrived, arresting forty or more. Twenty men and three women were committed to Durham jail for trial at the assizes. (quoted in Beynon and Austrin 1994 pp.33–34)

In 1844, a 17-week strike in Northumberland and Durham, involving 22 000 men and boys, led to evictions which were vividly described by Thomas Burt, a future miners' MP, in his autobiography:

> Nearly every house . . . had its contents thrown upon the roadway . . . The evictors consisted of a regiment of ragged ugly looking, ill bred, ill mannered fellows, locally called candy-men. They had been collected from the slums of Newcastle and other towns on Tyneside. They were accompanied by a strong force of police armed with cutlasses and stout formidable looking staves. The policemen for the most part looked quietly on while the candymen carried the furniture out of the houses . . . Active resistance was there none, nor was there violence . . . Some of the pitmen had strongly and skilfully barricaded their doors and windows from inside, and before an entrance could be affected the doors and windows had to be broken in pieces . . . Such evictions are always touchingly pathetic, sometimes almost tragic. Hundreds of helpless children cast upon the bare shelterless roads, the mothers standing disconsolately beside their household goods . . . presented a picture at once sombre and pitiful. Friends and sympathizers were not lacking among the farmers and shopkeepers who generously shared their houses with the evicted families . . .
>
> But the very magnitude of the evictions, extending over nearly the whole of the mining districts of Northumberland and Durham, made it impossible to find house accommodation for a twentieth part of the evicted. Scores of . . . families camped out by the roadside. The scene was novel and picturesque. No small

degree of architectural taste and skill were exhibited in arranging the household furniture. (Burt 1924 pp.34–37)

Companies routinely evicted widows of miners who died or were killed at work, and also threatened eviction if sons were not sent down the pit. Overcrowding was also a common problem for mining families. At the beginning of the twentieth century, in Whickham Urban District, Durham, most of the mining families' houses comprised just two rooms which could be occupied by up to 12 persons. In South Wales the average number of people in each house was over seven. The coal company, anxious to house as many miners as possible, made it a condition of many rental agreements that rooms should be sub-let (Lieven 1994).

Most miners lived in either large urban areas or isolated villages. 'Company' villages were common in the North East, South Yorkshire and the Rhondda valley in Wales where, at the turn of the century, 95 per cent of the population belonged to families engaged in or dependent on mining. Some mining settlements were 'model' villages – the Glamorgan Coal Company built Llwynypia in the Rhondda, the Bolsover Company built Creswell in Derbyshire and Brodsworth Main Company built the Woodlands village near Doncaster. Other villages were simply owned as rather poor collections of houses with miner tenants – Denaby in South Yorkshire was one of these. The lodge secretary in 1885 pointed out that the Denaby Colliery Company owned all the property in the village except two houses (Benson 1980).

Around three-quarters of miners lived in colliery houses in Ayrshire, the Lothians, and Northumberland and Durham, and about a third to a half in Lanarkshire and Central Scotland. In some areas coal companies used houses to attract labour and to retain particular skilled workers, but colliery houses were more scarce in West Yorkshire and in most areas of South Wales (Benson 1980). Most colliery houses were small, poorly designed and in poor repair. As pits were worked out these houses were simply abandoned and repairs remained undone. A Durham tenant of the Derwent Iron Company complained in 1864 that the housing manager:

cannot give anybody a civil answer, his insults are base to anyone who does not suit him or crosses him. There are some can get anything done to their houses, alterations or repairs for their comfort, such as call him Mr, and ask for favour, while others who don't do this or lick the dust at his feet, ask the most necessary repairs done to their houses, get insulted for their audacity, and told in the coarsest language to repair their own house, and do their own glazing and if they remonstrate with him he will threaten to shift them away from the place. (quoted in Benson 1980 p.97)

A year earlier, at the Yorkshire Miners' Conference of 1863, the South Yorkshire delegates reported that:

> Miners houses in many instances were unfit to live in, and that even where this was not so there is . . . an objection to living in a coalowner's house, no matter how excellent the accommodation may be, and that is, that such an arrangement places every man's domestic arrangements in the hands of the employer, gives that employer enormous powers and destroys the chances of the miner so situated to make a fair bargain for wages with his master. (Machin 1958 p.303)

This power afforded to the employer was used in 1866 to evict Derbyshire miners who joined the union. Staveley and Clay Cross Companies gave 200 men eviction notices in one week. But such actions were not always met passively. For instance, in 1878 in Stirlingshire, while the officer was engaged serving warrants upon a community of about 120 miners a large crowd collected and he was obliged to flee from the place. The houses of five colliery owners and managers were attacked, the windows broken, shrubs and trees destroyed, and furniture and other property smashed to pieces (Benson 1980). In the great coal industry lockout of 1893 police evicted miners from their homes and local churches and charities set up 'tent cities' to offer emergency accommodation. Miners dependent on private landlords were also often grossly exploited – in South Wales at the end of the nineteenth century key money and compulsory purchase of useless furniture were common. In 1911, during miners' 'riots' in Ebbw Vale, Bargoed and Tredegar, landlords charging inflated rents for cottages had their houses attacked.

Workers in other industries experienced similar difficulties. In the railway sector companies used housing policy as a means of staff control and for the preservation of company loyalty (McKenna 1980). At the start of the railway boom the Eastern Counties Railway had built 300 homes in Stratford, East London, the Great Western had built a good deal of new Swindon, and the Great Northern Railway had built a military-style estate of 226 brick-and-slate houses known as 'The Barracks' in Peterborough. At Wolverton in 1855 'a little red-brick town composed of 242 little red-brick houses . . . the whole lately built by orders of a railway board, at a railway station, by a railway contractor, for railway men, railway women, and railway children: in short, the round cast-iron plate over the door of every house, bearing the letters LNWR, is the generic symbol of the town' (quoted in McKenna 1980 p.51). The railway centre of Crewe became 'the archetypal Victorian company town'.

Some railway housing was of very poor quality. For instance, the brick tenement in St Pancras known as Polygon Buildings was divided into flatlets, suitable for only the smallest families. There were no bathrooms:

toilets and water taps were amenities to be shared (McKenna 1980). However, there were a number of 'model' railway estates and villages – for instance, in 1888 Harwich village had a mechanics hall, a technical school and a public hall seating 900; the North British Railway's development at Riccarton, Scotland, had a school house, a company recreation hall and a co-op store. But, as in the coal industry, the reality of eviction was an ever-present threat. In 1871 the London and North Western Railway (LNWR), one of the richest limited companies in Europe at the time, evicted enginemen in Camden Town for embarking on strike action. And in Scotland:

> In 1890 strikers at Motherwell were evicted with great violence from their rented cottages. Police and army were called in to carry out the eviction, and by way of retaliation the strikers did great damage to the glass roof of Motherwell station. A medallion inscribed 'Remember Motherwell 1890' was later struck to mark the occasion. (McKenna 1980 p.53)

The struggle against tied housing was waged by tenants largely through their trade unions. Employers had only rarely provided 'model' housing to unionized labour. The Fitzwilliams, Earls of Rockingham, provided good-quality housing on their estate at Elsecar near Rotherham for skilled miners – but at the expense of open union membership. Lord Lever at Port Sunlight took a similar position with employees in his soap and chemicals firm. However, miners' unions gradually started to influence tenants' rights. In Durham, the trade union played an important role in regulating allocations and tenure arrangements. A large part of the lodge secretary's time was taken up with the question of justice in relation to allocations and the 'Coal and House Agreement' made between the union and the company (Beynon and Austrin 1994).

By the end of the nineteenth century the unions had become the national 'tenants' organization'. There had been various attempts made by trade unionists throughout the latter part of the century to campaign for legislation preventing the eviction of tenants of company housing during industrial disputes. The Scottish Trade Union Congress took up the issue again in 1898 and two years later its proposals were contained in the Workmen's Houses Tenure Bill. One Home Office civil servant argued against the 1900 Bill, suggesting:

> It is possible that the Bill might have the effect of discouraging the excellent work which railway companies and other large employers of labour are doing in the way of providing comfortable houses for their workpeople. This proposal might also, if it becomes law, operate very considerably to the disadvantage of an employer of fresh hands if he were unable to provide them with accommodation; and would clearly therefore put a powerful weapon in the hands of the strikers. (Englander 1983 p.126)

After the First World War large-scale tied housing went into decline. Council housing was slowly replacing company housing – particularly in the heartlands of 'paternalism' like Durham – although after the Second World War, at the nationalization of the coal industry, the National Coal Board (NCB) still inherited 140 000 houses from the coal companies, of which 37 per cent were classed as 'poor' and only 34 per cent 'reasonably modern and in fair condition'. Their sale or transfer to local authorities was rejected and in 1952 the NCB set up the Coal Industry Housing Association to start building again. As late as 1974 the NCB still had 90 000 houses, half of which were over 50 years old. It was only in July 1976 that the decision was taken to dispose of all workmen's houses as rapidly as possible (Ashworth 1986). Since the 1960s, British Coal has progressively disposed of its housing and in the 1980s it sold stock through auctions at London hotels – a degrading end to a chequered history of miners' housing. In 1987 some tenants in Thurnscoe near Barnsley reacted on hearing about plans to auction their houses by stopping the sale and organizing themselves into the largest housing co-operative in the UK, managing 361 homes (see Chapter 10, pages 224–233).

A good example of a union acting as a 'tenants' federation' can be found in the case of agricultural workers. Tied housing in agriculture had been a feature of country life since the seventeenth century and by the 1800s rural housing was often in a worse condition than urban housing. Farm workers in the 'open' hamlets rented from small tradespeople and, in some cases, got their cottages 'rent free' in return for their labour (Morgan 1982). In 1843, agricultural workers' houses in Dorset were described as 'squalid mud huts'. A Parliamentary Commission found in nine villages out of ten the cottage was still nothing but a slightly improved hovel while, in the 1860s, Shaftesbury described cottages on his own estate as filthy, close, indecent, unwholesome – stuffed like figs in a drum (see Snell 1985). Such conditions were not perhaps so surprising when one considers the attitudes of some landlords. A Miss Boucherett, sister of the owner of the parish of Willingham in Lincolnshire, told a Parliamentary Commission of 1867:

> No sink or other communication with drains ought to exist in labourers' houses, the inhabitants have not intelligence enough to keep such things in order. The more intelligent of our poor know this and beg not to have sinks; all refuse should be carried out by hand. (quoted in Russell 1956 p.9)

In Scotland and Ireland rural tenant issues were at the forefront of political concerns over land ownership and famine. In 1882, crofter tenants in Skye revolted over grazing rights and rents, with 500 people accosting the sheriff officer serving eviction summonses. This protest was the prelude to more widespread acts of insubordination sustained on many Highland estates for several years and was reflected in later years when links were forged between the nineteenth-century 'land question' and the organization of tenants in towns and cities of lowland Scotland in the early twentieth century. While similar rural protests occurred in Ireland, there the most remarkable demonstration of a collective response was through mass emigration rather than physical resistance (Devine 1994).

In England, farm workers responded to the problem of poor housing conditions through their unions. In the 1870s the 'Revolt of the Field' led to the dramatic evolution of Joseph Arch's union, particularly in the Eastern Counties. However, the tied-cottage system contributed to its defeat with farmers locking out union members. In 1874 over 10 000 men were thrown out of their jobs and in many districts families were evicted from their homes because fathers or sons belonged to a trade union. Bitterest memories of these evictions remain in Dorset. Even today in many a Dorset cottage the visitor will come across a faded photograph of an eviction of the great lockout (Groves 1981). The agricultural workers started to campaign officially in 1909, alongside the emerging ILP, for improvements in tenure rights. The repressive nature of landlord–tenant relationships in rural communities at the time is illustrated in a 1912 tenancy agreement:

> I, the undersigned, agree to give the cottage up held by me, with all its apartments, to the landlord or his agent, at a week's notice.
>
> I also agree, on quitting my cottage, not to damage the property in any way. If the copper, oven stoves, etc., are my property, I undertake not to remove them without first offering them for sale to the landlord or his agent.
>
> I undertake not to take in any lodger without first obtaining the consent of the landlord or his agent.
>
> I promise not to harbour any of my daughters who may have committed a breach of morality, nor yet any of my sons who may have broken any of the game laws.
>
> I promise not to receive into my home any members of my family, with their wives and their families, without first obtaining the consent of the landlord or his agent.
>
> I promise to act as game watch on the estate when called upon to do so. (see Groves 1981 pp.125–126)

The agricultural workers failed to persuade the Labour governments of 1924 and 1929–31 to bring in protective legislation and in 1931 the National Union of Agricultural Workers defended 300 cases of eviction. A similar annual 'caseload' appeared in union activities into the 1950s. In 1964 the union at last saw a Protection from Eviction Act. The proportion of farm workers in tied accommodation had actually risen from 34 per cent in 1947 to over 60 per cent by the early 1970s. By 1975, 1268 possession orders were granted to farmers with 'only' about 20 evictions a year. It was the Labour government of 1974–79 which finally addressed the stranglehold of the tied-cottage system by giving councils a duty to house workers displaced from such accommodation (see Armstrong 1988).

Rent strikes and the struggle for council housing

Between 1900 and the outbreak of the First World War there was a mounting tide of militancy and dissatisfaction with governments and trade union leaders. Between 1910 and 1913 there was an explosion of trade union militancy: 'their organization and industrial activity proceeded with an explosive, self-sustaining momentum. Clashes with police and "blacklegs", and the intermingling of strikers and town mobs, were seen again, this time on a far greater scale. The slightest reason for ceasing work now became sufficient' (Hunt 1981 p.320). Ten million days were lost in strikes in 1911, forty million days in 1912. Trade union membership rose from two to four million between 1910 and 1913. This 'resort to direct action which characterized the industrial unrest of these years found a parallel in the housing reform movement' (Englander 1983 p.142). George Lansbury, founder of the *Daily Herald*, Poplar Labour councillor and eventual leader of the Labour Party, advocated the 'rent strike' as a weapon in the fight for 'Socialism'. In the *Daily Herald* of 10 May 1912 he asked:

> Has not the time come for organizing a strike against paying rents to slum landlords? . . . We are of the opinion that the formation of Tenant Societies to resist the exactions of landlords by all possible means might wring great benefits from that selfish class, even as Trade Unions have extorted concessions from grasping employers . . . Such an organization, powerfully directed, might make history.

Furthermore, in the *Daily Herald* of 19 May 1913, Lansbury detected 'welcome signs throughout the country of an impending strike against rent'. These signs included the inaugural meeting of the Scottish Federation of Tenants' Associations in the autumn of 1912, with 23 delegates attending from a range of tenant organizations in the West of Scotland including over 1000 tenant members from Clydebank and over 600 from Paisley; the activities of the Amalgamated Society of Engineers (ASE) which, by the spring of 1912, was actively promoting tenant organizations; and the local trades council in Wolverhampton which in 1913 set up the Wolverhampton Tenants' Defence League to organize a rent strike in response to rent increases by the local Property Owners Association – albeit unsuccessfully. Similar responses to rent increases occurred elsewhere in 1913. A Tenants' Defence League formed in the Erdington district of Birmingham, while in Yorkshire, John Lake, Secretary of the East Leeds constituency of the Labour

Party, advocated militant action and rent strikes as an alternative route towards the destruction of capitalism. However, a rent strike in the Holbeck area of Leeds failed to gain the support of the local Labour Party hierarchy. In January 1914 the Leeds trades council assisted in forming the Leeds Tenants' Defence League which supported 290 tenants in the Burley area in organizing a rent strike – but this again proved unsuccessful.

Tenant organizations in the pre-war period were linked to the trade union movement, the ILP and other sections of the Labour Party. With the outbreak of the First World War national organizations which had lobbied for better housing conditions, such as the WNHC, gave way to wartime organizations. The Workers' National Committee (WNC) became a co-ordinating organization for tenant activities and pressurizing government. In the first months of the war the Courts Emergency Powers Act was passed, making it easier for landlords to collect rents and seek evictions. In areas where workers were recruited for war industries, landlords began to exploit the shortage of accommodation. This simply fuelled tenants' militancy and in London tenant organizations threatened action on rents in Shoreditch, Bethnal Green and Camberwell. In Woolwich, a centre of munitions production, there were calls for a rent strike. In Edmonton 1000 tenants were on rent strike in 1914, while in Tooting tenants formed the War Rents League. In Birmingham, 130 tenants in Lozells were on rent strike in October 1914 while Aston and Handsworth tenants' associations also threatened action.

Eventually, the wartime government was forced to act and rents and mortgages were frozen under the Rent and Mortgage Interest (War Restrictions) Act 1915. This piece of legislation can be seen as the culmination of a long pre-war struggle between landlord and tenant. But the militant struggle of Glasgow tenants proved to be a crucial element in defeating profiteering landlords and the government, and needs to be considered as a unique and special case. Before the First World War the class hatred of the rentiers of Glasgow had produced its own 'war mentality' between landlord and tenant. Landlords generally managed their properties through 'factors', who mostly held a low opinion of tenants. A spokesperson for the Glasgow Factors Association told a commission in the 1890s 'that the root of the evil in the housing of the poor is the thriftlessness, intemperance and want of self respect of a considerable class among tenant occupants' (Damer 1980 p.83). Many Glasgow properties were allocated on 'long lets' – renewed annually – which was clearly a problem for tenants with irregular employment patterns. Landlords could sequester property and furniture and sell it if tenants got into rent arrears. Also, around 22 000 properties were 'ticketed' in the early years of the twentieth century – these were tenements where overcrowding was monitored by the police, sometimes in the middle of the night, leaving tenants in fear of constant harassment. The House Letting and Rating Act 1911 reduced long lets following agitation from the labour movement. In 1911 a City Labour Party had formed in Glasgow 'with housing as a central plank' of its policies. In 1913 John Wheatley, an ILP Councillor, published his *£8 Cottages for Glasgow Citizens* pamphlet, and the revolutionary John Maclean helped to organize a Scottish Federation of Tenants' Associations. Glasgow trades council, with its regular meetings of 400 delegates, also organized legal action against rent increases before the First World War.

Labour Party politics was largely founded on the 'housing question' and women were to play a central role in the development of its early position on housing. Glasgow ILP women had strongly developed links with the suffrage campaigns. Sylvia Pankhurst had prepared a 'People's Army' under the direction of her East London Federation of Suffragettes to resist police brutality and to implement a 'No Vote, No Rent' strike in the East End. Glasgow's *Labour Weekly* had carried a report on this action before the War. Women had also joined the Tenants' Defence Associations in Clydeside before 1914 and were also active in the co-operative societies of the area which were to act as the core of much of the agitation in 1915. Women's Labour League activists, like Agnes Dollan and Mary Barbour, founded the Glasgow Women's Housing Association on the eve of the First World War. As Ben Shaw, the then Secretary of the Glasgow Labour Party, put it in 1913, 'housing is, above all, a woman's question . . . If every ill-housed woman who cherishes a housing ambition can be brought to demand it fiercely, and collectively, its realization will be assured' (Melling 1983 p.33).

The First World War brought the munitions industry to Glasgow, with about 16 000 munitions workers moving to the city and around another 4000 moving to the surrounding areas. In a situation of near monopoly, the Glasgow landlords put up their rents and there was a concerted roar of protest. In 1914, an official corporation inquiry into rent increases investigated 2000 complaints, finding a clustering of overcharging in the heavily industrialized areas of Govan and Partick where the housing stock was under severe pressure. The Glasgow Women's Housing Association took up the rents issue and committees were formed in the working-class districts to resist increases. Cards were printed with the words 'RENT STRIKE – WE ARE NOT REMOVING' and placed in the windows of all the houses where rent increases were demanded. Other grass-roots organizations played a critical role in mobilizing support for the rent strike – the ward committees, the labour representation committees, and the tenants' defence and protective societies. The importance of these various committees is that they were all democratic collective organizations located directly within working-class neighbourhoods and with a capacity for mass mobilization.

In the early summer of 1915 there was a huge demonstration on Glasgow Green where again workers stated their refusal to pay increased rents. The rent strike was spreading and by August 1915 there were strikes all over Glasgow – in Govan, Partick, Parkhead, Pollokshaws, Pollok, Cowcaddens, Kelvingrove, Ibrox, Govanhill, St Rollox, Townhead, Springburn, Maryhill, Fairfield, Blackfriars (the Gorbals) and Woodside. The excitement and tension of the period strike the reader in all the contemporary accounts. All day long – in the streets, halls and houses – meetings were held. Kitchen meetings, street meetings, mass meetings, meetings of every kind. No halt, no rest for anyone. In October 1915, 15 000 Glaswegians were on rent strike including five Labour councillors. By this time the women were assaulting the factors and bailiffs, pelting them with rubbish and flour. Elsewhere, in other munitions areas, particularly Sheffield, there was similar if less intense unrest. By November 1915, 20 000 people were on strike in Glasgow. The government had established the Hunter Committee in the previous October to review the situation, but the rent strikes continued to escalate – particularly around the trials of rent strikers. A General Strike was threatened after a mass demonstration on 17 November and eight days later, on 25 November 1915, a Rent and Mortgage Interest Freeze Bill was introduced, becoming law in four weeks flat, receiving the Royal Assent on 25 December. This was a famous victory (Damer 1980 p.101).

The emergence of the council tenant

Local councils had made only limited progress in the direct provision of housing before 1919. The London County Council (LCC) and other London boroughs had done more than most, building over 12 000 dwellings before the war (Wohl 1971). However, pre-war pressures and the tenants' challenge in Glasgow produced a major Royal Commission for Scotland (the Ballantyne Commission 1912–17) and, as we have seen, the Hunter Committee (preparing the way for the 1915 Act and the Tudor Walters Committee of 1918, which recommended improved standards for housing under the influence of Raymond Unwin and his vision of 'Garden Cities'). The 'Addison Act' 1919, named after the Minister of Health responsible for its introduction, was passed in a year of significant social conflict – major strikes in mining, transport and engineering, mutinies in the army and even a police strike! The Act came into being only two years after the 1917 Russian Revolution and Lloyd George and his Cabinet were well aware of the 'Bolshevik' menace. As one Home Office paper warned, in the event of rioting, for the first time in history, the rioters would have been better-trained than the troops (see Swenarton 1981).

Lloyd George, with his much misquoted pledge to provide 'habitations fit for the heroes who have won the war', believed that he could win over 'the sane and steady leaders among the workers' by state spending on housing and other social measures. 'Even if it cost a hundred million pounds, what was that compared to the stability of the State?' His Parliamentary Secretary summed up the government's position in April 1919, stating that 'the money we are going to spend on housing is an insurance against Bolshevism and Revolution' (quoted in Swenarton 1981 p.79). The Addison Act simply by-passed the local political minefields by guaranteeing central government subsidies and limiting local authority contributions to a penny (1d) rate. Local councils were instructed to undertake urgent surveys of housing need – and to build. Between January 1919 and March 1923, 154 500 houses were built by local authorities. Continued pressure from tenant organizations ensured that the Rent Restrictions Act 1915 was renewed in 1920 and remained in force until 1923. As tenant activity declined and unemployment weakened the influence of the trade union movement, the government reduced subsidies in 1921 and Addison was replaced – but 'council housing' had arrived.

In 1918 a number of women in the Women's Labour League (WLL), authors of a pamplet published in January 1918 called *The Working Women's House*, joined a Women's Housing Sub-Committee (WHSC) set up by the Ministry of Reconstruction. In its campaign the WLL argued that 'women ought to be the housing experts and consider what they want, and leave compromises on one side. Do not carry your flag too low' (Matrix 1984 p.28). The women on the WHSC had already had experience of documenting the lives of working-class women. Women in Lambeth had been described in Maud Pember Reeves's *Round about a Pound a Week* (1913). The WHSC had also visited estates built with government subsidies in London and Gretna Green for munitions workers and had stressed in its findings that 'it is important to find out the candid opinion of the housewife . . . [and] take into account the average and representative view held by the bulk of the tenants' (quoted in Matrix 1984 pp.29–30). When the Ministry of Reconstruction refused to publish the WHSC's findings in full in May 1918 the sub-committee decided to campaign with and consult working-class women, women's groups, mothers' and infant clinics, women's suffrage societies and women's co-operative guilds, encouraging them to organize, meet and discuss the type of houses that women wanted. Drawing on these consultations the WHSC compiled a report emphasizing the need to design houses that were low cost and provided separate cooking facilities and hot water. The report also considered co-operative housekeeping arrangements, referring to a co-operative scheme developed at Meadoway Green in Letchworth Garden City. Here, tenants had a communal dining room, employed a cook and a part-time cleaner, and organized the kitchen on a rota basis. Although enthusiastic about communal housekeeping, the report stressed that 'successful experiments can only be made after consultation with working class women and full co-operation with them', recognizing that 'English women do not under present conditions regard communal arrangements with favour' (see Matrix 1984 p.36).

The first wave of tenants in the new council 'cottage' estates of the 1920s were ex-servicemen and their families. Rents were high and certainly in most parts of the country council housing was largely confined to a limited range of income groups; that is, in practice, the better-off families, the small clerks, the artisans, and the better-off semi-skilled workers with small families and fairly safe jobs (Bowley 1945). Ernest Barker, a Manchester politician looking back in 1933, admitted that Manchester had hitherto been housing the middle class and the aristocracy of labour, and had done almost nothing for the low-paid workers (Manchester WHG 1987). An LCC survey of five major estates in the late 1930s showed that 22.6 per cent of the households were skilled workers, 31.3 per cent semi-skilled, 17.1 per cent transport workers, 10 per cent black-coated workers, 5 per cent retail traders and 5.6 per cent postal workers, police or servicemen. In Liverpool 20 per cent of tenants were from non-manual backgrounds. The social character of estates was thus by no means strictly a reflection of those most in need (Cronin 1984). High rents in Bristol meant that only a small proportion of the waiting list of 3000 could be offered tenancies and tenants on the newly occupied estates at Fishponds and Knowle formed the first corporation tenants' associations to press for rent and rate reductions. In March 1922, the Hillfields Park Tenants' Association was founded as a result of a mass meeting of 300 tenants to protest at high rents. A committee of 20 (including five women) was elected to lobby the council. They worked with the Housing Committee and won rent reductions. The tenants continued to lead a movement for further rent reductions and also organized campaigns for better facilities on estates and the right of tenants to buy their own houses (Dresser 1984).

Private rents in the Gateshead, Jarrow and South Shields areas in 1912 were between 15 and 25 per cent of average miners' earnings; by the 1920s, in council housing in relatively prosperous Easington, 23–27 per cent of average earnings; in redundancy-hit Auckland, 45–50 per cent of average earnings. On the Mount Pleasant estate in Stockton, a survey showed tenants moved from rents of 4s 8d to council rents of 9s – almost double. The 1926 General Strike and miners' strike caused chaos in some regions. For instance, in Sunderland Rural District 87 per cent of tenants went into arrears. It was to be the miners' 'tenants' association', the Durham Miners' Association, which came to the rescue, paying off nearly half the arrears to the council of £1500 in 1927. In 1930, Easington decided to send eviction notices to 400 tenants in arrears, but quickly withdrew them when a local miners' lodge politely enquired what provision the council was making for the families which would be displaced (Ryder 1984). Some councils responded to the affordability problem by offering 'half tenancies' – literally doubling up in houses, two families in each! By 1930 a quarter of Brandon Council's houses were shared, allowing the relatively poor working-class tenants to be housed.

Many local authority landlords in the 1920s operated in a similar way to private landlords of the period. Even before the First World War in Liverpool, between 1905 and 1909, 42 per cent of tenants leaving council houses were evicted! Manchester in the early 1920s employed 'private-sector agents' to manage part of its stock. Chester-le-Street hired a firm of private estate agents to handle all rent collections on a 3 per cent commission basis. Early in the history of council housing some local housing committees opted for 'right to buy' policies. The 1923 Chamberlain Act allowed subsidies to be passed on to private builders and, in Birmingham, to tenant purchasers. Birmingham City Council had decided in 1922 that these facilities should be offered to its tenants to buy the houses in which they lived. The City Estates Department handled sales and in 1925 published a booklet called *How to Be Your Own Landlord*. By 1929 the Birmingham Municipal Bank had loaned £1 million to 3314 purchasers of council houses (Chinn 1991).

In 1923 the Conservative government began to reverse the progressive housing legislation introduced after the war, Chamberlain's Act lifting rent restrictions on the next change of tenancy. This encouraged landlords to evict tenants from restricted tenancies. From August 1923 to March 1924 there were 35 000 court hearings for possession, 21 326 orders for possession and 3835 actual evictions. The worst affected area in Britain was again Clydebank and Glasgow, where between January 1923 and March 1924 there were 4936 orders and 1000 evictions. These figures underestimate the true scale of the landlords' campaign because many tenants left prior to legal proceedings (see Lyman 1957).

In 1924 the first Labour government was elected. This was a minority administration mainly notable for its Housing Act, the Wheatley Act, piloted by John Wheatley, a champion of council housing since the Glasgow rent strike days. The Wheatley Act restored and increased council subsidies and rents were controlled. The Act embodied a view of council housing as a major tenure offering accommodation to a wide cross-section of the British population (Cole and Furbey 1994) and led to a major expansion in council housebuilding – over 500 000 houses were built up to 1933 under the Wheatley subsidies, despite some pruning by the Conservative government in 1929. The 1924 Labour government also passed the Prevention of Eviction Act, giving limited protection to tenants. Following the election of a second Labour minority government in 1929 the Greenwood Act was passed in 1930, emphasizing slum clearance and prioritizing low-income families. The high standards of the Tudor Walters Committee were abandoned and councils were encouraged to bring in differential rents – a move that undermined Wheatley's vision.

Tenant organizations in the 1920s held high expectations of the Addison and Wheatley Acts. However, they were more often than not disappointed by the lack of facilities on the new estates. The Watling Residents' Association was formed in 1927 on a new LCC estate in Middlesex and pressed the LCC for necessary facilities, like a meeting place, and also began generating schemes of co-operatives and mutual aid, like a loan and share-out club and collective lawn mowing (Yeo and Yeo 1988). Tenants in Hillfields, Bristol, campaigned for such basic facilities as schools, playgrounds and shops, and in 1928 they successfully negotiated electric lighting in council housing. Facilities on Bristol estates were still extremely limited with virtually no shops, libraries, community halls or pubs for several years after the first tenants had moved in. Up to 1930, not one cinema or social centre was provided on a corporation estate in Bristol (Dresser 1984). In Leeds only one municipally operated community facility was built on a council estate before 1939 – the Meanwood community hall and branch library in September 1936 (Finnigan 1984). In 1932 a comparative study was conducted between Kingstanding, a Birmingham City Council estate with about 30 000 people, and the slightly smaller town of Shrewsbury. Shrewsbury had 30 churches, 15 church halls, 4 picture houses, 159 public houses and parks, sports grounds and hospitals. Kingstanding had one church, one hall, one picture house, one pub and no parks, sports grounds or hospitals. The council planned a community centre but it was never built, so tenants organized their own – the Perrystanding Community Centre. It was not until 1936 that Birmingham's first council-funded community centre opened in Billesley. Throughout the city in 1936 tenants' associations and charitable groups had provided four other community centres – in a city where one in six of the population was a council tenant (Chinn 1991).

Some councils actively discouraged the development of essential shops and services on estates – such as pawnbrokers. In the same way that the loss of the pub on the new estates was a serious blow to working-class communal life, the elimination of the pawnshop represented to a lesser extent a similar disruption of familiar social patterns. Customers relocated on the Wythenshawe estate outside Manchester still journeyed to their old pawnbroker in Hulme, even after the Second World War (Tebbutt 1983). Women in particular felt cut off from old networks, with one woman on Wythenshawe observing that 'a lot of people . . . eventually went back to what we used to call the "corner shop". You see, they didn't like the atmosphere here, because it was a bit lonely, and you know this idea of the corner shop not being there' (quoted in Tebbutt 1995 p.152). The first residents to move to Wythenshawe also had to cope with unmade roads and a poorly developed public transport network. Furthermore, for women, informal methods of getting extra money, company, or a change from domestic duties were also banned at Wythenshawe (Manchester WHG

1987). Lodgers were not allowed and the tenancy rule forbidding the carrying out of a business activity from home was rigorously enforced – even women's hairdressers were investigated.

Tenants' associations themselves began to take action to improve their social facilities. Birmingham City Council had launched the *Municipal Tenants Monthly* in 1922 which 'encouraged gardening on council estates, distributed useful information to tenants, and tried to foster a spirit of neighbourliness amongst them'. The magazine was short-lived but the tenants recognized the need for communal action on estates where the housing was good but where facilities were lacking. Various associations were formed – such as that for gardening on the Linden Road estate, and that on the Pineapple estate which aimed to protect tenants' interests, arrange lectures and to forward complaints to the housing department. Pineapple tenants managed to get a postbox and telephone box on the estate, indicating the importance of tenants' pressure to establish essential facilities (Chinn 1991).

Thus, tenants' associations developed in a form in the 1920s instantly recognizable to the present generation of tenant activists. But as housing management developed in this period, middle-class observers again responded with anxiety to working-class organizations in working-class districts. 'Community Associations' were deliberately organized to undermine tenant organizations. The Liverpool Council of Social Services tried to head off the tenants' associations by recruiting them into a Liverpool Community Committee in 1927. Ernest Barker, at the time a member of the National Council for Social Services, advocated a 'Community Council' on the Norris Green Estate in Liverpool, arguing:

> The title 'Tenants' Association' does perhaps suggest as the basis of your union that you are a tenant, and have a landlord confronting you, and that there is antagonism between landlord and tenant. I know the Tenants' Associations transcend their names. They are in effect Community Associations. But I have a sneaking preference for the title 'Community'. It has a deep human effect – that you have a neighbourhood feeling towards each other as good neighbours. (quoted in Yeo and Yeo 1988 pp.243–244)

Middle-class voluntary workers could not accept conflict, nor did they accept the traditional 'mutual aid' networks established by women on estates, preferring the formal committees of community associations. These attitudes were to influence early housing management practices. The ideas of Octavia Hill were continued by her pupils in the Women House Property Managers Institute. Bristol appointed a 'Lady House Visitor' from the institute in 1928 to continue the idea that the education and moral improvement of the tenant should be part of housing management. In Bristol housing officers seemed to believe in neat and tidy gardens as evidence of moral respectability. The local housing manager reported in 1930 that 'contrary to the prophecies of pessimists, picture rails are used, and baths are not misused. Gardens are generally very well cultivated and prove of great service to the tenants. Horticultural societies have been formed on the large Estates, and the results obtained are most gratifying.' As Dresser points out, 'this emphasis on the state of tenants' gardens is significant. Nowhere, it seems, was the transforming power of the garden more taken for granted than by those involved in corporation housing. The garden was seen implicitly as a major moral regenerator, and a well-kept garden was repeatedly assumed to be the sign of a "good" tenant' (Dresser 1984 p.207).

Local authorities also refused licences for pubs on council estates. In Leeds the early estates were 'dry' – in the Watling estate, tenants refused to accept a house offered for use as a club because an alcohol licence was unavailable. In Bristol, on the Sea Mills and Horfield estates, tenants campaigned unsuccessfully for pub and off-licence premises and had to resort to vans selling alcoholic drinks around the estate. Middle-class residents living near Horfield believed that the tenants had come from districts which were slums and if drink were to be brought into the area, conditions would deteriorate (Dresser 1984). Such class hostility was openly displayed in some areas. In Leeds the City Council planned an estate at Moortown adjoining prosperous middle-class suburbs. When the Conservatives returned to power the estate was 'moved' to a remote site at Cookridge. In Lewisham, the two 'cottage estates' built by the LCC, Bellingham and Downham, were greeted with fears of crime, unruly children, unemployment and associated charges on the rates. 'Residents in an adjacent private estate in Bromley did all they could to exclude Downham tenants, building a concrete wall, with broken glass embedded in the top, across the connecting road. Despite considerable controversy . . . the wall was not demolished until 1946' (Jeffery 1989 p.212). This was a theme to be repeated after the Second World War – in Cardiff, for instance, and with the famous Cutteslowe Wall in Oxford in the 1950s (see Collison 1963).

After 1930, with the influx of poorer households from slum clearance areas on to council estates, attitudes hardened towards these 'slum-minded' tenants. 'The opinions of Dr Hanschel, who described slum-dwellers as a "sub-species of *Homo sapiens*", found some support. "There exists evidence for the probability that some, at least, of this sub-species' young are like the parent, hopeless and helpless by reason of stamped-in mental defect"' (quoted in Burnett 1986 p.242 – original emphasis). This perspective influenced the housing management thinking of a number of local authorities in the 1930s, some of whom adopted the Octavia Hill system where women housing managers were employed to train the tenant in good housekeeping and 'decent' living (Power 1987). However, it must be stressed that the pre-war experience of council tenants was not entirely one of disaffection and that by 1941 they were settling in to their new estates. Mass Observation, a survey organization, published *Inquiry into People's Homes*, a study of 12 working-class communities which actually found that 'of many types of working-class housing examined, satisfaction was highest (80 per cent of the sample) on housing estates and lowest (62 per cent) in privately rented old houses' (Burnett 1986 p.237).

Tenants and the political movements of the unemployed

The tenants' movement of the 1920s and 1930s continued to be linked to trade union and political movements of the period. As we have seen, the 'rent strike' had been advocated by some socialists as a self-conscious tactic to undermine the capitalist state. Other tenant groups advocated the tenants' movement model as a paradigm for future social organizing – similar to the 'workers control' theories of syndicalists in the trade union movement. In Merseyside, the Larkhill and North-East Liverpool Tenants' Association:

> once formally constituted in 1922 . . . acted as a tenants' trade union, pressing the Corporation about rents, contracts and decorations. Besides this . . . the Association organized educational and recreational activity. Some activists even envisioned the tenants' associations replacing political parties in a new state consisting of local and national parliaments with representatives from consumers' and producers' organizations. (Yeo and Yeo 1988 p.242)

The close co-operation with the Labour Party was a feature of early tenants' organizations. As the Party became a membership organization, the new council estates provided many of its subscribers. In Lewisham, Herbert Morrison built up 2500 Labour Party members for the East Lewisham constituency as a 'result of conscious and concentrated effort involving the development of local drama, choral, and sporting societies, political education and intensive canvassing, with each road on the estates managed by a "street captain"' (Jeffery 1989 p.196). In echoes of more recent 'gerrymandering' allegations in Westminster, Pavnall, a London Conservative MP, led a delegation to the Prime Minister in 1937 asking for LCC estates to be hived off the marginal Conservative seats of Hendon, Romford and Lewisham. In Bristol the Conservative Council, in the bitter days after the General Strike in 1926, simply refused to allow a Labour Party meeting on a corporation estate. The 'model tenant' it seems was assumed by Bristol housing officials to be a clean-living and right-minded family man who was to be 'diverted from the pub, protected against agitation, advised on housekeeping and tempted into horticulture' (Dresser 1984 p.208).

In Leeds as early as 1922 the Conservatives had resisted pressure to build under the Addison Act and had introduced a municipal housebuilding programme to promote owner-occupation through 'rental purchase'. The *Yorkshire Post* saw the political value of small-scale property owners as 'possibly the best and surest safeguard against the follies of Socialism' (quoted in Finnigan 1984 p.109). The owner-occupier was seen as a natural Conservative voter. There was indeed a massive boom in private building for owner-occupation – from 130 000 in 1931 to an annual average of 260 000 a year between 1935 and 1939, with building society funding rising from £87 million in 1920 to £756 million by 1940. But even here the authorities met some collective resistance. The building boom in the private sector saw many examples of jerry-building and the quality of housing produced was very poor. Consequently, the new owners of these properties could often not afford both their mortgage repayments *and* the cost of repairing their homes to an acceptable standard. Thus, there were widespread mortgage strikes with several thousand people withholding payments until their housing defects were corrected. Elsie and Jim Borders, communist activists and founders of the Coney Hall District Residents' Association in Kent, fought the building societies through the courts. The dispute continued for months, rousing suburban dwellers throughout the country (Piratin 1948). This strike eventually forced legislation in the form of the Building Societies Act 1939 (see Boddy 1992).

The Greenwood Act 1930 had divided some Labour authorities from their tenants because it paved the way for the introduction of rent rebate schemes. Eleanor Rathbone, best known for her role as a champion of family allowances in 1945, was the chief advocate of what she described as 'children's rent rebates' (Malpass 1992 p.69). Some Labour authorities did bring in rebate schemes, but overall only 80 local authorities out of 1400 had schemes by 1939 (see Finnigan 1984). The best known of these was in Leeds where the council, under its radical Chair of Housing, Councillor Rev Jenkinson, introduced a scheme which involved higher rents for the better-off tenants and some living rent free. By October 1935 the scheme covered 10 960 council properties and 11 per cent of the tenants in these houses were living rent free. Many tenants bitterly resented the 'means test' required by the rebate scheme, while the Leeds Tenants' Association opposed it totally and went to the courts to have it declared unlawful. The case failed in the Court of Appeal in October 1934 and consequently the Association was forced into an alliance with the Conservatives against rebates. The Conservatives favoured lower-standard council houses to save money while opposing the political implications of the rebate scheme. Alderman Davies, the Conservative leader, saw the scheme as the first step towards 'communal socialism in Leeds'. Despite Jenkinson's record of clearing slums, rebuilding 6000 council houses and planning a major building programme that included the famous Quarry Hill flats, the tenants' opposition to rent rebates helped the Conservatives to return to power in 1935. Labour were not to regain control of Leeds City Council until 1945. In 1939 the Birmingham Conservatives had also tried to introduce a rent rebate scheme which caused a prolonged rent strike involving 7000 tenants. The council dropped the scheme when war broke out (see Malpass 1992).

In Manchester, where the council had built more homes than the private sector in the inter-war period (20–30 000 by 1939), the Labour Party and women's organizations were jointly involved in a number of housing campaigns. In particular, the Labour Party Women's Advisory Council (WAC) opposed flatted schemes – 2000 of which had been built in the city by the Second World War. It had launched a determined campaign between 1934 and 1936 against the Smedley Point development in Wythenshawe 'for being too large and like a barracks [and] for not having the most modern facilities in kitchens and communal washhouses, and especially for not having lifts' (Manchester WHG 1987 p.33). Women were heavily involved in the housing politics of the city, not only through the WAC but also the Manchester branch of the National Council of Women and the Women's Citizen Association. They demanded opportunities for women housing managers, campaigned on design factors and tenancy issues, and offered housing advice services.

The Communist Party of Great Britain, founded in 1920, was also involved with tenants' campaigns in the inter-war period. Phil Piratin, later a Communist MP, organized tenants in Stepney from 1934 and in 1937 the Stepney Tenants' Defence League was formed. Michael Shapiro, a university lecturer, engaged with the Stepney activists to set up the National Tenants' Federation with offices in Holborn. In August 1938 Bethnal Green tenants in Quinn Square organized a rent strike of 230 tenants. At the same time 300 council tenants were on rent strike in Welwyn Garden City. In November and December 1938 a whole rash of rent strikes was organized throughout the private sector of Limehouse, then throughout most areas of East London. By 1939 some of these rent strikes had become very protracted – one for eleven weeks, another for five months. 'Barbed wire barricades were placed around the entire blocks. Pickets were on duty day and night. At Langdale Mansions in June 1939 there were pitched battles between police and tenants who defended themselves with saucepans, rolling pins, sticks and shovels.' A massive demonstration and march of 10 000 supporters was broken up by the police. But the Stepney events had gained national publicity and by 30 June 'the twenty-one weeks' rent strike, bitter, bloody, had been won'. In January 1939 'action began among 50 000 Birmingham municipal tenants. Similar action took place in Sheffield, Huddersfield, Liverpool, Aberdeen, Sunderland and Oxford' (see Piratin 1948 pp.35–41).

Tens of thousands of working class men and women had organized themselves for common struggle . . . Committees were formed and hundreds of people who had never been on a committee and had no experience of organization or politics, learned those things and learnt them well. Outstanding were the women. Every feminist claim was proved . . . They were mostly more enthusiastic, and hence more reliable . . . it was the women who did most of the picketing. (Piratin 1948 p.46.)

The president of the Stepney Tenants' Defence League, Fr. John Groser, and many of the activists were Jewish. The Stepney Tenants' Defence League had three full-time organizers, including their secretary, Ella Donovan (Piratin 1948).

The East End tenants co-operated with the National Unemployed Workers' Movement (NUWM), founded in 1921. In various parts of the country, the NUWM worked with tenants' defence organizations to prevent evictions of unemployed tenants. In Bradford, the Unemployed Association and its organizer, Harry Goldthorpe, confronted the city bailiffs who:

had to put wire mesh guards in front of their offices for safety . . . Big Norton was one of them . . . he was the man who scared the womenfolk with his chalk marks on their furniture. But he met his match in the Unemployed Association. We had a second-hand Jowett van . . . and with some loyal colleagues I took many 'marked up' homes from under Norton's feet, to return them later to their rightful owners. Our van, with its frequent loads of chalked furniture snatched out of further reach of the bailiffs, became known as 'the Bailiff's Runner'. (Goldthorpe 1959 pp.12–13)

Bert Edwards organized similar resistance in Southwark in the 1920s with the NUWM. When bailiffs threatened 'we would put into the house a defence committee of ten to twenty members, according to the size of the house. We would supply them with a bucket and a rope . . . When we had barricaded the front door and the ground-floor windows, back and front, we would fill the street with unemployed workers or sympathetic neighbours . . . Another tactic was to organize a rent strike. We said that the rents were too high, so the tenants decided to withhold paying it. They would pay it to me and I'd put it in the bank . . . The strike didn't last long . . . we won our demands and that was that' (Edwards 1982 pp.31–32).

In July 1939 a National Tenants' Federation convention was planned for Birmingham to demand a new code for tenants and residents, a new Rent Act and improved housing standards. A 'Housing Charter' was drawn up and campaigning started. In the same month, on the eve of the Second World War, a demonstration was held at Hyde Park with Communist Party speakers standing alongside Aneurin Bevan and Ellen Wilkinson of the Labour Party. The government, learning from the experiences of 1915, eventually froze rents at their September 1939 levels.

The squatters, tenants and the state

The massive loss of housing during the long and protracted Second World War produced a major national crisis and it was therefore not surprising that housing was to become such a dominant issue in the 1945 election campaign. The bombing raids of the war destroyed and damaged enormous numbers of houses. There were already a large number of poor-quality and unfit houses in Britain at the onset of war. By the end of 1942 around 300 000 families were living in houses condemned as unfit – representing well over a million people. In addition, after the raids of 1940 and 1941, 2.5 million people lived in occupied bombed houses which had received only patchwork repairs. Early in 1943 the War Cabinet started repairing the 100 000 bombed houses which were uninhabitable. Housing shortages meant that the 'social ulcer of overcrowding spread from the industrial conurbations to smaller country towns' (Calder 1969 p.316). In the same year V1 and V2 rockets had destroyed many more Londoners' homes. By the end of September 1943, 25 000 houses in the London region had been totally destroyed or damaged beyond repair, adding to the 84 000 written off after earlier raids (Calder 1969). By January 1945, 130 000 building workers were employed in repair work in London alone, but many bombed-out families were still living in huts erected with the help of American troops and Italian prisoners of war. Returning servicemen were thus confronted with overcrowding and an acute shortage of accommodation. Labour's landslide victory in the 1945 election – the first majority Labour government – increased expectations and reflected the popular mobilization characteristic of the war years. During the London Blitz the underground stations of the East End were occupied by families who elected their own shelter committees (Hinton 1988). In April 1945, as the war drew to a close, demobbed servicemen occupied empty property in south coast resorts. Churchill, then Prime Minister, referred to these people as 'vigilantes':

> I deeply regret to see the continued prominence of the vigilantes, as reported in the newspapers. This is a matter of considerable importance, and lawlessness should not be allowed. The law officers and the police should consider all means of putting an end to these pranks; and the newspapers should be induced . . . to curtail their publicity. (quoted in Dickens 1977 p.219)

These 'vigilantes' were actually organized by Harry Cowley, a former chimney sweep and market trader from Brighton. He and his group 'had similarly appropriated houses in 1920 for returning servicemen. On that occasion, Cowley, with a fake bomb in each hand, threatened to blow up an estate agent who tried to evict an elderly lady squatter' (Dickens 1977 p.220). There had in fact been other examples of squatters taking over camps after the First World War. At Birtley in County Durham, 600 two- and three-bedroomed huts built to house a colony of Belgian refugees working in munitions were squatted in by families until Chester-le-Street Council took them over in 1924 (see Ryder 1984). Cowley's group inspired a range of other groups in South London and other towns to seize empty houses in 1945. In response to this Churchill's coalition government gave local authorities powers to requisition empty properties. *The News Chronicle* (24 July 1945) greeted this decision with enthusiasm as 'the first instance of really successful pressure by public opinion in relation to a major domestic issue. Dissatisfaction with government policy has forced these major concessions' (quoted in Dickens 1977 p.200).

Squatting died out soon after this until the summer of 1946 when groups began to occupy empty military camps and prisoner-of-war camps and – when these camps filled up – empty houses, flats and hostels. In May 1946 a cinema projectionist taking up a new job in Scunthorpe and unable to find any accommodation moved, with his wife and four children, into the officers mess of an abandoned military camp. The word spread and by July another twenty families had joined them. This was the start of the squatters' movement (Hinton 1988). News spread, triggering further occupations in Scunthorpe itself, Doncaster and Sheffield. Durham miners occupied camps, and Bristol and Birmingham followed. By 25 August a meeting in Birmingham representing 257 families in 12 camps around the city established the Birmingham and District Squatters Association. Birmingham City Council cut off services to the camps, refusing to negotiate with the Association because of its Communist Party support. In September in London squatters involved in occupations of the Duchess of Bedford House flats in Kensington were charged with conspiracy. The squatters withdrew from these 'demonstration' occupations, but in Birmingham the council agreed to negotiate with squatters and in the rest of the country squatters continued occupying camps. The *Daily Mail* praised the squatters for their 'robust common sense' and their ability when governments fail them 'to take matters quietly but firmly into their own hands'. It was 'a refreshing example of what ordinary people can do when they have a mind to do it' (quoted in Hinton 1988 p.116). Support for the squatters was widespread. Even *The Economist* commented that their action, taking the law into their own hands, was socially just (see Addison 1985). By 10 October 1946 the Commons was informed that some 46 335 people were in occupation of 1181 camps. Gradually, the camps were transferred to local authorities and services were provided.

Squatter families spent many years in the camps – in 1954 there were still 23 000 families in over 1000 camps in England and Wales (see Dickens 1977). In Glasgow 1500 families had squatted and the authorities were still evicting squatters in the city centre areas throughout 1949. This era of working-class squatting has disappeared from our social construction of the image of the tenant activist. As Johnstone remarks:

> Squatting is sometimes portrayed in the media as anarchistic and individualistic. However the squatting that took place in Glasgow and other towns and cities throughout Britain between 1946 and 1950 was the antithesis: it was collectively based, organized from within the working class and had a collective goal in mind: public sector housing for all. (Johnstone 1993 p.14)

When squatting returned on a mass scale in the 1960s and 1970s, highlighting the plight of the homeless and the large number of empty houses, it failed to ignite the same public sympathy or a wider movement of action among tenants – although this was clearly the aim. Ron Bailey, a 'leader' of the squatters, was clear about the movement's wider aim:

> Obviously we hoped that our action would spark off a squatting campaign on a mass scale, and that homeless people and slum dwellers would be inspired to squat in large numbers by small but successful actions. But the main purpose of the movement was even wider than this – we hoped to start an all out attack on the housing authorities, with ordinary people taking action for themselves. Finally, and closely in conjunction with this, we saw our campaign as having a radicalizing effect on existing movements in the housing field – tenants associations, action committees, community project groups, etc. If these could be radicalized and linked together then we would really have achieved something.
>   It is important that these wider aims be understood because many people feel that the squatters, even if they succeeded in launching a mass campaign, can do little more than Shelter to solve the housing problem. Squatting, after all, is only concerned with existing empty property. But this is to miss the point. Squatting should be the movement of ordinary people to challenge the authorities on the whole issue. It must become the living demonstration that ordinary people will no longer accept the intolerable housing shortage. It must become the threat that will compel government, national and local, to change its priorities. (Bailey 1973 p.34)

Although by 1976 there were estimates of between 10 000 and 50 000 squats throughout Britain, the movement failed to mobilize a wider campaign for 'public-sector housing for all'. But arguably this wave of squatting was influential – along with the television programme *Cathy Come Home* – in the formation of Shelter and the passing of the Housing (Homeless Persons) Act 1977.

Tenants and the 'New Jerusalem' – 1945–60

Aneurin Bevan, who became Labour Minister of Health with responsibility for housing in 1945, had a vision of council housing which included high-quality houses and socially 'mixed' communities. He insisted on national projects giving priority to public authorities and their housing programmes. Between 1945 and 1951, 80 per cent of housing completions were in the public sector – in 1951 almost 90 per cent. Bevan pushed up space standards from the Addison average of 750 square feet per dwelling to 900 square feet and by 1949 the average had risen to over 1000 square feet, producing some of the most spacious council houses ever built. As Bevan said, 'we shall be judged for a year or two by the number of houses we build. We shall be judged in ten years time by the type of houses we build' (quoted in Hennessy 1993 p.172). Bevan also disliked the 'prefab' concept introduced as an emergency housing solution in 1944. He called them 'rabbit hutches', although some 125000 had been built by 1948, many of which are still occupied today. In the initial post-war period 600000 damaged houses had been brought back into occupation and 70000 requisitioned by local authorities. In 1940 there were 55400 public-sector completions, rising to 175213 by 1948 and then settling at around 150000 a year until 1951. The incoming Conservatives increased housebuilding under Macmillan as housing minister – although this was at the expense of quality and space. The Conservatives completed 220924 public-sector houses in 1954. After 1955 more traditional Conservative Party policies took over, with lower subsidies and rent decontrol in 1957.

Tenants' associations continued to develop after the war and the National Association of Tenants and Residents was founded in 1948. The tenants' movement continued to be linked to some degree with its pre-war Communist predecessor and this link meant that tenants' networks were caught up in the anti-Communist 'witch-hunts' of the 1950s. In 1953 the Annual Report of the Yorkshire Regional Council of the Labour Party reported that the Leeds Federation of Municipal Tenants' and Householders' Associations had been 'exposed' as being 'Communist controlled'. The report also noted with satisfaction that the idea for an All Yorkshire Committee of Tenants' Associations had been defeated (see Grayson 1991).

On the new estates tenants again had to grapple with the problem of a lack of facilities and building new communities. Lewis Silkin, then Minister of Town and Country Planning, brought in a New Towns Act in 1946 which envisaged 14 new towns. Immediately there was middle-class opposition. A Residents' Protection Association was set up in Stevenage and members changed signs at the local railway station to 'Silkingrad' (see Hennessy 1993). Mary Tabor, the first Housing Manager at Stevenage, remembers:

> . . . how easy it was to get a group of people together, in response to a need that had come to light, an injustice that had been perceived, indignation at proposals or neglect of action by the statutory authorities, or simply to encourage action and

stimulate interest in the development and planning of the Town. Most of the groups at first were ad hoc. Later they became established as a Residents Federation and Community Associations. (quoted in Ward 1993 p.53)

Len White, who later became Social Development Officer in Stevenage, argued in two publications for the National Council for Social Service (*Community or Chaos: Housing Estates and their Social Problems*, 1950, and *New Towns*, 1951) that councils should avoid 'the defects of inter-war housing, with its shortsighted emphasis on mere housing and its lamentable failure to plan for social needs', adding that 'even in the large post-war schemes all the essential community services, shops, transport, schools, recreation and churches have fallen hopelessly behind the build-up of population' (quoted in Ward 1993 p.51). As one early resident of Stevenage recalls, her 'outstanding memory is of *dust* and *mud* [original emphasis]. We had no gardens, no roads, no pavements or footpaths, no telephones, no shop' (quoted in Ward 1993 p.50). Some of the architecture was designed to 'engineer' new communities. Some developments in Hertfordshire in the 1940s and 1950s were constructed with what were called 'anti-gossip' walls to discourage the kind of intimacy associated with the slums (Tebbutt 1995). A whole series of surveys and research in the estates of the 1950s – in Coventry, Sheffield, Liverpool, Manchester and Surrey – found young families struggling to establish new networks and communities. But 'estates which allowed the inhabitants a far greater degree of space than their old housing were likely to be welcomed with some relief' (Tebbutt 1995 p.155). Tenants celebrated the move to new council estates, particularly the 'respectable' ones. The Housing Act 1949 had removed the requirement to house the 'working class' and the new tenants were from the 'respectable' section of the working class – not the 'rough slum dwellers' housed in the 1930s. This changing orientation of council housing was acknowledged in the 1959 Central Housing Advisory Committee Report on *Councils and their Houses* which stated that 'tenants today are much more representative of the community as a whole and are, for the most part, independent, reliable citizens who no longer require the support and guidance which was often thought necessary in the past' (cited in Clapham *et al.* 1990 pp.209–210).

But class divisions were still evident on the boundaries of the estates. In 1955 in Cardiff 'the City Council built a six foot high wall across the road between the council estate at Llanishen and a double row of privately owned houses'. Leo Abse, then a local councillor, protested that 'this is the most silly monument to snobbery imaginable. You are trying to transform the council estate into a ghetto' (Allaun 1968 p.92). But the wall was still standing in 1968. This kind of social snobbery remained evident in recent years in Leeds. In 1990 a wall was built across a street on the Belle Isle estate, separating housing association tenants and owner-occupiers from the existing council tenants.

The tenants' movement developed on the new post-war estates and in 1957 tenants across London formed the Association of London Housing Estates (ALHE). The gradual reversal of housing policies in the 1950s renewed the militancy of the movement. In Glasgow, a city still suffering appalling housing conditions, 'peripheral' estates had been built at Castlemilk, Drumchapel, Easterhouse and Pollok. A 'progressive' council was elected in 1951 and it backed the Conservative Opposition nationally in building for sale and selling council houses. It proposed to sell the Merrylee Road housing scheme on the south side of the city. Shop stewards at a firm near Merrylee called a meeting of trade unions' Labour and Communist representatives and tenants' associations at which a demonstration was planned for 6 December 1951. Between 2000 and 5000 people attended, including 'five processions of "housewives" from Bridgeton, Gorbals, Anderston, Partick and Tradeston . . . Most of the women were active in local tenants' associations and had a deeper understanding of the appalling conditions in the city' (Johnstone 1993 p.17). Protest meetings continued after the decision to sell and strikes and demonstrations in January 1952 provided the first use of·the Public Order Act of 1936 in Glasgow. Some houses were being processed for sale by April, but the issue remained central to the May elections and Labour was returned to power. 'It was through the campaign organized by building workers, tenants' associations, women's groups and other working class organizations in Glasgow that the real opposition to the sale of the Merrylee houses was mobilized' (Johnstone 1993 p.23).

Where authorities were building council housing for rent tenants were often impatient about the pace of slum clearance. In 1953 in West Ham, 300 people from the Tenants' Association of Radland Road and affiliated roads called for the resignation of the West Ham Council *en bloc* and for a government inquiry into local housing conditions. In August 1954 the tenants of Jidal Basin, a low-lying area of poor housing, were being championed by the local prospective Conservative MP against the Labour council. In 1955 tenants called for central government to take over the borough's housing function. The Minister of Housing refused the request, lodged by 2000 tenants, but promised to put pressure on building rates (CDP 1976).

Between 1953 and 1957 the Conservatives passed a series of Housing and Rent Acts cutting council subsidies, encouraging the sale of council houses and, in the 1957 Rent Act, decontrolling rents in the private sector and increasing rents in the council sector. Tenants' organizations joined building-trade unions and trades councils in mobilizing opposition. In Manchester the city still had 60 000 unfit houses and the Trades Council set up a Rents Advice Bureau in 1953 which joined the national campaign against the Rent Act. After the Act it continued advice services and in 1958 was reporting that landlords were also taking advantage of the situation to impose new agreements (Arnison *et al*. 1993). The legislation also had an effect on council rents. In St Pancras, London, in 1958 the Labour group split and 'Communists' who had fought the 1957 Act were expelled. Labour increased rents and the Conservatives won the borough in May 1959.

The Conservatives immediately put up rents: most of the rents on pre-war estates were trebled, and those on the post-war estates doubled. There were already some small tenants' associations, but the rent increases galvanized tenants throughout the estates. In August 1959 the St Pancras United Tenants' Association (UTA) was formed, to which 25 tenants' associations were affiliated. The UTA campaigned throughout the autumn with demonstrations and took out every night as many as 60 women, banging on the councillors' doors. The police were less likely to arrest the women and the women themselves were very keen and formed the backbone of the movement, keeping everything going in the day and giving each other mutual support. In November a meeting of 165 delegates from 35 associations gave delegates a free hand to negotiate *and* to organize a rent strike if this failed. A last-minute petition of 16 000 signatures failed to have an effect. The rent strike started with about half the 4200 tenants affected but, by the end of January, 624 were on strike (see Burn 1972).

The council started proceedings for evictions for the rent strike arrears and most tenants withdrew, leaving only two leading members of the UTA facing eviction after a court hearing in May 1960. One of them was Don Cook, a tenant since 1947 and secretary of the UTA, who faced a rent increase of 100 per cent. The blocks of flats where the tenants lived were barricaded and the attempts by the council to evict them revived the campaign. All the tenants in the affected blocks went on rent strike again – local railwaymen organized a strike in support, council workers went on strike for two days and demonstrations were held. 'Distress rockets and cars equipped with loudspeakers were used to rouse the tenants against the bailiffs, one "false alarm" bringing over 1000 people into the area around one besieged flat at midnight' (Moorhouse *et al*. 1972 p.139). After six weeks the two UTA members were evicted amid violent scuffles. Building workers led a march of 2000 people to the Town Hall in protest and at least 50 people were arrested, five of whom were later sent to prison. The rent strike then petered out with agreements on arrears, but the strike was 'notable for the overt violence it produced between tenants and "authority" – action unusual in the British context' (Moorhouse *et al*. 1972 p.140).

Black tenants organize

In 1958, in Nottingham and Notting Hill, there were street riots targeting black tenants, many of whom had recently settled in these areas. Britain in the 1950s had been accustomed to a 'colour bar' operating against black settlers and black Britons established in many working-class areas since the early years of the century. Trevor Carter, who moved from Guyana in 1956, remembers:

> In the inner-city areas to which we were drawn by the light manufacturing industries, we competed with the Irish and others for bedsit accommodation. Council housing was not an option for us: most were single and in our twenties. But even families with children could not get council housing because of the residence qualification.
>
> Most private landlords did not want black tenants any more than the local authority. Often their insulting signs in the window included 'No Irish' and 'No children' along with the proscribed blacks and dogs. The rents for the flats and rooms we did get were grossly inflated, sometimes four times the amount charged to white tenants. 'Black tax' it was called. (Carter 1986 p.31)

Excluded from mainstream housing opportunities, migrants from the Caribbean were forced into the hands of loan sharks to get mortgages. In 1957 the Bradford Equitable Building Society was able to explain in writing to a 37-year-old Jamaican civil servant and London School of Economics graduate that: 'It is the policy of the society's directors not to approve advances to coloured people' (*Sunday Pictorial* 21 July 1957, quoted in Smith and Hill 1992 p.106). Asian settlers of the period found a similar situation and thus the 'tradition' of owner-occupation and multi-occupation developed. Pubs refused to serve black customers and thus 'we were forced to develop the habit of holding parties at home' (Carter 1986 p.39). Notting Hill proved a turning point in black organizing. Three local black groups were formed in North Kensington: the Racial Brotherhood Movement, the Coloured People's Progressive Association and the Afro-Asian Club. By the end of 1959 a co-ordinating committee had been set up, the Committee for Inter-Racial Unity in West London.

Claudia Jones, a black American Communist expelled from the USA, established the *West Indian Gazette* in 1958 and the Notting Hill Carnival by 1960. In 1959 Pansy Jeffries, the first black woman worker at the Citizens' Advice Bureau, helped to develop the Notting Hill Housing Trust as an advice and social centre and to campaign on issues such as discrimination in housing. In the 1960s further black organizations emerged from meetings in the Notting Hill area, notably the Mangrove Restaurant, which opened in 1969. Furthermore, a vigorous black housing association movement was established, and it flourished towards the end of the 1950s (Smith and Hill 1992).

Discrimination continued through the 1960s. There were 'colour bar petitions' to exclude black people from council accommodation – 500 tenants in the Loughborough Road Estate, Brixton, signed a petition in September 1964. Residential qualifications were common, with Birmingham retaining a five-year qualification until 1977. Overtly racist adverts excluding black tenants were quite legal until 1968 and in that year a quarter of adverts in one East London newspaper had the phrase 'no coloureds' included. By the mid-1960s only 6 per cent of the black population born overseas had secured access to council housing, compared to 28 per cent of Irish immigrants and about one-third of the rest of the population. This is not the place to rehearse the history of black people in Britain in the post-war period but, as outlined in Chapter 11, it is abundantly clear from a number of research studies that structural, subjective and institutional racism has produced ethnic cleavages in terms of both residential experience and opportunities to participate in tenants' organizations.

In the 1950s almost half of all housing was still in the hands of private landlords and the Rent Act 1957, although not fully implemented until 1961, had a significant impact by decontrolling rents at the next change of tenancy. This permitted landlords such as Peter Rachman to 'winkle out' established tenants to take advantage of higher rent possibilities (Kemp 1992). In 1957 private tenants in the North Kensington Tenants' Association had started to organize against the Bill, linking up with a West London Rent Bill Action Committee. Out of this campaign two tenants' groups emerged: the St Stephen's Garden Tenants' Association and the Powis and Colville Residents' Association. Both groups stressed anti-racist and anti-fascist policies and the defence of private tenants and council tenants. In April 1960, 11 tenants went on rent strike in one block and in August 1963 a family faced with eviction were barricaded in – the barbed wire barricades were up for six days and a system of alarm bells was rigged up (O'Malley 1977).

By 1967, the Notting Hill People's Association had been formed around the struggles of 72 tenants in Colville Gardens. The Association spawned a range of other initiatives – neighbourhood councils, a People's Centre, playschemes, and a range of original tactics including a housing register of ownership in the area, 'auction busting' (stopping the auction of homes requisitioned by the council in the war) and squatting campaigns. In May 1973 the local community forum organized an all-night 'lock-in' of councillors and officials during 'consultations' with the local community about redevelopment plans. The leader of Kensington and Chelsea Borough described the community tenant organization as 'a gang of organized thugs and anarchists . . . [who have] created a general atmosphere of anarchy and terrorism in North Kensington' (quoted in O'Malley 1977 p.137).

The return of the rent strike – 1968–73

In the late 1960s the British and international political scene was in ferment – trade union strikes, student uprisings, anti-Vietnam movements, the women's movement, Black Power and so on. Tenant activities and campaigns became linked to and mirrored these general political trends in society. For instance, with reference to Northern Ireland in October 1971, *The Guardian* reported that 'the civil disobedience campaign, which involves the non-payment of all rents, rates and bills to public bodies, has been running for seven weeks . . . The Government reckons that local authorities have lost more than £400 000 in council rents alone . . . Officials estimate that about 140 000 people living in council houses have been taking part in the campaign' (quoted in Moorhouse *et al.* 1972 p.153).

Council housebuilding had taken off again with the election of a Labour government in 1964. The government opted for a policy based on the rapid expansion of mass housing achieved by concentrating on the construction of tower blocks using industrialized 'system building'. Council housebuilding rose to a peak of 159 300 in 1967, many of these in tower blocks. However, in May 1968, after the Ronan Point gas explosion in West Ham saw the partial collapse of a 22-storey tower block, high-rise housebuilding was to slow down and was eventually abandoned. The legacy of the 'great British housing disaster' was to haunt tenants' organizations throughout the next 20 years. In West Ham, in response to the Ronan Point disaster, 700 tenants attended a meeting in July 1968 in Custom House and decided to refuse rehousing in tower blocks. Arthur Carr, the prospective Conservative MP for East Ham, organized what he called 'the peasants' rebellion' – involving tenant activists in clearance schemes – to encourage resistance to rehousing in tower blocks (see CDP 1976). However, while no more tower blocks were built in West Ham, tenants continue to be moved into them today.

Tenants' associations started to spring up in the tower blocks. In June 1969 in Glasgow as many as 22 of the 34 associations believed to be active in the city were in areas containing multi-storey flats. Of these associations 13, with a total of 7000 members, had activities very familiar 30 years on. They met monthly and collected annual subscriptions of 12.5p per family. Half of their 96 office-holders were 50 years old or over, and more than half of them were men – mostly skilled manual workers. Attendances were around 50 a meeting and activities were focused on complaints, condensation, transport issues and rent increases. Their link to political movements survived, often a cross-link between committee members and those of trade unions and Municipal Ward Committees. The Glasgow Council of Tenants' Associations was often accused of never having shaken off the communist sympathies which had coloured its early days. The council had fairly meagre resources compared with the Association of London Estates, which received £9000 towards its £11 000 expenditure in 1969 from grants from local authorities and the Council of Social Service. The London association had 90 affiliated organizations and full-time staff, two of whom were trained in community development and who provided training for associations. In contrast, the Glasgow tenants were facing difficulties in finding rooms and halls in which to meet. In London, for estates over 400 dwellings, the GLC would usually have built and furnished simple premises for any association that had proved itself viable. In Birmingham in 1969 the council aimed at a hall of some kind for every 2000 of its 140 000 tenants, and had provided 35 of these (Jephcott 1971). By 1973, an extensive web of 'tenant participation schemes' had emerged in London boroughs (Richardson 1983) with tenants' representatives as observers on housing committees, sitting as co-opted members on sub-committees, and attending a whole range of joint consultative committees and meetings with councillor landlords and housing officers. Certainly, the language of tenants' organizations had started to change, housing management practices began to be more responsive and 'community development' started to be mentioned in housing circles – these latter trends being primarily the result of tenant militancy over the previous five years.

The Conservatives won control of the GLC in April 1967 and decided to phase in a 70 per cent increase in council rents over the next three years. Tenants on ten estates immediately reacted and formed the Tower Hamlets Federation. Later another 19 estates affiliated: Hackney Federation and some individual estates formed the United Tenants' Action Committee and the Becontree Co-ordinating Committee formed to represent tenants in Dagenham. They all came together in a demonstration at Tower Hill. The tenants' organizations lobbied, demonstrated, attended council meetings, and finally organized a Trafalgar Square rally of between 10 and 20 000 people. In October 1968 the rent increases were brought in, tenants organized and, by November, 5 per cent of all GLC tenants (around 11 000 families) were on rent strike. After a protracted battle with demonstrations and lobbies, tenants threatened with eviction retaliated by threatening industrial action (which had already been promised by dockers' leaders) and launched a £5000 fund to finance legal action. In January 1970 their legal actions failed but after 15 months 3000 tenants were still withholding rents. The tenants had raised £10 000 for the campaign and, although some of the associations wound up, many continued. At the same time as the GLC tenants were on strike, in Liverpool increases had precipitated a rent strike which lasted six months and had won a small concession – a reduction of 12.5p a week in rent (see Moorhouse *et al.* 1972). In smaller housing authorities there was a similar pattern. For instance, in Batley in the early 1960s, council rents were among the lowest in the country. But by 1968 large increases had led to the formation of tenants' associations on all the large estates. Some of 'the most vociferous objections came from tenants on the inter war estates who because of rent pooling had to bear their share of the cost of the new building programme by paying higher rents for relatively sub standard housing' (CDP 1976 p.40).

Conservative cutbacks in subsidies at the end of the 1950s had started to push council rents towards market levels. Government advice to councils was to reduce rate subsidies (compulsory under the Labour government of 1945–51) and to bring in rent rebate schemes. In some Labour authorities this was seen as the reintroduction of a 'means test' for housing. In 1960, Roy Hattersley, then Deputy Chair of Sheffield's Housing Committee, argued that rent differentials would impose 'inexcusable indignities on the tenants'. However, the Labour government of 1964 continued to issue the same advice on rebates. Rent rises in Sheffield resulted in problems in lettings which led Alderman Dyson to introduce a review of housing finance in the city in February 1966. A questionnaire was sent to tenants and a rebate scheme proposed for July 1967. The Trades and Labour Council only narrowly accepted this policy. In January 1967, the Arbourthorne Tenants' Association was founded, rapidly recruiting 500 members and an influx of trade union and left-wing Labour support. During the May elections of 1967 a mass meeting of tenants at Sheffield City Hall attracted 1000 people and the Sheffield Federation of Tenants was launched. The Conservatives, as a result of the furore, had come within one seat of controlling the city in the elections and Communist candidates, active in the tenants' movement, had seen their votes increase substantially. After the elections the Trades and Labour Council swung against the local authority while tenants' organizations mushroomed – Shiregreen had 1500 members on 15 May and 2000 members by 21 May. Tenant discontent with the council's policy forced the Labour group to make concessions, which included a modified rebate scheme proposal and Alderman Dyson resigning the Chair of Housing.

Negotiations were held with tenants to discuss the modified rebate scheme. By January 1968 the tenants' federation in the city was divided into two factions following the breakaway of the Democratic Federation. The Democratic Federation was opposed to the Communist influence in the tenants' federation and planned to put up its own tenant candidates against Labour if negotiations with Ron Ironmonger, the Labour leader, broke down. Negotiations did break down and five tenant candidates and eleven Communists stood in the 1968 local elections. One tenant candidate received over 600 votes. The Conservatives won 19 of the 27 seats and Labour was out of power in Sheffield for the first time since 1932. Although these results need to be set within the context of a massive national swing against Labour, the election result in Sheffield stunned the Party. In 1969 a rent freeze was promised and constructive work began with the co-ordinating committee of a unified tenants' federation. Labour returned to power in 1969 and organized joint action on the Conservative Housing Finance Bill 1972 and, eventually, support for a revived tenants' federation in 1978 (see Lowe 1986 and Baldock 1982). Peter Baldock, a local community worker looking back at the militancy in the 1980s, argued:

> The movement was in its origins . . . a movement of women. Men may have taken it over to a large extent, but the origin remained important . . . In Sheffield at least, tenants' associations were successful as militant organizations precisely to the extent that women secured and maintained positions of power in them. Moreover, where women did retain some degree of control of the movement, they developed modes of organization based on local housewives' networks, modes that were more informal, put more emphasis on mutual support, were more openly democratic than the models imposed by men with mainly trade union experience. They thus anticipated . . . the women's liberation and community action movements [of the 1970s]. (Baldock 1982 p.124)

By 1974 the co-ordinating committee had disbanded and, although individual tenants' associations continued, a Sheffield Federation of Tenants was not revived until 1978.

If rent rebates and rent increases had already angered tenants' organizations, the Conservative government's Housing Finance Bill 1972 sparked off a national campaign. During 1972 and 1973 at least 80 separate rent strikes were organized. The Bill proposed a rapid move to market or 'fair rents' in council housing, threatening large rent increases. In June 1972, 233 delegates from 87 ruling Labour groups met in Sheffield and voted overwhelmingly not to implement the Act. Harold Wilson met the leaders of Manchester, Leeds and Liverpool City Councils and advised caution; 32 councils held out but eventually implemented the Act between October 1972 and January 1973, 13 held out to 1973, and two (Clay Cross, and Bedwas and Machen) never implemented the legislation. The first serious move in the campaign was a National Conference to decide tactics called by the National Association of Tenants and Residents for the end of July 1972 in London. A national rally in Trafalgar Square on the Sunday before the rent rises came into force, 2 October 1972, was the most concrete consequence of the NATR's efforts over that summer. Although this rally attracted an estimated 3000 people from tenants' organizations around the country, the demand for a national rent strike against the increases was not met. This was the only time a tenants' organization was in a position even to consider this on a national scale – but it was rejected largely because of a lack of resources to co-ordinate such a campaign.

If the national tenants' campaign never really got off the ground, scores of affiliated tenants' associations went ahead on their own initiative and tenants of at least 80 local authorities concluded that the only way left to fight the Housing Finance Act was to withhold the rents imposed by it. On Merseyside the Kirkby rent strike on the Tower Hill estate lasted a year and involved several hundred tenants. The Kirkby tenants made alliances with trade unionists at a local Birds Eye factory who undertook to organize joint action. The Tower Hill Unfair Rents Action Group (THURAG) blocked traffic in and out of the town during one rush hour. However, the number of tenants on rent strike declined over the winter of 1972–73 to between 500 and 800. By the end of 1973 seven rent strikers had been imprisoned for arrears and contempt. THURAG finally agreed to open discussions.

In Dudley, 15000 tenants had withheld rent increase payments from the end of 1972, but by October 1973 the Dudley Tenants' Association decided to recommend paying the increase and the £300000 arrears. There were still 2000 tenants not paying the original increase and 2000 not paying arrears. The council began to break the rent strike by trying to incorporate as many of the tenants' leaders as it could into the local Labour Party, thereby splitting the tenants. In other centres there were some well-organized rent strikes. In Bolton, 500 tenants were withholding the increases in October 1972, organized by the newly formed Bolton and District Tenants' Federation. For the first few weeks of the rent rises between 3650 and 5500 tenants withheld increases in Oldham. The Oldham and District Association of Tenants and Residents organized a campaign involving a march, supported by about 3000 people, which saw women spit on placards containing the names of the 31 implementing councillors which had been placed in a coffin along with the rent increase notices. By February 1973 there were still between 1500 and 2000 tenants involved. The council issued 400 summonses in September and, following the Kirkby climbdown in December, the strike was called off. In Sheffield several hundred tenants withheld increases for about a month, but there were obvious divisions on the co-ordinating committee. By June 1973 there were probably around 150 'withholders' remaining. As in other large cities – such as Liverpool, Manchester, Birmingham and Leeds – groups of withholders were scattered around rather than centrally co-ordinated. Some of the smaller mining housing authorities in South Yorkshire were ironically much less sympathetic to withholders and Kiveton, Knottingley and Hoyland all threatened eviction action immediately. In Barnsley a joint NUM and Tenants' Co-ordinating Committee was set up in November 1972 to organize the campaign in branches and through the South Yorkshire Tenants' Association. At Wombwell, where the NUM was organizing to fight evictions, all 15 councillors were NUM members. In fact, the 500 Wombwell tenants only withheld increases for about a month so confrontation was avoided.

In London the main campaigns were in the East End. The broad-based

Hackney United Tenants' Federation organized a total rent strike for two weeks, with 3500 tenants and 20 councillors participating. In Scotland some councils, such as Clydebank, held out until late on in the national campaign. But although there were examples of withholding and partial rent strikes, there seems to have been confusion in the Scottish tenants' movement and their national organization – the Scottish Council of Tenants (SCT) – and most activity had ceased by the summer of 1973. In Wales, councils initially had 'no eviction' policies but later started actions against withholders. In Llantrisant and Llantwit an original 2000 tenants joined a campaign organized by five miners' lodges. By March, 600 tenants faced legal proceedings and by July, only one person – Alf Williams, Chairman of the local Tenants' and Residents' Association – remained. In the Rhondda, about 300 tenants withheld increases and the Swansea Valley Tenants' Federation co-ordinated the action of around 2000 tenants taking action in October/November 1972. But even in this area tenants failed to mobilize effective support from local unions and the strike was called off in January 1972 (see Sklair 1975).

The emergence of 'tenant participation'

The majority of tenant federations and co-ordinating organizations established during the resurgence of tenant militancy between 1968 and 1973 were disbanded after 1974. However, at the level of individual tenants' associations, campaigns on local issues continued throughout the 1970s. Sklair points out that an examination of the rents campaigns of that period demonstrates that 'the precipitating factors in the rent strikes . . . were not only the rent rises but also a worsening of repairs and maintenance on the estates' (Sklair 1975 p.270). Tenants were now confronting the effects of the mass building of the 1960s. However, the character of tenants' organizations started to change. One of the main effects of the Housing Finance Act 1972 was to create a new social cleavage on housing estates based on who paid rents and who received benefits – just as tenants and politicians had foreseen. In 1974 in England and Wales local councils were reorganized and reduced in number – from 1385 to 422 – and consequently the number of housing authorities was dramatically cut, making them even more remote from tenants' interests. Rent strikes declined and, although there was a spurt of militancy with strikes in Walsall and Kirklees in the early 1980s, and again in January 1992 when a tenth of council tenants in Camden refused to pay rent following rent increases of up to 19 per cent, the tactic does seem to have been shelved. As Lowe remarks:

A degree of activity re-emerged in the late 1970s in response to some new issues –

the possibility of a tenants' charter, dampness, repairs and heating being the main concerns. The rents issue had been decisively lost and was largely stripped from the tenants' movement agenda. (Lowe 1986 p.93)

In 1977 a conference organized by the National Consumer Council reopened discussions on national and regional organizing. The National Tenants' Organization (NTO) emerged, as did the North East Tenants' Organization and a South Wales Association of Tenants. In April 1976 the Scottish Council of Tenants had organized the first annual conference of tenants' groups in Scotland with 100 delegates attending from 80 groups. In Sheffield, with the help of community workers, a powerful new federation emerged after 1978 with a tenants' levy. The role of housing authorities and community workers became increasingly important in the development of tenants' organizations, while 'tenants' charters' were negotiated to give clearer tenants' rights and improvements in repairs – Newcastle, Basildon and Scunthorpe are examples. A major success for tenants' organizations in the 1970s was their campaign on security of tenure. A Shelter Report of 1975 pointed out that, although tenants were given protection against private landlords under the Rent Acts 1965 and 1974, it was assumed that tenants did not need to be protected against councils, since they were not business orientated. This meant that council tenants had no security of tenure and could, in effect, be evicted without reason (Griffiths 1975). Campaigns by tenants' organizations and the establishment of the NTO in 1977 persuaded the Labour government to include 'security of tenure' in its Housing Bill 1979, subsequently included in the Conservatives' Housing Act 1980.

The 1970s also marked the last major slum-clearance and demolition programme in Britain. The Compulsory Purchase Order (CPO) used by councils, and the rather arbitrary approach to the declaration of improvement areas, were often opposed by poorer owner-occupiers and private tenants. The Federation of Associations of Redevelopment and Rehabilitation Areas in Southwark was launched in 1974 and, in the same year, a similar federation was organized in Nottingham. The Burnley Federation of Tenants and Residents formed in 1974 to fight the planning 'blight' caused by the building of the M65 and other redevelopment, developing a 'Clearance Code' for the council to follow. *Community Action* magazine, a major chronicle of tenants' activities in the 1970s and 1980s, reported in 1974 that 'Manchester has recently experienced a proliferation of strongly organized residents' groups determined to make a stand to save their own particular area from the bulldozer' (*Community Action* 16 November/December 1974 p.33) – a campaign led by the Manchester and Salford Housing Action group. The long struggle on the redevelopment of London Docklands began with the formation of the Isle of Dogs Action Group in 1974.

The new council estates of the 1960s and 1970s also presented tenants with fresh challenges. In 1974, on a three-year-old estate in Moss Side, the Hulme Tenants' Society and the Moss Side Community Council campaigned against 'appalling conditions . . . from severe infestation by bed bugs, mice and beetles, to repeated lift breakdowns and the lack of any amenities on the estate' (*Community Action* 16 November/December 1974 p.3). The Hulme tenants were faced with huge heating bills from unsuitable electric central-heating systems and the Hulme Electric Action Campaign was formed after 90 of the 900 tenants faced disconnection. They organized a 'camp-in' outside the electricity board offices and forced concessions. In 1976 in Cardiff, 100 tenants from the Pentwyn Estate burnt their heating bills outside the City Hall; 150 tenants refused to pay heating charges on their rents, with another 250 refusing to pay heating bills. The Hunslet Grange Heating Action Group forced concessions from the Yorkshire Electricity Board on an estate which was to become one of the first of the 1960s estates to be demolished. A national 'Rights to Fuel' campaign raised support in Newcastle, Liverpool, Manchester, Birmingham and London. Tenants' groups also organized around 'dampness' issues. The Hutchesontown and Laurieston Tenants' Association in Glasgow campaigned over 1200 flats built between 1971 and 1976, but already suffering from severe dampness by the end of that decade. The council blamed the tenants' social habits for the problem and 40 tenants went on rent strike. In 1979 the Craig tenants in the Afan Valley in South Wales combined with the new South Wales Association of Tenants to fight a militant campaign on dampness. 'A dozen women supported by tenants from other South Wales estates stormed the council offices, barricaded themselves into a committee room, chained themselves to radiator pipes and stayed in occupation for 3 days and 2 nights' (*Community Action* 48 March/April 1980 p.14). Six days later the occupation was repeated for a further three days. The council backed down and installed damp-proof courses. A national 'Campaign Against Dampness' produced a 'charter' in 1979 on which local groups could base their own campaigns. In May 1979, the North East Tenants' Organization brought together tenants from Newcastle, Gateshead, Wallsend and Sunderland to link with Sandwell and Edinburgh tenant campaigns on dampness (*Community Action* 43 May/June 1979).

By 1979 tenants in Lambeth and Loughborough were publicizing the widespread use of asbestos in council housing. Some tenants' organizations were forced to the ultimate campaign – for the demolition of their own council flats. The long campaign for the demolition of the Divis flats in Belfast began in 1979. In Liverpool, the first council to demolish flats built in the 1960s and 1970s, the Netherley Tenants' Association were faced with an estate completed in 1973 which only a year later had 90 per cent of its dwellings suffering from extensive cracks and 50 per cent from water penetration. The women in the group 'blocked roads, organized petitions, kidnapped rent officers, dumped rubbish and bugs in the town hall, disrupted council meetings, picketed council offices, lobbied councillors and MPs' (*Community Action* 47 January/February 1980 p.15). They were finally forced into a campaign for demolition.

Tenant campaigns led to concessions from councils in the form of 'tenant participation' schemes – although the tenants of the ALHE wrote a damning report about these in 1973. Hague suggests:

> The pressure for tenant participation was being led by tenants and their political allies. Their calls for tenant involvement coincided with the more general development of community action in British cities, much of which was focused around the experience of urban renewal and rehousing. They were part of a much wider international call for participation in many aspects of social life. (Hague 1990 p.247)

However, as the ALHE report on tenant participation observed, despite the considerable investment of time and effort into such schemes, there had been little or no improvement in services or communication between landlord and tenant. Few of the schemes had given tenants any meaningful executive responsibilities (Griffiths 1975).

Even so, with Colin Ward's influential *Tenants Take Over*, published in 1974, tenant 'control' and tenant 'management' were firmly on the housing agenda by the early 1970s. From this time a small number of tenant co-operatives were established including the Granby Co-operative Housing Ltd in Liverpool in 1971 and the Holloway Tenants' Co-op in London in 1972. The Campbell Report of 1976 recommended further encouragement for management co-operatives. However, tenants were suspicious of the government's motives, particularly in a period of public spending cuts, and queried the meaning of a circular issued in 1976 which stated that 'the introduction of co-operative schemes would be a means of bringing additional personal resources into housing' (*Community Action* 31 May/June 1977 p.16). The 'pros' and 'cons' of co-operative housing schemes were to be debated fiercely within the tenants' movement. *Community Action* argued:

> The distinction between a tenants association and a co-op is that a tenants association is a form of political organization which *can* be *entirely* focused around campaigns, deciding their own tactics, action, organizations etc. which can lead to challenging fundamental aspects of capitalism. In contrast a tenant co-op has first and foremost a responsibility to acquire, manage and maintain housing and other property. It can only be involved in campaigns on other issues when it has first carried out these duties. (*Community Action* 31 May/June 1977 p.17 – original emphasis)

Tenants' organizations had become linked to a wider range of community movements by the 1970s. Radical community workers had become involved in the government's Community Development Project (CDP) from the late 1960s. A number of housing campaigns developed on the foundation of the CDPs, including Batley and Oldham tenants' organizations. The National Co-ordinating Committee Against Housing Cuts organized a national campaign in 1975 against the Labour government's planned cuts in public expenditure. In Liverpool, the Tenants' Co-ordinating Committee emerged as a federation for tenants and rent strikes were organized in protest at the Liberal council's policies. In Birmingham in 1975, where community workers had exposed a 'dispersal policy' for black applicants for council housing, there was little in the way of tenants' reaction to the policy – although a Housing Advice Liaison Group and Black Self-Help Groups co-ordinated a campaign (*Community Action* 23 December/January 1975). Tenant links were also forged with the network of Claimants Unions, formed by benefit claimants and welfare rights workers. In May 1974, 30 Claimants Unions held a national conference in Birmingham. The women's movement also continued to have an impact on tenants' campaigns in the 1970s, with radical and socialist feminists particularly focusing on domestic violence and the plight of 'battered' women – a campaign that led to the development of the Women's Aid Refuges network. New resource and information centres, such as those in Coventry, Leeds and Tyneside, developed to link trade union activists and other community organizations, including tenants, in a range of community campaigns. Community newspapers and newsletters mushroomed and Nottingham tenants published their own *Housing Action* newspaper, with 10 000 free copies distributed around 15 estates in June 1977.

Despite the different campaigns and the existence of the NTO, the 1970s never really produced an effective national tenants' organization. Tenants in South Wales attempted to form a National Housing Liaison Group in 1979 which did briefly attract a wide range of campaign and trade union groups. But the political climate was already changing. The sale of council houses had expanded in the early 1970s, with 61 957 houses sold in 1972. Although this dropped to 3000 in 1975, by 1978 sales had risen again to around 18 000. The GLC was proposing sales and Liverpool was planning to sell the 'Piggeries' flats. Although tenants organized campaigns against the sales policy it was, ironically, the 'right to buy' policy which enabled the Conservatives to return to power in 1979 with, arguably, the support of a large number of council tenants. A new national tenants' organization failed to emerge in opposition to the Conservative government's right to buy policy and, by 1982, a national demonstration against sales, organized for Walsall, could only attract around 2000 people. Although there was to be a revival of tenant campaigning in 1988, 1979 proved to be a watershed in the history of the tenants' movement in Britain. Council housing, which had been at the centre of tenants' campaigns since the 1890s, now became the prime target of Conservative government policy.

From the 1980s, tenants had a new agenda in the face of the mass privatization of council housing, attempts to develop and transform the housing association movement, stock transfers, massive reductions in state spending on housing, the compulsory competitive tendering of housing management, residualization and poverty, and racism and harassment. At the same time, new policies of 'tenant participation' and 'tenant management' emerged in an attempt to incorporate campaigning tenants. It is ironic and not a little confusing to tenants that the Conservative administrations of the 1980s stressed consultation and participation. Few tenants would presumably be opposed in principle to the views of the Earl of Ancram who, as Conservative Scottish Minister for Local Government, stated in the *Scotsman* of 11 November 1986:

> Consultation alone is not sufficient. What is required is the direct involvement of tenants wherever possible in the actual management and delivery of the housing service . . . It means devolving real control over policy and resources at the local level, leading to programmes which are better targeted and more suited to tenants' requirements and indeed resulting in a strengthening of local responsibility and democracy. (quoted in Hague 1990 p.250)

However, on closer scrutiny it appears that the Conservatives' policies were a little more consistent on privatization than on empowerment of tenants and their organizations. As Hague argues:

> Through the 1980s the Conservatives were able to use tenant participation to their political and ideological advantage . . . In the Housing Act of 1988 tenant participation became intricately and explicitly interwoven with the ending of local authorities' role as landlords. (Hague 1990 p.250)

Tenants' rights, as Stuart Lowe illustrates in Chapter 6, allow tenants the privilege to move to home-ownership or a new quasi-private-sector landlord – but the move is one-way, out of the municipal sector. By forcing up council rents and restricting the power and resources of local authorities, the choice facing tenants is increasingly 'Hobson's' – that of staying with rising rents and falling standards or selecting to purchase or rent from a new quasi-private landlord. Indeed, as Hague concludes, 'through the 1980s the Conservatives were able to use tenant participation to their political and ideological advantage' and in practice 'the new rights for the tenants will mean new investment opportunities for the private sector of the economy, while re-emphasizing the inadequacy of the provision and management for social need by the state' (Hague 1990 pp.250–251).

Conclusions

Despite the ambiguity of current tenant-participation policies and practices in the 1980s and 1990s, tenant campaigns have continued to focus on the threats that transfers out of council housing pose to them. Indeed, a 'further feature of tenant participation in the late 1980s was the rising level of tenant activism. It is estimated that there were about 300 active tenants' groups in Scotland in 1980, 950 in 1985, and 1800 in 1989' (*Observer* Scotland 16 July 1989 p.3, quoted in Hague 1990 p.252). The security of tenure won as late as 1980 is given up only very reluctantly by tenants faced with the insecurities of redundancy, unemployment or low wages. After a million council homes were sold in the 1980s tenants still launched effective local and national campaigns against the Housing Act 1988, forcing a major retreat by the government on 'Tenants' Choice' and Housing Action Trusts (HATs). A number of tenants' federations, such as Kirklees and Sandwell, were developed through this campaign, as were the Estate Management Board in Belle Isle in Leeds and hundreds of other tenants' associations and federations. Hulme tenants defeated a HAT proposal and forced major concessions and changes to the redevelopment of their estates; Calderdale tenants developed a federation from campaigns on unfit council housing; and Walterton and Elgin tenants defeated the developers and Westminster Council to win control of their own homes. Campaigning tenant organizations have survived the 1980s – it may well be that an understanding of their 'pre-history' might encourage them to thrive again beyond 2000.

References

Addison, P. (1985), *Now the War is Over*, London: Cape/BBC.

Allaun, F. (1968), *Heartbreak Housing*, London: Zenith.

Armstrong, A. (1988), *Farm Workers in England and Wales: Social and Economic History 1770–1980*, London: Batsford.

Arnison, J., Frow, E. and Frow, R. (1993), *And the New Paths are Begun*, Manchester: Manchester Trades Union Council.

Ashworth, W. (1986), *A History of the British Coal Industry Vol.5 1946–1982*, Oxford: Oxford University Press.

Bagguley, P. and Mann, K. (1992), 'Idle Thieving Bastards? Scholarly representations of the "underclass"', *Work, Employment and Society*, 6(1), pp.113–126.

Bailey, R. (1973), *The Squatters*, London: Penguin.

Baldock, P. (1982), 'The Sheffield rent strike of 1967–8' in Henderson, P., Wright, A. and Wyncoll, K. (eds), *Successes and Struggles on Council Estates*, London: Association of Community Workers, pp. 118–131.

Benson, J. (1980), *British Coal Miners in the 19th Century*, London: Gill and Macmillan.

Beynon, H. and Austrin, T. (1994), *Masters and Servants*, London: Rivers Oram Press.

Boddy, M. (1992), 'From mutual interests to market forces' in Grant, C. (ed.), *Built to Last?*, London: Shelter, pp.40–49.

Bowley, M. (1945), *Housing and the State*, London: Allen and Unwin.

Burn, D. (1972), *Rent Strike: St Pancras 1960*, London: Pluto.

Burnett, J. (1986), *A Social History of Housing 1815–1985*, 2nd edn, London: Methuen.

Burt, T. (1924), *Thomas Burt – An Autobiography: Pitman and Privy Councillor*, London: T Fisher Unwin.

Calder, A. (1969), *The People's War: Britain, 1939–45*, London: Jonathan Cape.

Carter, T. (1986), *Shattering Illusions: West Indians in British Politics*, London: Lawrence and Wishart.

Chinn, C. (1991), *Homes for People: 100 Years of Council Housing in Birmingham*, Birmingham: Birmingham Books.

Clapham, D., Kemp, P. and Smith, S.J. (1990), *Housing and Social Policy*, Basingstoke: Macmillan.

Cole, I. and Furbey, R. (1994), *The Eclipse of Council Housing*, London: Routledge.

Collison, P. (1963), *The Cutteslowe Wall*, London: Faber.

Community Development Project (CDP) (1976), *Whatever Happened to Council Housing?*, London: CDP.

Cronin, J.E. (1984), *Labour and Society in Britain 1918–79*, London: Batsford.

Damer, S. (1980), 'State, class and housing: Glasgow 1885–1919' in Melling, J. (ed.), *Housing, Social Policy and the State*, London: Croom Helm, pp.73–112.

Daunton, M.J. (1990), 'Housing' in Thompson, F.M.L. (ed.), *Cambridge Social History of Britain 1750–1950 Vol.2: People and their Environment*, Cambridge: Cambridge University Press, pp.195–250.

Davin, A. (1996), *Growing Up Poor*, London: Rivers Oram Press.

Devine, T. (1994), *Clanship to Crofters' War*, Manchester: Manchester University Press.

Dickens, P. (1977), 'Squatting and the state', *New Society*, 5 May, pp.219–221.

Dresser, M. (1983), 'People's housing in Bristol 1870–1939', *Bristol's Other History*, Bristol: Bristol Broadsides, pp.129–160.

Dresser, M. (1984), 'Housing policy in Bristol, 1919–30' in Daunton, M.J. (ed.), *Councillors and Tenants: local authority housing in English cities, 1919–1939*, Leicester: Leicester University Press, pp.155–216.

Edwards, B. (1982), 'Organizing the unemployed in the 1920s' in Craig, G., Mayo, M. and Sharman, N. (eds), *Jobs and Community Action*, London: Routledge & Kegan Paul, pp.27–32.

Englander, D. (1983), *Landlord and Tenant in Urban Britain 1838–1918*, Oxford: Oxford University Press.

Finn, M.C. (1993), *After Chartism*, Cambridge: Cambridge University Press.

Finnigan, R. (1984), 'Council housing in Leeds, 1919–1939: social policy and urban change' in Daunton, M.J. (ed.), *Councillors and Tenants*, Leicester: Leicester University Press, pp.101–153.

Goldthorpe, H. (1959), *Room at the Bottom*, London: Independent Labour Party.

Grayson, J. (1991), *Solid Labour*, Wakefield: Yorkshire Regional Labour Party.

Griffiths, P. (1975), *Homes Fit for Heroes – a Shelter Report on Council Housing*, London: Shelter.

Groves, R. (1981), *Sharpen the Sickle! The History of the Farm Workers Union*, revd edn, London: Merlin.

Hague, C. (1990), 'The development and politics of tenant participation in British council housing', *Housing Studies*, 5(4), pp.242–256.

Hennessy, P. (1993), *Never Again: Britain 1945–1951*, London: Vintage.

Hinton, J. (1988), 'Self help and socialism – the squatters movement of 1946', *History Workshop*, **25**, Spring, pp.100–126.

Hunt, E.H. (1981), *British Labour History 1815–1914*, London: Weidenfeld and Nicolson.

Jeffery, T. (1989), 'The suburban nation – politics and class in Lewisham' in Feldman, D. and Stedman Jones, G. (eds), *Metropolis*, London: Routledge, pp.189–219.

Jephcott, P. (1971), *Homes in High Flats*, London: Oliver and Boyd.

Johnstone, C. (1993), 'Early post-war housing struggles in Glasgow', *Journal of the Scottish Labour History Society*, **28**, pp.7–30.

Jordan, J. (1989), *Moving Towards Home – Political Essays*, London: Virago.

Joyce, P. (1980), *Work, Society and Politics: The Culture of the Factory in Later Victorian England*, London: Methuen.

Kemp, P. (1992), 'The ghost of Rachman' in Grant, C. (ed.), *Built to Last?*, London: Shelter, pp.110–121.

Knee, F. (1977), *The Diary of Fred Knee (ed. D. Englander)*, London: Society for the Study of Labour History.

Lieven, M. (1994), *Senghennydd – The Universal Pit Village*, Cardiff: Gomer.

Lowe, S. (1986), *Urban Social Movements: The City After Castells*, Basingstoke: Macmillan.

Lyman, R.W. (1957), *The First Labour Government 1924*, London: Chapman and Hall.

Machin, F. (1958), *The Yorkshire Miners*, Barnsley: Yorkshire National Union of Miners.

Malpass, P. (1992), 'Rents within reach' in Grant, C. (ed.), *Built to Last?*, London: Shelter, pp.67–76.

Manchester WHG (Women's Housing Group) (1987), 'Ideology in bricks and mortar – women's housing in Manchester between the wars', *North West Labour History*, **12**, pp.24–28.

Matrix (1984), *Making Space: Women and the Man-Made Environment*, London: Pluto.

McKenna, F. (1980), *The Railway Workers 1840–1970*, London: Faber.

Melling, J. (1983), *Rent Strikes*, London: Polygon.

Merrett, S. (1979), *State Housing in Britain*, London: Routledge & Kegan Paul.

Moorhouse, B., Wilson, M. and Chamberlain, C. (1972), 'Rent strikes – direct action and the working class' in Miliband, R. and Saville, J. (eds), *Socialist Register 1972*, London: Merlin, pp.133–156.

Morgan, D.H. (1982), *Harvesters and Harvesting 1840–1900*, London: Croom Helm.

O'Malley, J. (1977), *The Politics of Community Action*, Nottingham: Spokesman.

Piratin, P. (1948), *Our Flag Stays Red*, London: Lawrence and Wishart.

Power, A. (1987), *Property Before People: The Management of Twentieth-Century Council Housing*, London: Allen and Unwin.

Richardson, A. (1983), *Participation*, London: Routledge.

Rodger, R. (1989), *Housing in Urban Britain 1780–1914*, London: Macmillan.

Russell, R.C. (1956), *The Revolt of the Field in Lincolnshire*, Lincoln: Lincolnshire NUAW.

Ryder, R. (1984), 'Council house building in County Durham, 1900–39: the local implementation of national policy' in Daunton, M.J. (ed.), *Councillors and Tenants*, Leicester: Leicester University Press, pp.39–100.

Sklair, L. (1975), 'The struggle against the Housing Finance Act' in Miliband, R. and Saville, J. (eds), *Socialist Register 1975*, London: Merlin, pp.250–292.

Smith, S. and Hill, S. (1992), 'An unwelcome home' in Grant, C. (ed.), *Built to Last?*, London: Shelter, pp.101–109.

Snell, K.D.M. (1985), *The Annals of the Labouring Poor*, Cambridge: Cambridge University Press.

Swenarton, M. (1981), *Homes Fit for Heroes*, London: Heinemann.

Tebbutt, M. (1983), *Making Ends Meet*, Leicester: Leicester University Press.

Tebbutt, M. (1995), *Women's Talk? A social history of gossip in working class neighbourhoods 1880–1960*, Aldershot: Scolar Press.

Thompson, E.P. (1993), *Customs in Common*, London: Merlin.

Ward, C. (1993), *New Town, Home Town: The Lessons of Experience*, London: Calouste Gulbenkian Foundation.

Wohl, A.S. (1971), 'The housing of the working classes in London 1815–1914' in Chapman, S.D. (ed.), *The History of Working-Class Housing: A Symposium*, London: David and Charles, pp.13–54.

Yeo, E. and Yeo, S. (1988), 'The meaning of "community"' in Yeo, S. (ed.), *New Views of Co-operation*, London: Routledge, pp.229–258.

3 Tenants' choice and tenant management: who owns and who controls social housing?

Paul Lusk

From 1986 there was a continuing commitment from the Conservative-controlled British central government to promoting forms of tenant control as an option for the 20 per cent of the population still occupying state-owned council estates. The government provided funding for the training and promotion of 'tenant management', where tenants run their estates by making a tenant-controlled organization the managing agent. In 1993, tenant management became a statutory right. From 1988 to 1991, there was active support for tenants to transfer the ownership of their estates to their own tenant-controlled organization. This support lapsed from 1992, and the legislation permitting it was repealed in 1996. The Labour government plans to restore a right for tenants to enforce a transfer of ownership to a new landlord, provided it is supported by more than half of all tenants – which would put such a power on the same basis as the Right to Manage passed in 1993. Labour has also criticized the exclusion of tenant control in the arrangements for local housing companies – the system created in 1995 for councils to bid for capital subsidy for new, subsidized private-sector landlords of council housing needing repair.

So a government of the right – a government famous for privatizing state assets in numerous fields, not least housing – showed consistent support for an option which enabled tenant-controlled organizations to manage, but not to own, their estates. Its support for the ownership option was shorter-lived. It seems probable that this ownership option will, on policies stated in 1996, receive revived support from the new Labour government. This chapter seeks to explain this perhaps surprising set of alignments. We will trace some of the key episodes, to tease out how politicians and the wider policy and housing worlds responded to opportunities at moments of transition. But first, we consider how current tools of analysis can be used to make theoretical sense of these responses. Readers uncomfortable with theoretical

67

discussion may wish to skip the first section! We also review the experience of reforming council housing since 1986 and consider the practical implications for the future prospects for tenant control. In addition, we will argue for the viability and application of the theoretical scheme introduced in the first section, before drawing together our overall conclusions.

Citizens and markets – or customers and consumers?

A prominent theme in the political sociology of advanced urban systems since the early 1980s has been the characterization of users of state-sponsored services as 'consumers'. Recent work has focused on two issues: a revived interest in 'citizenship', and a consideration of 'customer' and 'consumer' orientations in public service delivery. One common approach is to draw a critical distinction between on the one hand the 'citizen' achieving his or her ends through political action, and on the other hand the 'consumer' who enters into a market relationship with the providers of state services (see for example Lowndes 1995). This analysis is presented diagrammatically in Table 3.1. From this point of view, both 'customer' and 'consumer' orientations in social provision are equally the result of a 'commercial' construction of the provider/user relationship. This 'commercial' model sees services as provided to discrete individuals, and does not admit the substantial role for collective user action which is allowed by the alternative 'citizen' model (Cairncross *et al.* 1994). Communitarian hostility to consumerism is neatly summed up by Selbourne (1995), for whom 'customer' and 'consumer' are the translations of 'citizen' in the 'vocabulary of a corrupted politics'.

In this context, discussion of tenant participation and control faces a puzzle: are tenant-controlled housing projects examples of the 'citizen' or the 'consumer' models of political behaviour? Policies and organizations that foster tenant control seem to conform to the 'consumer' model insofar as they seek and gain freedom to procure services in a competitive market, but

Table 3.1 The 'citizen' vs 'market' analysis

citizen =	consumer =
collective action =	customer =
community	market =
	individualist

also to the 'citizen' model insofar as they depend on collective action and voluntary mutual aid, and promote reflection on the social and political context for material choices. Analysis is caught between these alternatives and finds it difficult to make significant progress, able to explain outcomes only as 'unpredictable' responses by individuals to an accidental set of relations with trainers (Furbey *et al.* 1996).

An alternative approach is to draw a distinction between 'customer' and 'consumer' roles. The two terms, 'customer' and 'consumer', have different meanings, whether in everyday usage or in the language of political economy (Clarke 1994). 'Consumers' have rights over their expenditures, to translate purchasing power into 'demand' for alternative goods and services and thus to force producers to adjust the mix of supply to match that demand. The 'consumer' can then choose among competing suppliers for a particular good. Neither of these two powers belongs to the 'customer'. The 'customer' by definition exists only in relation to the operations and imagination of a specific supplier. A trading firm would naturally speak of 'our customers' but not of 'our consumers'. 'Consumers' do not belong to anyone. They are only potential customers, to be won in a continuous process of product adjustment and competition with other would-be providers. This alternative scheme, as developed in the discussion in this section, is illustrated in Table 3.2.

A successful business is customer centred when it responds to this reality. It knows that its customers have choices and that they will revert to being consumers at large if they are not continuously satisfied by the product and service. The normal situation with public services is different. The 'customers' of hospitals, schools and housing departments cannot readily find an alternative supplier, although market policies may give them such a choice by a more remote process such as periodic tendering or longer-term transformations in structures of provision. The 'customers' of public services usually do not pay for them directly, and do not have the freedom to use their spending power to force supply to adjust to demand, since prices are not set by the market but are determined by the state (Le Grand and Bartlett 1993 p.23). In the case of housing services, although a rent is paid, it is paid

Table 3.2 The 'customer' vs 'consumer' analysis

customer =	consumer =
rights to supply =	choice =
rights to 'voice' =	rights to 'exit' =
externally controlled prices	market prices

by the state on behalf of the customer in most cases, and is set by a political rather than a market process.

When public servants are urged to construe users as 'customers', it means they are to treat them in the way that a competitive business must do if it is to survive: to be sensitive to customers' needs, to provide satisfaction and so on. The public servant may be motivated by a broader sense that, ultimately, a competitor may win a tender for the whole service if overall customer satisfaction falls. But rarely is there a prospect of immediate loss of a dissatisfied customer to a competitor. The public servant may respond to a policy agenda that requires her or him to respond to user needs and requirements. But there is no way for the supplier to gain more business by refining the service to meet detailed changes in user preference.

It is clear then that in any conception of market transactions there must be an important distinction in meaning between customers and consumers, and that this distinction is particularly important in a public service environment. 'Consumers' have a choice of supplier – not under some broad, service-wide long-term plan, but in an ability to implement choice more or less immediately in relation to a specific item or product. 'Consumers' can deploy their spending power to influence the mix of goods and services that constitute the output of suppliers. 'Customers' lack these two powers.

Consumer choice is, however, a two-way process. Suppliers also have a choice over the sector of the market place at which they aim, and exercise this choice by price and specification. Prices in a free market are determined by not only competition among suppliers for customers, but also competition among consumers for products. For the market to work, both sides must be price-takers and not price-setters. If any party to a transaction can determine the price at which exchange takes place, they will exploit that power to deprive the other of a legitimate return. This will bring rewards in the short term, but in the longer term will not support a sustainable pattern of exchange.

A rational reason for users to fear the consequences of marketization in public services would be that suppliers of an acceptable product may exclude users with weaker purchasing power. This is obviously likely to be so with British public housing, a product which (unlike public health or education) is directed exclusively at poorer users. A 'customer' orientation may therefore be more attractive than a 'consumer' orientation if users fear the weakness of their bargaining position in a competitive environment. Thus, commentators on tenant participation use the language of the economist Hirschman (1970) to suggest that the 'voice' option has proved more sympathetic to users than the 'exit' alternative (Stewart and Taylor 1995, Foley and Evans 1994). As Clarke (1994) notes, the 'voice' option is for customers, while 'exit' is for consumers. It may well be more rational for activists seeking greater participation or control in housing to choose a customer rather than a consumer orientation. The customer gains rights over quality of supply without taking responsibility for budget control or for the selection of supplier – responsibilities that carry risks as well as rewards.

By using tenant management to take control of budgets, or Tenants' Choice to take control of estate ownership, communities opt for a 'consumer' role, because they take power to control expenditures and select providers of housing management and repairs services. A tenant management organization takes control primarily over revenue expenditures, its budget being related (under the Right to Manage) to what is regularly spent on the estate by the landlord. A transferred ownership organization buys the property at a price which is the present value of the future net rental income stream less a discount for necessary repairs and possibly improvements. By acquiring on these terms the new owner also takes control of a capital investment programme. Tenants who choose the alternative solution of an estate committee, agreement or other accommodation with a landlord are generally tending to the 'customer' role. They acquire a right to be treated in a certain way, for their views to be taken into account and so on, but not control over the allocation of money or choice of service supplier.

The next section reviews the political processes which drove the introduction of tenant-controlled alternatives into the public housing arena from 1986 to 1996. Then this discussion is related to the analytic scheme previously considered.

Tenant control and housing policy – 1986–96

The Conservatives were returned to power under the leadership of Margaret (later Lady) Thatcher in 1979. At the forefront of their electoral programme was a promise to give all tenants of council houses – then comprising 35 per cent of all households – the right to buy their own homes at a discount. This was part of a 'Tenants' Charter' which also conferred security of tenure to both council and housing association tenants, with accompanying rights for occupying relatives to inherit tenancies, and for tenants to sub-let and to exchange their homes with each other.

Initially the new government concentrated its reforms in the public rented sector on this individual right to buy and other measures to shift the balance from social renting to individual property ownership. Both council and housing association rental programmes experienced deep cuts in capital investment. For the first half of the 1980s there was no strong government preference for housing association over local authority provision. Nor was there an agenda to reform the structures of provision for rented housing. Heavy private-sector rent controls were untouched (the 1980 Act did contain a provision for private landlords to join a special register in order to benefit from deregulated 'assured tenancies', but there was little take-up). Fair rents for housing association tenants remained in place, these low rates being achieved with grants close to 100 per cent of capital cost. Meanwhile Labour, under the left-wing leadership of Michael Foot, opposed the right to buy in its 1983 general election manifesto, in Gerald Kaufman's words the 'longest suicide note in history'.

New legislation introduced in 1985 as the Housing and Planning Bill was the first time the Conservative government signalled an intention to restructure the system for social rented housing provision. It created a framework for ministers to approve schemes from councils to transfer the ownership of stocks to outside bodies (to make 'voluntary transfers'). It also enabled councils to delegate management of estates to outside bodies. This latter feature was an extension of a power originally created by the previous Labour government in the Housing Rents and Subsidies Act 1975, for councils to delegate management of estates to tenant co-operatives. Together these indicated a government programme to bring private agencies and housing associations into both the ownership and management of existing council estates. All these powers were 'permissive', in other words councils could not be compelled to diversify the management or ownership of estates.

By the mid-1980s, the Labour opposition had learnt the lesson of its over-identification with traditional council provision, in particular the political consequences of previous opposition to the right to buy. The new Labour opposition leader, Neil Kinnock, appointed as his 'shadow' housing minister Jeff Rooker, a radical whose longstanding non-statist instincts anticipated features of later 'New Labour'. Labour did not oppose the 1985 Bill by proclaiming the virtues of council housing and condemning the right to buy. Instead, it outbid the government in attacking the failures of centralized council landlords, for instance arguing for higher discounts for tenants buying hard-to-let homes.

Labour's response to the proposals to diversify management agents in the public sector was to argue for greater tenant involvement in management as a better alternative to privatization. In the committee stage of the Bill, Labour moved an amendment to give council tenants a right to manage their own estates as co-operatives. Government backbenchers were reluctant to vote the idea down. The housing minister, John Patten, offered a compromise, giving council tenants the right to demand a management co-operative and receive a reasoned response from their landlord. This became Section 11 of the Housing and Planning Act 1986. (The government had previously defeated a Lords amendment for a 'right to manage' in 1984.)

Section 16 of the same Act allowed ministers to give grants for housing management training. This power was later used mainly to support training for tenant management organizations.

But the main legislative effect was to extend an existing provision for tenant management to cover management by other bodies including private businesses. So it is interesting that, in the run-up to the 1987 general election, the government chose to emphasize its new commitment to co-operatives rather than to signal an agenda for privatization. On 8 January 1987 *The Times* ran a front-page lead, signed by its political correspondent Robin Oakley and based on an interview with Mr Patten. Headed 'Tories want to break up large council estates', it continued:

> A little noticed provision in the Housing and Planning Act . . . allows local authorities to delegate the management of houses and flats to . . . tenant management co-operatives . . . Mr Patten's outline plans are likely to provoke an angry reaction from the Labour Party, fearful of seeing its political strength on the council estates . . . broken up.

This provision was indeed 'little noticed' – so much so that it had evidently escaped the attention of *The Times* when passed in the Housing Rents and Subsidies Act 1975, renewed in the Housing Act 1980 and consolidated in the Housing Act 1985! The proposition that this 'outline plan' would anger the Labour Party was absurd insofar as the legal provision simply reiterated one which Labour had itself enacted 11 years earlier, and that the Labour opposition had demanded to be strengthened. But, in turning Labour's position to its own advantage, the government was exploiting a deeper confusion in Labour ranks: the statist interests represented by the big-city local authorities were lobbying for Rooker's dismissal (reported in *The Guardian* under the heading 'Labour spokesman under fire for backing council flat sales', 8 September 1986). John Patten followed this coup with a signed article in the Labour-inclined *Guardian* ('Room for a new view', 30 January 1987 p.23) making five separate references praising collective tenant control of ownership or management of council housing:

> I want us to think increasingly in terms of transferring ownership of estates or parts of estates in small units . . . I am particularly keen to encourage co-operative management or ownership . . . It certainly is exciting when one sees groups of people in co-operatives wresting control of their own destinies.

In the 1987 general election, the Labour manifesto reiterated the Party's commitment to a right for 'tenants who want to take over the running of their homes' to do so through a management co-operative (p.10). In their manifesto, *The Next Moves Forward*, the Conservatives said:

We will give groups of tenants the right to form tenant co-operatives, owning and running their management and budget for themselves. They will also have the right to ask other institutions to take over their housing . . . We will give each council house tenant individually the right to transfer the ownership of his or her house to a housing association or other independent, approved landlord. (p.14)

This curious formulation is worth examining closely. There are three separate ideas here. The first sentence seems to imply a right to manage but is ambiguous (in what sense is management 'owned'?). The second sentence offers a collective right to invite other landlords or agents. The third sentence is the clearest linguistically but the oddest in its depiction of commercial realities: council tenants would each individually invite their own personally appointed landlord to assume ownership.

It was this third sentence that most closely reflected the mind of the Thatcherites, one of whom was the Environment Secretary (the Cabinet minister in overall charge of the policy) Nicholas Ridley. Collective rights, co-operatives and management agreements were part of the Labour agenda borrowed by Ridley's housing minister John Patten, a member of the centre-left Tory Reform Group. For the right, the new agenda would be about landlords scurrying around council estates touting for tenants, rather like the private buses that roamed city streets after Ridley had deregulated them in his previous post as Transport Secretary.

This vision drove the highly controversial Part IV of the Housing Act 1988, the so-called 'Tenants' Choice' scheme. Prospective landlords, approved by the Housing Corporation, could bid for estates or areas. Individual tenants could opt out of the move. Tenants' groups could veto the whole transfer only if a majority of all tenants voted against. The scheme could have been purpose designed to discredit the whole notion of ownership change in social housing and this was how it turned out.

Numerous campaigning groups sprang up and virtually every council estate in the land was festooned with posters proclaiming 'our estate is not for sale'. The problem for ministers was summed up on one page of the social housing trade paper *Inside Housing* on 4 March 1988. John Patten's successor, William Waldegrave, told the House of Commons that new landlords 'would first have to accept a "social landlords charter" which would incorporate safeguards for tenants. Criteria would include . . . treatment of existing tenants.' On the same page it was reported that Shelter, the respected (and supposedly non-political) housing charity, was distributing posters with slogans that included: 'They're passing a law that could lose you your home'; 'Ten million people call a council house home. In the City they call it a nice little earner'; and 'The Housing Bill could make you homeless.'

Voluntary transfers proceeding under the 1986 Act arrangements faced the backlash of tenant hostility to the new mechanisms. One Conservative council (in the south coast region of Torbay) attempted to run a voluntary ballot using the 1988 Act rules, but the result was discredited and the exercise abandoned. The government was forced to back down from imposing Housing Action Trusts (HATs – central-government holding companies) on estates without majority support in a tenant ballot, and successive proposals to set up HATs in five inner-city areas failed despite an offer of half a billion pounds in public investment.

In February 1991 the Department of the Environment (DoE) received a research report which showed that, of 61 active cases being handled under the Tenants' Choice scheme early in 1990, 47 were cases of 'tenants wishing to establish their own landlord organization' in the form of a co-operative or neighbourhood association. Fieldworkers charged with implementing the policy were drawn into community-development work in support of these grass-roots initiatives. Staff responsible for considering applications for approved landlord status from established organizations had little to do. The research showed that 'a central problem was that procedures are generally geared to transfers to an existing landlord whereas the majority of active cases were seeking tenant control' (CURS 1991). In discussions between officials responsible for the policy, one option considered was to change the procedures in order for Tenants' Choice to produce results. Ministers decided against this, on the grounds that new legislation would be too soon after the passage of the 1988 Act.

On two estates (one in Coventry and one in Hackney), where tenant groups were advancing outline proposals to acquire ownership using the Tenants' Choice system, the DoE accepted alternative local council proposals to finance repairs through Estate Action funding, with further work on ownership transfers specifically precluded by the introduction of this mechanism. An unofficial agreement was reached between the Housing Corporation and the DoE at the end of 1991 that further Tenants' Choice projects would not receive support in the form of revenue funds for training and promotion. The decision was made to concentrate on one scheme to revive the ownership transfer in Torbay, which was eventually overwhelmingly defeated by the tenants after the Housing Corporation had spent £1.7 million on promoting it. Tenants' Choice changed the ownership of 981 homes in three transfers – 918 of them in one scheme in Walterton and Elgin block in Westminster, where the main motive was to prevent the Thatcherite local council marketing the estate for private ownership and to procure instead substantial resources for repairs for the estate to remain as social rented housing under the control of Walterton and Elgin Community Homes (WECH).

One other large transfer was in practice the fruit of Tenants' Choice, although in the event it proceeded as a voluntary transfer. This was at

Glyntaff Farm, an estate of 536 homes on a hill outside Pontypridd in South Wales. At first the tenants had hoped that repairs to remedy serious structural and drainage problems and poor insulation could be generated through tenant management. When they realized otherwise they pursued Tenants' Choice. Eventually the estate was sold for a negative valuation of £19.6 million, – money that had to be given by the Welsh Office to the local council after slicing it out of the whole housing investment programme for Wales.

WECH and Glyntaff Farm were examples of tenants using transferred ownership to lever in resources through a negative valuation. This works because the market price for social rented housing is the value of the future net cash-flow assuming that the homes are rented to people in housing need, and are routinely repaired and managed to an acceptable standard. From this value is deducted the cost of any major repairs or improvements that may be deemed necessary. For housing that is below an acceptable standard – because of disrepair or design faults – this figure easily becomes negative, meaning the landlord is forced to hand a sum of money over to the new owner along with the properties. Furthermore, there is scope for considerable legal argument over what repairs or other work might be necessary to achieve an acceptable standard. The 1988 Act created a framework for disputes about property values to be settled in court. Tenants contemplating a stock transfer benefited from early advice from surveyors, valuers and lawyers about the repairs they could expect to be granted, so that revenue costs for pre-transfer consultancy quickly reached hundreds of thousands of pounds.

The decision to abandon tenant-led, estate-based urban stock transfers, and to concentrate the Tenants' Choice budget on reviving a borough-wide transfer in a prosperous coastal resort, made little sense if the intention was to support the mandatory Tenants' Choice concept as a tenant-controlled alternative to the oversubscribed voluntary transfer programme. On the other hand, it made excellent sense if the intention was in fact to allow Tenants' Choice quietly to wither away. Which agenda was at work? The evidence for the following analysis is circumstantial. There clearly was a strong structural imperative at this point to see the concept fail. Suppose the Thatcherites and a few dozen inner-city Glyntaffs had encountered each other: what would have been the unplanned costs to the public purse? Clearly, Tenants' Choice had the potential to make a hole in the public finances to the extent of several billion pounds, devoted to tenant-controlled urban regeneration. That such a hole never materialized is partly due to the complexity of the procedures, but substantially due to two political forces.

The first was Lady Thatcher herself. She left office in 1990 with regrets over the failure of Tenants' Choice and HATs. For her, the obstacle to both was 'the deep rooted hostility of the Left to the improvement and enfranchisement of those who lived in the ghettos of dependency which they controlled'. She opposed tenants being required to give majority support to transfer proposals, since 'This would have been an impossibly high hurdle, given the apathy of tenants and the intimidation of the Left' (Thatcher 1993 p.601). Thus the Thatcherites faced profound conceptual problems with the notion that tenants could take collective control over their destinies, since tenants *en masse* could only be conceived as the lifeless puppets of the left. The idea that Tenants' Choice could be saved by amending the procedures to facilitate tenant control – as the research showed – would have been alien to this mind-set.

The second was what might loosely be called the public housing establishment, which immunized tenants against transfer by the campaign summed up in the Shelter posters quoted earlier. Using private money to finance urban stock transfers was no more liable to make anyone homeless than using the same resources to finance housing associations or voluntary transfers in rural areas, neither of which attracted anything like the same assault from Shelter, but Thatcher's hostility to an effective tenant veto inevitably created space for an intimidating campaign to succeed.

Tenant control in practice – a review

The 1986 Act promoted 'voluntary transfer'. This power was used mainly by smaller Conservative councils with higher-value, often rural stock, to earn capital receipts. These ownership transfers also tended to shift housing benefit costs away from the council's other rent-payers and on to central government. For this reason, in 1992, the government introduced controls rationing permission for transfers to a planned target of 25000 homes per year (Wilcox *et al.* 1993). As we have seen, the mandatory system for transfer introduced in 1988 had the potential to apply stock transfer to urban estates in need of investment, but under the ownership of Labour councils hostile to ownership change. The system failed due (I have suggested) to a combination of the authoritarian attitude to tenant involvement embodied in the 1988 Act, and the capacity of mandatory privatization to suck in unplanned investment. Voluntary transfers later proceeded only if majority tenant support was gained in ballots, but had to be rationed because of the way in which they were enriching councils at the expense of the social security budget.

In 1995, the government announced plans to direct future stock transfer at urban priorities. For the first time, a budget was set up to meet the costs of negative valuations of these portfolios. Bids for this – known as the Estate Renewal Challenge Fund (ERCF) – could only be made by councils, who must prepare balanced transfers in which the costs of repairs were to some extent offset by mixing in higher-value stock. Councils could take substantial ownership stakes in the new landlord bodies. The right of tenants to initiate and control such transfers – through Tenants' Choice – was repealed in 1996. Tenant control of the new landlord entity was not permitted.

The ownership reforms initiated in 1986 thus proceeded fitfully, reflecting the Conservative government's successive attempts to control and direct the financial flows generated by movements of housing stock. The price of directing a manageable flow of public expenditure at urban (and rural) priorities was to concede a commanding position to local government interests. Tenants gained recognition of their right to endorse or reject transfers in a democratic ballot, but lost the right to create and control their own regeneration projects through transfer.

The management provisions of the 1986 Act laid the foundations for a new and continuing commitment to promote tenant management of estates. While the 1974–79 Labour government legislated for council tenants to control their own estates through management co-operatives, it left it to councils to promote this option if they chose. Few did, with Glasgow and Islington being the main exceptions. After 1986, the government funded a network of agencies to promote tenant management – either through Tenant Management Co-operatives or Estate Management Boards – and to provide training to tenants. In 1993, Parliament legislated for a Right to Manage. To the end of 1995, over 100 council estates had signed tenant management agreements, with a further 100 in the development and negotiation processes. Originally tenant management was incorporated into Conservative thinking in an almost casual fashion, as a by-product of registering a wider – but little fulfilled – ambition to diversify ownership away from councils. Since 1986 it has been allowed to develop in a consistent fashion, with control rights for tenants being strengthened.

The obvious problem for government in granting ownership rights to tenant-controlled bodies lies in the financial issues arising from negative valuations. A renewed government commitment to a right to change landlord is unlikely to be sustainable if these issues are not addressed. No government is likely to live for long with a situation where valuations are subject to legal argument with billions of pounds of unplanned public investment potentially at stake. In the view of this writer, the supporters of tenant control will best serve their objectives by developing an alternative which works by bidding for resources against a planned public budget for major repairs.

Tenant control as a consumer orientation

Earlier we saw that analysts of tenant-controlled housing have used two alternative theoretical frameworks. The 'citizen' or 'market' approach, when applied to tenant control, presents the problem that more 'market' does not necessarily mean less 'citizenship' as the model would predict. An alternative is the 'customer' or 'consumer' approach, distinguishing between groups who concentrate on achieving a 'voice' in services which they do not control, and those who gain the right to 'exit' using control over their expenditures. Both tenant management and Tenants' Choice enabled tenants to adopt a 'consumer' role.

One reason for the failure of Tenants' Choice was the ambiguous position of the Conservative government over enfranchising tenants as 'consumers'. The structure was designed for tenants to be admitted to the process, at best, as 'customers'. Through a process of state sponsorship and approval, an alternative landlord would present itself to tenants who had the option to reject this alternative. The way in which Tenants' Choice was used by groups developing and arguing for their own proposals was a major problem for the authorities. While Thatcherism and the Shelter campaigners may have held radically different views about 'citizenship', they clearly concurred on one crucial point: that tenants should be 'customers', not 'consumers', in relation to their landlord. Voluntary transfer and the ERCF process continued this emphasis on tenants accepting customer rights but not having those of consumers.

Tenants' Choice empowered tenants as consumers because, among other things, they could value their consumption demands (especially for repairs) and argue this into the price-setting process. This produces potentially enormous negative valuations. There is a conundrum here. A 'market' price cannot, in general, be negative, since no market can be made if there is no incentive for supply to take place. To understand the paradox of the negative price we have to remember that a market system works in two ways: consumers compete for supply just as producers compete for demand. Transferred ownership begins from the premise that existing tenants have property rights. The market for the right to occupy a rented home is not like markets for bread or petrol, where traders are free to sell their goods to whichever consumers present themselves each day and pay the going price. Tenants of estates do not compete with other consumers who may appear and offer a higher price. Nor, of course, does anyone think they should.

Tenants' Choice was an inherently unstable system because it allowed for a 'market' price to be determined in a market which was in fact heavily weighted by the property rights given to tenants by regulation. This Thatcherite project failed not least because the Thatcherites, supposedly the apostles of market economics, failed to understand how this market would work. Tenant management provides a stable means of empowering tenants as 'consumers' since the purchasing power it generates is determined by existing revenue budgets – in other words, prices are consistent with the regulated nature of the market in which consumers and producers operate. Using the right-to-manage structure, tenants can manipulate rents, budgets and expenditures to build up surpluses and direct resources at chosen priorities. The right to manage provides a framework for tenants to identify future repairing needs, and to bid for capital expenditure. It does not, however, confer an open-ended entitlement to capital, in the way that transferred ownership rights threatened.

Conclusions

I have proposed that tenant control can be analysed in a framework of 'consumer' empowerment and that this 'consumer' or 'customer' model has analytic value. I have suggested that the tenant management model which the state incorporated from the centre-left proved more durable than transferred ownership models conceived on the right, because the management model is a better adaptation to the constraints of the regulated market in publicly assisted housing. If this analysis is correct, any future development of tenant-controlled ownership by transfer will have to take account of the need to ration investment, rather than allowing it to be determined by a market which is (rightly) distorted in favour of sitting tenants.

References

Cairncross, L., Clapham, D. and Goodlad, R. (1994), 'Tenant participation and tenant power in council housing', *Public Administration*, **72**(2), pp.177–200.
Centre for Urban and Regional Studies (CURS) (1991), 'Tenants' Choice: The Role of the Housing Corporation' (unpublished research for the Department of the Environment), Birmingham: CURS, University of Birmingham. Quoted by permission.
Clarke, J. (1994), *Capturing the Customer: Consumerism and Social Welfare*, paper for ESRC Seminar 'Conceptualising Consumption Issues', University of Lancaster, December.
Foley, B. and Evans, K. (1994), 'Tenant control, housing co-operatives and government policy', *Local Government Studies*, **20**(3), pp.392–411.
Furbey, R., Wishart, B. and Grayson, J. (1996), 'Training for tenants: "citizens" and the enterprise culture', *Housing Studies*, **11**(2), pp.251–269.
Hirschman, A.O. (1970), *Exit, Voice and Loyalty: Responses to Decline in Firms, Organizations and States*, Cambridge, Mass: Harvard University Press.

Le Grand, J. and Bartlett, W. (1993), 'The Theory of Quasi-Markets' in Le Grand, J. and Bartlett, W. (eds), *Quasi-markets and Social Policy*, Basingstoke: Macmillan, pp.13–34.
Lowndes, V. (1995), 'Urban politics and its citizens' in Judge, D., Stoker, G. and Wolman, H. (eds), *Theories of Urban Politics*, London: Sage, pp.160–180.
Selbourne, D. (1995), 'Rights and duties', *New Statesman & Society*, 11 August, pp.13–14.
Stewart, M. and Taylor, M. (1995), *Empowerment and Estate Regeneration: A Critical Review*, Bristol: Policy Press.
Thatcher, M. (1993), *The Downing Street Years*, London: HarperCollins.
Wilcox, S., Bramley, G., Ferguson, A., Perry, J. and Woods, C. (1993), *Local Housing Companies: New Opportunities for Council Housing*, York: Joseph Rowntree Foundation.

4 Concepts of community involvement, power and democracy

Charlie Cooper and Murray Hawtin

This chapter explores the meaning of community involvement by examining the concept from a range of ideological, sociological and political positions. The analysis sets out to unravel the inherent contradictions underlying the idea of community involvement and reconstructs a framework to clarify how the participation process in different contexts can be understood. In achieving this, concepts of community involvement will be connected with broader ideas about empowerment and democracy, the justification being that analyses of community involvement practice need to be informed by a greater understanding of the way in which power and accountability operate in society.

Concepts of community involvement

Political theorists in ancient Greece stressed the importance of direct participation in democratic processes and that this should be achieved by establishing accessible mechanisms through which *all* citizens could negotiate *directly* with policy-makers (Rousseau 1973). This view of democratic involvement is shared by Richardson's conceptualization of participation as *direct action* as distinct from indirect action or political representation. Direct action involves people collectively engaging in direct contact with elected or appointed officials to determine policies for service delivery, and service consumers participating in the implementation of those policy decisions. The forms and levels at which participation can take place may vary, with people either negotiating within existing organizational arrangements such as local authority sub-committees, or within newly established structures such as neighbourhood committees (Richardson

1983). However, for others widespread direct involvement is seen as impractical in modern states and *representative* democracy is viewed as being more manageable and desirable. Political representation addresses the practical problems of involving large numbers of people who may be geographically dispersed. At the same time it permits a broader view of national and local interests to be incorporated into policy-making. The danger of direct democracy is that minority interests may be outweighed by a vociferous majority (Schumpeter 1943).

More recently debates on community involvement have focused on the rights of citizens as either *consumers* or *communities*. The consumer perspective fits easily within the neo-liberal position, emphasizing individual freedom, choice and the sovereignty of the market. People's rights are maintained through consumer power and the opening up of public services to greater competition, complaints procedures and redress. Involvement is based on the process of consumption by individuals rather than on collective choice, a basis which depoliticizes community participation (Marcuse 1964). In contrast, the community perspective focuses on the notion of citizenship and collective interest. Within this perspective there are different interpretations of how community participation can be achieved. For example, the communitarian movement associated with the ideas of Etzioni calls for a realignment of individual and collective obligations based on moral values and a sense of responsibility – the 'what can you do for your country' approach (Etzioni 1995). Alternatively, Castells saw community action as a force for social change in which disadvantaged people can challenge and confront the hegemony of the capitalist state. Participation is seen as a means of redistributing power and resources in society (Castells 1977). Some commentators have justified community participation on technical grounds, largely to increase management efficiencies. Involving communities (or more specifically consumers) in service delivery can provide decision-makers with a deeper understanding of what people want from a service and, consequently, how it might be improved. Furthermore, allowing involvement in service delivery can lead to greater consumer satisfaction as people feel a sense of control (TPAS/CIH 1989).

Arnstein's classic model offers a vertical description of the objectives and implications of different forms of participation, from 'manipulation' and 'therapy', where there is little or no redistribution of power, through to 'delegated power' and 'citizen control', where there is some redistribution of power (Arnstein 1969). This model has been adapted by some advocates of tenant participation to illustrate the incremental stages through which tenants might become involved in housing (see Packard's horizontal description in Ward 1974, Willcox 1994). However, conceptualizing community involvement as a ladder is simplistic and could be misinterpreted. For instance, the lower rungs of the ladder may not necessarily imply a lack of control: they may offer opportunities for residents to get involved at a level appropriate to their needs and wishes. It could also be argued that some of the examples of involvement identified by Arnstein as empowering communities (such as partnership approaches) may be designed to placate or manipulate troublesome communities, or to undermine the power base of local authorities. As Marsh and Murie observe:

> Partnership approaches and enabling are now widespread in the delivery of a range of welfare and other services which have conventionally been located in the public sector. We would suggest that it is important not to accept the rhetoric of partnership uncritically and to retain a concern with issues of control. Although in principle strategies can be formulated jointly, this ignores the reality of social interaction in the sense that it is typically the relatively powerful players in a particular situation who shape the agenda. (Marsh and Murie 1996 p.6)

The concept of community participation therefore needs to consider the political convictions shaping community-participation strategies as well as concepts of 'power'. The following section explores the notion of community involvement in the context of competing ideological perspectives drawn from the neo-liberal/Conservative New Right, Marxist, social democratic and anarchist positions. A broader critique of these viewpoints, drawn from the position of gender, 'race' and disability, is developed in Chapter 11.

Ideological perspectives

Neo-liberal/Conservative New Right perspectives

The neo-liberal/Conservative New Right ideology which emerged in Britain out of the recession of the 1970s was built largely on a critique of the so-called post-war consensus, opposing state dependency in favour of independence, freedom, self-reliance, individual responsibility and social inequality (George and Wilding 1991). Nozick believed that state intervention to achieve social equality was in itself an attack on the rights and entitlements of individuals to retain what they had acquired justly through free exchange (Nozick 1974). Nozick justified extreme social and economic inequality on the basis of the need to protect individual freedom, a view shared by the Conservative New Right. Indeed, the existence of inequality is justified from this viewpoint as evidence of freedom in society. The Thatcher administrations after 1979 advocated free-market principles, individual choice, the 'trickle-down' theory of wealth, anti-state welfare and privatization, and reduced trade union power. Despite this, community-development strategies did survive the Thatcher years, partly as a result of urban unrest and violence in 1980, 1981, 1985 and 1986 (Popple 1995).

From the perspective of the political right, participation strategies are largely employed as a means to achieve consensus, social stability and economic efficiencies. The Conservative New Right is generally opposed to participatory democracy because it would place an undue burden on the state, encouraging excessive demands to be made and forcing governments to make promises in order to retain power. This would cause economic inefficiencies due to excessive taxation to pay for these demands, thereby leading to *dis*investment. However, for the New Right, there is a role for participation in managing social divisions and conflict. In addition to the traditional formal institutions in democratic societies there are cultural elements which are important in preserving the social order. As Almond and Verba suggest, 'if the democratic model of the participatory state is to develop . . . it will require more than the formal institutions of democracy – universal suffrage, the political party, the elective legislature . . . A democratic form of participatory political system requires as well a political culture consistent with it' (Almond and Verba, quoted in Thornley 1977 p.15).

A 'political culture' could be seen to comprise the following elements:

- the *parochial culture*, where communities are apathetic about the political system and traditional values prevail;
- the *subject culture*, where a community holds no desire or expectation of taking an active role in societal decision-making, remaining passive and deferential; and
- the *participant culture*, where communities hold expectations of participating in political activities, although this is at best limited to single issues (for instance housing, health, the environment and crime).

The ideal neo-liberal democratic society requires a balance between these three cultures, with no one of them particularly dominant. For order to be maintained there needs to be a mix of apathetic, deferential and participative cultures. On the one hand, if there are too many apathetic and deferential communities this could lead to the development of authoritarianism – there need to be sufficient active citizens to prevent dictatorship. On the other hand, if there are too many demands from participative communities this will lead to the 'overloaded state' (Habermas 1976). Furthermore, Almond and Verba suggest that in reality even those who lean towards the participative culture need not actually participate in a democracy. The crucial point is that policy-makers and citizens need to believe that people *could* participate if they needed to – so democracy need only exist as a 'myth' for social stability to be maintained. Indeed, Almond and Verba argue that community participation should remain as a myth because of the impracticalities of organizing it and 'thus it is only an attitude that is needed for stable democracy, that is, a belief in the myth' (Thornley 1977 p.16). The Conservative New Right conceptualizes participants as 'dutiful citizens' where individuals, as members of society's component parts (families, professional bodies, trade unions, churches and so on), perform roles and duties prescribed by their group. The emphasis is on the contribution which individuals can make (rather than their rights). Consequently, the political right is circumspect about participatory democracy (which might lead to more claims than could be met) and hostile to social planning (which distorts the natural order). Democracy for them should be achieved through political representation, ordered hierarchically, and through giving people a material stake in the country – for instance, through participation in property or share ownership (Scruton 1984, Hayek 1944/1976).

Neo-liberal support for community involvement does not require any change in the balance of power relations. Indeed, from a functionalist perspective, the empowerment of socially excluded groups in society can be achieved without threat to the status quo. Once empowered, poorer sections of society merely become more self-reliant and less dependent on the state. Such a view assumes that empowerment does not necessitate the loss of power by one group so that power can increase within society as a whole. This contrasts with the view that the total amount of power in any society is fixed and that the empowerment of one group necessitates the loss of power by another group – power conceived in 'zero-sum' terms (Craig and Mayo 1995).

Institutional support for community participation in the early 1990s can therefore be understood largely in the context of neo-liberal reforms and the New Right Conservative government's political agenda. The Conservatives aimed to restructure the welfare state and to create what some observers termed 'welfare pluralism' (Johnson 1987), where decentralized and participatory structures of provision replaced centralized and bureaucratic local state structures, producing a diversity of providers in a competitive market. Other commentators interpreted this change as the emergence of a 'shadow state'. In this view the centre increased its control over welfare provision through the imposition of regulations and constraints on service providers (Warrington 1995). These reforms have been pushed at a time when most western European societies have been experiencing economic crisis, increasing poverty, social polarization and the contraction of state welfare provision. Community involvement in housing projects, therefore, can be understood in relation to the wider goals of reducing public expenditure and withdrawing state intervention in the provision of rented housing. The key objective in Conservative housing regeneration initiatives can be seen to be largely about creating neighbourhoods that could survive without a long-term commitment to public subsidy. The defining characteristics of community regeneration organizations involved in urban programmes in Britain in the 1980s and 1990s were financial independence and entrepreneurship. Such initiatives witnessed a high degree of government support for community and tenant involvement, reflecting the antipathy of the Conservatives to municipal landlordism which they believed had denied people individual freedom and choice. Housing policies since 1979 aimed to introduce pluralism into the housing system through the collective (stock transfers) and individual (right-to-buy) privatization of council housing alongside the creation of self-governing tenant management organizations. As Meekosha argues, these changes have to be seen in the context of a broader restructuring of the welfare state:

> Governments are increasingly using *community strategies and the language of community practice* as part of a reformulation of the welfare state. One of the main avenues for the implementation of this community perspective remains the family, as the concept of the 'community caring' becomes translated into caring by families (principally women), without support, outside institutions, in the 'community'. (Meekosha 1993 p.177 – original emphasis)

Another avenue for the implementation of this community perspective has been the dismantling of traditional state institutions. Indeed, the erosion of local government's power and resources under the Conservatives meant that the ability of the public to influence local services was severely diminished. Urban Development Corporations, Housing Action Trusts, Training and Enterprise Councils, Task Forces and housing associations all received considerable resources and support from the centre, yet they had no obligation to account directly to their local constituencies. In effect, housing and related welfare services were being de-democratized. In contemporary British society, only those with adequate consumption power hold the necessary preconditions for making effective choices.

Marxist perspectives

For traditional Marxists community involvement is a means of changing the social order by heightening class consciousness through the participation process itself. The means of change in modern societies is class struggle, out of which Marx saw the emergence of a more harmonious and participatory society in which decision-making would be decentralized to local communes elected by universal suffrage. Communes would comprise a body of delegates (rather than representatives) and senior administrators (the police, magistrates and so on). All delegates would be bound by the mandate of their constituencies. Marx proposed a system of mandated delegates rather than universal participation as the first stage of the transition from capitalism to socialism. Later, under communism, state institutions would wither away and universal participation would occur. Accounts of the Marxist dimension of participatory practices can be found in the discussions of Poulantzas (1980), Macpherson (1973), Pateman (1970) and Arendt (1959), characterized in Butcher *et al.* (1993) as notions of public citizenship where individuals act collectively through direct political participation in the public policy-making arena. Consensus is arrived at through rational public debate and dialogue.

Recent Marxist accounts discuss the question of community involvement in the context of the role of the state and the manipulation of radical social movements. By co-opting representatives of community movements into formal state institutions, the government is able to neutralize social discontent and defuse community protest. Therefore, state-sponsored community-participation projects diminish rather than enhance community empowerment and self-reliance by institutionalizing grass-roots movements in the mainstream – for instance, local authority housing departments legitimizing 'squats' through granting licences to the occupants; incorporating discontented council tenants on to sub-committees of housing departments (see Lowe 1986). Thus, by encouraging participation the state can nurture its own ideological values among community leaders, thereby 'integrating' protest movements into the dominant social and political structures generally. State-sponsored participation is rejected by many Marxists on the premise that it inevitably leads to the dilution of genuine participatory ideals, and it works to stabilize capital itself.

The concept of 'community' itself is problematic and ambiguous to some Marxists. Marxists generally view market capitalism as alienating – as a system which isolates people and produces antagonistic relationships between them – and consider that the creation of mutually supportive communities can support an individual's sense of ontological security. However, communities can also be exclusive. Black people, for instance, have largely been excluded from tenant participation processes in Britain (see Chapter 11). Furthermore, as some libertarians have argued, communities might stifle individual development. According to Miller (1989), the only way in which the tension between competing interests in communities can be reconciled is through the constitution of a citizenship which allows for individual self-realization *and* equality of political status. This reconciliation, Miller argues, can be achieved through the *politics of dialogue*, described by Mayer as:

> an alternative to interest aggregation politics. Under interest aggregation politics, actors are irredeemably egoistic and have essentially immobile opinions grounded in fixed interests. The essence of politics is reconciling interests to forge a coherent

majority coalition. Dialogue politics, on the other hand, assumes that political actors seek the common good and that opinions can change drastically as a result of communication. Political dialogue succeeds when a proposal not only commands majority support but can be accepted by the minority as well. Legitimacy of decisions in dialogue politics derives not mainly from adherence to proper procedure but from honestly presenting the reasons behind a decision, thus making it easier for opponents to accept. (Mayer 1994 p.270)

Applying this concept to community development, Miller argues that tightly knit communities are not the ideal setting for dialogue politics because the constitution is too small for objective debate. Communities must have the right to connect with a wider constitution through active participation if they are to engage in meaningful political dialogue, and this right must be institutionalized through the rule of law (Miller 1989). The influence of much of this thinking can be attributed to the rise of the New Left movement which, although currently in the wane, has contributed significantly to current democratic thinking. Throughout their treatise on human need, Doyal and Gough stress 'the importance of individuals being able to explore their intellectual and emotional capabilities in optimal ways. To do so, they must have the right to as much self-determination as is consistent with their not violating the basic needs of others' (Doyal and Gough 1991 p.298). Held argues that an equal right to self-determination can only be achieved in a 'participatory society', a society that fosters a concern for collective problems and nurtures a proficient citizenry capable of taking a sustained interest in the democratic process. This would require a constitution and bill of rights that offered people:

not only equal rights to cast a vote, but also equal rights to enjoy the conditions for effective participation, enlightened understanding and the setting of the political agenda. Such broad 'state' rights would, in turn, entail a broad bundle of social rights linked to reproduction, childcare, health and education, as well as economic rights to ensure adequate economic and financial resources for democratic autonomy. (Held 1987 p.285)

This leads to the inevitable conclusion that effective community involvement in Britain cannot be achieved without far-reaching social, economic and constitutional changes.

Social democratic perspectives

The social democratic perspective on community participation is founded largely on Marshall's ideas on 'citizenship'. Marshall believed that social disadvantage could be minimized by allowing all to participate in the essential elements of society. All citizens should be allowed equal rights to protection under the law, the ballot, and to the social necessities of life (education, health care, a minimum income and decent housing). Furthermore, citizenship should embrace the right to participate in politics and policy-making processes, either as a member of a political authority or through the election of such an authority. These rights should be regardless of people's individual circumstances (Marshall 1950).

The political centre, as represented by the social democrats, advocates community involvement as a means of ensuring social justice, democracy and economic efficiency (Clapham *et al.* 1990). Conflict in society causes inefficiencies and therefore needs to be managed through conciliation, mediation and arbitration – otherwise, more violent forms of protest might emerge. To achieve this, while they accept that the responsibilities of government will be carried out largely by an élite, social democrats argue that state institutions should be open and representative (that is, pluralistic). Power in society should not reside with any single interest group, and policy-making decisions should reflect the outcome of bargaining between numerous interests to ensure accountability. Community participation, alongside the decentralization of policy-making structures, is crucial to this process. Community groups not only influence decisions made by the ruling élite, but also act to manage sudden and radical demands from their membership – that is, the 'politics of regulated conflict' that ensures evolutionary change (reformism) rather than a radical rupture with the past (revolution). Social democrats therefore support community participation, but only if it is organized in a structure of bodies which regulate its membership. They oppose the Marxist notion of mandated delegates on the grounds that such a system would be slow, cumbersome and inefficient (due to its lack of decision-making abilities). Instead, they prefer the idea of elected representation and delegated authority (George and Wilding 1991).

The social democratic model for housing includes the decentralization of service provision, tenure diversification to allow 'tenants as consumers greater choice of provision', and rights to tenant participation (Clapham *et al.* 1990 p.246). These characteristics are largely reflected in current Labour Party thinking. Addressing the Labour Housing Conference on 5 March 1996, the Labour Party Leader Tony Blair announced that:

> Many parts of our country have housing estates facing huge problems of multiple deprivation. The war on this deprivation has to be led not by government or councils but by tenants themselves. The state will play a role but the tenants must take the lead. It is only by empowering the people who live in deprived urban estates that they can be turned around.

At the same conference, the then shadow housing spokesperson Nick Raynsford, addressing Labour's main policy challenges, stated that:

we are committed to a pluralist approach. We see the merits of harnessing the resources of many different providers not just to give greater choice to the public but also to ensure that we all learn from both the successes and the failures of other organizations working towards similar goals . . . The wider involvement of people in all the key decisions affecting their homes – the way they are designed, financed, built, managed and maintained – is an essential ingredient in the creation of a really effective and responsive housing policy. Gone are the days when the providers of housing could simply tell the public what was good for them . . . Where tenants want to assume a greater degree of direct control over their housing either through co-operatives or tenants participation initiatives or, for the very brave, through self-build, then they should be helped and assisted to do just this. Where they want merely to be kept informed and consulted by their landlord then that option should equally be available. There is no single standard pattern of tenant participation. What we should be seeking is an appropriate range of responses in which the tenants themselves are determining the degree and the extent to which they are in control.

Ostensibly, these approaches to tenant involvement contrast significantly with those implemented under the Conservatives in that they allow greater discretion for tenants themselves to determine what style and degree of participation and/or consultation they wish to see. However, social democrats share the New Right view that democratic processes should be administered through representative rather than participatory democracy (Rawls 1971, Titmuss 1968), although their perspective moves beyond the legal and political realm towards one that embraces the social and economic. For instance, Gould argues that freedom 'should be interpreted as the activity of self-development, requiring not only the absence of external constraint but also the availability of social and material conditions necessary for the achievement of purposes or plans' (Gould 1990 p.32). This can only be achieved through a model of social relations founded on equal rights of participation in the political, social and economic arena – achieved largely through the state acting to minimize social and economic hardship and enhancing choice through skills development and education. This view reflects the Fabian tradition within social democracy and comes closer to the neo-Marxist position. However, in contrast to neo-Marxism, social democrats do not question capitalism as 'potentially the most efficient form of economic organization' (George and Wilding 1991 p.67). As Hague suggests, this effectively denies the very existence of 'those structured patterns of power which do seem relevant to an understanding of tenant participation' and, consequently, the social democratic analysis of social relations in the housing system 'can too easily be confined to the knee-jerk rejection of "bureaucratic paternalism"' (Hague 1990 p.253). In turn this leads social democrats to advocate policy prescriptions calling for the dismantlement of state welfare institutions in favour of more pluralist forms of provision (Clapham *et al.* 1990, Commission on Social Justice 1994). However, existing power relationships remain untouched.

Anarchist perspectives

Anarchists have argued that all forms of authority are incompatible with individual freedom. Consequently, if the concept of freedom is to have any real value all forms of authority have to be rejected. The political ideology of anarchy is influenced by liberalism, socialism and a critique of Marxism. In 1872 Bakunin attacked Marx's ideas on socialism – not for wanting social and economic equality but for wanting such equality through the power of a state dictatorship. Bakunin argued that state control was anathema to liberty, and therefore genuine equality and autonomy could only be achieved through the abolition of the state apparatus and the reconstruction of society from the 'bottom' upwards (see Ward 1982). Instead of state institutions controlling political, social and economic processes, anarchists believe that power should be given to a federation of workers' associations free from the central state. While anarchists support the socialist ideal of equality, they differ from the traditional British labour movement (who, at the Labour Party Conference of 1918, committed the party to establishing 'socialism' through state-controlled bureaucracies) in how it should be achieved. Anarchists argue that where socialist parties have gained control (either through parliamentary democracy or following a popular revolution) individuals and the mass of the working classes have remained powerless because they have surrendered power to the state. What is needed, according to the anarchist perspective, is a new form of human relationship built on a popular, communalist, self-governing mode of socialism involving direct action, autonomy, workers' control, decentralization and federalism (Ward 1982).

Wieck defines *direct action* as action which 'realizes the end desired' (so long as it lies within the power of a group to achieve this), as opposed to *indirect action* which 'realizes an irrelevant or even contradictory end' (Wieck, quoted in Ward 1982 p.23). He illustrates this distinction with the case of a cheating butcher. If the butcher weighs out your meat with his/her thumb on the scale – and you spot this – you can complain that he/she is a bandit robbing ordinary people, or report him/her to the Weights and Measures department. These are forms of indirect action. However, if you picket the shop, or get involved in setting up a workers' co-operative butchers' shop, these would involve direct action. Because most of us have delegated power to state institutions, and because it would be impractical in all situations, we rarely consider taking direct action. To overcome this, anarchists argue that the autonomy of the worker and decentralization are essential for self-reliance and genuine democracy. Workers should organize themselves into local councils linked through 'federalism' (involving a network of local, regional, national and international councils, unfettered by the state). In this way, participatory democracy can be achieved (Albert and Hahnel 1991).

Another element in anarchist thinking is the theory of 'spontaneous order', a process whereby people improvise and experiment collectively (through trial and error) to create order out of any adverse situation. This order will be more durable and sustainable in the long term because it will be one that is more closely related to the majority of people's needs. This view is based on observations of the history of human society: for example, the post-war squatting movement of 1946, when ex-servicemen and women squatted in army camps (40 000 homeless people in England and Wales occupied over 1000 army camps) and established a Squatters Protection Society, a federation of squatting groups (see Chapter 2); this movement cut across a wide range of social groups, from tinkers to university dons, operating as leaderless and non-hierarchical collectives. Such organizational cultures are often found in inventive and imaginative occupations, such as architecture or scientific research (Handy 1985). In such situations the main factor holding the organization together is the 'task' (be it the building of houses, finding a cure for a serious disease or, in the case of squatters, a solution to a social problem) rather than a rigid managerial pyramid of authority (which tends to kill off innovation and the capacity to be creative). As Ward states, 'the system makes its morons, then despises them for their ineptitude, and rewards its "gifted few" for their rarity' (Ward 1982 p.43).

While anarchy as a social theory can be applied at the level of the organization, to highlight the benefits of collective working in project teams, its applicability to organizing modern western societies at the macro level appears doubtful. However, social anthropologists have identified a range of successful and sophisticated societies, such as the African Bush tribes and the Innuits of the Arctic, where order is maintained through kinship ties and mutuality rather than formal legislation, social class and political élites. Non-hierarchical forms of social organizing have also been advocated by theorists applying the laws of 'cybernetics' – the study of communication systems applied to managing organizations. Stafford Beer, for instance, argues that organizations and societies should be ordered in a similar way to biological systems and the human senses. Human senses work in harmony, co-ordinated by the brain. But the brain does not act as a leader and the body is free to interpret its instructions and directives. Society and organizations should be similarly free to work in self-determined and flexible ways so that they can deal effectively with the complexities of the changing external environment. This flexibility would be achieved in modern societies through networks of interdependent groups made up of the entire population. Equilibrium would be maintained through perpetual adjustment and readjustment between a multitude of influences organized as an interdependent network of federations involved in various activities (production, consumption and exchange; communications; education; defence; housing and so on). This organic view of social order sees society as comprised of mutually dependent organs and cells forever adapting and rejuvenating themselves to meet new situations (Beer 1971). In territorial terms, the anarchist system would be organized at the neighbourhood level (as near as possible to the direct control of people) through communes and co-ordinated (rather than managed) at the regional level by federations of communes. These regional federations would be co-ordinated at the national level by a confederation of regions (replacing the nation-state) and at the European level by a confederation of confederations (Ward 1982).

Anarchists have distinguished 'housing' as a *noun* from 'housing' as a *verb*. The noun describes a commodity or product ('a house'), while the verb describes a process ('to house' – the activity of housing someone). Despite the fact that adequate housing is an important intermediate need which must be met if our basic individual needs for health and autonomy are also to be satisfied (Doyal and Gough 1991), the great majority of us have no control over this process. It is done to us by others – be they mortgage lenders, developers, estate agents or housing departments – and we have to accept their decisions and submit to their control. Consequently, the outcomes of the process frequently fail to meet our needs, desires or interests, as Dunleavy's account of the politics of mass housing provision in the late 1950s and early 1960s so clearly demonstrates (Dunleavy 1981). But it is possible for people to take control over their own housing activities. Today, a third of the world's population house themselves. New technology in housing production, such as the Walter Segal method, has allowed more and more people to control the housing development process and, through direct action, to house themselves. The developing countries of Africa, Asia and Latin America have, over the last 40 years, witnessed enormous population shifts from rural to urban areas, resulting in the development of large squatter settlements on the periphery of existing cities. Here, people have utilized whatever materials they could find (straw, timber, old bricks, corrugated iron, beaten-out cans or oil drums) to construct their own homes. In addition, these communities have developed their own local economies – generating work by growing food, raising chickens or selling home-produced goods – alongside sophisticated internal political organizations and electoral procedures. These squatter movements can achieve higher rates of literacy, employment skills and income than the poor in inner-city slums, as well as relatively lower levels of crime – challenging popular myths about such developments being dens of vice and social disorganization (Turner and Fichter 1972, Turner 1976, Ward 1976, Ospina 1987).

A London Churches Group report, *From Sympathy to Solidarity* (1996), based on a survey of 187 homeless projects helping 5000 people a day in São Paulo, offers a comparison of approaches to tackling homelessness in Brazil and Britain. In Britain, approaches are characterized as sympathetic, top-down and paternalistic, with the homeless perceived as passive recipients of a service. In contrast, service-users in Brazil are seen as partners in innovative projects aimed at helping people to become politically active on their own behalf. Monsignor Lancelotti describes the aim of a social centre for the homeless in São Paulo as getting 'the street people involved in political action' and helping them to 'organize so they can represent themselves'. Therefore, it can be argued that the poor of the developing world – by acting in an anarchic way – have gained three freedoms which the poor in rich developed countries have lost: first, the freedom of community self-selection and determination; second, the freedom to control their own resources; and third, the freedom to shape their own environment ('Brazil offers way to help homeless', *The Guardian* 21 February 1996). In the developed world most land is owned by someone else who controls its use backed up by the law and state agencies (planners, the police, the judiciary and so forth). There is little common land. Housing disadvantage in the developed world can therefore be partly explained by the state's denial of self-determination.

Ideological positions summarized

Applying these ideological positions on community participation to an analysis of housing policy and practice in Britain, it can be concluded that resident involvement initiatives have largely had similar functions to play in the strategies of both mainstream political parties. While collective forms of housing provision, permitting genuine control for residents, have been part of the mainstream tenure patterns in Scandinavian countries (see Chapter 5), in Britain these have consistently remained marginal. As McDonald observes in his discussion on collectively run housing schemes:

> in Britain the consensus between right and left is so strong that both ends of the political spectrum find the idea incomprehensible and, perhaps, threatening. To the right it's an initiative in self-help that won't be allowed to disturb the mainstream; to the left it's a remarkable, perhaps opportunist, experiment that won't be allowed to disturb the mainstream. (McDonald 1986 p.16)

The mainstream in British housing is a system dominated by mass home-ownership, some market renting and a 'residualized' social sector (Malpass and Murie 1994). There is little scope for democratic and collectivized forms of provision. Participation strategies for the Conservatives have been predominantly about depoliticizing housing through restructuring the state sector, reducing the state's financial role in housing provision, and creating new development opportunities for the private sector. The Labour Party's proposed housing policy agenda in 1996 – set out in the speeches of Tony Blair and Nick Raynsford to the Labour Housing Conference mentioned above – gave prominence to supporting 'the aspiration of the majority of people to own their own homes' (Blair) and to 'engineer a sustained recovery in the housing market' (Raynsford). There was no clear commitment to re-democratize the housing system.

While an understanding of the ideologies underpinning housing policy-making helps to explain why participation is being advocated and identifies in whose interest it is being promoted, it cannot be assumed that the aims of different forms of participation will produce the intended outcomes. Although particular organizations and residents may well engage in a community-participation project with particular goals in mind, the eventual outcomes may not be the same as those initially determined. This is because participation is essentially about negotiating and bargaining and therefore the outcomes can be indeterminate and unpredictable. While ideology may seek to determine the structures within which participation processes take place, the role of human involvement may result in different effects to those intended. The process of participation itself can work to increase political consciousness and thereby lead to conflict (Thornley 1977). Consequently, a broader understanding of the participation process requires a sociological consideration of the connection between structure and agency.

Sociological perspectives

Giddens's structuration thesis focuses on the role of actors in re-creating the means whereby they express themselves as agents ('agency') and the edifices set in place to monitor and control their behaviour ('structure'). While agency involvement is largely constrained by the structure – which is firmly established in time and space – people have the capacity to change their social environment. We all retain some autonomy as thinking and acting beings, so that while the structure may appear strong and control by dominating agents may seem complete, there is always the potential for subversion (Giddens 1984). A number of sociological studies have focused on the capacity of community-development approaches to redefine collective consciousness around housing tenure. These studies are rooted in the 1960s when sociological attention began to focus on how conflict over scarce urban resources was mediated. Much of this work applied a Weberian analysis of class struggle to developing a systematic urban theory. Struggles over the use of scarce urban resources were seen as leading to new forms of 'social cleavage' and new locations for collective action which cross-cut and, to some extent, superseded class. For instance, Rex and Moore's notion of 'housing classes' (Rex and Moore 1967), together with Pahl's subsequent critique (Pahl 1975), highlighted how housing-distribution mechanisms left particular groups socially and spatially disadvantaged. In turn, this can induce the development of a new collective consciousness based on a shared understanding of residential experience, leading to new forms of political protest aiming 'less to reduce inequalities at the work place than to reduce inequalities at the place of residence' (Pahl 1975 p.257).

These debates drew a number of responses from neo-Marxists in the 1970s which contributed further to the idea of new possibilities for collective action. Of particular relevance to an understanding of community participation is Castells's analysis of the 'urban', urban conflict, and urban social movements (Castells 1977). In developing his thesis Castells drew largely on the neo-Marxist view that for modern capitalist societies to be successful the state has to perform two critical functions: *accumulation* (the reproduction of labour power and the extraction of profit for reinvestment to perpetuate economic growth) and *legitimation* (the retention of social cohesion and the co-operation of the working classes). However, these two functions are contradictory or incompatible. In order to ensure accumulation and the retention of legitimacy the state has to provide what Castells describes as *collective consumption* facilities – that is, for labour power to be reproduced there must be the means whereby workers are able to offer their labour for sale day after day. This requires that they consume – food, housing, transport, health care and education. All these items are provided in the urban setting, the provision of which has becoming increasingly a matter for the state as individual private investors find such activities unprofitable. Consequently, subsidized council housing emerged after 1919 and the welfare state expanded after the Second World War. These collective forms of state provision become the subject of political debate and action. The more the state is involved in the provision of welfare services, the more difficult it is to raise the money by taxation to meet the cost without reducing the profits of the capitalist class. This leads to what Marxists call the *crisis of capitalism*. As the state tries to cut back its expenditure on public services political protest, and the mobilization of what Castells called *urban social movements*, occurs. As these cutbacks affect all social groups, urban social movements cross-cut traditional class divides.

The *urban* is therefore seen by Castells as a specific spatial formation reflecting the need of the dominant class to organize effectively the processes of reproduction and legitimation. This idea can be seen as a rudimentary attempt at changing the focus of urban sociology by understanding cities as arenas for political conflict and class struggle. However, it appears that

Castells's concept may be overstated as a general urban theory, since conflict over scarce resources is not necessarily confined to the urban setting (for example, conservationists versus housebuilders in rural communities). Furthermore, while social movements may organize around specific consumption issues such as housing, these movements are generally small-scale and short-lived. They rarely lead to a long-term ideological shift in consciousness or demands for wider structural change.

The notion that consumption is crucial to shaping collective consciousness was developed by Dunleavy in his own urban political analysis. He suggested that the significant growth of urban social movements in Britain from the late 1960s reflected 'the increasing displacement of social crisis into consumption processes' (Dunleavy 1980 p.164). The ideological hegemony of the post-war welfare state began to break down in the 1960s as it became increasingly evident that the state was failing to deliver the goods. The 'rediscovery of poverty', rising unemployment, slums and homelessness, flawed public housing schemes and unpopular private-sector office developments led to a number of urban protest movements seeking major changes in the way urban services were delivered. In housing, such protests involved tenant action groups, squatting campaigns and co-operative movements. However, more recently the utility of the concept of urban social movements for understanding collective consciousness among council tenants has been brought into question. Cairncross *et al.* (1993) argue that council tenants in Britain are divided on the basis of class, social status and consumption position, and rarely have a strong orientation towards collective protest action.

Dunleavy argues that the significance of analysing urban social movements is not so much to do with their potential to achieve social change, but more to do with examining whether they 'may hold the key to the intractable problems of studying non-protest and quiescence in urban politics' (Dunleavy 1980 p.158). He suggests that urban social movements, by being drawn into a network of institutionalized influence, offer a mechanism by which social grievances are effectively managed by state agencies. Lowe's study of urban social movements illustrates how tenants' grievances in Sheffield at the end of the 1960s were institutionalized in the local state apparatus (Lowe 1986). Tenant representatives, previously hostile to local housing policies, were incorporated within the local council's management committee structure. In a similar way, the Community Development Projects (CDPs), initiated in 1968 in the aftermath of Enoch Powell's 'rivers of blood' speech and growing urban tensions, can be seen to represent an attempt by government to pre-empt further urban problems by achieving social cohesion through community participation. This inter-relationship between community groups, urban social movements and the state apparatus, which effectively maintains the status quo, has led some commentators to question whether or not such movements should operate at a distance from the state apparatus rather than within it. Craig and Mayo suggest that community action organized at a distance from state institutions would be unlikely to achieve success, arguing that:

> without engaging with the state and with political processes at different levels, localized community actions risk remaining marginalized, if occasionally incorporated. The importance of developing strategies to link local projects and movements into wider strategies and movements for change at both national and international levels is clearly defined. (Craig and Mayo 1995 p.9)

However, others have argued that it is difficult to envisage how such associations can be formed without the unity of the social movement becoming subsumed into the state system (see Gyford 1985). Feminist and anti-racist perspectives in particular have recommended separatism as a means of achieving emancipation (see Chapter 11). In practice, community participation in Britain in the 1980s can be characterized in terms of a closer working relationship between communities and the local state, portraying a pragmatic response from local government to an attack on its power from central government. In defence of their position many local authorities sought to gain the support of their local communities by working closer with them, establishing new possibilities for community involvement (Hoggett and Hambleton 1987). New Left authorities in particular were keen to use powers contained in Section 137 of the Local Government Act 1972 'which enabled a council to spend up to the proceeds of a 2p. rate on anything related to the needs of local residents' (Lansley *et al.* 1989 p.67). The conflicts of the 1960s and 1970s, where community workers were often at odds with the local state, were redirected in the 1980s towards addressing the tension in central–local relations. An acceptance that community action must engage with the local state grew as even those activists who had previously adopted a confrontational stance saw the opportunities presented in working with local government (Taylor 1995a).

However, since the 1980s the ability of local government to act for the community has diminished following numerous measures to replace council functions with new forms of service provision. Housing services and urban regeneration activities have been taken out of municipal control in various ways including the right to buy, Tenants' Choice, stock transfer, Housing Action Trusts, compulsory competitive tendering, the cessation of council housebuilding, urban regeneration joint venture companies, and an enhanced role for the housing association movement. The introduction of business management practices (such as business planning, performance indicators, the three 'Es' and 'value for money') into the public and voluntary sectors has diverted them away from their original welfare objectives. If community work is to survive such changes it will, according to Taylor, have to take on board a number of roles including 'a *market development* role. Community work can capitalize on the current emphasis on service user involvement and help user organizations to develop their own services, to make sense of the new institutional environment, to offer advocacy and to take up new opportunities for participation in service planning.' In addition, Taylor refers to the role of ' *"managing deprivation and urban dissent"*: to participate in government programmes to address the dislocation caused by economic change, particularly crime and urban decay' (Taylor 1995a p.105 – original emphasis). These policy prescriptions, nevertheless, need to be evaluated in the broader context of diminishing resources, piecemeal area-based regeneration programmes (many of which do not affect most social housing areas) and the increasing social exclusion of significant sections of the population. Given these structural limitations, the opportunities for disadvantaged communities to influence the direction of government policies and programmes remain remote. In addressing this dilemma it is critical to establish a clear understanding of how power operates in society and how, subsequently, certain communities continue to be socially excluded. The next section explores different concepts of power.

Concepts of power

Sociological attention to the concept of power emerged out of the growing discontent with bureaucratic state institutions in the late 1960s. Traditional democratic theories, based on liberal individualism and Marxist communitarianism, were seen as failing to reconcile the dual rights of individualism and collectivism. On the one hand, liberalism conceptualized the individual as essentially motivated by self-interest and justifies social and economic inequalities – ideas which undermine political equality. On the other hand, Marxist interpretations appeared to condone authoritarianism and the repression of individual liberties. Subsequently, a sociological critique of power evolved focusing on three key issues: first, that power represents the legitimate regulation of societies based on consensus; second, that power reflects the ability of dominant interest groups to prevent any opposing views from being voiced; and third, Foucault's notion that power and resistance is present in all areas of society and that the exercise of power is not merely the preserve of state institutions. Morgan and Stanley (1993) describe the development of this critique as it appeared in the pages of *Sociology*, starting with *consensus theory*.

Consensus theory is based on a pluralist view of power and argues that genuine power comes with holding a mandate from those represented to make decisions, legitimated through the ballot box. Parsons suggests that political power is analogous to the banking system, where electors bank their deposits (through the ballot) with their elected representatives and, if they are dissatisfied, can withdraw their deposits at the next election (see Morgan and Stanley 1993). Schumpeter (1943) claimed that periodic elections ensured political accountability because they required power-seekers to gain the support of a diverse range of interests. However, consensus theory fails to account for the existence of unequal power relationships which permit the electoral process to be manipulated by dominant interest groups. Furthermore, some electoral systems, such as 'first-past-the-post' majority rule, deny representation in parliament to a number of political interests while fostering the illusion of democracy. Consensus theory also assumes that people are free to understand and express their needs and common interests, which may not always be the case.

Lukes turns consensus theory on its head by suggesting that power exists when people's interests and needs are frustrated. He refocuses the power debate on to the question of why so many oppressed groups fail to mobilize around their interests, suggesting that power is exercised through the denial of access to knowledge and through the manipulation of understanding and perception. It is the freedom to choose from a range of options that confers power and influence – if this is denied, so too is power. Therefore, the oppressed put up with their situation because they are unaware of their real interests and, because of this, there is a failure to act (Lukes 1974). Gramsci's notion of *hegemony* takes a similar view of power residing beyond economic-corporatist roots. He considered the way in which the ideological agenda is set and how this becomes perceived as legitimate and non-contestable by those subjugated to it. For Gramsci, power is abstruse, pervasively diffused as a 'system of ideas' throughout all manifestations of individual and collective life: in the family, schools, universities, the media, the workplace, the judiciary, everyday cultural practices and so on. Power is transmitted as 'common sense', to provide ways of thinking and behaving that seem so natural that they are not subject to scrutiny (Gramsci 1971). Working-class self-determination, therefore, can only be achieved through contesting the dominant hegemonic culture spread throughout the entire social order. 'The power of the ruling class is spiritual as well as material; and any "counterhegemony" must carry its political campaign into this hitherto neglected realm of values and customs, speech habits and ritual practices' (Eagleton 1991 p.114). In contrast, Hindess argues that the focus of enquiry should not be why certain interests are *not* pursued but, rather, why other interests *are* pursued. He suggests that explanations of power relationships must focus on the activities of the executors of power – not on why those subordinated fail to mobilize in their own defence (Hindess 1983).

Marxist interpretations of power in modern societies have largely focused on the way in which the economic structure determines the superstructure that stabilizes class relationships. Marx believed that capitalism alienated and exploited the labouring classes, but that the proletariat would develop a collective consciousness of their situation and mobilize in defence of their self-interest. However, as this did not happen, Marxists had to reconsider their position. Lenin identified the emergence of a *labour aristocracy*, a bribed power élite within the proletariat who stood between mass working-class consciousness and the bourgeoisie. He predicted the emergence of a proletarian dictatorship through class struggle within 15 years of the Bolshevik Revolution. But again this did not happen and, following Lenin's death, more totalitarian regimes emerged in the eastern bloc (Dallin 1992). By the late 1960s the dichotomy between notions of individual freedom and egalitarianism became a preoccupation of neo-Marxist thinking, particularly in the light of extreme forms of state socialism under Stalin's influence. One of the most coherent formulations of this Marxist revisionism can be found in the writings of the Yugoslavian *Praxis* movement, named after the title of their journal. The two central themes of the *Praxis* philosophy are its rejection of authoritarian state socialism (which it sees as denying people their creative potential), and its call for self-management in all spheres of decision-making – social, economic and political – through the mechanism of a multicameral political body (Gould 1990).

Building on the ideas of the *Praxis* movement and the work of Macpherson, Gould argues for the need to develop a new theory of freedom and social co-operation. She calls for greater *self-development*, a concept close to Macpherson's notion of *developmental power*, where people have equal rights to the conditions that allow them to live as fully as they wish (Macpherson 1973). The point of departure between Gould and Macpherson is the latter's attempt to specify the capacities which individuals need to develop if they are to attain self-realization. Gould prefers to leave these specifics to human choice. Macpherson argues for democratic participation in political decision-making and, unlike Gould, holds back from extending this to self-management in wider economic and social processes. Gould's model of democracy hinges on four inter-related principles:

First, that freedom should be understood as an activity of self-development, requiring the availability of conditions; second, that the principle of equality should be understood as one of *prima facie* equal rights to the conditions of self-development; third, that reciprocity and common activity serve as social conditions for freedom . . . and fourth, that democracy should apply not only to the political domain, but to the economic and social domain as well. (Gould 1990 p.80)

For Gould, the democratization of economic and social life is a prerequisite for the elimination of political alienation and the distorted influence which capital holds in decision-making.

More recently, some Marxists have adopted a 'game-theory perspective' to give greater emphasis to the role of agency in social processes. Urry (1995) examines aspects of this debate as it was explored in *Theory and Society* and *Politics and Sociology*. A fundamental stance common to this discussion is that traditional Marxism simply *assumed* that structures in capitalist societies were functional for capitalism (it did not offer evidence to prove that they were) and that greater attention needs to be given to the role of agency and the games which people play within the wider social structure.

Olson (1965), in considering why people do not mobilize in defence of their interests, argues that *non*-collective action is a rational choice. People will generally perceive that the benefits which they are likely to derive from involvement in collective action will be minimal in comparison with the personal cost of their individual efforts. Furthermore, the collective benefits derived from each individual's contribution will be perceived as slight. Consequently, it is rational for individuals to view their investment of time and effort in collective action as largely pointless, particularly in large organizations or committees where peer-group pressure may be less obvious. (For a broader consideration of the psychology of participation see Chapter 8.) If these perceptions of the benefits of collective action exist at the level of the firm, then it is no wonder that the broader labour movement has not mobilized at the macro level to improve its situation. Urry, however, challenges Olson's position on two counts. First, he suggests that it ignores those occasions where workers *have* organized collectively on a significant scale (as demonstrated by John Grayson in Chapter 2). Second, it discounts the possibility that individuals may perceive the benefits of 'synergy' which collective action can bring (Urry 1995).

Elster (1979) argues that humans act with intent, within a 'strategic environment', and that individuals will choose actions which they believe will bring about the best results for them. This concept of power is based on rational relativity, where non-participation is conceived as a calculated response rather than as apathy. The decision to participate is dependent on a group's perception of their capacity to exercise any significant influence on outcomes. Elster presents a game-theory framework within which an analysis of rational choice and the interdependency of decisions can be made. He suggests that if certain conditions co-exist collective action in a group is more likely to occur. These conditions would include:

- the actors in the group perceive a contradiction in their present circumstances;
- the actors in the group are not distant from each other;
- the group has a low rate of turnover in membership; and

- there are possibilities for reversing the perceived contradiction (Elster 1978).

Urry argues that Elster ignores the ideological conditions shaping human behaviour (Urry 1995). The New Right ideology that found favour in both Britain and the USA in the 1970s and 1980s promoted market-led individualism at the expense of social democracy, making the choice of 'free-riding' a more likely option. Furthermore, Elster overlooks the resources, knowledge, skills and capabilities required for collective action to be effective, factors that have been increasingly diminished in certain communities during the latter part of the twentieth century.

Richardson suggests that any meaningful analysis of the participation process must examine *how* groups strive to fulfil their aims and the factors affecting the outcomes of the bargaining process. Her examination also deploys a game-theory analysis, which she defines as:

> the study of strategic choice and its consequences in circumstances whose outcomes are not based primarily on either skill or chance. In its own terms, it is concerned with 'games of strategy' which are those 'in which the best course of action for each player depends on what the other players do'. The decisions of the respective parties are thereby interdependent, that is, they are based on each party's respective expectations of the others' actions. (Richardson 1983 p.83)

Negotiations between groups may proceed in an atmosphere of pure conflict, where gains made by one party correspond to a direct loss by the other (the *zero-sum* perspective). Alternatively, negotiations may occur in a climate of collaboration, where the interested parties identify that they will both gain through co-operating or both lose by not co-operating. (An application of the game-theory framework to an understanding of cross-national comparative tenant-participation processes is discussed by Bo Bengtsson and David Clapham in Chapter 5.) If tenants feel that participation offers a genuine opportunity to influence policy outcomes, collective action is more likely to happen. However, while game theory offers an important framework for evaluating the rules and conditions under which opportunities for effective collective strategic action exist, it does not adequately address the key factors shaping the outcomes of bargaining processes. To achieve this requires a closer examination of the question of power relationships in the housing system and what resources (financial, political, skills, knowledge and so on) each actor can bring to bear on the bargaining process. Furthermore, there is a need to establish appropriate performance indicators, qualitative as well as quantitative, to evaluate the outcomes of participation processes.

Somerville and Steele suggest three criteria for evaluating the effectiveness of tenant-participation processes. First, 'the effectiveness of institutional techniques for initiating and developing tenant participation . . . in terms of the satisfaction of tenants generally with specific forms and processes of collective action'; second, the 'representativeness of those who actually participate' measured by the degree of consensus between those who participate and those who do not; and third, the extent to which there is a genuine balance of power measured by tenants' responses to 'the question of whether they feel they have sufficient say in decision-making processes' (Somerville and Steele 1995 pp.266–267). Overlaying these indicators with ideas from democratic theory, Somerville and Steele apply their framework for evaluation to three different models of tenant participation in British council-housing management – compulsory competitive tendering (defined as a 'marketized arrangement'), tenant management organizations (defined as 'tenant-controlled management') and landlord–tenant partnerships (such as estate agreements) – suggesting that, in this way, the collective quality of service provision can be measured.

While Somerville and Steele offer an appropriate framework for comparing the performance of different models of tenant participation at the micro level within the existing institutional arrangements for housing provision, they fail to address the nature of power and influence in the wider policy-making community. Although sustainable structures for a representative sample of tenants might be established, the agenda that landlords and tenants are able to address will be largely prescribed by broader power structures at the macro level. Somerville and Steele's focus is on participation within existing structures of housing provision and there is no attempt to include notions of empowerment, or to see the possible need for changing the social relationships within the existing structures. They therefore fail to address the problem highlighted in Saunders' study of tenant participation in Croydon which concluded that tenants have:

> confronted the local authority, not as challengers, but as supplicants. Far from representing a challenge to the prevailing pattern of resource allocation, they have strengthened the pattern of distribution by competing for the crumbs while resolutely ignoring the cake. (Saunders 1979 p.288)

Furthermore, the constituency defined by Somerville and Steele comprises existing tenants and landlord representatives and ignores the wider community (including the homeless, others who aspire to become tenants and those indirectly affected by housing-related policies). Their framework therefore remains problematic. What is needed is a model which allows an examination of the *way* in which power is exerted over disadvantaged communities to exclude them. By developing a coherent understanding of the processes of social exclusion, it will be possible to design appropriate strategies for genuine community empowerment.

Freire suggests that if the oppressed are to overcome their disadvantage they must not only understand the way in which power is exerted, but also conceptualize their disadvantage as a 'limited situation which they can transform' (Freire, quoted in Rees 1991 p.7). Rees, alluding to Gramsci's claim that 'everyone is a philosopher', highlights the importance of *biography* and giving voice to the experiences of individuals. Individuals should be encouraged to make sense of their own world and be enabled to overcome perceived obstacles to empowerment. Freire saw this happening through a process of *conscientization* whereby people would gain political literacy and change their perception of their situation – for instance, from one that sees their problems and failings as the result of their own social pathology to one that sees them as being the product of externalities beyond their control (see Rees 1991). Once disadvantaged individuals and communities develop a political understanding of their circumstances, they can prepare to take action against the sources of power which cause their social exclusion. Freire suggests that one critical source of power excluding individuals and communities is located in their own interpretation of their social condition. This explanation moves into the realm of more opaque instances of social exclusion – that is, those as perceived by excluded people themselves.

Fromm identifies three perceived sources of power: first, *external authority*, where power comes from people's perceptions of hierarchical authority; second, *internal authority*, where power comes from people's self-perceptions of their own authority; and third, *anonymous authority*, where power comes from assumed and unchallenged 'truths' (representations rather than reality) such as the primacy of majority rule, sound economic management principles and 'value for money' (Fromm 1969). Internal perceptions of authority invariably reflect external and anonymous forms of control, leading Rees to suggest that effective empowerment strategies should give greater emphasis to enabling people to realize their *own* internal authority (Rees 1991).

However, if internal perceptions of authority are ultimately shaped and controlled by external factors, realizing self-determination would appear to be an impossibility. Foucault's examination of the way in which power has been exercised throughout history highlights how human beings are transformed into subjects and, ultimately, disempowered. He identifies three objective processes which 'subjectify' the human body. The first occurs through modes of enquiry which have claimed, at different moments in time, the status of 'science' and which serve to generate new *specifications* of the 'individual'. These modes are presented in the form of written technical discourses, with each period of history defining its own discourse knowledge base. For example, throughout the nineteenth century educationalists, physicians and administrators incorporated issues of sexuality into their discourse to specify the homosexual as 'a personage, a past, a case history . . . in addition to being a type of life, a life form, and a morphology with an indiscreet anatomy and possibly a mysterious physiology' (Foucault 1984 p.43). These various discourses operated together to determine a norm of sexual development, one that could be defined and all possible deviations from it identified and proscribed. Similarly, discourses since the industrial revolution have specified the 'residuum' (as distinct from the 'respectable') and the 'underclass' (as distinct from 'mainstream society'). Foucault suggests that it is chiefly through these technical fields of knowledge/discourse that the structures of society and power relations are formed. Concurrently, power is exercised in a second way through the process of *dividing practices*, where the subject is divided within herself or himself and from other people. So we have, for instance, mad people/sane people, sick people/healthy people, criminals/saints, deserving/undeserving, decent tenants/problem tenants and so on. At the same time, a third process of social control occurs where a human being 'turns himself into a subject', such as homosexuals who 'recognize themselves as subjects of "sexuality" and become incarcerated by their identity' (Foucault 1982 p.778).

This third process has been recognized in explanations of how the consciousness of some tenants on unpopular housing estates is shaped, where 'a sense of failure is internalized and reinforced by stereotyping' (Taylor 1995b p.6). Once subjectified in these ways individuals are then subjected to further exercises of power: the psychiatrist over the 'mental patient', the social worker over the 'single-parent mother', the housing manager over the 'tenant' and so on. These notions of power represent a departure from those traditional Marxist theories which see power as a unitary measure residing in the lap of the state. Foucault argues that power is omnipresent, applying itself:

> to immediate everyday life which categorizes the individual, marks him by his own individuality, attaches him to his own identity, imposes a law of truth on him which he must recognize and which others have to recognize in him. It is a form of power which makes individuals subjects. There are two meanings of the word 'subject': subject to someone else by control and dependence; and tied to his own identity by a conscience or self-knowledge. Both meanings suggest a form of power which subjugates and makes subject to. (Foucault 1982 p.781)

Foucault rejects as too simplistic the traditional image of power as monolithic, clearly visible and embodied in the law. Power in modern society is a more subtle phenomenon operating through processes of normalization (rather than punishment), exerted at all levels of society in different and largely covert guises. Power is not hierarchical – flowing down from above as the 'ladders of participation' imply – but localized (in the family, in the school, in relationships between men and women, on the estates and in relationships between landlords and tenants). Foucault argues that this power technique, this individualizing form of power, originated in Christian institutions which aimed to save individuals by exploring their souls through the confessional and directing their consciousness. From the eighteenth century the modern state's primary objective changed to one of meeting more temporal needs, achieved through the mechanism of a multitude of statutory and voluntary agencies deploying the same individualizing tactic – only this time through the family, doctors, psychiatrists and administrators rather than the priest. By the late twentieth century power relations and the discourse through which power is exerted have become 'progressively governmentalized . . . elaborated, rationalized, and centralized in the form of, or under the auspices of, state institutions' (Foucault 1982 p.793).

Since the mid-nineteenth century a multitude of images and notions about housing have been filtered through a range of discourses (founded largely on sociology and the political sciences). These have served to 'fetishize' tenure forms, subjectify individuals, prescribe measures of environmental and social control, delineate social relationships and enforce 'natural forms' of social organizing. Teymur argues that a clearer understanding of housing strategies requires an analysis of the 'housing discourse' that scrutinizes:

> its *objects*, the points of view (problematics), the textual and discursive *structures* of arguments and statements, the *mechanisms* and the media through which these statements gain plausibility, the *effects of* the discourse on, and the *effects on* the discourse by, non-discursive domains, the various *translations* and *transformations* between discursive and non-discursive, between discursive and spatial, and between verbal and visual domains, and culminating in the common socio-spatial bases of pathology in the lives, homes and minds of those who support the different sides of the discourse. (Teymur *et al.* 1988 pp.21–22 – original emphasis)

An archaeological trail through housing discourses constructed by practitioners, professional institutes and academics uncovers a range of objectifying practices and instances of social control. These include 'destructive patterns of symbolizing homelessness' (Daly 1996 p.8), the 'problematization' of the council tenant as part of the 'residuum' or 'underclass' (Murray 1990), the differentiation of deserving and undeserving (Macey and Baker 1973), the determination of 'natural' tenure forms (Saunders 1990), the planning of settlements to order societies and space (Sibley 1995), the design of housing to reinforce gender roles (Roberts 1991), the symbolic construction of community (Cohen 1985) and so forth. Jacobs and Manzi (1996) argue that housing discourse grounded in the ideology of the New Right has been used by policy-makers and professionals to nurture a particular perspective. For example, the use of the term 'customer' rather than 'client' changes the perception of housing practitioners towards consumerism and the marketization of the housing service. Similarly, the 1995 Housing White Paper committed the Conservatives to generating housing-allocation schemes that reflected the 'underlying values of our society. They should balance specific housing needs against the need to support married couples who take a responsible approach to family life, so that tomorrow's generation grows up in a stable environment' (DoE, quoted in Jacobs and Manzi 1996 p.556). Housing therefore becomes a reward for subscribing to family values.

In the nineteenth century the urban poor became the target of a scientific discourse that subjectified them as 'outcasts . . . [and] hopeless subjects of reform' (Booth, quoted in Sibley 1995 p.56). As we approach the end of the twentieth century a similar process of subjectification is occurring – only this time the concept has changed to 'social exclusion'. While a historical analysis of housing policy displays a wide range of discourses and sub-discourses, with different disciplines attaining supremacy over the debate at different moments in time, they often display a surprising degree of consensus as to the nature of the 'housing problem' – be it due to flawed architectural concepts, the social pathology of certain individuals, or the inherent deficiencies of the public housing sector – and what specific policy prescriptions are needed to solve it. However, despite these agreements, society has never managed fully to eliminate 'the problem'. Teymur suggests that this is because unequal power relationships and unequal access to opportunity have been sustained through the continual existence of private privileges represented, through discourse, as a natural right (Teymur *et al.* 1988). Additionally, the use of technical language, a significant feature of the housing debate, has been 'used to prevent outsiders from the "linguistic community" gaining access' (Jacobs and Manzi 1996 p.547).

While Foucault helps us to see the role which subjectifying practices play in the exercise of power, he never really identifies *who* is exercising power or for what reason. However, Foucault has defended this position by arguing that attempts to identify who are the power-holders would be a futile exercise. The *task* is to understand the processes of power and to resist these – resistance occurring *within* the system of power relations themselves. The way to empowerment is through strategies that seek to enable oppressed communities to participate in, influence and ultimately take control of the discursive practice through which power is exercised. Foucault is in no doubt that the appearance throughout history of a whole range of scientific discourses has allowed the advance of social control over all areas of people's lives. But this has also made possible the formation of a 'reverse' discourse whereby people who are excluded can speak on their own behalf, demand that their legitimacy be acknowledged:

> often in the same vocabulary, using the same categories by which [they are] disqualified. There is not, on the one side, a discourse of power, and opposite it, another discourse that runs counter to it. Discourses are tactical elements or blocks operating in the field of force relations; there can exist different and even contradictory discourses within the same strategy; they can, on the contrary, circulate without changing their form from one strategy to another, opposing strategy. (Foucault 1984 pp.101–102)

Rees advocates a similar device – which he terms 'reverse thesis' – in arguing for the need to demystify the language of experts and to challenge the rationale of policy evaluations that ignore the wastage of a significant minority of unemployed and marginalized people and the social, psychological and economic constraints that this imposes on community empowerment. This requires a reverse discourse to challenge the stereotypical assumptions about public-sector inefficiency and private-sector enterprise alongside:

> the achievement of the more equitable distribution of resources and non-exploitative relationships between people and the enabling of people to achieve a creative sense of power through enhanced self-respect, confidence, knowledge and skills. (Rees 1991 p.66)

Foucault's account, therefore, presents a starting point for developing community resistance at the local level, where power in its most modern form operates on its subjects. In the longer term these smaller sites of resistance will need to become incorporated into a broader strategy, through engaging with a wider network of insurgency aimed at challenging power relations at the global level. In the context of housing, therefore, the long-term strategies of tenants on run-down housing estates might be to engage with movements with policy objectives on homelessness, negative equity, sub-standard housing, fuel consumption, health care, crime, poverty, unemployment, transport, education, income support, racism, gender issues, childcare, disability, sexuality and the environment.

Putting these ideas into a more practical framework, and building on notions of liberation through dialogue (Freire 1972), advocacy and action (Rose and Black 1985) and partnership and co-production (Rosenfeld 1989), Rees suggests a number of key stages in the empowerment process. These involve communities in the following:

● gaining a clear understanding of the key themes or issues relevant;
● evaluating self-image and knowledge;

- developing an awareness of policies and the notion of choice;
- experiencing solidarity with others (networking);
- acquiring and using appropriate language;
- developing a resistance to a return to powerlessness;
- developing interactive and political skills; and
- establishing evaluative mechanisms for measuring progress (Rees 1991).

Rees suggests that this empowerment process needs to be implemented with the support of community-development practitioners.

Conclusions

The concept of community involvement cannot be characterized by a single theory. The nature of community participation is multi-faceted, with many variants depending on: histories and stage of development; ideological, political, economic and cultural context; institutional arrangements and so forth. The outcomes of participation practices will also have different consequences, some intended and some not, some successful and some less so (depending on one's ideological perspective) and some winners and some losers. Participation can lead to shifts in the balance of power (albeit small) between élites and poorer communities by raising self-consciousness, stimulating collective action and encouraging creative energies. Alternatively, participation techniques may be imposed to achieve the acquiescence of local communities and their co-operation in strategies designed to meet the wider aims of structural adjustment, including the transfer of responsibility for the delivery of welfare services from the state to unaccountable private/quasi-private-sector agencies, community groups, families and individuals. This latter arrangement appeared to be in the ascendancy in the late 1990s as 'community organizations are invited to become "agents" of the state, to take over services that an increasingly disempowered local government used to provide, and to do so in a climate of financial restraint' (Taylor 1995a p.99).

The revival of community politics in the 1990s partly reflected the wider concerns of the state over the side-effects of unbridled self-interest promulgated in the 1980s. Etzioni has argued that there is:

> now near universal agreement that the resulting world of massive street violence, the failing war against illegal drugs, unbridled greed, and so on, is not one we wish for our children or, for that matter, ourselves.

And that to solve these problems we must:

shore up the moral foundations of our society . . . start[ing] with the family. The
family was always entrusted with laying the foundations of moral education. In
the renewed communities we envision, raising children is a job for both parents.
(Etzioni 1995 p.29)

Under Etzioni's scheme, moral upbringing in the family will be reinforced in
schools, neighbourhoods, at the workplace, in ethnic clubs and in other
social and professional associations. This style of communitarianism was
reflected in the Department of Education's guidance for schools, issued at
the end of October 1996, on what to teach pupils about morality, including:

> We value truth, human rights, the law, justice and collective endeavour for the
> common good of society. In particular we value families as sources of love and
> support for all their members and as the basis of a society in which people care for
> each other. (quoted in *The Independent* 31 October 1996 p.6)

Responsibility for dealing with the neglect of the 1980s will increasingly fall
on local communities and families rather than state institutions – a new
mode of regulation in response to changing 'post-Fordist' economic
circumstances. However, it is questionable how realistic it is for such a
prescription to work in poor neighbourhoods – basically, disadvantaged
families and communities pulling themselves up by their bootstraps.

The globalization and increasing mobility of capital in the late twentieth
century have led to the erosion of old power structures in both capitalist and
former central-eastern European socialist countries. In Britain, there has
been a clear shift away from the power of labour and its political
representation through both trade unions and municipal socialism in favour
of the power of the consumer. The impact of this change has been spatially
and socially uneven. Among the winners are the new shareholders of
privatized industries and utilities, and the managerial classes who retain
access to employment opportunities in the new technical and service-sector
growth regions. The main losers are the unemployed and dispossessed left
behind by the flight of capital from run-down deindustrialized regions.
Power has become increasingly concentrated in multinational companies
and central state institutions. Underpinning this transformation is the notion
that society in Britain is fragmenting and that democracy itself is being
eroded.

Unable to participate in the consumption process or to pay taxes, the
marginalized and economically inactive are excluded structurally and
through internalized feelings of worthlessness from other rights of access –
to employment, knowledge, skills development, education, healthy
neighbourhoods, status, information, new technology and, significantly,
decision-making structures. In addition, people who work face increasing

job insecurity and a loss of control over decision-making in the workplace and in their neighbourhoods. A large proportion of electors lack confidence in the political system, a situation not helped by the Scott Inquiry on aspects of ministerial accountability to Parliament, or the Nolan Committee's findings on democratic accountability in quangos. These developments are not conducive to a sustainable future or a free democracy.

Residential experience offers a coherent focus for illustrating the extent to which social, economic and political well-being is distributed in society. In Britain, 1.6 million home-owners moved into negative equity during the recession of 1990–92, severely constraining their freedom (Hutton 1996). In parallel, the quantity and quality of social housing have fallen, restricting the freedoms of those unwilling or unable to gain access to home-ownership. The main providers of new social housing – housing associations – have no statutory or constitutional obligation to be accountable to their local communities. Private tenants have lost rights in relation to independent rent-setting and security of tenure. There is an increasing polarization between good and bad neighbourhoods, a duality that incorporates unequal access to health, education, leisure, transport and employment opportunities.

At the heart of the process of social exclusion is the persistence of unequal power relations, a situation explained largely by reference to ideology. Social inequality is perpetuated through ideological processes which maintain 'meaning' in society and which, through the proliferation of ideas and the systematic control of discourse, legitimize a dominant social, economic and political system. However, as Eagleton suggests, the exercise of power in modern societies cannot be explained solely in terms of ideological hegemony. Other more mundane factors are important – for instance the eccentricity of electoral systems, the demoralization of the working classes, exhaustion and fatalism, fear of superiors or feelings of indifference (Eagleton 1991). Indeed, some commentators, while recognizing that dominant ideologies exist, express doubt as to whether they are transmitted into the consciousness of those subordinated to them. They prefer to account for domination by reference to the logic of capitalism and the fragmentation of the opposition (Abercrombie *et al.* 1988). Others have argued that power systems do not maintain themselves merely through the imposition of ideas but through *techniques of domination* – for instance detailed discourses prescribing our everyday behaviour, keeping us unaware or making us deny our true wants and needs; or practices of exclusion based on judgements as to deviance and normality (Foucault 1982, Lukes 1974).

The key to genuine community empowerment would seem to lie in a strategy which exposes the processes of social exclusion and which begins to counter these effects. We have seen that these processes are not merely controlled by ideologies, legal systems and the practices of state agencies.

They occur routinely through language, moral judgements, the production of knowledge, the media, self-perception, spatial boundaries and cultural norms. All these forces combine to underpin power relationships in society, resulting in the disqualification of low-ranking popularist forms of discourse. Throughout history, administrators and academics particularly have developed their own ritual practices and maintained a monopoly over social actions and areas of knowledge about the world, allowing them to establish and control the processes of exclusion (see Sibley 1995). Mainstream community participation in housing and urban policy in the 1990s largely continues these practices, with social policy-makers, practitioners and academics acting together as advocates on behalf of disadvantaged communities.

A number of detailed studies of community involvement in housing regeneration, launched by the Joseph Rowntree Foundation (JRF) in 1992 under its *Action on Estates* programme, resulted in a summary report on 33 research projects covering more than 100 small-area-based initiatives (Taylor 1995b). This report prescribes seven key ingredients for successful community development in housing regeneration:

● a detailed analysis of an area's problems and the assets available to tackle these;
● the development of solutions based on the local community's own priorities and linked to the wider local and regional economy;
● support for communities in developing their confidence and competencies;
● the development of locally based services which permit residents to choose an appropriate level of involvement;
● investment in local jobs and training to allow residents access to employment opportunities in the wider economy;
● the development of new forms of local governance based on the concept of partnership and power-sharing; and
● long-term strategies to sustain opportunities for future investment.

There are a number of problems with these recommendations. First, there are obvious contradictions, such as the potential tension between a local community's priorities and the needs of the wider business community. Second, there is the more general problem associated with small-area-based targeted regeneration projects, such as displacement and inter-area conflict. Third, these policy prescriptions assume no need for broader changes at the macro-political and economic level. Existing power relationships and the structural causes of urban deprivation are not questioned and therefore remain intact. In this context the long-term aim of sustainable regeneration through community development is unlikely to be achieved because the structural causes of neighbourhood decline – economic downturn, de-skilling, political and social exclusion and so forth – are not being addressed.

In response to these and other limitations of contemporary approaches to community participation, we argue the case for an alternative strategy for incorporating disadvantaged groups into mainstream social, political and economic activities. This strategy needs to start from a coherent understanding of the structural determinants of social inequality, the failings of selective urban policies and the non-transparent instances of social exclusion. Greater attention needs to be given to addressing the barriers to inclusion as perceived and articulated from the perspective of the excluded themselves. This requires giving greater currency to populist forms of understanding to break down the existing boundaries of 'knowledge' which exclude concepts perceived as a threat to the status quo.

References

Abercrombie, N., Warde, A., with Soothill, K., Urry, J. and Walby, S. (1988), *Contemporary British Society*, Cambridge: Polity.

Albert, M. and Hahnel, R. (1991), *The Political Economy of Participatory Economics*, Princeton: Princeton University Press.

Arendt, H. (1959), *The Human Condition*, New York: Anchor.

Arnstein, S. (1969), 'A ladder of citizen participation', *Journal of the American Institute of Planners*, **35**(4), pp.216–224.

Beer, S. (1971), *Brain of the Firm*, Harmondsworth: Penguin.

Butcher, H., Glen, A., Henderson, P. and Smith, J. (eds) (1993), *Community and Public Policy*, London: Pluto Press.

Cairncross, L., Clapham, D. and Goodlad, R. (1993), 'The social bases of tenant organization', *Housing Studies*, **8**(3), July, pp.179–194.

Castells, M. (1977), *The Urban Question*, London: Edward Arnold.

Clapham, D., Kemp, P. and Smith, S. (1990), *Housing and Social Policy*, Basingstoke: Macmillan.

Cohen, A.P. (1985), *The Symbolic Construction of Community*, London: Routledge.

Commission on Social Justice (1994), *Social Justice: Strategies for National Renewal*, London: Vintage.

Craig, G. and Mayo, M. (eds) (1995), *Community Empowerment: A Reader in Participation and Development*, London: Zed Books.

Dallin, A. (1992), 'Causes of the collapse of the USSR', *Post-Soviet Affairs*, **8**(4), pp.279–302.

Daly, G. (1996), *Homeless*, London: Routledge.

Doyal, L. and Gough, I. (1991), *A Theory of Human Need*, Basingstoke: Macmillan.

Dunleavy, P. (1980), *Urban Political Analysis*, London: Macmillan.

Dunleavy, P. (1981), *The Politics of Mass Housing in Britain: A Study of Corporate Power and Professional Influence in the Welfare State*, Oxford: Clarendon Press.

Eagleton, T. (1991), *Ideology*, London: Verso.

Elster, J. (1978), *Logic and Society*, Chichester: Wiley.

Elster, J. (1979), *Ulysses and the Sirens*, Cambridge: Cambridge University Press.

Etzioni, A. (1995), 'Just a social crowd of folk', *The Guardian*, 18 February, p.29.

Foucault, M. (1982), 'The subject and power', *Critical Inquiry*, **8**, Summer, pp.777–795.
Foucault, M. (1984), *The History of Sexuality Vol. I: An Introduction*, Harmondsworth: Penguin.
Freire, P. (1972), *Pedagogy of the Oppressed*, Harmondsworth: Penguin.
Fromm, E. (1969), *Escape from Freedom*, New York: Avon Books.
George, V. and Wilding, P. (1991), *Ideology and Social Welfare*, London: Routledge.
Giddens, A. (1984), *The Constitution of Society*, London: Polity.
Gould, C.C. (1990), *Rethinking Democracy: Freedom and Social Co-operation in Politics, Economy and Society*, Cambridge: Cambridge University Press.
Gramsci, A. (1971), *Selections from the Prison Notebooks*, London: Lawrence and Wishart.
Gyford, J. (1985), *The Politics of Local Socialism*, London: George Allen and Unwin.
Habermas, J. (1976), *Legitimation Crisis*, Boston: Beacon.
Hague, C. (1990), 'The development and politics of tenant participation in British council housing', *Housing Studies*, **5**(4), October, pp.242–256.
Handy, C. (1985), *Understanding Organizations*, Harmondsworth: Penguin.
Hayek, F.A. (1944/1976), *Road to Serfdom*, London: Routledge and Kegan Paul.
Held, D. (1987), *Models of Democracy*, Cambridge: Polity.
Hindess, B. (1983), *Parliamentary Democracy and Socialist Politics*, London: Routledge and Kegan Paul.
Hoggett, P. and Hambleton, R. (eds) (1987), *Decentralization and Democracy: Localizing Public Services*, Bristol: School of Advanced Urban Studies, University of Bristol.
Hutton, W. (1996), *The State We're In*, London: Vintage.
Jacobs, K. and Manzi, T. (1996), 'Discourse and policy change: the significance of language for housing research', *Housing Studies*, **11**(4), pp.543–560.
Johnson, N. (1987), *The Welfare State in Transition: The Theory and Practice of Welfare Pluralism*, Brighton: Wheatsheaf.
Lansley, S., Goss, S. and Wolmar, C. (1989), *Councils in Conflict: The Rise and Fall of the Municipal Left*, Basingstoke: Macmillan.
Lowe, S. (1986), *Urban Social Movements: The City After Castells*, Basingstoke: Macmillan.
Lukes, S. (1974), *Power: A Radical View*, Basingstoke: Macmillan.
Macey, J.P. and Baker, C.V. (1973), *Housing Management*, 2nd edn, London: The Estates Gazette.
Macpherson, C.B. (1973), *Democratic Theory: Essays in Retrieval*, Oxford: Oxford University Press.
Malpass, P. and Murie, A. (1994), *Housing Policy and Practice*, 4th edn, Basingstoke: Macmillan.
Marcuse, H. (1964), *One Dimensional Man*, Boston: Beacon.
Marsh, A. and Murie, A. (1996), *Citizenship, Choice and Control in British Housing Policy: Changing Concepts and Contexts*, paper presented at the Housing Studies Association Conference on 'Housing and Social Exclusion', Birmingham, 16–17 September.
Marshall, T.H. (1950), *Citizenship and Social Class*, Cambridge: Cambridge University Press.
Mayer, T. (1994), *Analytical Marxism*, London: Sage.
McDonald, A. (1986), *The Weller Way: The Story of the Weller Streets Housing Co-operative*, London: Faber and Faber.
Meekosha, H. (1993), 'The Bodies Politic – Equality, difference and community practice' in Butcher, H., Glen, A., Henderson, P. and Smith, J (eds) *Community and Public Policy*, London: Pluto Press, pp. 171–193.

Miller, D. (1989), *Market, State and Community: Theoretical Foundations of Market Socialism*, Oxford: Clarendon.

Morgan, D. and Stanley, L. (eds) (1993), *Debates in Sociology*, Manchester: Manchester University Press.

Murray, C. (1990), *The Emerging British Underclass*, London: IEA Health and Welfare Unit.

Nozick, R. (1974), *Anarchy, State and Utopia*, Oxford: Blackwell.

Olson, M. (1965), *The Logic of Collective Action: Public Goods and the Theory of Groups*, Cambridge, Mass: Harvard University Press.

Ospina, J. (1987), *Housing Ourselves*, London: Hilary Shipman.

Pahl, R. (1975), *Whose City?*, Harmondsworth: Penguin.

Pateman, C. (1970), *Participation and Democratic Theory*, Cambridge: Cambridge University Press.

Popple, K. (1995), *Analysing Community Work: Its Theory and Practice*, Buckingham: Open University Press.

Poulantzas, N. (1980), *State, Power, Socialism*, London: Verso/New Left Books.

Rawls, S.J. (1971), *A Theory of Justice*, Oxford: Oxford University Press.

Rees, S. (1991), *Achieving Power: Practice and Policy in Social Welfare*, London: Allen and Unwin.

Rex, J. and Moore, R. (1967), *Race, Community and Conflict*, London: Institute of Race Relations/Oxford University Press.

Richardson, A. (1983), *Participation*, London: Routledge.

Roberts, M. (1991), *Living in a Man-made World: Gender Assumptions in Modern Housing Design*, London: Routledge.

Rose, S. and Black, B. (1985), *Advocacy and Empowerment: Mental Health Care in the Community*, New York: Routledge and Kegan Paul.

Rosenfeld, J.M. (1989), *Emergence from Extreme Poverty*, Paris: Science and Service Fourth World Publications.

Rousseau, J.J. (1973), *The Social Contract and Other Discourses*, London: Dent.

Saunders, P. (1979), *Urban Politics: A Sociological Interpretation*, London: Hutchinson.

Saunders, P. (1990), *A Nation of Homeowners*, London: Unwin Hyman.

Schumpeter, J. (1943), *Capitalism, Socialism and Democracy*, London: Allen and Unwin.

Scruton, R. (1984), *The Meaning of Conservatism*, London: Macmillan.

Sibley, D. (1995), *Geographies of Exclusion: Society and Difference in the West*, London: Routledge.

Somerville, P. and Steele, A. (1995), 'Making sense of tenant participation', *Netherlands Journal of Housing and the Built Environment*, 10(3), pp.259–281.

Taylor, M. (1995a), 'Community work and the state: the changing context of UK practice' in Craig, G. and Mayo, M. (eds), *Community Empowerment: A Reader in Participation and Development*, London: Zed Books, pp.99–111.

Taylor, M. (1995b), *Unleashing the Potential: Bringing Residents to the Centre of Regeneration*, York: Joseph Rowntree Foundation.

Tenant Participation Advisory Service/Chartered Institute of Housing (TPAS/CIH) (1989), *Tenant Participation in Housing Management*, Coventry: TPAS/CIH.

Teymur, N., Markus, T.A. and Woolley, T. (1988), *Rehumanizing Housing*, London: Butterworth.

Thornley, A. (1977), 'Theoretical perspectives on planning participation', *Progress in Planning, Vol.7 Part 1*, London: Pergamon.

Titmuss, R. (1968), *Commitment to Welfare*, London: Allen and Unwin.

Turner, J.F.C. (1976), *Housing by People: Towards Autonomy in Building Environments*, London: Marion Boyars.

Turner, J.F.C. and Fichter, R. (eds) (1972), *Freedom to Build*, New York: Macmillan.
Urry, J. (1995), *Consuming Places*, London: Routledge.
Ward, C. (1974), *Tenants Take Over*, London: Architectural Press.
Ward, C. (1976), *Housing, An Anarchist Approach*, London: Freedom Press.
Ward, C. (1982), *Anarchy in Action*, London: Freedom Press.
Warrington, M.J. (1995), 'Welfare pluralism or shadow state? The provision of social housing in the 1990s', *Environment and Planning A*, **27**, pp.1341–1360.
Willcox, D. (1994), *The Guide to Effective Participation*, Brighton: Partnership Books.

5 Tenant participation in a cross-national comparative perspective

Bo Bengtsson and David Clapham

Tenant participation in public rented housing is a widespread phenomenon in many different countries, and a body of literature is emerging looking at its different experience within individual countries. Nevertheless, tenant participation remains a relatively under-researched area and there are considerable gaps in our knowledge even in comparatively well-covered countries such as Britain or Sweden. The aim of this chapter is to expand the horizons of research on tenant participation by exploring the potential for international comparisons. This is very much an initial exploration because there have been few, if any, international comparisons of this kind and we are restricted to using empirical data already collected – with all its gaps!

The chapter starts with a review of three types of comparative research, which we have called *theoretical comparison*, *policy-oriented comparison* and *contrasting comparison*. The reasons for undertaking each of these types of comparison vary, with each being appropriate in certain circumstances and to meet particular objectives. In the rest of the chapter we confine ourselves to discussing and attempting to undertake a *contrasting comparison*. This is less demanding than a *theoretical comparison*, which to be successful would require the collection of new empirical material.

Most studies of tenant participation, whether comparative or based within an individual country, have concentrated on examining the administrative arrangements or structures for involvement. The drawbacks of these approaches are discussed in the next section and two alternative methods are considered which concentrate more on the *process* involved in tenant participation. These are the *circuits of power* approach, used by Cairncross *et al.* (1994) in their analysis of tenant participation in Britain, and the approach based on *game theory*, used by Bengtsson (1995) to examine housing policy in Sweden. The two approaches are outlined and compared. The conclusion reached is that they share sufficient similarities for us to put forward an integrated framework based on the two approaches. This integrated framework is then used to examine the experience of tenant participation in public rented housing in Britain and then in Sweden, based on existing research. More emphasis is placed on the Swedish experience because it will probably be less familiar to readers of the book. Finally, conclusions are drawn by contrasting the experiences of the two countries. In addition, we reflect on the usefulness of the integrated framework in undertaking international comparisons and present ideas for further comparative research.

Before we begin this discussion, some justification is warranted for why we chose Britain and Sweden as comparisons. Of course, the nationalities of the two authors and their knowledge from earlier research of tenant participation in Sweden and Britain respectively make these two countries the obvious choice. Notwithstanding this practical motive, we would argue that Sweden provides a very interesting comparison with and valuable lessons for Britain in this specific field (see Cooper 1996 for another example). Since we are undertaking a contrasting comparison, we need to select countries with systems of tenant participation that are not too similar, otherwise the 'counterfactual relief' wanted would not be provided. On the other hand, the cultural traditions should not be so different that the object of the study, in our case tenant participation, is an unknown concept in one of the countries or has quite different meanings between them.

Although there are important differences in how tenant participation is perceived in Britain and Sweden, there is an understanding in both coun!ries that it is about the involvement of tenants in decision-making on their housing conditions and that this is an issue of some importance. On the other hand, the models of tenant participation are rather different in the two countries. In Britain they are based largely on legislation and local tenants' associations, whereas in Sweden they are based mainly on collective agreements and organized within the national tenants' movement. Hence, both the general similarity and the specific divergence that should make a contrasting comparison meaningful are there.

The common social definition of tenant participation and the different models employed not only make Sweden an ideal case to compare with Britain but also mean that our theoretical model of analysis will be put to the hardest test that is possible within the framework of a contrasting comparison. If a comparative analysis based on our theoretical model would not prove to be fruitful in bringing out new perspectives on tenant participation in Britain and Sweden, it would not be possible to account for the failure by arguing that the cases compared are either too different or too similar. Instead, it would indeed be an indication that the theory is not suited for our purpose. In this respect our contrasting comparison could be seen as a first step on the road to theoretical comparison.

Three types of comparison

There are three good reasons for international comparison in social research – first, to advance social theory; second, to develop a better understanding of the situation in the individual countries studied; and third, to make policy recommendations for one country based on the lessons experienced in other countries. We can call these three types *theoretical comparison, contrasting comparison* and *policy-oriented comparison* respectively. The same comparative study could contribute towards one or more of these three goals, but in principle they should be kept apart, since they call for different approaches, different types of comparison, and sometimes even different types of countries to be compared.

To develop theory is always at the heart of social research and this is the aim of theoretical comparison. International comparison of tenant participation could be used to find out more about the general conditions of the subject matter *per se* – for example, what cultural, political or economic prerequisites would favour or work against collective action among tenants; or how local norms of co-operation could be developed in housing; or under what conditions tenant participation may lead to the empowerment of tenants. A more ambitious theoretical aim with comparative studies of tenant participation may be to make a contribution to more general theoretical discourses – for example, on power, collective action or bargaining. Kemeny is probably the most ardent advocate of using housing as a substantial field in which to develop general social theories and concepts (see Kemeny 1991).

Whatever the ambitions in terms of theoretical generalization, the empirical comparison must be structured in such a way that the result could say something of importance about the theory at hand. The comparison must be based on variables derived from the theory, and the focus must be on the aspects of the cases that can be translated into those variables. Ideally, even the choice of countries to compare should be done with the theoretical aims in view. It should be meaningful to apply the central concepts of the theory to the countries studied, and some variation between the cases should also be expected (or at least conceivable) in terms of those concepts. Otherwise, it would be impossible to translate the empirical conclusions into a relevant theoretical statement. In comparative studies aimed at developing theory, it may sometimes be fruitful to compare countries that are quite different in economic and institutional respects in order to highlight the theoretical generality.

If researchers should be concerned with using comparison as a tool to develop theory, policy-makers and practitioners are often more interested in the possibility of learning from other countries. In policy-oriented comparison the structure and focus do not have to be quite as strict as in the theoretical comparison. Learning from others always has a heuristic element. It is obvious that in most cases, nationally specific cultural, economic and political factors make it almost impossible to import institutional devices from another country directly. (For an example of policy failure in this regard see Clapham and Kintrea 1987.) But if the only solution to that problem was trying to control for all such differences in the pursuit of academic purity, we would probably never learn anything from others. Instead, the impact of the particular national context should be considered by examining carefully the potential problems of imitating – or even applying in modified form – a successful institutional solution in another national setting. This examination may be undertaken by researchers, or policy-makers, or both. Notwithstanding the importance of such 'contextual analysis', it is fair to say that normally the prospects of 'learning from others' are best if there is some general similarity between the countries included in the study.

The third type of comparative study, the contrasting comparison, is perhaps the least discussed in methodological terms. By contrasting the situation in our own country with other countries we may gain a better understanding of what is unique and what is universal. What is taken for granted nationally may be less self-evident in an international context, and this awareness may often have an impact both on comparative analysis and on the discussion in specific countries. In this case the function of the comparative analysis is to supply what may be called *counterfactual relief*, indicating what the national situation might have been 'if things had been otherwise'. Instead of using theory or history as such relief, we may use comparison with other countries to give perspective to current national institutions and practices.

In contrasting comparison the cases should preferably be neither too similar nor too dissimilar. The very point of making the comparison is that we expect some difference between the countries, and that we want to know something about the impact of that difference. On the other hand our counterfactual relief is not worth much if the countries that we compare differ too much in terms of general cultural, social, political and economic background. But how can we compare if our crucial variable must be dissimilar? How can we even know what to compare? Again, we must turn to theory to focus the comparison and to develop a relevant relief. In contrasting comparison the relation between theory and comparison is the opposite to the one in theoretical comparison. In the latter, comparison is used to shed light on theory and, if possible, to develop it. In contrasting comparison, theory is used to shed light on the cases compared. This indicates that the two approaches cannot be combined, since in one case the theory is tested, and in the other it is taken as given. In practice, however, the development of theory and the increased understanding of the empirical cases may sometimes contribute to each other in a circular process.

Although seemingly less ambitious than both other variants, the comparative advantages of contrasting comparison should not be underestimated. To develop general theory in social research is always an uncertain project, and to do it by comparing extremely complex entities like nation-states may often be totally in vain. On the other hand, the heuristic learning from other countries might be a task better suited to pragmatic and context-conscious policy-makers than to academic researchers. Indeed, the contrasting comparison rather makes the best of the fact that nation-states are complex entities. By focusing on one crucial differing element, and the effects of that difference, the comparison may be carried out without paying attention to all other differences between the cases.

In this chapter we will discuss tenant participation in a comparative perspective mainly from the viewpoint of contrasting comparison. That is also the perspective which we will be using in our illustrative comparison between tenant participation in Britain and Sweden.

The formal approach

There have been few attempts to compare tenant participation between different countries. This is not surprising given the difficulty in defining and understanding what tenant participation is (see Chapter 4). The most common approach has been to think of tenant participation as a set of administrative arrangements or structures. It would be possible to compare the formal structures of tenant participation between different countries. What are the institutional arrangements defining the relations between landlords and tenants? Do tenants' representatives have a place on decision-making committees? What is the extent of tenant association membership and what is the attendance at tenant meetings? But this exercise would be insufficient for two main reasons. First, it would not take into account what happens when tenants and landlords come together in meetings. It is theoretically possible, and as our research in Britain showed was relatively common (see Cairncross *et al.* 1996), for tenants' associations to achieve more of their objectives when they are operating outside of formal meeting structures than within them. There may be informal contacts with the landlord, or associations may engage in a public campaign and enlist the help of the media. The processes of tenant participation, or the ways in which the parties interact, are important factors in understanding the nature of tenant participation. Because tenants in one country have reached a higher step on some ladder of influence does not necessarily mean that the relationship with the landlord allows them to achieve more of their objectives than will tenants in another country without these formal powers. Second, the simple comparison of tenant-participation structures does not take into account the social, political and economic context within which they are situated. It may be that tenants have extensive formal powers, but the context of the tenure is such that the landlord is not able to respond to any tenant requests. For example, demands for low rents or for increased capital investment may be met by landlords in some countries, but not in others because of central government financial controls.

Both these factors mean that the comparison of tenant participation between different countries is a complex and difficult task which involves many layers of analysis. A comparative study of tenant participation in 'social housing' in the four Nordic countries (Sweden, Denmark, Norway and Finland), in which one of the authors of this chapter was involved, tried to take some of these problems into account. In this particular comparative study the customary ladder of formal participation was supplemented by an analysis of legal, technical and economic restrictions on the scope of decision-making, and of the bargaining resources available to the landlord and tenants respectively (Cronberg 1986).

However, even with such contextual complements, the institutional approach cannot fully account for the social and political complexities involved in the interaction between landlords and tenants in housing provision and management. The objective of this chapter is to indicate how social theory can help to integrate such concepts as power, institutions and social norms into the analysis of tenant participation. With that purpose we put forward a framework for comparative analysis and try to demonstrate how it can be applied by using the examples of public rented housing in Sweden and Britain.

Two frameworks

The authors have separately put forward two frameworks for the analysis of tenant participation. Cairncross *et al.* (1994) have built on the concept of 'circuits of power' put forward by Clegg (1989) to view tenant participation as an ever-changing power game between different actors which takes place within a context which is partly contingent and partly exogenously determined. Bengtsson (1995) draws on 'game theory' to conceptualize the activities of tenants' organizations as a series of nested games in different arenas (see Tsebelis 1990). In this section the two frameworks will be described in turn and then an attempt will be made to reconcile them.

The analogy of tenant participation as a power game is based on a view of power as originating not from any single source but existing in a world of shifting and unstable alliances in a state of flux – 'power is approached through a view of more or less complex agents engaged in more or less complex, organized games' (Clegg 1989 p.20). In the study of tenant participation this focuses attention on the agents involved (tenants, housing officers and local councillors) and their relationships. In playing the tenant-participation game the key elements are the *resources* of the parties, the *tactics* they employ, and the *rules* of the game. The resources include time, money, knowledge and expertise (for example, of legislation or current housing-management practices), premises (for tenants' associations, access to somewhere to meet or to a photocopier or computer) and, crucially, legitimacy. For housing managers, legitimacy tends to come with professional status, but for tenants it is often dependent on factors such as the degree of support they have from the wider body of tenants.

All or some of these resources may be deployed in the participation game by the parties involved. They may have a strategy and certainly will pursue certain tactics to achieve their objectives. Some strategies or tactics may work better than others in particular situations. For example, will tenants be more likely to get the landlord to change his/her mind through a media campaign or by quietly speaking to an influential councillor? Many factors may influence the answer to this question, which may vary considerably between different situations. The ability to weigh up the possibilities and make an appropriate choice of tactics in a particular situation is a crucial skill.

The game is played according to a set of rules which are partly set by the participants and partly exogenously determined. They are made up of the accepted places and forms of interaction. The organizational structures for involvement are part of this, as are the acceptable participation processes, which may include consultation, dialogue or joint decision-making. (For a full list of processes see Cairncross *et al.* 1994.) A final element is the objectives of the parties involved. What is the intention of involvement in tenant participation? Is it to promote community development or better housing management, or to increase tenant satisfaction? On the basis of these three elements of structures, processes and objectives, Cairncross *et al.* (1994) identified a typology of three different forms of tenant participation which were common in local housing authorities in Britain at the end of the 1980s. These were labelled the *traditional*, the *consumerist* and the *citizenship* models.

These typologies are simplified abstractions from reality, or ideal types in the Weberian usage. Therefore, they do not accurately reflect the totality of the complex interaction which in most cases consists of elements of all three models. Nevertheless, the typologies are useful in drawing attention to the different nature of the interactions and in providing a general picture of experience.

These models were partly the result of the interactions of the parties themselves in the participation game. For example, the political allegiances and ideologies of local councillors influenced which model was applied, as did the views of key housing professionals and tenant representatives. The housing and general economic and social environment were also important. For instance, it was found that citizenship participation was more common in large urban local authorities with major housing problems, which were more likely to be controlled by the Labour Party.

The rules of the game are strongly influenced by the wider context in which the game takes place. At a specific level certain forms of participation structure, such as the presence of tenant representatives with voting rights on statutory committees, are illegal in Britain (as is the case in Sweden). At the same time there is a legal duty on local housing authorities to consult tenants on some issues such as significant changes in housing-management practice, whereas other issues such as the determination of rent levels are specifically excluded. In more general terms the position of the public rented sector is important in structuring the nature of the interaction between the parties, as we shall show later.

Therefore, the rules of the game are produced and reproduced through a complex interplay of agency action and structure – in other words, a process of structuration. Factors such as the national political culture both constrain and influence tenant participation and are influenced to at least some degree by the outcomes of tenant-participation games, among many other factors. Therefore, any analysis of tenant participation should examine both the participation game itself and the exogenous or structural influences on the rules of the game.

The circuits-of-power framework provides a useful way of analysing tenant participation at a number of levels. At the level of the housing organization it can be used as a guide to understand the relationship between tenants and their landlord. An analysis of resources and how they are deployed can shed light on why particular games had the result they did. At the same time the framework provides a mechanism for analysing the context within which particular games take place. Therefore it can be used to analyse changes in tenant participation over time or, as in the case of this chapter, for international comparisons. Before undertaking a more extensive evaluation of the use of the framework for this purpose, another possible and similar framework is outlined.

Bengtsson (1995) puts forward an approach to understanding the housing system based on game theory. He argues that the predominant approach to investigating housing systems in the past has been to stress the dualism of the state and the market. Such an approach has generally failed to examine the complex interactions between actors involved in *both* sectors. Bengtsson also takes the 'game' as an appropriate analogy for interactions in housing, but rather than taking his framework from theories of power he looks to game theory. The drawback of much work in the game-theory tradition is that it assumes that actors are perfectly rational and have simple one-dimensional goals. An example of this is the budget-maximizing models for public organizations. Bengtsson proposes a game-theory model based on Elster's concept of 'thin rationality' where actors are assumed to have some logical consistency in the pursuit of their goals, whereas the nature of those goals (the preferences of the actors) is not assumed *a priori* by the researcher but is open to empirical examination (see Elster 1983).

The main problem with the thin rationality approach is that it makes it harder to analyse the outcome of games. The fully rational approach allows games to be analysed formally because the motivation of actors is assumed to be simple and predictable. Once these assumptions are relaxed it becomes more difficult to predict behaviour in a given situation. If, on the other hand, the purpose of the analysis is not prediction, but explaining and understanding observed behaviour, the assumption of thin rationality makes it possible to reconstruct both the attitudes and preferences of an individual actor, and the interaction between several actors (for example, between landlords and tenant representatives). Again, since models based on thin rationality are open-ended as regards the preferences of different actors, empirical observation is of crucial importance in the reconstruction of the games.

Bengtsson discusses the role of Swedish tenant and housing co-operative organizations on the national level, but his general framework may be used on the local level as well. He identifies three arenas in which housing agencies operate simultaneously, and which help shape their objectives. They are the organizational arena, the market arena and the political arena. The *organizational arena* is concerned with the internal capacity of the organization in mobilizing its members and recruiting new ones. There are parallels here with the concern about resources in the power approach, in which tenants' associations attempt to build up their capacity for action by recruiting a large membership and by mobilizing it on specific issues. Bengtsson discusses these issues in terms of the prospects of overcoming the free-rider problem of collective action, which he argues could be achieved, for example, by the development of social norms of co-operation or by designing institutions enabling (or even encouraging) tenant activities. The *market arena* is where the actors attempt to achieve value for money. For instance, in this arena tenants may be involved in negotiating an appropriate trade-off between the quality of the service received and the rent paid. For landlords, it may be about maximizing revenue from tenants and from government. The *political arena* is where housing organizations form different kinds of relationship to further their own members' interests. One example of this in Sweden is the creation of large national and regional co-operative organizations such as HSB and *Riksbyggen* and the forging of what has been described as a corporatist relationship between *Hyresgästernas Riksförbund* (the tenants' union) and the government over rental policy.

Bengtsson sees games operating at a number of levels in what he calls 'nested' games. The idea is that games which may seem to be independent are in fact linked. For example, the strategies chosen by a tenant association in the game against the landlord in the market arena may not be understood if one does not take into account what the organization wants to accomplish in the other arenas, such as changes in housing policies or increased tenant activity. This approach has strong parallels to the power approach, where the rules of the tenant-participation game are seen as being at least partly dependent on other games played elsewhere and at different levels. An important element of the nested-games approach is that the result of one game may be a change in the rules of future games, what Tsebelis (1990) calls 'institutional design'. Over time a historical chain of games, institutions, new games and new institutions may be developed.

Bengtsson argues that the only way to understand the complexity of the interplay between games in different arenas, at different levels and at different points of time is through what he calls 'process tracing' (see George and McKeown 1985). This involves a detailed historical study of the complex games, particularly looking to identify 'critical junctures' (see Collier and Collier 1991), which Bengtsson defines as points of historical change decisive of further development. In particular he argues that the aim is to identify the games which change the rules of future games. At the national level, the most important games played in this respect are those over tenure. At the local level, changes in the formal institutions may also be the result of games of tenant participation, but the rules of future games may also be changed by the development of local social norms about the forms and content of tenant participation. Bengtsson summarizes his approach as follows:

> Housing provision as nested games is seen as an ongoing strategic interplay between politicians, bureaucracies, organizations, firms and individual households. These actors meet in different types of games in a number of interrelated arenas, games that from time to time result in institutional change, in particular changes in the tenure structure. (Bengtsson 1995 p.240)

With some modifications, owing to the fact that the actors and institutions are to some extent different at the local level, the same general idea of housing provision as nested games may be applied to tenant participation. In this case, however, a fourth arena should be added to the model, which could be called the participation arena or, more generally, the *estate arena*. This is where the interplay takes place between the individual landlord and his/her tenants concerning housing conditions on a particular estate. As in the market arena, the aim of the tenants is to achieve value for money, but the rules of the game are different from those in the market arena where other landlords and other tenants are also involved. For example, the landlord's and the tenants' respective positions in the market arena may be used as power resources in the estate arena.

The idea of process tracing in order to find critical junctures may also be applied at the estate level. One empirical difficulty would of course be that it may be more difficult to trace the history of participation on a housing estate than to identify critical junctures in national housing policies.

The two frameworks compared

The similarities between the two frameworks presented are obvious. The metaphors of actors and games are at the core of both the circuits-of-power perspective and the nested-games perspective. However, there are two main differences between the frameworks. One concerns how the different elements of the interaction are perceived (and labelled), while the other relates to what elements of the interaction are treated as exogenous or endogenous. These differences are derived from the fact that the ultimate aim of the circuits-of-power model is to provide, more or less, general causal explanations in terms of institutional structures, power resources and norms of co-operation, whereas the game model has the more modest aim of providing a tool for interpreting and analysing specific cases of interaction. To serve these different aims, power models must be open-ended – that is, open to empirical testing – while game models are more useful as tools the more tautological they are, since only a closed model makes it possible to reconstruct the preferences of actors from their behaviour. As we have seen, the nested-game model as applied by Bengtsson is not completely tautological, based as it is on the less demanding assumption of thin rationality. The price of this concession to realism is that we always need specific empirical evidence of actors' preferences in order to reconstruct the game.

Let us see how some of the concepts of the circuits-of-power model may be translated into the game perspective. First, in the game model, unlike the power model, power resources are treated as exogenous to the game. Second, if actors are defined as being perfectly rational, tactics would of course be of no avail, since your opponent is certain to see through all tactics. With thinly rational actors, on the other hand, successful tactics may be of great importance to the result of the game, and a difficulty in the empirical study of a particular game may indeed be to distinguish between behaviour that reveals the actors' preferences and behaviour that is only part of some tactical device.

Seemingly more problematic is the concept of rules of the game. In the game-theory perspective the rules of the game are often defined rather formally as the players taking part, their alternative strategies and the information available to them (Tsebelis 1990). In the power perspective, the rules of the game may include more dynamic, social-interactionist elements, illustrated by the three models of traditional, consumerism and citizenship which can be seen as a discursive result of the interplay between landlord and tenants.

However, if we hold on to the assumption of thin rationality, this type of social interactionism may also be integrated in a nested-games perspective. One important type of nested game is what Tsebelis calls institutional design, where the result of one game is that the 'rules' of later games are changed. Tsebelis defines institutions as formal rules (including only players, alternatives or information), but if actors are less than perfectly rational the result of one game may also be a change in their preferences or their definition of alternatives and outcomes. Such change could, of course, affect the power and power resources of the actors just as much as a change in the formal rules.

Thus, given thin rationality, differences between the two approaches in definitions of the rules of the game are only ones of terminology. If we accept that the rules of the game include both formal and informal elements, both social institutions (such as tenure forms) and social norms, the power perspective and the games perspective may be quite comfortably integrated. Once this has been settled, none of the three elements of the rules of the game in the circuits-of-power model (that is structures, processes and objectives) presents any problem. The *organizational structure* affects preferences, alternatives and outcomes in the game perspective: the *participation process* may be seen as a 'game in extended form', that is, an analysis of a game that takes the time dimension into account. Timing, like tactics, gets more important the less omniscient the actors are assumed to be. The *objectives* are simply what game theorists would call *preferences*.

Towards an integrated framework

The analogy of the game used by both frameworks provides a useful mechanism for a comparative analysis of tenant participation in different countries. It both provides a framework for the analysis and highlights the key issues which need to be considered. The analysis can be approached from a 'bottom-up' or a 'top-down' perspective. Whichever is chosen the same factors need to be considered. The bottom-up approach starts with the game between an individual landlord and his/her tenants and broadens the analysis to examine the wider factors which influence it. This is the approach taken here.

The analysis can start with a review of the rules of the game which frame the interaction between a landlord and his/her tenants. This may include institutional prerequisites such as tenure forms and other formal rules of decision-making. But the ambition should be to go beyond that to include existing social norms of local participation and other cultural elements. Clearly these will vary considerably between different landlords and different groups of tenants, but it is possible to provide a general picture by constructing typologies of different combinations of structures, processes and objectives, as was done by Cairncross *et al.* The extent of these different typologies can then be gauged to provide a general picture for the country. It is to be expected that the pattern would be very different for different countries.

The next element is to examine the resources which the actors in the game can deploy. In the terms of the nested-games model an actor's access to and influence on other arenas can be used as a power resource in the game between landlord and tenants in the estate arena. This is most obvious in the case of the central and local political arenas. But the alternatives provided to landlord and tenants respectively in the market arena should also be of importance to the outcome of the participation game. Another key element is the ability to overcome barriers to collective action in the organizational arena and to mobilize members, whether tenants or workers of the landlord (Bengtsson 1994). In principle, all types of power resources may even be described in terms of access to and influence in social arenas, money to other market arenas, formal rights to judicial arenas, legitimacy to different social or political arenas and so on.

The analysis therefore needs to be broadened to examine the wider games which influence the rules of the game and the ability of the actors to operate effectively within them. Again, the framework for this analysis can be taken from the arenas identified by Bengtsson. Power relations in each of the arenas may be different in different countries, and can be used as an indicator of country differences.

Empirical research in Britain has shown that most tenants' associations have only one general objective, to improve the housing conditions of their members. This is equivalent to the economic criterion identified by Bengtsson and puts the emphasis on the estate and market arenas where this criterion is dominant. However, this does not necessarily mean that the other criteria, the organizational and the political, are irrelevant because they can be seen as subsidiary goals which are necessary for the primary goal to be achieved. In practice most tenants' associations attempt to engage in all these arenas. In order to understand and explain power relations in the different arenas, the historical analysis advocated by Bengtsson can be employed to identify the crucial factors in the rule-setting games. The best way to elucidate this framework further is to explore the approach applied to the example of tenant participation in Britain and Sweden.

Although in principle the circuits-of-power perspective is one of explanation and the nested-game perspective one of interpretation, the distinction is to some degree dissolved by the assumption of thin rationality (which is also implied in the power perspective). As we have seen, this makes the integration between the two models unproblematic, and the choice of one or the other when it comes to concepts and terminology is more or less a matter of taste – perhaps the main thing in which the authors of the chapter disagree! In the following illustrative comparison between Britain and Sweden, we take our point of departure in the circuits-of-power model, while making use of the concept of games on multiple arenas when we discuss power resources.

Tenant participation in Britain

Tenant participation has been widely advocated in Britain for over 20 years. In a survey carried out in 1986/87, 80 per cent of local authorities had formal arrangements for tenant participation (Cairncross *et al.* 1990). Therefore the main issue is the kind of participation which is pursued. Three models of tenant participation in local authorities have been identified. These are the traditional, the consumerist and the citizenship local authority models. Details of these are given in Table 5.1.

It is not possible to say precisely how many local authorities fall under each of the models, because the incorporation of information on objectives and processes is difficult to collect accurately from a wide survey. However, there is some reliable information on tenant-participation structures. Just under half (47 per cent) of local authorities said that they had regular discussions with tenant groups in 1991, compared to just over a third in 1986/87 and only 3 per cent in 1977 (Bines *et al.* 1993). It is difficult to conceive of a citizenship model without regular discussions taking place, but these by themselves do not necessarily constitute the processes of citizenship. Therefore, while we know that the structures of tenant participation are growing, it is less clear what objectives and processes are being pursued. We can safely assume that the extent of the citizenship model is limited and the traditional and consumerist models are more illustrative of the relationship between tenants and their landlord. Furthermore, the consumerist model was actively supported by the Conservative government.

Table 5.1 Models of tenant participation in local authorities

Traditional local authority models

Structures	*Processes*	*Expressed objectives*
		(Councillors, officers)
Letters	Providing information	Better housing
Leaflets	Listening	management
Handbooks	Seeking information	Tenant satisfaction
Tenant surveys	Choice	Community development (tied to previous two)
Most participation around:		(Tenants)
Modernization		Better housing
Difficult-to-let estates		

Consumerist local authority models

Structures	*Processes*	*Expressed objectives*
		(Councillors, officers)
Letters	Providing information	Better housing
Leaflets	Seeking information	management
Handbooks/information packs	Listening (to individuals)	Expand choice
Advertisements/ newsletters	Choice	Tenant satisfaction
Tenant surveys		
Meetings with individual tenants		(Tenants)
		Better housing
Most participation around:		
Issues which impact on individual tenants rather than general policy		

Citizenship local authority models

Structures	Processes	Expressed objectives
		(Councillors, officers)
Letters	Providing information	Community
Leaflets	Seeking information	development
Handbooks	Listening	Better housing
Newsletters	Consultation	management
Tenant representation	Dialogue	Empowered tenants
Regular meetings	Joint management	Tenant satisfaction
	(Control)	
		(Tenants)
		Better housing

Most participation around:
Covers whole range of issues
   from practical to policy

Within the consumerist model the emphasis is on tenants as individuals exercising choice and expressing views on the services provided through market-research mechanisms. This leaves little room for collective action by tenants, which is at best tolerated and at worst actively resisted by many landlords. Even where collective action is possible, in any type of authority tenants' influence is constrained by the limited resources available. In Britain, tenants' associations are generally poorly resourced, with most having little financial support and difficulty gaining access to basic facilities such as office equipment and a meeting room (see Cairncross *et al.* 1992). This is in contrast with the relatively strong economic and political position of the Swedish tenants' movement.

There is considerable support for tenants' associations from the main body of tenants. For example, Cairncross *et al.* (1993) report that over two-thirds of the tenants they surveyed agreed with the statement that tenants' associations were a way to get the council to do something on an estate. However, this support is often passive, with many associations having difficulty in finding active members, which seems to indicate the existence of a 'prisoners' dilemma' problem of collective action. In the same survey, less than a third of tenants in areas where there was a tenant association had ever attended one of their meetings. Also, support for collective action by tenants is relatively weak – only 10 per cent said that they would contemplate stopping paying rent, and only 7 per cent said that they would think of going on a protest march. Tenants said that they would mostly take individual action by contacting a councillor or member of parliament if they had a problem.

Therefore, tenants in Britain are in a relatively weak position in playing the participation game and have little influence in shaping the rules. This situation is created and reinforced by the weak position of local authority housing generally, which has resulted mainly from central government policies. The council housing sector is declining in size and status because of the sale of its better-quality housing stock under the right to buy, stock transfer and restrictions on new capital investment. Council estates are increasingly inhabited by marginal groups in society. Council housing is increasingly a stigmatized sector of last resort for those who cannot own their own house (Cole and Furbey 1995). This may, of course, place public-sector landlords in a weaker position in the general housing market arena, since they would have difficulty finding more 'profitable' tenants. On the other hand, political support for the tenure has also been weak and, as it has declined in size and status, putting forward policies to revive it will gain few votes. Some of the issues which were the subject of national campaigns prior to the 1980s (see Chapter 2) have since been defused. For example, tenants once protested over rent rises, but now the vast majority get all or part of their rent paid through housing benefit payments. This not only makes rent increases a 'non-issue'. It also removes the key weapon of the rent strike from the armoury of tenants.

There is evidence that the perception which tenants have of council housing varies considerably, depending on their experience of their own landlord and conditions on their own estate. The sector is split by many cleavages which make collective action above the level of the individual estate or the individual landlord very difficult (Cairncross *et al.* 1993). There have been a number of attempts in Britain to establish a national tenants' organization, but none has met with any lasting success. The picture is one of a weak tenants' movement which has few resources to play the game and has a set of rules which limit the issues which can be discussed and constrain the possibilities for collective action (see Chapter 6). The game takes place within a context in which council housing is under threat, severely constrained in its activities and marginalized in political importance. It has not always been like this and national tenant campaigns in the 1970s were common, if not particularly successful (see Lowe 1986). Since then collective tenant activity has been marginalized in the same way as collective trade union activity in the workplace.

We can now examine the possible resources of tenants in the four arenas. In the organizational arena, tenants' associations act to achieve the recruitment of new members and the mobilization of old ones. Here tenants' associations in Britain have had mixed success in building power resources. The number of tenants' associations has increased considerably in the last 20 years and membership has probably grown in proportion, although there has been no systematic survey. There is considerable support for associations from tenants but mobilization has been very difficult and associations have not built up the organizational resources which would make mobilization easier and more effective.

The second significant arena was the market or economic arena, in which Bengtsson argues that the main aim of a consumer organization is to help its members obtain good value for money. Clearly, tenants' associations in Britain have not been successful in achieving this for their members. Rents have increased substantially in real terms in the last 20 years and it is generally perceived that owner-occupation offers better value for money for those who can afford it. Many factors are at work here, but it is evident that tenants have not been able to exert sufficient political pressure, either by themselves or in coalition with other agencies such as Labour local authority landlords or the Labour Party nationally, to prevent this happening or even to challenge it in any effective way. In addition, a number of studies have claimed that housing associations offer a better standard of service to their tenants and at rent levels which are increasingly competitive with local authorities, albeit achieved with higher subsidies and substantially more expenditure on housing management (see DoE 1989). There is considerable concern about housing conditions in the council sector, particularly in system-built and high-rise dwellings, and dampness seems to be an endemic problem in much council housing. The social, economic and environmental conditions on many council estates are also a cause for concern and in some areas there is a problem of difficult-to-let property. Despite these problems a large majority of tenants have expressed satisfaction with their local authority landlord and when given the opportunity to opt for another approved landlord – through a voluntary transfer or Housing Action Trust ballot – in only a few cases has there been a majority of tenants who have chosen to make a change.

The third arena was the political one, in which Bengtsson argues that the objective of any organization is to support policies and institutions which can serve to help the members. Tenants' associations in Britain have had few friends within mainstream politics in the past few years and the lack of a viable and effective national organization has meant that they have been unable to forge the alliances which would possibly have been able to resist the assault on council housing by central government.

In the fourth arena of the estate, tenants' associations have been more successful in some areas, although there has been no systematic survey of their experience. At the estate level, there has been considerable spread of tenant-participation structures, although this has not occurred in the systematic way it has in Sweden. Intensive, local housing management involving tenant participation has become the norm on estates considered to be problematic or difficult to let. There has been a steady if unspectacular growth in the number of tenant management co-operatives (see Clapham and Kintrea 1992). Nevertheless, the power resources of tenants have been constrained by the limited spread of the citizenship model as well as by problems of lack of material resources at the estate level and problems of mobilization. The fostering of consumerist innovations such as compulsory competitive tendering of housing management have served to limit collective representation.

It is difficult to isolate a critical juncture in the story of British council housing unless one takes the election of a Conservative government in 1979 as that point. Since then the position of the sector has steadily declined through a series of Acts of Parliament and executive measures which have marginalized council housing. Tenants' rights have been viewed as individual rights, such as the right to buy one's council house (see Chapter 6). So even though landlords in England and Wales were given the statutory duty to consult tenants over significant issues of housing management in 1980, this has often been interpreted as consulting individual tenants by post rather than engaging in a dialogue with tenants' associations. There has been no national promotion of a particular model of tenant participation at the estate level in Britain as there has been in Sweden and so practice has varied widely, depending on the rules of the game constructed at the local level.

Tenant participation in Sweden

The formal basis of local tenant involvement in Swedish public housing is the Central Agreement on Tenant Participation that was signed in 1979 (and revised in 1986) by SABO, the umbrella organization of the municipal housing companies (MHCs), and the National Union of Tenants. Four years later, in 1983, a corresponding agreement was reached on tenant participation in the private rental sector. Both agreements are structured in a similar way, although the formal rights of participation are more limited for tenants in the private sector. That agreement has also had much less impact at the local level. While local agreements on tenant participation, based on the central agreement, have been established for almost the whole Swedish public housing stock, only a small number of private landlords have signed such local agreements.

To understand the Swedish structure of tenant participation in public housing some background knowledge of the system of housing provision in general is necessary. Public rental housing in Sweden is organized mainly in the form of MHCs, which are owned and controlled by the local municipalities but run as independent enterprises on a non-profit basis. The total number of such companies can be estimated as 400, of which 320 are members of the umbrella organization SABO. There is one MHC – and sometimes more than one – in almost every Swedish municipality. The total stock of the SABO companies is about 910 000 dwellings. The spread in size between MHCs is considerable, ranging from some 20 dwellings in the smallest companies up to 53 000 in the largest one.

The MHCs were given their present role in the comprehensive housing policy introduced by the Social Democratic government in the years after the Second World War. During the following three decades the MHCs experienced a rapid growth, culminating in the so-called 'Million Programme' when MHCs accounted for almost 40 per cent of the one million new dwellings built between 1966 and 1975. Today more than 20 per cent of all dwellings and some 40 per cent of multi-family dwellings are owned by MHCs.

Two important particulars of the Swedish public rental sector should be pointed out. One is that Sweden has no 'social housing' in the sense that certain tenures or housing estates are intended for people of limited means. There are no income limits or other socially defined criteria for getting an MHC dwelling. Second, and as a consequence, MHCs have not – at least in principle – received any special financial support from the state. The official political goal of 'tenure neutrality', laid down in 1974, means that the state finance of housing should be designed to counterbalance differences due to taxation rules with the aim of generating 'equal costs for equal dwellings'. State housing loans used to be available for all types of tenure and, after the abolition of those loans in the early 1990s, the remaining subsidy system is still allocated in accordance with the principles of tenure neutrality.

Tenant participation was not placed on the political agenda until the 1970s, after the Million Programme had helped to solve the most urgent problems of housing shortage – and created new ones of large-scale anonymity. Although relatively new in the rental sector, the tenants' right to decide collectively on important housing questions has a longstanding tradition in the co-operative sector, which is one of the largest in the world with some 15 per cent of the total Swedish housing stock. To some extent the strong position of housing co-operatives is due to the fact that in Sweden owner-occupation in multi-family housing is forbidden by law. The specific co-operative Swedish tenure is *tenant-ownership*, meaning that co-operative estates are jointly and severally owned by the tenants and all important decisions concerning the management of the co-operative are taken either at a general meeting or by a board elected by the tenant-owners. Thus, in this sector the law guarantees a minimum level of co-operative participation based on a combination of direct and indirect democracy.

It is clear that the democratic traditions of the co-operative sector have had an important impact on discussions on tenant participation in the rental sector. For example, in the 1974 Governmental Proposal on housing policies, where tenant participation ('housing democracy') was put forward as a new goal – alongside the more traditional ones of living space, physical standards and housing costs – reference was made to the democratic traditions within the co-operative sector. Sometimes the conversion of rental estates to co-operative tenant-ownership has even been put forward as the best way to provide tenants with a reasonable control over housing management, in particular by the non-socialist parties.

Another important institutional prerequisite of tenant participation is the collective system of rent-setting (the so-called 'use-value system'), which in turn is based on the existence of a strong and unitary tenants' movement. The regional *tenants' associations* (TAs) belonging to the National Union of Tenants have a total membership of more than 630 000, which means that 45 per cent of all Swedish tenant households are members. The organization is particularly strong in the public sector, where more than half of all households are members. This internationally unique following has guaranteed the tenants' movement an influential position in the political arena, where it has acted as an important member of the so-called Popular Movements Coalition supporting the Social Democratic party in housing policy matters.

Notwithstanding its achievements in the organizational and political arenas, even more impressive is the position that the Swedish tenants' movement has attained in the rental market. Today almost all rents on the Swedish market are set in collective negotiations between landlords and the regional TAs. Those negotiations are based on the use-value system of rent-setting, which has been described as a 'third way' between market rents and state-controlled rents. The rent levels in the public sector should reflect the total costs of the MHC, whereas the rent structure should reflect not the costs of individual flats and estates, but their relative use value. The general idea is that dwellings estimated to be of equal value to the average consumer should have the same rent, regardless of the actual costs. (For a more comprehensive description and analysis of the use-value system see Bengtsson 1993.) The corporatist role of the tenants' movement is further underlined by the fact that the organization is represented – together with the public and private landlords – in the regional rent tribunals responsible for investigating legal disputes on rents and other housing conditions.

When tenant participation came on to the political agenda in the 1970s a number of different models were discussed and tested. Some but not all of them were based on the *contact committees* (CCs), which are the local unit of the tenants' movement. (Starting in 1988, the contact committees have been successively reorganized into *local tenants' associations* with formal democratic statutes and elected boards responsible to annual meetings of members – for the sake of clarity, however, we will use the term contact committee throughout the chapter.) After the central agreement was signed, however, most models where the right of participation was executed by independent bodies of tenants were successively replaced by the CC model prescribed by the agreement. As we will see there still exist other forms of participation, but those are exceptions.

According to the central agreement, the stock of an MHC should be divided into a number of management units, corresponding to the geographical area of responsibility of a CC (in most cases comprising between 100 and 500 dwellings). According to the agreement the CC has the right to consultations with representatives of the MHC on developments in general in the housing area, as well as on any important changes in the management of the estate. At least twice a year the CC is to call all tenants in the estate to a general meeting. While the CC, as part of the TA, consists only of members of that association, non-member tenants may also take part in the general meeting. Sometimes, active non-members are also called in as additional members of a CC.

Some characteristics of the central agreement should be noted. In principle the CC has what might be called a 'preferential right of interpretation'. The agreement states that, in the consultations between the MHC and the CC, the tenants' demands should be met as long as (a) this is possible within the economic resources available and (b) it would not conflict with the MHC's responsibilities to other parties, such as collective agreements with the trade unions. Furthermore, the MHC's responsibility for implementing the housing policies of the municipality cannot be set aside in favour of the demands of a CC. Of course, due to these reservations, the exceptions may well be more important than the general presumption in favour of the views of the CC. If the MHC and the CC are unable to reach an agreement in the consultations, the question is referred for arbitration to the parties involved in the rent negotiations. This means that an unsettled question about the management of a specific housing estate may be raised by the TA in the bargaining on the rent levels and rent structure of the whole MHC.

While the central agreement prescribes that the CCs have a right of information and consultation, more far-reaching rights may also be granted through complementary agreements between the MHC and the TA. These may include the choice of levels of housing management, linked to different rent levels. They may also delegate a right of decision-making to the CC within a local management budget. Such special complementary agreements have been reached in a number of MHCs, although in most cases only for a few CCs in each company.

The central agreement in the private sector has great similarities with the MHC agreement. However, there are also important differences. For example, private tenants may be represented by other types of organizations than CCs belonging to the regional TA. Also, private landlords may deny tenants access to information on the financial affairs of the estate (which a public landlord is not allowed to do). The formal rules of the central agreement indicate a possible tension within the CC between its role as part of the tenants' movement and its role as representative of all tenants living on an estate. This tension is reflected in the 'pros' and 'cons' of the strong links through the system of tenant participation with the national tenants' organization and the use-value system of rent-setting. On the one hand, these links make it possible for CCs to take up local matters at a higher level if they are unable to persuade the landlord in negotiations. On the other hand, tenants who are not TA members have a less favoured position than those who are members, which is rather dubious from a democratic perspective and which may also be an obstacle to high degrees of local activity.

There are also some examples of tenant participation within the public rental sector based on general co-operative principles. Legislation in 1986 made it easier to start new housing co-operatives based on rental tenure instead of the special Swedish co-operative tenure of tenant-ownership. Probably the best known examples are two *tenant management co-operatives* (TMCs). These are rental co-operatives where the tenants take over the responsibility for some or all of the management by signing an agreement with the MHC which retains the role as landlord in relation to individual tenants. Both existing TMCs have, however, experienced internal and external problems that may indicate the difficulty of organizing tenant participation in other forms than the established one within the auspices of the tenants' movement. (For details about TMCs see Svensson 1993.)

Tenant participation went through a crisis in the early 1990s when the bourgeois parties came into power both nationally and in many municipalities. A number of the local agreements were cancelled by MHCs. Often economic arguments were presented to justify this, but in some cases there were also ideological doubts about a system of tenant participation being based on the perspectives of a predominantly social democratic tenants' movement. It seems, however, that in most places participation continued in similar forms as before, with or without a formal agreement (Lind *et al.* 1996). Today, as already mentioned, agreements on tenant participation exist almost throughout the public rental sector. In a number of cases some form of decision-making power has also been delegated to the CCs. There are a total of almost 3000 CCs in the public rental sector, and almost every one of them has the minimum right to consultation granted by the central agreement.

However, not much is known about the actual activities at the estate level. At the time of writing, no Swedish survey corresponding to the British one by Cairncross *et al.* (1990) has been carried out. What we do know about tenant participation in Swedish public housing has either been gleaned from 'common knowledge' (which in reality almost always means anecdotal evidence) or has come from case studies of individual estates, often carried out some years ago and examining early experiments in participation. Our knowledge of the more established forms of tenant participation is surprisingly limited and unsystematic. To some extent, however, this situation has been improved by a more recent study of 32 CCs by Lind *et al.* (1996).

Most of the earlier case studies on tenant participation in Sweden are summarized and evaluated in a literature review by Uggla (1993). The review includes 25 case studies on 45 housing estates, dating from the period 1975 to 1993. Some 30 of the estates studied are in the public rental sector. One general observation from Uggla's review is that the case studies seldom covered a longer period than one or two years from the initiation of tenant participation. This means that neither the sustainability of participation, nor its possible long-term effects, were really investigated. As a corrective to this lacuna a follow-up study is now being carried out on the same cases by Bengtsson with Uggla and Svensson. Still, some general conclusions may be drawn from Uggla's study:

- In most cases, tenant participation has been the result of 'top-down' initiatives coming from municipalities, MHCs and other professional bodies, rather than 'bottom up' from the local tenants.
- In most cases, participation was dominated by a small number of active tenants, while tenants in general were said to be rather passive or even ignorant of their new collective rights.
- While participation rates were generally low, they tended to be higher on small estates and in housing areas where the turnover of tenants was low.
- Some tenants preferred to get involved in activities other than decision-making – for example, it was claimed that ethnic minorities were more often than not 'reluctant' to attend formal meetings and preferred to take part in common work on the estate (see also Liedholm 1991).
- The most intense examples of collective action by tenants were reported from so-called collective housing units – estates with a high degree of common services, such as restaurants and childcare arrangements, organized by the residents themselves. To some degree this may be explained by self-selection effects, as people with communitarian ideals may be more likely to choose to live on such estates.
- Sometimes the staff working for MHCs – in particular middle-level white-collar staff – saw tenant participation as a threat to their positions and professional status. Generally, the organization and budget systems of MHCs used to be centralized and therefore not adapted to local tenant participation. In this respect, important changes took place in the 1980s

and today most large MHCs have a district or area-based organization (see Lindberg and Karlberg 1988). This decentralization has diminished, but not completely abolished, the problems of implementing decisions taken by – or together with – the tenants (Lind *et al.* 1996).

● In cases where participation was organized through local bodies of tenants not attached to the TA, the support from that organization was often weak and sometimes non-existent.

According to Lind *et al.* (1996) the extension, content and intensity of tenant participation in Swedish MHCs still varies considerably between companies and housing areas. An increasing number of CCs have some form of right to direct influence over their local budget and rent levels. In some CC areas attendance at meetings and other common activities is on the same level as in the housing co-operatives. Many CCs are also active in fields other than housing management, which may indicate that tenant participation may in fact function as a participative 'school of democracy'.

If we analyse the experience gathered from tenant participation in Sweden in terms of power resources, the first thing that comes to mind is the dominant role of the strong and centralized tenants' movement. This resourceful professional organization can help local tenants by providing important support services, from office facilities to legal and economic expertise. The TA could also help legitimize the local activists in the eyes of the MHC. When it comes to legitimacy in the eyes of the tenants in general, however, the strong links between local tenant participation and the traditionally social democratic tenants' movement may have more double-edged effects. In estates where tenants are sceptical of the tenants' movement, the link may even serve as an obstacle to collective action.

In cases where tenant participation is not based on CCs within the TA, the situation is, of course, different, and the local tenants may sometimes face two opposite parties instead of one. There are cases where active tenants in local estates have been reported to have better relations with the MHC landlord than with the regional TA. In recent years, however, reports on conflict between local tenants and regional TAs are definitely fewer than in the late 1970s.

In terms of resources in different arenas, the links to the TA would seem to give local tenants a stronger position in the *estate arena* than in Britain. The CC receives an annual budget from the MHC and the TA of some 50 Swedish Crowns per dwelling, which guarantees some resources for its activities (Lind *et al.* 1996). The CC probably has a better situation in the *political arena* as well, since the regional TA is in a position to act as a strong advocate for the interests of complaining local tenants. Probably the position of tenants in the general *market arena* is also stronger in Sweden than in Britain. In Sweden most tenants are still in a position where they can choose between a public and a private rental dwelling, since neither sector is marginalized in the same way as in Britain. In some cases, the 'exit' possibility may be used as a power resource in the participation game against the landlord. The exception may be immigrant households who often have quite a weak position in the housing market – and who are seldom organized in TAs or active in tenant participation. The strong, monopolistic (or rather monopsonistic) position of the TA in the rental market may also have an impact on the result of consultations on the estate level. This is implied in the formal rules, since only the TA (not the CC) can refer an unsettled issue to the rent negotiations at the MHC level.

If we turn to the *organizational arena*, it is easy to observe that tenant participation *per se* has not been very successful in initiating and retaining collective action among tenants. With the collective housing units as the most important exception, the general activity seems to be quite low, both in collective decision-making and in common work. Breaks in the continuity of the activities of CCs and other local tenant bodies have often been reported.

It may be said that the relative strength of Swedish tenants in other arenas – through higher levels within the tenants' movement – may make collective action on the estate level unnecessary in a pure power perspective. On the other hand, increasing tenant activities, creating local networks and improving social control have often been seen as important goals of participation. It may be that the strong negotiating position of Swedish tenants could be working against the fulfilment of those goals. To some extent, however, this somewhat gloomy picture regarding the intensity of collective action should be modified by recent reports from a number of active CCs with different forms of economic influence. So far these CCs must be seen as exceptions, but they may indicate a future development with higher degrees of tenant activities, if and when more CCs are given economic influence.

The three different ideal type rules of the game suggested by Cairncross *et al.* (1990) and outlined above may be applied to tenant participation in Swedish public housing. It would seem that the consumerist view, although often referred to in the current debates on Swedish public housing, is seldom dominant in tenant participation *per se*. On the other hand, the low priority given to tenant participation in recent years, and the growing interest in the more individualistic idea of 'treating tenants as customers', may be seen as expressions of an emerging consumerist view. However, market-oriented devices such as the British compulsory competitive tendering model have not been introduced within the Swedish system of tenant participation. Thus, the existing Swedish cases of tenant participation in the public rental sector can probably be distributed somewhere along the axis between the traditional and citizenship models, probably with the centre of gravity considerably nearer the citizenship pole than in the British case. As no systematic survey has been done, such an empirical generalization must be tentative and the low degree of 'citizen activity' in participation detracts from the citizenship experience. The most obvious exceptions are the collective housing units described above, and probably also some estates where rights of decision-making on economic matters have been granted to the tenants. These estates may well qualify as examples of the citizenship rules of the game.

Conclusions

This chapter has outlined the main differences between tenant participation in public rented housing in Britain and Sweden. In Sweden, the tenants' movement has achieved a strong position in the organizational arena and so has been able to exert considerable influence on policy towards the sector at a national level and to obtain a dominant position within the rental market. This power in other arenas has enabled the movement to negotiate a national framework for the rules of the game in the estate arena at the local level, which has been applied almost universally. This framework is based on an ideology of collectivism which is close to, but not identical to, the citizenship ideal type identified in Britain. The main difference is that the embeddedness of tenant participation within the strong and professional tenants' movement may sometimes weaken the incentives for collective action on the local level.

In Britain, the tenants' movement has been very weak at the national level and the position of public rented housing has declined considerably in the last 20 years. These two factors are interwoven in a web of causality with many other factors, including broader political philosophies. There has not been the same national framework for the estate arena in Britain as in Sweden. This has allowed a wide variety of different practices at the local level. However, there has been a strong cultural pressure towards a consumerist approach and this has been reinforced by consumerist mechanisms of performance assessment and contracting. These have made the citizenship model more difficult, although not impossible, to implement. There has been some resistance to a sole preoccupation with consumerist ideas in local government which has become increasingly controlled by the Labour Party. Therefore citizenship ideas have survived, even if they have not exactly flourished.

The comparison between Britain and Sweden is limited by the constraints of our existing knowledge. There are substantial gaps in, for example, our knowledge of the workings of tenant participation in the estate arena in Sweden. A more meaningful comparison would need the collection of new empirical material in both countries with the type of information being collected guided by our framework. However, the main aim of this chapter has been to put forward a theoretical framework for international comparisons. We have described two different approaches and combined them into a unified framework. In our view this enables tenant participation to be examined on a number of levels, including that of international comparison. The framework offers a way of examining the nature of the relationship between a landlord and his/her tenants and the factors which influence this. It provides a way of considering the actions of the parties and the wider factors which shape this action.

Clearly, there is substantial room for the development of the framework put forward here. In particular, the ideal types identified from the British experience need to be refined and expanded on the basis of the rules of the game in other countries. It will only be possible to judge the potential usefulness of the approach suggested here when comparative studies have been undertaken which involve a directed collection of empirical material rather than relying on existing information, much of which has been collected with other objectives in mind. Only in this way will we be able to move beyond 'contrasting comparison' and towards 'theoretical comparison' to deepen our understanding of tenant participation. The theoretical framework identified here needs to be tested and developed through comparative research.

References

Bengtsson, B. (1993), 'Swedish rental policy – a complex superstructure with cracking foundations', *Scandinavian Housing and Planning Research*, **8**, pp.113–127.

Bengtsson, B. (1994), *Tenants' Dilemma: On Collective Action in Housing*, paper presented at the ENHR Conference on 'Housing: Making the Connections', Glasgow, 29 August–2 September.

Bengtsson, B. (1995), 'Housing in game-theoretical perspective', *Housing Studies*, **10**(2), pp.229–243.

Bines, W., Kemp, P., Pleace, N. and Radley, C. (1993), *Managing Social Housing*, London: HMSO.

Cairncross, L., Clapham, D. and Goodlad, R. (1990), *The Pattern of Tenant Participation in Council Housing Management*, Discussion Paper No. 31, Glasgow: Centre for Housing Research, University of Glasgow.

Cairncross, L., Clapham, D. and Goodlad, R. (1992), 'The origins and activities of tenants' associations in Britain', *Urban Studies*, **29**(5), pp.709–725.

Cairncross, L., Clapham, D. and Goodlad, R. (1993), 'The social bases of tenant organization', *Housing Studies*, **8**(3), pp.179–194.

Cairncross, L., Clapham, D. and Goodlad, R. (1994), 'Tenant participation and tenant power in British council housing', *Public Administration*, **72**(2), pp.177–200.

Cairncross, L., Clapham, D. and Goodlad, R. (1996), *Housing Management, Consumers and Citizens*, London: Routledge.

Clapham, D. and Kintrea, K. (1987), 'Importing housing policy – housing co-operatives in Britain and Sweden', *Housing Studies*, **2**(3), pp.157–169.
Clapham, D. and Kintrea, K. (1992), *Housing Co-operatives in Britain: Achievements and Prospects*, London: Longman.
Clegg, S. (1989), *Frameworks of Power*, London: Sage.
Cole, I. and Furbey, R. (1994), *The Eclipse of Council Housing*, London: Routledge.
Collier, R.B. and Collier, D. (1991), *Shaping the Political Arena: Critical Junctures, the Labor Movement, and Regime Dynamics in Latin America*, Princeton: Princeton University Press.
Cooper, C. (1996), *Tenants' Choice or the People's Home: Resident Involvement in England and Sweden*, Occasional Paper No. 4, Hull: Policy Studies Research Centre, University of Lincolnshire & Humberside.
Cronberg, T. (1986), 'Tenants' involvement in the management of social housing in the Nordic countries', *Scandinavian Housing and Planning Research*, **3**, pp.65–87.
Department of the Environment (DoE) (1989), *The Nature and Effectiveness of Housing Management in England*, London: HMSO.
Elster, J. (1983), *Sour Grapes: Studies in the Subversion of Rationality*, Cambridge: Cambridge University Press.
George, A.L. and McKeown, T.J. (1985), 'Case studies and theories of organizational decision making' in Sproull, L. and Larkey, V. (eds), *Advances in Information Processing in Organizations, Vol. 2*, Santa Barbara: JAI Press, pp.21–58.
Kemeny, J. (1992), *Housing and Social Theory*, London: Routledge.
Liedholm, M. (1991), *Boinflytande och deltagande som fenomen och process* (Tenant involvement and participation as phenomenon and process), Lund: Institute of Sociology, University of Lund.
Lind, J.-E., Lennartsson, H. and Soidre-Brink, T. (1996), *Lokalt boendeinflytande efter ett kvartssekel* (Local tenant participation after a quarter of a century), Gothenburg: Institute of Sociology, University of Gothenburg.
Lindberg, G. and Karlberg, B. (1988), 'Decentralisation in the public housing sector in Sweden', *Scandinavian Housing and Planning Research*, **5**, pp.85–99.
Lowe, S. (1986), *Urban Social Movements: The City After Castells*, Basingstoke: Macmillan.
Svensson, K.A.S. (1993), *Co-operative Housing in Sweden: A Building with Many Façades – On the Diversity of Co-operation*, Stockholm: Co-operative Institute.
Tsebelis, G. (1990), *Nested Games: Rational Choice in Comparative Politics*, Berkeley: University of California Press.
Uggla, C. (1993), *Forskning om boendeinflytande – en litteraturöversikt* (Swedish research on tenant participation – a literature review), Gävle: National Swedish Institute for Building Research.

6 Tenant participation in a legal context

Stuart Lowe

This chapter focuses attention on the legal context in which, broadly defined, tenant participation occurs. A single, key message emerges from the discussion – the law matters. While 'strict law' is best left to lawyers, there is no doubt that the legal framework of both statutory and individual rights is seminal to how relations between tenants and landlords are defined and have been acted out. The legal context is generally neglected in social policy analysis and none more so than in the field of housing. That having been said, there is an equal danger in isolating legal formulations from the political and policy framework. It is hoped that the chapter strikes a balance between providing a reasonably comprehensive summary of the legal position on tenant and landlord relations, insofar as they relate to tenant participation, but also shows how the law fits into the wider issues as they appear from the perspective of the summer of 1996, when the Housing Act 1996 had only just arrived on the statute books.

The chapter begins by outlining some of the broader, more conceptual issues on tenant participation, particularly the social context relating to council housing, before engaging in a fairly detailed account of the main parts of public-sector housing law in which the development of participation is set. This requires an examination of the principal individual rights of tenants – or rather lack of them – before exploring those more or less collective rights shared by the body of tenants. One of the key points to be made is that the individual and the collective are never very clearly separated and it is not possible to understand collective rights in isolation from the dominant framework of individual rights. Moreover, at the time when tenants' rights achieved a firmer foundation in statute through the Housing Act 1980, the primacy of individual rights was asserted as against those of a collective nature.

The Housing Act 1980, *inter alia*, established a near revolution in social housing law through the creation of secure tenancies and achieved a significant re-balancing of tenant–landlord relations, acting in part to confirm the new era of the 'consumer-tenant'. Whatever may be argued about this new form of citizenship and its sources and purpose, there is no doubting that it comes readily packaged with a bundle of legal rights which clearly define its practical limits. The scope for debating the higher concepts of the meaning of citizenship is very much brought down to earth by the legal framework established in the 1980 Act and developed subsequently. It is almost as though when there is a conceptual difficulty or an ideological confusion, the fundamental law remains as a foundation. Perhaps this is best posed by asking why, in an era of 'consumers' and 'customers', the notion of 'participation' is necessary at all? It might be logical to assume that it is redundant conceptually. In fact it has been growing in significance just at the time when new consumerism is at its zenith. The reason for this would seem to be that it has been inserted into the highly equivocal sets of relationships that have evolved between the *unaltered* status of council house tenants as tenants – for that is what they remain – and the idea of them as customers or citizens. Both of the latter clearly imply rights and choices which in the case of social housing tenants in Britain do not exist. 'Participation' is in this sense an invention to give voice to this conceptual confusion.

The social context

As John Grayson illustrates in Chapter 2, tenant participation has, in its wider meaning, existed throughout the history of social housing provision. It was common following the advent in 1919 of mass council housing for tenants' organizations to emerge on newly built estates. They often assisted in the 'settling-down' process, which sometimes took place in the face of hostility from neighbouring owner-occupiers. Frankenberg sums up the situation thus: 'there is a familiar pattern of initial loneliness followed by unity against the outside world giving rise to an agitational Residents' Association' (Frankenberg 1966 p.214). These agitational groups normally then became little more than social organizations and running through the history of the tenants' movement is a tendency for protest groups to metamorphose in this way. Indeed, as this author pointed out elsewhere, the most militant tenants' associations leave few traces, either documentary or organizational (Lowe 1986). The characteristics of council estates as social entities created a specific kind of social formation within which associational activity was characteristically informal and instrumental. The significance of this to contemporary interest in tenant participation is that the great plethora of activity has largely gone undocumented and, crucially, occurred *outside* the formal frameworks of central and local authority policy. In addition, as a number of authors have pointed out, council housing has not had the invigorating power of middle-class self-interest to support it (Saunders 1979, Cole and Furbey 1994).

Thus for most purposes most of the time proactive tenants' activity has been in *reaction* to outside pressures and interests. The rather uneven ebb and flow in this long history also stems from the essentially *individual* nature of the occupancy of a dwelling, which has been crucially underpinned by the legal framework of the tenancies which are based on an individual property relationship between landlord and tenant. An illustration of this is a problem that lies at the heart of militant tenants' action – the rent strike. Many of the most bitterly fought actions involving tenants' associations, as John Grayson's chapter depicts, have been over levels of rent set by local authorities. Almost without exception such campaigns have floundered on the rock of the individual tenancy. Who was to say during a rent strike who was or was not paying rent to the landlord? The truth was that there was no way of knowing and invariably such action failed to halt increases. This is not the place to pursue the point but the nature of the occupancy of a home – an inherently individual act – and the nature of the estate as a collectivity of families sharing a common landlord have endowed council housing with a very special set of legal and organizational structures, tactical dilemmas and a highly complex sociological context. Debates about tenant participation need constant sensitizing to this and to how this tradition and cultural context have evolved up to the present.

A further point here is that, read in this way, much of what is labelled in recent years as 'tenant participation' is no such thing but rather an encounter of tenants in general with officially defined structures and approved forms of involvement. Tenant mobilization outside institutional structures is, as Furbey *et al.* observe, very different from 'top-down sponsorship of tenant involvement by the state' (Furbey *et al.* 1996 p.252).

The rights of tenants

As important to an evaluation of tenant participation as the social context of council housing is the legal construction of the tenancy. The very foundation of the relationship between tenants and the landlord is encapsulated in the tenancy agreement and by tradition this is essentially a relationship of individual contract. The long tradition of English law has always allowed the ownership and control of property to be vested in the landlord, and as a landlord to others his rights have been paramount. Collective rights, where they affect the totality of tenants in relation to the landlord, were almost non-existent before the Housing Act 1980 and subsequently have only been very weakly developed.

From the outset of modern 'housing policy', normally taken to begin with the Housing of the Working Classes Act 1890, the legal emphasis in the provision of housing has been on the duties and powers of the local authority. The 1890 Act barely mentioned the supposed beneficiaries – the 'working classes' – except as households displaced following 'improvement' (generally meaning slum clearance). And the same is apparent in the Housing, Town Planning Act 1909 and on into the housing legislation during the inter-war period. Scant attention was paid to this after the Second World War, notwithstanding that the Housing Act 1949 removed the reference to the 'working classes' which had featured in most housing legislation until then. The concept of the 'working classes' was never statutorily defined and in fact as it appears in litigation referred to people in unskilled, poorly paid jobs (Hughes 1991). This interpretation would seem to be at variance with reality, at least in the 1920s and early 1930s when council housing was too expensive to be occupied by such a class of person. Early council housing residents were skilled artisans, teachers, postal workers, lower white-collar employees and so on.

Be that as it may, the key point here is that the rights of social housing tenants were very poorly developed and this is an important context to the modern period. The reason for this is that throughout the nineteenth century tenants' and landlords' legal relationships were mediated by *common law* procedures in which the presumption was that both sides were equally able to make or break the contract. Such a view in law was clearly upheld by the *laissez-faire* economy of the time and there was strenuous resistance in Parliament and in the legal system to challenges to this fundamental point. (Read *Hansard* on the debate over the 1890 Act for a sniff of the vitriol reserved for those who dared argue for state intervention in the housing market.) It is essentially from *this* tradition – based on common law, not statute – that the landlord–tenant relationship was learnt and adopted for the new municipal housing sector. Somewhat paradoxically, this situation arose at a time when statutory regulation in the privately rented sector began – notably in the rent controls imposed during the 1914–18 war. Thus, because the prevailing view was that council housing had a role to serve only certain types of people and as such was not in the market, common law continued to govern the 'social housing' sector. Rights of succession or security of tenure are alien to the common law and it is this tradition – ironically, derived from nineteenth-century private landlordism – that governed tenant–landlord relations in social housing until the Housing Act 1980 began to establish a limited range of rights; albeit, as we shall see, individual rights.

Tenants of local authorities also laboured under a second legal presumption. Under public law the courts *monitor* the administrative procedures and political apparatus to make sure that this system is acting appropriately. Basic rights – such as they are – are defined in standardized tenancy agreements over which the individual tenant has no control except indirectly through challenges in public law. The law, however, hardly ever intervenes, because the presupposition is that the system of public administration is controlled and directed through political accountability. For example, public landlords are legally bound by statute to set a 'reasonable rent', with a significant adjunct from the Local Government and Housing Act 1989 to take into account local property values in the private sector. Rents, as an element of tenancy agreements, are set by an administrative/political procedure and in law there is no challenge to this or defence against excessive increases for individual tenants. In 1992, in the case of *R vs London Borough of Ealing ex parte Jennifer Lewis*, the Court of Appeal – the second highest court in the land – held that large rent increases were not a consideration for the courts and that only the legal structure of the authority's Housing Revenue Account was open to question.

The secure tenancy

As the privately rented sector continued to decline in the post-war period, it began to be recognized that the polarization between state housing and the rapidly increasing owner-occupier sector was creating a very clear two-nation effect, with the legal rights of the latter very highly developed against those of the former. From about 1960 onwards – when this polarized system was more obviously apparent – there was concern to redress the balance between the tenures and this is the source of the recognition that tenants' rights needed some statutory recognition and support. The problem was tackled in a number of ways, including the development of tenant consultation and participation procedures, but principally in the creation of the 'secure tenancy' – something of a legal revolution.

The 1979 Green Paper on Housing (Cmnd 6851) argued for legislation to provide council tenants with security of tenure and this was a central part of the Callaghan government's Housing Bill of 1979. The Green Paper and the Bill provoked a wide-ranging debate about council housing and it was in this context that some Conservatives put forward the rights of tenants to buy their home as a mechanism for bringing the benefits of home-ownership into the state rental sector. The weak position of public tenants compared to the Rent Acts (controlling the privately rented sector) was also argued as an overdue reform.

An important step announced in the Bill was the proposal to create Joint

Estate Management Committees (JEMCs) which would have been required in every local authority area and giving a small element of representation to council tenants through their elected tenant representatives. At the time a few authorities set up their own JEMCs and others encouraged the formation of tenants' associations and city-wide federations. The Bill fell with the Labour government and with the advent of the Thatcher administration all such notions were superseded by a new basket of *individual* rights built around the concept of the secure tenancy – as derived from the original Bill. It hardly needs to be said that principal among these rights was the 'right to buy', the ultimate individual right to cease to be a tenant. Equally, however, other rights retained from the original Bill and incorporated in the Tenants' Charter were essentially those of an individual nature – security of tenure, rights of succession and exchange, sub-letting, billing landlords for repair work and so on. The secure tenancy thus put in place for the first time statutory rights for council house tenants and has generated a new stream of litigation previously unknown. The central point in this context is that, while the granting of such rights is undoubtedly progressive, virtually all the newly codified rights are of an individual nature. This clearly reflects the prevailing political and ideological context of the era and the scale of what they imply corporately for tenants is limited.

Collective rights

Collective rights, through which the tenant body as a whole exercises an influence over the landlord, were hardly developed at all in the 1980 Act. Five, arguably six, very short sections gave authorities an obligation to consult tenants in relation to management changes, maintenance, improvement or demolition of the buildings, and the provision of certain services. The obligation, however, is one of consultation only and there is no duty in law to take notice of such opinion, merely to take such dialogue into consideration. The courts also determined that there is no requirement to involve tenants in the policy-making process (*Short v Tower Hamlets LBC* [1985]). The duty is to consult with secure tenants or a 'group' of them, a group being defined as tenants forming a distinct social cluster or in occupancy of a distinct area or type of building, estate or larger area.

Section 104 of the Housing Act 1985, into which the terms of the 1980 Act were consolidated, also imposes a duty on authorities to publish up-to-date information about secure tenancies, including a specified range of information from the provisions of Parts IV and V of the 1985 Act and Sections 11 to 16 of the Landlord and Tenant Act 1985. Section 167 of the Local Government and Housing Act 1989 also imposes a duty on local housing authorities to publish an annual report to most tenants (in fact only those living in dwellings incorporated into the Housing Revenue Account) on housing-management performance or other information that the Secretary of State requires. This, however, is hardly a system of fundamental accountability and the quality of publications is very variable.

Although such rights as these are often deemed to be collective, the extent to which the tenant body as a whole experiences them is limited. Even on those issues which are more inherently participative, the fact of the essentially individual nature of tenant–landlord relations impinges. For example, apart from the right to buy, tenants have been offered a number of other 'exit' strategies, usually requiring the wholesale transfer of an estate or the whole stock, through Tenants' Choice, voluntary stock transfers or Housing Action Trusts (HATs), each requiring a ballot of tenants to approve the transfer. Even though none of the first round of HATs went ahead, the events surrounding this outcome established the conditions and context for the other forms of transfers. Balloting of tenants under the Housing Act 1985 created a new set of relationships in which the collective will of tenants could be more fully felt. In the case of the HATs it allowed quite favourable conditions, from the tenants' point of view, to be negotiated with the Trusts as a precondition for the transfer out of authority control. The problem was, *inter alia*, that such bargains could not be incorporated into tenancy agreements because the tenants were not legally party to the contract between the HAT and their current landlord (Stewart 1994). Agreements based in effect on promises which affected the existing rights of secure tenants and the apparent lack of accountability of the post-HAT landlords caused the tenant body to back away from the HAT mechanism. Tenants continued to confront the dilemma that what was offered by way of deals and packages of improvements could not, according to their status as tenants, ultimately be enforced in practice. When it came to Tenants' Choice – through which tenants selected a new landlord for themselves – this same problem arose. Although it was the Housing Corporation which had to approve the new landlord, and the ballot of tenants had to produce a clear majority, this exit option also made very little impression. Considerable efforts were made to counter the problem that negotiated packages were unenforceable. The Housing Corporation concocted a complex legal procedure essentially compelling contractors to adhere to the terms of agreements as a condition for approving take-over companies. Nevertheless, Tenants' Choice floundered and sank almost without trace. This failure in practice is sealed in Schedule II of the Housing Act 1996 in which Part IV of the Housing Act 1988 (dealing with changes of landlords, Tenants' Choice and so on) is repealed. It was not of course the only reason, but underlying these failures was undoubtedly tension between the essentially individually constructed tenancies and the essentially collective nature of such transfers.

Voluntary stock transfers have made a much bigger impact and, as has been observed by several commentators, it is ironic that its success was derived from procedures not intended for this purpose but to enable authorities to dispose of land and also dwellings under the terms of the Housing Act 1985 (Mullins *et al.* 1993, Hughes and Lowe 1995). The motivation for Large Scale Voluntary Stock Transfers (LSVT) concerned the anxieties of smaller local authorities about Tenants' Choice, the potential threat arising from compulsory competitive tendering (CCT) for housing-management services and, particularly, the consequences of the 'new financial regime' under the Local Government and Housing Act 1989 (notably the scale of rent increases necessitated by the incorporation of Housing Benefit Subsidy into the Housing Revenue Account). A clear motivation was the possibility of generating large capital proceeds from the sale of housing stock. LSVT was almost always an officer-led initiative and initially mainly in rural authorities with small housing stocks. Between 1988 and 1994, 31 authorities transferred their stocks in this way involving some 140 000 tenants (Hughes and Lowe 1995). The procedural requirements for LSVT are similar to those for the establishment of a HAT and meant that whatever the tenants agree the conveyance of the properties is between the old and the new landlord. In many cases this would in fact be the same managers often reconstituted into a new housing association, so there was a greater element of security in the situation from the tenants' point of view. Comment was also made on the fact that the transfer entailed a change from being a secure tenant to being an 'assured tenant'. Tenants' Charter rights under the 1980 Act were substituted for the somewhat different and arguably stronger conditions of the Housing Corporation's 'Tenants' Guarantee'.

The Tenants' Guarantee occurs through Section 36A of the Housing Associations Act 1985. This provides a considerable body of guidance on such issues as allocation policies, terms and conditions of tenancies, rent and service-charge determination, and complaints and consultation procedures. The Housing Corporation encourages consultation particularly regarding new management procedures and maintenance policy, and it can further *insist* that such views are taken into account. Arbitration mechanisms through which landlords' and tenants' disputes can be settled are also encouraged. The guidance on such matters given by the Housing Corporation is detailed and non-compliance can be a factor in the exercise of the Corporation's powers, for example over the registration of associations. The Tenants' Guarantee thus provides tenants of housing associations with a considerable body of rights through express conditions in their tenancies and it seems likely that the enhancement of the rights of council house tenants should, as a first step towards improvement, move in this direction. It is also worth noting the role of the Housing Corporation in this process –

operating rather on the lines of regulators in the utility services, providing statutory monitoring of best practice with some powers of intervention.

Thus, through the 'exiting' process, there is no doubt that the legal status of the tenants of local authorities has improved – principally through the right to buy and in the collective influence they can exert in the negotiations that surround balloting procedures. However, it cannot be stressed too often that all this is conducted in the shadow of essentially individual terms – to quit council housing or to enter, despite the Tenants' Guarantee, what Stewart refers to as 'the uncertain regulatory framework of the housing association' (Stewart 1994 p.277).

Tenant management organizations

The development of tenant participation has been most clearly developed in the context of government initiatives to transfer council housing management into some form of tenant management. The idea was not unknown but had previously been unsuccessful. The first significant experience followed the promotion of co-ownership and cost-renting housing through terms in the Housing Acts 1961 and 1964. By the mid-1970s there were about 40 000 co-ownership dwellings, but this figure fell dramatically after the Housing Act 1980 enabled co-owners to buy out the remaining share 'on the basis of the outstanding debt' (Smith 1989 p.227). The house-price boom of the early 1970s had already created a considerable incentive for co-owners to capitalize their equity and move into mainstream owner-occupation.

The introduction of housing association grant in 1974 stimulated a new form of co-operative with no equity stakes through the development of 'par value' co-ops. The Housing (Rents and Subsidies) Act 1975 gave local authorities discretionary powers to delegate management of council housing to co-ops. Indeed, the Department of the Environment (DoE) Working Party on Housing Co-operatives (the Campbell Committee) recommended that 10 per cent of the Housing Corporation's Approved Development Programme (ADP) should be devoted to co-ops. Some powers were also given to local authorities to do this (Circular 8/76), but very little use was made of these powers. Thus, for over a decade, despite powers under the 1975 Act, tenant management through the mechanism of co-operatives made no more than a token impact. Par value co-ops and some short-life co-ops (using vacant and derelict dwellings) were the only significant, if minor, activity.

This situation, however, changed dramatically in the late 1980s and early 1990s arising from Section 27 of the Housing Act 1985, which gave local authorities powers to transfer specific housing-management functions to 'another person'. The mechanism for such transfer was the 'management agreement'. This legislation further enabled local authorities to put management functions out to tender through CCT and Statutory Instrument (SI) 1994/1671 under the Local Government Act 1988 defined those activities. Management agreements made as a result of CCT have to conform to a consultative framework similar to that under a voluntary transfer under Section 27 of the 1985 Act. This framework was subsequently inserted into Section 131 of the Leasehold Reform, Housing and Urban Development Act 1993. Local authorities need to inform tenants of agreements and the identities of the managers. Tenants are entitled to make their view known, but there is no right for tenants to veto a proposed management agreement. The limited power of the tenants' ballot to block management changes was not in this case to be allowed to override the government's intention to bring the benefits of the market to council housing.

The situation in which the tenants themselves proactively serve notice on a local authority proposing a management agreement is regulated under the Housing (Right to Manage) Regulations 1994, SI 1994/627. Thus, a tenant management organization (TMO) serves a right-to-manage notice on the authority giving details of the estate or geographic area defined. At least 20 per cent of all tenants must be members of the TMO and it must deliver to every household a copy of the proposal. Only TMO members can vote in the first ballot and a majority must support the proposal for it to progress to the next stage. If the outcome is successful the TMO selects a training agency from the DoE's approved list and a feasibility study is mounted – funded by a grant under Section 429A of the 1985 Act. If the study concludes that there are reasonable grounds to proceed, a full ballot of *all* tenants is conducted. There follows a further training period to help develop the requisite management skills among the tenant body. (A more detailed examination of training for tenant participation can be found in Benita Wishart's and Rob Furbey's discussion in Chapter 9.)

Further assistance for tenant training has been given through Section 16 of the Housing and Planning Act 1986. Resources have been given to tenant bodies exploring the idea of establishing a TMO to assist with skills training and working towards establishing a management agreement. A wide variety of agencies have sought to take advantage of Section 16 finance – nationally the Priority Estates Project (PEP) and the Tenant Participation Advisory Service (TPAS) have been significant, and locally, community development groups, consultant training specialists, housing associations, adult education colleges and even universities have been funded. Section 16 funding was also used to support tenant bursaries on the National Certificate in Tenant Participation course, organized as part of the Chartered Institute of Housing's certificated training programme (see Chapter 9). The Section 16 budget expanded to £4.9 million in 1991–92, aimed primarily at developing tenant involvement in estate regeneration schemes. The motivation behind such an apparently generous increase in state support for tenants' organizations is, however, clearly aligned to the government's desire to encourage 'citizenship' and foster its ideological ambition of developing independence, initiative and breaking the mould of welfare dependency.

By the early 1990s there was a considerable scale of activity focused on TMO initiatives involving Estate Management Boards (EMBs), mainly under the auspices of the PEP which aimed to shelter tenants from the full burden of estate management. DoE research identified 117 TMOs already established or under preparation and a further 54 local authorities were actively engaged in helping set up a TMO (DoE 1994). Such a scale of activity is unprecedented. The whole face of housing management was considerably changed even where these initiatives were not mounted. Everywhere tenants became known as 'customers' and the impact of this central framework, with financial incentives suitably deployed (with the implication of penalties), drew even the most reluctant authorities into the era of the tenant-customer. The range of responses has, accordingly, been very varied. At one extreme there has been little more than tokenism (such as 'satisfaction surveys' or 'user panels') but at the other extreme enthusiastically embraced – although even here a glance over the shoulder at the proposal for Local Housing Companies, mooted in an early 1995 Consultation Paper but, in the end, not given force in the Housing Act 1996, had some influence.

Conclusions

As has been stressed throughout this chapter, tenants of municipal authorities and housing associations are and remain just that – tenants. It has been shown how the tradition of English law was to neglect tenants' rights, being based fundamentally on common-law principles derived from nineteenth-century private landlordism. It was only in the Housing Act 1980 that tenants' rights began to be shaped in a statutory form. This happened, however, at a time when the emphasis in policy switched very firmly towards individualism. Hence, the principal right enshrined in the Tenants' Charter was the right to buy – the right to cease to be a tenant. Collective rights were also consequently very undeveloped, remaining merely at the level of consultation procedures. Even when collective force could be exerted in the context of negotiations leading to a ballot, tenants could not enforce any agreements unilaterally because they themselves were not the contracting party and were precluded from inserting negotiated outcomes into their tenancy agreements.

Latterly the centrally constructed frameworks for tenant participation have allowed for a greater volume of activity – notably the mushrooming of TMOs. But here too the message is cautionary, because there is no doubt that the context for this was the desire of the former Conservative government to continue its deconstruction of the welfare state, create individualized consumers and 'independently minded' citizens, and above all a centralization of control from which to launch varieties of 'market solutions'. The constant theme behind all housing policy was how to bring the benefits of the market to tenants. Participation, if indeed this is an accurate label for what has taken place, is a far cry from the autonomous tenants' movements, described by John Grayson in Chapter 2 and which have been a longstanding feature of the social history of housing in Britain. Let it not be forgotten, however, that this tradition is one of great flexibility, instrumentality and adaptability. It may be that from within the highly circumscribed position of the management agreement the vision and creativity of the tenant body will release new approaches and new forms of activity, engendering greater control over their own lives and the lives of their neighbours. It is a latent and powerful tradition.

As to the law, it has at least moved much more centrally into the statutory regulation of tenancies and there is no doubt that for the future a more fully blown Tenants' Charter is needed, involving more than mere consultation to include a sharing of decision-making, rights to representation on statutory committees and so on. The gains in recent years have been almost entirely those of an individual nature and these now need to be enhanced by a range of collective rights which reflect more accurately and fairly the truly collective nature of social housing. It might have been that Local Housing Companies under the Housing Act 1996 became a nascent version of the Swedish Municipal Housing Companies, analysed by Bo Bengtsson and David Clapham in Chapter 5, or the Danish housing association movement, where tenants are able to negotiate with their landlords from a position of power. In this way the yawning gulf between the rights of the public and private sectors in housing can begin to be narrowed. Indeed, it would be entirely possible to harmonize the public and private rental sectors – as is the case in the Scandinavian and Austro-German traditions of housing – through legal terms and conditions that are common to both public and private tenants, as well as an equalization of the housing subsidy system. Such a form of 'social market' is surely the way forward, but requires the jettisoning of what Kemeny calls the 'command system' of housing in which housing tenures are rigidly demarcated (Kemeny 1992). Thus, it is probably appropriate not to end on a point of law but to acknowledge that, whatever else happens, without sustained investment in and financial support for housing as a whole, no amount of tenant participation or any number of tenant-management agreements will be of any use in developing a more equitable housing system.

References

Cole, I. and Furbey, R. (1994), *The Eclipse of Council Housing*, London: Routledge.

Department of the Environment (DoE) (1994), *Training for Management*, London: HMSO.

Frankenberg, R. (1966), *Communities in Britain*, Harmondsworth: Penguin.

Furbey, R., Wishart, B. and Grayson, J. (1996), 'Training for tenants: "citizens" and the enterprise culture', *Housing Studies*, 11(2), pp.251–269.

Hughes, D. (1991), 'Tenants' rights' in Lowe, S. and Hughes, D. (eds), *A New Century of Social Housing*, Leicester: Leicester University Press, pp.90–99.

Hughes, D. and Lowe, S. (1995), *Social Housing Law and Policy*, London: Butterworth.

Kemeny, J. (1992), *Housing and Social Theory*, London: Routledge.

Lowe, S. (1986), *Urban Social Movements: The City After Castells*, Basingstoke: Macmillan.

Mullins, D., Niner, P. and Riseborough, M. (1993), 'Large-scale voluntary transfers' in Malpass, P. and Means, R. (eds), *Implementing Housing Policy*, Buckingham: Open University Press, pp.169–184.

Saunders, P. (1979), *Urban Politics: A Sociological Interpretation*, London: Hutchinson.

Smith, M.E.H. (1989), *Guide to Housing*, London: Housing Centre Trust.

Stewart, A. (1994) 'Rethinking housing law: a contribution to the debate on tenure', *Housing Studies*, 9(2), pp.263–279.

7 Transforming estates

Jerry Smith

The question of whether to involve residents in estate regeneration and tenure change is no longer at issue. For several years programmes such as Estate Action have required resident involvement as a funding criterion, while mandatory ballots and the provision of independent information, advice and support to tenants are enshrined in regulations governing large-scale voluntary transfers (LSVTs), moves to establish tenant management organizations (TMOs) and the transfer of estates to Local Housing Companies (LHCs). The question which persists is 'how?'.

This chapter will examine what we can learn from a wealth of experience of community involvement in estate regeneration going back over 20 years – a period in which mistakes have too often been repeated, wheels reinvented and good ideas lain stillborn for lack of funding or influential support.

Policy background and context

The first serious attempts at the modernization of the oldest large council estates began in the early 1970s when some local authorities declared their own pre-war estates as General Improvement Areas (GIAs) under the Housing Act 1969, thereby obtaining central government support for their improvement. Since the properties in question invariably had outside toilets, and sometimes lacked bathrooms, they were not of an acceptable standard. However, the 1969 Act was clearly aimed at the improvement of much older areas of private housing and the loophole was soon closed. The 1969 Act was one of the first to recognize the importance of resident consultation, at a time before tenant participation became commonplace in housing departments.

For many thousands of tenants, the fact that their landlord was seeking their views was an important novelty which arguably played a part in the growth of the tenants' movement at the time (although a bigger factor was undoubtedly the rent rises introduced in the Housing Finance Act 1972).

The housing and urban policy focus of the 1970s, however, was the discovery of the 'inner city' and, for the remainder of the decade, council estates were out of vogue. Housing departments were aware of the problems on estates but saw them in terms of management, or in the worst cases simply blamed the tenants and saw no particular reason to change their own practices. Tenants, too, were aware of the problems and often organized themselves to tackle them. But without a sympathetic ear they tended to be unsuccessful, ending up as short-lived movements or marginalized 'militant' pressure groups, or moving in the direction of 'safe issues' such as providing community services (for instance, play provision or welfare rights).

The growing housing profession and the Department of the Environment (DoE) were by the end of the decade beginning to take the problems of council estates seriously. A programme of DoE research ultimately led to the creation of the Priority Estates Project (PEP) within the department in the early years of the 1979 Thatcher administration. The PEP programme was the first to include tenant participation as a key element in a package of wider housing management and urban design reforms aimed at 'turning around' estates which had become 'difficult to let' (Power 1984). The terminology in quotes indicates that the focus remained on the concerns of those managing council housing rather than those living in it, but the importance of including tenants for the first time as stakeholders in finding solutions to the problems of run-down estates is difficult to overestimate.

In the original PEP model tenant participation was justified in terms of value for money. Given the housing-management orientation of the message this is entirely understandable. But despite some attempts to list the potential financial benefits of tenant involvement (such as lower maintenance costs of environmental improvements), no serious research was done or, so far as the author is aware, ever has been done, comparing the long- or medium-run costs of estate management of improved estates which had had tenant involvement with those which had not. While the arguments were logical and sound, the sceptics were not convinced and for some time afterwards the proven elements of the PEP approach were increasingly adopted while the more fragile ones, including tenant participation, were too often ignored.

Tenant participation, long established in some localities, first gained general recognition in the Duke of Edinburgh's *Inquiry into British Housing*. The recommendation of this Inquiry led directly to the establishment of national organizations, Tenant Participation Advisory Services (TPAS) agencies, to promote, support and develop tenant participation in England, Wales and, for a time, Northern Ireland. These followed the successful example of TPAS Scotland which had been established some years earlier (JRF 1985).

The inner city is, perhaps, a metaphoric rather than a geographic construct. During the 1980s, peripheral estates gradually supplanted inner areas as a concern of urban policy. From the 1981 Census data it became clear that in many cities and large towns it was these areas of (largely) council housing which figured most prominently in the indices of economic and social deprivation. The only missing element was race. By the end of the decade crime, rioting and other disturbances had become more commonplace on outlying council estates than in inner areas (Campbell 1993). This was not just a housing problem. It was not even 'about' unemployment, or poverty, or the chronic lack of facilities for young people. It was about the alienation of a significant section of the population in such estates from any concept of society or community. Crime, anti-social behaviour and disturbances on estates are directed at least as much against the communities living in those estates as against the police or other representatives of external authority.

These issues, of crime, security and anti-social behaviour, have long been at the top of the agenda of estate residents. In recent years they have also found their way into a range of policy initiatives focused on estates, from City Challenge to the Safer Cities Programme, and have also been reflected in housing-led programmes such as Estate Action. The solutions, however, have tended to be seen in physical or 'hardware' terms rather than in terms of involving residents. From the 'designing out crime' approaches of influential researchers such as Alice Coleman (1985) to the 'target hardening' (window locks, stronger doors, CCTV, entry-control systems) so favoured by Safer Cities and others, the only people who are deemed to have nothing to contribute to solving the problems are the victims. Neighbourhood Watch schemes, so commonplace in most urban and rural areas, are notably absent from the worst council estates (Mayhew *et al.* 1989). Community-development approaches to crime prevention and, latterly, drugs issues are remarkable as much for their rarity as their success (Lightfoot 1994).

Top of the housing-management agenda in 1996, however, is the closely related problem of 'neighbour nuisance', encompassing both criminal activities (such as drug-dealing and vandalism) and non-criminal activities (such as excessive noise and unruly dogs or children). While it is gratifying to note that local authorities, some housing associations and even, up to a point, government in the form of the Housing Act 1996 and Labour's subsequent proposals are belatedly taking seriously one of the longest-held grievances of tenants, examples of solutions which involve tenants themselves (as opposed to new or stronger forms of enforcement by public authorities) are rare. A tenants' conference on the subject in April 1996, sponsored by the Local Authorities Working Group on Anti-Social Behaviour, made a number of demands, but all are aimed at central and local government or the police rather than giving tenants' organizations a direct role; very understandable, but disappointing from a tenant-participation perspective.

The other non-housing issue which attracted serious policy attention from the 1980s onwards was economic development. Several Scottish estate initiatives, culminating in the 'New Life for Urban Scotland' programme, featured community enterprise development. This has been much less common south of the border, although there have been prominent exceptions such as the regeneration of Hulme in Manchester. The more typical pattern has been that of local economic development agencies, often sponsored by government departments other than the DoE, sometimes focusing their attention and resources on housing estates. Examples include several Inner City Task Forces, Urban Development Corporations, English Partnerships and City Challenge schemes. The approach taken by most of these bodies has concentrated heavily on creating training and employment places for residents in target areas, rather than the development of community enterprise.

The DoE itself was responsible for developing the Estate Action programme and its predecessor, Community Refurbishment Schemes (CRS). Both CRS and the early Estate Action projects made attempts to connect physical improvement with jobs and training. There were also connections made between CRS/Estate Action funding for housing and environmental improvements and Urban Programme funding for refurbishing or creating community facilities. Later, resident involvement was made a requirement of Estate Action funding. The DoE seemed to be getting somewhere near to the kind of approach which estate residents wanted and which a host of underfunded but innovative community projects had been pioneering for some years. But a series of unconnected government policy changes rendered the new approach stillborn. CRS and Estate Action employment initiatives depended, first, on using the Community Programme to provide short-term employment for residents on a variety of schemes (mainly concerned with environmental improvements and running community facilities and activities) and, second, on local authorities requiring outside contractors to use local labour where this could be demonstrated to be appropriate. The closure of the Community Programme and the outlawing of local labour clauses in local authority contracts effectively killed off the initiative. A few years later, the Urban Programme itself was abandoned, thereby removing the links between improving homes and improved community facilities.

The DoE had a few other cards to play. In its promotion of TMOs the department used promises of Estate Action funding as an enticement to tenants and local authorities to establish either tenant management co-operatives (TMCs) or estate management boards (EMBs). This inducement, however, was withdrawn with the introduction of the right to manage regulations in 1994, severing any links that existed between estate regeneration and tenant management.

In the handful of areas where they have been established, Housing Action Trusts (HATs) have a broad responsibility for economic and social development, as well as housing, in addition to a remit to involve tenants. However successful HATs have been (and opinions differ sharply) they are not, nor were they designed to be, a generally replicable approach.

In the wake of an influential report pointing out the dangers inherent in housing associations developing estates almost exclusively for low-income households and without accompanying social, educational or employment opportunities (Page 1994), and of the positive lessons from the 'People for Action' organization (McArthur 1995), the Housing Corporation has established its 'Housing Plus' initiative, providing funding for housing associations wishing to promote and develop such opportunities. While the objectives behind 'Housing Plus' are laudable, the small scale of the funding and its insistence on innovation at the expense of replicating and building on established good practice mean that it is doomed to play only a very marginal role in this important field.

The final area of housing policy which has an effect on estate regeneration is stock transfer. Until recently this has been restricted to sales to private developers (for improvement or redevelopment for sale) or to housing associations (for a combination of rented, shared ownership and housing for sale). The housing association transfers are of three kinds: 'trickle transfers' of individual properties as they become vacant; small-scale voluntary transfers of perhaps a few hundred properties which could be better managed outside the local authority portfolio for a variety of geographical and other reasons; and large-scale voluntary transfers (LSVTs) of up to 5000 properties. Although such transfers rarely involve a full-scale modernization package, housing associations have access to private finance and are able to offer tenants the chance of having outstanding repairs cleared up and some improvements done. The LSVT process is governed by regulations which require independent advice to tenants on the options available (in terms of rent and service-charge levels, repairs and improvements, tenancy conditions and tenant-participation arrangements) and a ballot of tenants to decide whether the transfer should go ahead. This process can be highly empowering but its relationship to estate regeneration is, to date, slight. Almost all LSVTs have involved the transfer of the entire stock of smaller local authorities, although there are signs that some larger authorities are considering LSVTs for large peripheral or overspill estates. The recent transfer of Manchester's Partington overspill estate to Manchester and

District Housing Association involved extensive tenant organization and participation in what will, for most purposes, be a community-based subsidiary body of the housing association (Bright 1995).

The Housing Act 1996 paved the way for the establishment of Local Housing Companies (LHCs) as a way of securing investment in large, run-down estates. While the precise details of how LHCs will operate are not yet clear, they will involve a 'partnership' between local authorities, financial institutions, developers, housing associations and residents. There are some examples of LHCs already in existence including a few which are community based, such as the Royds scheme in Bradford based on three adjacent peripheral estates. While there is serious interest in many local authorities (and within the Chartered Institute of Housing) in LHCs, at the time of writing, most were waiting on the outcome of the 1997 general election before making any firm commitment. If LHCs do become popular as an approach to estate regeneration under 'New Labour', they would seem to have some particular attractions. They will require tenant and resident involvement to a high degree, and will have a brief which encompasses economic and social development as well as housing renewal and management.

Summarizing the above, only rarely have estates as neighbourhood communities been the focus of policy attention. More typically, estate-based initiatives have been aimed at tackling one symptom of the malaise, rarely taking cognizance of other (previous or current) related policy initiatives. Too often the search for solutions within the DoE has been frustrated by the (unintended?) consequences of policy changes elsewhere – such as the closure of the Community Programme and the Urban Programme, or changes in local government legislation or the benefits system.

Ask almost any tenants' and residents' association what the problems of its estate are and housing will probably figure as but one of many, including crime and security, anti-social behaviour, the lack of facilities for children and young people, and unemployment. It is not surprising that housing-led 'solutions' have so often failed to engage the interest and commitment of residents. The Single Regeneration Budget (SRB) brought together a range of departmental programmes in an attempt to tackle these diverse and related issues holistically – although not only on estates, of course. Is the SRB the answer? On paper, the integrated approach is just what residents want. In practice, the SRB to date has been characterized as 'a missed opportunity' to involve communities (Clarke 1995). The drawbacks of the approach are:

● Short bidding timescales militate against community-based schemes and lead to overdependence on packages put together by local authorities using 'off-the-shelf' projects for which they have previously been seeking funding.

- The emphasis on economic development may well be correct, but from a community perspective this requires a fine-grained, community enterprise approach related to redressing the lack of social facilities, development of informal economic activities and the creation of community-owned assets.
- The SRB, in common with its predecessors, suffers from being largely a capital funding scheme, thereby running the risk of creating 'white elephant' community facilities without the staff or revenue to manage them effectively and efficiently.

In 1995 a report was published which summarized three years of action research into all aspects of estate regeneration (Taylor 1995). This was the final report of the Joseph Rowntree Foundation's (JRF) *Action on Estates* programme, which combined 33 studies of work on over 100 estates. The report calls for a national and regional policy framework for local regeneration to replace both the current and recent policy assumption that the market will ultimately produce solutions, and the rather more longstanding problem of separate departmental approaches which, as we have seen, only rarely connect with one another (despite the introduction of the SRB) and which are at the mercy of the unintended consequences of entirely separate policies. The report also points out that the root problem of such estates is not housing but poverty, and by implication that housing-led approaches will have at best only a partial impact. What is required is an inter-disciplinary approach to policy which Butcher (1993) calls 'community policy', characterized by the following:

- The pursuit of goals which embrace the 'community values' of solidarity, participation and coherence.
- The targets/beneficiaries of policy being seen as members of a community.
- Engagement with groups/organizations acting collectively at the community level.
- Priority given to disadvantaged, oppressed and marginalized sections of society.

Whilst a number of reservations have been expressed about the JRF studies' assumptions (see Chapters 4 and 12), it is with the more immediate practical conclusions of the report that the remainder of this chapter is concerned. These are the following:

- Estates contain substantial energies and skills which can be harnessed given the right approach.
- Providing technical and professional support to communities is essential.

- The ways in which mainstream services are delivered to estates need to change.
- Regeneration programmes need to create both long-term employment opportunities and community-owned assets.
- Long timescales are required for effective resident involvement.

The remainder of the chapter will consider these key themes in relation to: (a) holistic approaches to estate regeneration; (b) the role of professionals in estate regeneration; (c) building partnerships with the community; and (d) notions of sustainability.

Holistic approaches

Estates tend to be seen as the responsibility of the landlord, whether the local authority housing department or a housing association. It is not only other agencies which take this view but also many tenants and, crucially, housing authorities themselves. The tradition of bureaucratic paternalism in British public rented housing is long and deep, and its history is one in which tenants and landlord have been locked together in mutual dependence (see Chapter 2). Tenants have expected 'the council' (meaning the 'housing department') to solve estate problems; and landlords have needed a dependent body of tenants, especially in recent years, to fight off continued threats to the very provision of council housing, notably the ill-conceived 1988 'Tenants' Choice' legislation recently repealed.

Many landlords and tenants will bridle at this description of their relationship, and it is admittedly an oversimplification which has been changing since at least the early 1980s. But it remains the case that many, probably most, estate initiatives are based on improving the landlord–tenant relationship. What has changed, and it should not be underestimated, is that tenants are more likely to be treated as customers with consumer rights rather than as passive recipients of a housing service delivered by people who know 'what's best for them'. But this, as Hambleton and Hoggett (1987) point out, is a far cry from the 'collectivist' solution which treats tenants as 'citizens' with a wide range of concerns and helps them to organize both to meet these needs directly and to represent themselves to bodies other than their landlord.

Yet how realistic is it to make a hard-and-fast distinction between consumerism and collectivism? Projects designed to empower tenants as consumers of housing services may well have the effect of empowering them more broadly as citizens, often through the medium of training (see Chapter 9).

From the JRF research programme and from other examples it emerges that the estate initiatives most likely to break out of the consumerist, landlord/tenant strait-jacket are those which are led from the community itself. Examples of holistic approaches which are 'top down' are rare, but one exception is the Bell Farm project in York where a particularly enlightened and corporate local authority led the way in helping residents to negotiate a series of service agreements with a very diverse range of statutory and voluntary agencies. More common, although still all too rare, are community-led initiatives such as the Miles Platting Community Assembly (Manchester) which has harnessed local energies to deliver a wide range of services and community enterprises. Other examples are the work of residents of the Belle Isle estate in Leeds (discussed in more detail in Chapter 10), the Pembroke Street estate in Devonport (Watson 1994) or the Meadowell estate in North Shields (Gibson 1993). In all these cases, and many more, it was the residents who insisted on setting the agenda and refused to limit it to one of physical refurbishment.

Holistic approaches are most commonly characterized by a strong, committed local leadership with a 'vision' which enables it to link capital investment to jobs and training, and to use physical refurbishment to 'lever' funds from non-housing sources to provide for other community needs. But however strong the local leadership, it needs to find a response somewhere within the power structure. In practice, there are very few successful estate regeneration experiences which are purely either 'bottom up' or 'top down'. Success usually means combining both; whether this happens depends certainly on the quality of local leadership and community organization, but also on the response of professionals at all levels.

The role of professionals

One of the characteristics of estates, by contrast with most inner-city areas, is that very few professionals live in them (Holmes 1992). For professionals, housing estates are a workplace, not a community. Moreover, most day-to-day professional contact with estate residents concentrates on those who either have, or cause, problems. Housing officers see more of tenants with rent arrears, or who complain vociferously about repairs, than they do of the larger number of more satisfied tenants who pay their rent regularly. Social workers spend their time almost exclusively with individuals and families who are either physically or mentally infirm, or have serious emotional and psychological difficulties – a tiny minority of estate residents. The police and probation service get to know villains and their victims. All of this is likely to create a professional mind-set that people who live on estates need to be either helped, or managed, or both.

There are exceptions. The principal ones are the professionals whose work is in schools (especially primary schools) and places of worship, and to a lesser extent neighbourhood-based voluntary agencies. Many such professionals identify strongly with the communities they serve. This can be a mixed blessing. At best, they can provide the initial leadership, the ignition which sets in motion community organizations. At worst, they may either limit their role to providing services to the community in the most patronizing fashion, or else supplant or stifle the emergence of genuine local leadership.

How effectively professionals promote or hold back community regeneration depends on the stance they adopt. Wilcox (1994) identifies five distinct stances: providing information; consulting residents; deciding together; acting together; and supporting community initiatives. These should not be seen as either a simple hierarchy or mutually exclusive. In practice, 'deciding together' and 'acting together' with the community may be far more challenging to established ways of working than 'supporting community initiatives' with grants and other assistance, while 'information', as well as being a stance in itself, forms part of every other approach.

Community empowerment is more likely to result from professionals sharing problems, ideas, decisions and responsibilities with communities than from simply providing services and resources, no matter how sensitively delivered. There are, it is true, a very few well-organized and highly articulate communities which have the capacity to take on the management of their estates, or significant aspects of it, and require of professionals and agencies only that they provide adequate funding, information and other resources and do not get in the way. And there is no reason in principle why all neighbourhoods could not in time become equally self-reliant. In practice, the policy context is unlikely in the foreseeable future to permit more than a few 'experiments' at any one time. In any event, the long and often troubled history of community action in such estates, outlined by John Grayson in Chapter 2, is often forgotten or glossed over in the understandable desire to concentrate on current achievements and successes. The best option for most estates, then, is perhaps not community control but some form of community-based partnership, which we consider below.

Before leaving our discussion of the role of professionals, however, we need to consider the other main kind of professional intervention in communities – that of the external consultant or trainer. Such interventions are usually for a strictly time-limited period, ranging from one-off training sessions through to sustained but occasional consultancy support over a period of possibly two years. Hyatt (1995) studied six such interventions and found that their value to the community depended on the extent to which the community itself had sought the intervention (including the selection of the consultant and being signatory to the contract). Equally important was the presence of a 'community support worker' on a more permanent basis to help the community organization to maintain momentum in between the sporadic visits of the consultant. Both these elements were perceived to be as important as the abilities and qualities of the consultant or trainer.

The work of consultants and trainers ranges from simply providing digestible information on complex subjects through to using sophisticated operational research or organizational development techniques, taking in such disciplines as community arts, architecture and technical aid on the way. At their worst, such consultants can be insensitive, inflexible in their approach, or just downright lazy. At their best they can achieve more in a very short period of contact time than some locally based professionals achieve in years.

The contribution the arts can make to community regeneration is documented by Landy *et al.* (1996). They demonstrate that participatory arts programmes enhance social cohesion, improve the image of a neighbourhood (both to itself and outsiders), promote interest in the environment, enhance partnerships and local organizational strengths, and help residents to form a vision of their future which motivates and drives their efforts. Similar documented claims, although sometimes based on more limited experience, have been made for community technical aid (Watson 1994), community architecture (Kean 1992), 'Planning for Real' and associated techniques (Gibson 1991, 1993), community operational research (see Chapter 10) and community organizational development (Batson and Smith 1995).

While the use of consultancy techniques in regeneration is still in its infancy, training has long been seen as an important aspect of any regeneration agency's intervention strategy. The vision of training usually on offer, however, tends to be a limited one, confined to some combination of accredited, NVQ-based training aimed at employability and information provision. This is sometimes misleadingly referred to as 'capacity building'. Fordham (1995) teases out this vogue (and vague) term into four components:

- individual capacity (for instance personal skills, knowledge and confidence);
- collective or organizational capacity (for instance committee skills, financial management, and recruiting and retaining members);
- infrastructure (for instance access to networks or agencies providing technical or other specialist information, and advice and assistance); and
- institutional capacity (that is, developing community-based agencies

with the long-term potential to develop and manage the regeneration process).

Most training provided through estate regeneration has addressed the first of these while the others have remained under-resourced. A study by the Tenant Participation Advisory Service (TPAS) and Sheffield Hallam University (Phillips 1995) found that tenants rated training as their second highest priority, after having somewhere to meet, but that there was insufficient awareness: (a) by tenants of what training resources were available, especially in further and higher education; and (b) by trainers and adult educators of the existence or training needs of tenants' organizations. Developing a greater understanding of the potential role which training can play, and bringing together needs and resources from across a wide spectrum of provision, remain key tasks which estate regeneration programmes need to address. (For a fuller discussion of training strategies for tenant participation see Chapter 9.)

Partnerships with the community

The *Action on Estates* studies suggest that there is an enormous imbalance between residents and the other partners in terms of organizational capacity, time, access to money and staff resources, and legitimacy and power (Taylor 1995). 'Partnership' was the buzzword after 'empowerment' began to seem jaded and before 'stakeholder' took over. It is an easy concept to subscribe to, but the devil itself to realize. Our concern, like Taylor's, is with how communities can take an equal place in a 'partnership' whose activities increasingly govern the quality of their lives (Hastings and McArthur 1995). Before considering this, however, it is instructive to recognize the imbalances of power between the other partners. Most regeneration partnerships (and perhaps in the future Local Housing Companies) are dominated in practice by local authorities, despite government restrictions on the level of their formal representation. This is because local authorities have the experience, the key relationships and most of the knowledge, information and staff resources needed to make regeneration work. They lack, of course, the funding to do so and some of them lack both the skills and the vision, but the powers they do hold are quite sufficient to control the agenda and speed of the regeneration process. As one local government officer put it to the author recently, speaking of a specific project, 'If you think the community are out of their depth in this partnership you should see the private sector!' Whether a community regeneration partnership works, then, depends above all on the attitude of the local authority.

This factor can work to the advantage of the community, provided that they enjoy good relations with the local authority. Given that the local authority is the principal power-holder, this in turn requires it to be committed to devolving real power to communities, which it is only likely to consider if it is convinced of the reliability, representativeness and competence of the community organization(s) concerned. How, then, can communities achieve and demonstrate these qualities?

Reliability implies a consistent performance over time. Studies of community partnerships have identified one of the success factors as being a long tradition of community action and community projects (McArthur 1995, MacFarlane 1993). A short-term programme aimed at an estate with weak or non-existent tenants' and community organizations is unlikely to achieve anything in this sphere, even if much is achieved in terms of physical improvement. However, it is not only a question of longevity, but of the nature of community action and the activists attracted to it. A run-down and neglected estate is likely to throw up protest and campaign groups (if it produces any grass-roots activity at all). These may be articulate and effective, but often the leadership have an agenda of pressurizing the authorities to improve services and resources, and no interest whatever in playing a part in managing those services and resources. The real potential strengths may lie not in the high-profile campaigning groups, but in lower-profile community service organizations such as playgroups, advice centres and community centres. Community action on estates often flows through a sequence from campaigning to consultation to management. Different people in the community will be attracted to each phase and as the nature of the game inevitably changes new players must continually be sought.

Representativeness is at least as important as reliability. While sometimes used as a convenient stick with which to beat community activists expressing controversial views or demands, it is nonetheless reasonable to expect any community members being offered real power to be able to demonstrate that they are speaking for the majority of residents – provided, of course, that other partners are willing to offer the help and resources required to enable them to be both representative and accountable. There is also the issue of where the burden of proof should lie. It is too easily assumed that it is up to community leaders to prove that they are representative. Why should it not be the task of those who doubt them to prove (through surveys, for example) that they are not?

But the big question often begged is, just what do we mean by being 'representative'? Elected councillors are representative in a narrow, political sense. In a broader, sociological sense, they are often anything but, being overwhelmingly male, white and middle-aged. A community group with an imperfect constitution, but which draws its membership and its agenda from the residents for whom it speaks, is arguably more 'representative' than one which is scrupulously constitutional but elected at a poorly attended AGM and whose active members are disproportionately of one gender, ethnic or age group.

Nevertheless, the one source of power which community activists can draw on and point to is that of being democratically accountable. Donnison (1988) assessed the 'success factors' of community organizations as being very largely to do with their accountability and their political skills and connections (the other factors were charismatic, committed leadership and a tradition of community action in the locality). It is therefore in the interests of community partners to accept at least partially the requirement to be visibly representative and accountable, but to insist on a broad rather than a narrow definition which focuses on the agenda as much as on the formal trappings of democracy.

Competence is the third quality required of community partners. Competence is partly a function of experience (the question of a local tradition of community action again), partly something which can be gained through training and development which we explored in the previous section, but also partly a question of how easy or difficult other partners make life for community representatives. The overuse of jargon, over-reliance on the written word, unexplained technicalities, and the sheer volume of work laid at the door of busy volunteers (most other partners being professionals doing the job in their work time) are all unfortunate characteristics of too many estate regeneration programmes which demoralize, deskill and demotivate community activists (Hastings and McArthur 1995).

Far more attention has been paid to the 'structures' for community partnership than to the processes such as those discussed in this chapter and in Charles Ritchie's account in Chapter 10. This is probably another aspect of the local authority domination of the regeneration business. Local authorities are generally very good at structure and very poor at process. But, undeniably, structures are important. Taylor (1995) notes that 'the ideal partnership structure would . . . be light, flexible and focused'. MacFarlane (1993) suggests a strong central organization (in most cases, the Partnership Board) with a range of open, less formal 'focus groups' to develop work on specific issues, with links provided by a 'steering group' comprising the chairs of the 'focus groups'. This does indeed seem the best compromise between the requirements of the different partners, and the potentially conflicting demands of efficient decision-making and maximum participation. A comparative study of ten community regeneration partnerships in Scotland and England found little recognition of the need for agencies to change their practices to accommodate the community as an equal partner. As a result, the community had little input into strategic (as opposed to operational) discussions and were often (deliberately or not) cut out of important informal negotiations (McArthur *et al.* 1996).

Finally, 'partnership' should not necessarily be taken to mean 'consensus'. Each partner will have their own agenda and priorities and disputes are all but inevitable. If such disputes are resolved only through the exercise of power then the community, as the least powerful partner, will be the loser. More powerful partners, and local authorities in particular, must be willing to compromise more than is strictly necessary, for the sake of the partnership and the long-term future of the estate. The use of independent consultancy advice, or even mediation, can be productive here. For their part, residents may need training in negotiation skills and to learn that the most effective community representative is not necessarily the one with the loudest voice and the most adamant demands.

Sustainability

A word which is almost as perplexing to define as 'community', 'sustainability' can essentially be conceived in either of two ways: that is, either as a dynamic concept involving continual renewal and replacement (the sense in which it is used by ecologists and environmentalists, for example), or as a static concept of permanence. It is the first of these which is used here.

Sustainable estate regeneration on this model requires a community which has a real stake in the maintenance (in the broadest sense) of the improvements made – whether environmental, social or economic. There are a number of aspects to this question of 'stakeholding'. The one which finds most sympathy in current national policy is that of giving residents a financial stake, usually through tenure change and the encouragement of owner-occupation. While the logic of this seems unassailable at first glance, it is in practice dependent on ability to pay. The visual evidence on many estates is there to see: poorly maintained owner-occupied properties; empty, unsaleable houses; and undeveloped privatized land.

Aside from housing equity, then, how else can communities 'buy in' to the future of their estates? One answer is through collective ownership. This could take several forms. One would be through the transfer of land, housing and other assets, including community buildings, to some form of Local Housing Company with a community majority on its board, as has been done with the three estates forming the Royds Community Association in Bradford. On a less radical level, assets, such as community centres, youth and sports facilities, might be handed over to community ownership to be run as community enterprises (although subsidy would still be required). Community-owned umbrella organizations, such as Community Development Trusts, could be formed to manage a portfolio of assets including both social and community facilities, office and workshop spaces and parcels of land for lease or sale. Such trusts, which already have a substantial track record in some areas, might also act as holding companies for service-based community enterprises in such fields as security, environmental maintenance, community care, childcare, catering, and property maintenance and management. Any trading surpluses would be reinvested in the community. Self-build (new or refurbished) housing offers another way of giving residents an economic stake in the community (Levine 1994).

Having a stake in one's community can, however, mean more than simply community ownership of assets. Stakeholding also acts at a psychological level. This is harder to pin down and to exemplify, but involves what we might call a sense of belonging, a commitment to the future, or simply that old-fashioned but still popular term 'community spirit'. This sense of collective 'psychological ownership' of an estate cannot be defined directly, but might be glimpsed through such intermediate forms as strong, secure and well-supported community organizations, a high level of social and cultural activities, and positive media coverage.

The final way in which regeneration can be sustained is through the localization of service delivery under either community control or strong community influence. Within the housing field, successful TMOs achieve this, but so too can alternatives such as 'estate agreements' or other forms of service-level agreement, even when they are not legally binding, provided that their outputs and performance indicators are sufficiently clear and specific. There is no reason such agreements might not be extended to other local services such as policing, youth work or health.

Sustainability, as Fordham (1995) argues, cannot be achieved unless it is designed and planned for at the outset. As a strategy for estate regeneration it needs to be broadly constructed, taking in the three aspects of economic ownership (both individual and, especially, collective), psychological ownership, and community management of or influence over local service delivery.

Conclusions

The body of experience and, in recent years, research into community involvement in estate regeneration is considerable. The lessons from this experience and research may briefly be summed up in the following ten points – ten commandments for community-led regeneration, if you like:

- Local and national organizations must be integrated, to the extent of 'dancing to the same tune', if not more formally constituted.

- Every successful initiative has an influential and dedicated 'champion'.
- Agencies must be prepared to change the ways existing services are delivered and budgets structured – regeneration must be more than icing on the cake.
- Agencies must be prepared to make a long-term commitment to communities.
- Lead-in times must be sufficient to allow thorough resident consultation and, where necessary, the development of effective community organizations.
- Communities must be provided with dedicated professional and technical support.
- Communities must be provided with *independent* advice and information.
- Sustainability requires handing over real economic assets to community control.
- Community leaders require 'critical support' to ensure they are not only strong but flexible and accountable.
- Process is as important as structure.

A glance through SRB, Housing Plus or ERCF proposals indicates that most of these lessons have been absorbed, at least on paper. However, practice on the ground continues to lag seriously behind the aspirations. The reasons, as this chapter has demonstrated, are a combination of the financial, the organizational and the psychological. Financially, short-termism and uncertainty militate strongly against the timescales required for effective community involvement. Organizationally, despite the rhetoric, estate regeneration remains dogged by competition between agencies for resources and power. Psychologically, those in authority too often remain reluctant to hand over real power and resources to communities or to change traditional ways of delivering services.

Disentangling this web is the real challenge for those committed to community-led regeneration in the coming years.

References

Batson, B. and Smith, J. (1995), *Organizational Development in the Community: Application, Tools and Discussion*, Leeds: International Social Policy Research Unit, Leeds Metropolitan University.

Bright, J. (1995), 'Tenants back "new model" stock transfer', *Inside Housing*, 3 November, p.6.

Butcher, H. (1993), 'Introduction: Some Examples and Definitions' in Butcher, H., Glen, A., Henderson, P. and Smith, J. (eds), *Community and Public Policy*, London: Pluto, pp.3–21.

Campbell, B. (1993), *Goliath: Britain's Dangerous Places*, London: Methuen.

Clarke, G. (1995), *A Missed Opportunity: An Initial Assessment of the 1995 Single Regeneration Budget Approvals and their Effect on Voluntary and Community Organizations*, London: NCVO.

Coleman, A. (1985), *Utopia on Trial: Vision and Reality in Planned Housing*, London: Hilary Shipman.

Donnison, D. (1988), 'Secrets of success', *New Society*, 29 January, pp. 11–13.

Fordham, G. (1995), *Made to Last: Creating Sustainable Neighbourhood and Estate Regeneration*, York: Joseph Rowntree Foundation.

Gibson, T. (1991), *Taking the Neighbourhood Initiative: A Facilitator's Guide*, London: Department of the Environment.

Gibson, T. (1993), *Danger/Opportunity*, Telford: Neighbourhood Initiatives Foundation.

Hambleton, R. and Hoggett, P. (1987), *Decentralization and Democracy: Localizing Public Services*, Occasional Paper 28, Bristol: School for Advanced Urban Studies.

Hastings, A. and McArthur, A. (1995), 'A comparative assessment of government approaches to partnership with the local community' in Hambleton, R. and Thomas, H. (eds), *Urban Policy Evaluation: Challenge and Change*, London: Paul Chapman, pp.175–193.

Holmes, A. (1992), *Limbering Up: Community Empowerment on Peripheral Estates*, Middlesbrough: RIPE.

Hyatt, J. (1995), *Calling in the Specialist: The Value of Using Consultancy in Community Capacity Building*, London: Community Development Foundation.

Joseph Rowntree Foundation (JRF) (1985), *Duke of Edinburgh's Inquiry into British Housing*, York: JRF.

Kean, J. (1992), *Organizational and Operational Structures to Enable Community Participation in the Built Environment*, Newcastle: Newcastle Architecture Workshop.

Landy, C., Greene, L., Matarasso, F. and Bianchini, F. (1996), *The Art of Regeneration*, Stroud: Comedia.

Levine, D. (1994), *I've Started So I'll Finish: A Study of Self-build Schemes for Young People in Housing Need*, Worksop: Ryton Books.

Lightfoot, J. (ed.) (1994), *Towards Safer Communities: Community Development Approaches to Crime*, London: Community Development Foundation/Crime Concern.

MacFarlane, R. (1993), *Community Involvement in City Challenge*, London: NCVO.

Mayhew, P., Elliott, D. and Dowds, L. (1989), *The 1988 British Crime Survey*, Home Office Research Study No. 111, London: HMSO.

McArthur, A. (1995), *Housing Associations and Neighbourhood Regeneration: The People for Action Initiative*, Glasgow: Centre for Housing Research and Urban Studies.

McArthur, A., McGregor, A. and Hastings, A. (1996), *Less than Equal? Community Organizations and Estate Regeneration Partnerships*, Bristol: The Policy Press.

Page, D. (1994), *Building for Communities*, York: Joseph Rowntree Foundation.

Phillips, S. (1995), *Releasing the Resources*, Salford: Tenant Participation Advisory Service.

Power, A. (1984), *Local Housing Management*, London: Department of the Environment.

Taylor, M. (1995), *Unleashing the Potential: Bringing Residents to the Centre of Regeneration*, York: Joseph Rowntree Foundation.

Watson, D. (1994), *Putting Back the Pride: A Case Study of a Power-sharing Approach to Tenant Participation*, Liverpool: ACTAC.

Wilcox, D. (1994), *The Guide to Effective Participation*, Brighton: Partnership Books.

8 The psychology of participation

Johnston Birchall

Underpinning every text on tenant participation is the assumption that people will be prepared to participate in the process; obviously, without people to take part there is no participation. Yet there have been very few attempts to measure the level of participation in different types of tenant-controlled organizations, nor has there been a systematic attempt to understand the motivations behind participation or its lack. Why are motivations to participate important? There are at least five reasons.

First, and rather obviously, without it there cannot be any dialogue between landlord and tenant. Over the last decade or so, pressure has been building up for social landlords to make themselves more accountable to their 'customers', and many have been anxious to demonstrate that they are doing so (see Platt *et al.* 1990, Fraser and Gibson 1991). Yet even if the right policies are in place, appropriate structures set up and a genuine process of consultation engaged in, without participation there is, literally, nothing happening. The types of initiative promoted by local authorities and housing associations have generally been tailored to realistic assumptions of low levels of interest among tenants, and there has been little pressure to opt for high-participation options such as tenant management co-operatives (see Phillips 1992). Where participation has proved to be low, there has been the option of falling back on, or remaining at the level of, less stringent forms of participation, such as area forums or occasional estate meetings, and then gradually building up to more permanent representative forms such as a network of tenants' associations and a federation. But no matter how flexible the strategy, at some point landlords have to measure its success in terms of the level of tenant participation.

Second, as part of its wider drive for privatization, the Conservative government was interested in pushing council housing towards the high-participation options of full or partial tenant self-management on specific estates (DoE 1992a). This raised the problem of participation in an acute form. Following the 'Tenants' Choice' legislation brought in by the Housing Act 1988, several reports and 'how-to-do-it' manuals have tried to make this relationship between participation and structure explicit, in the form of generalizations about the level of participation needed to make certain options work: tenant management co-operatives are thought to require a high level, estate management boards less and other estate-based committees even less, implying a kind of hierarchy of commitment. Assessing the likely level of interest among tenants has come to be regarded as part of the process of advising and promoting these various options; promoters have had to make guesses about the level which participation can be expected to reach in any particular situation, and then to recommend an appropriate option for tenants to pursue (see DoE n.d.). When the process became systematized by access to funding from the Department of the Environment (DoE) for estate-based tenant management organizations (TMOs) under Section 16 of the Housing Act 1986, the level of participation reached at each stage and the level of commitment to a particular proposal actually became part of the funding process; participation became a hurdle over which TMOs and their promoters had to jump in order to qualify for further funding (see Crossley 1992).

Third, there is an important link between participation and equal opportunities (discussed in greater detail in Chapter 11). The problem for landlords (and indirectly for tenants) is that unless the various forms of participation reach a level where a genuine choosing of representatives by tenants takes place it is difficult to legitimize the consultation process (see AMA 1990). Even when tenants are elected to representative bodies, low turnouts can undermine their authority. This is particularly true when they represent tenants on a committee in which other interests are also represented and where the role of tenant representative remains ambiguous (see Platt *et al.* 1987). To avoid the problem of persuading tenants in general to elect representatives, indirect elections through tenants' associations can be used, but these only push the problem of legitimacy downwards to another stage. Serious doubts have been raised about the representativeness of estate-based associations, again highlighted in Chapter 11, and researchers have found ethnic and age biases. Occasionally the motivations for forming an association are explicitly racist or élitist. The more important tenant participation becomes as part of the policy process, the more difficult it is to defer these questions of legitimacy and representativeness.

Fourth, tenants became an important part of the policy-making process in two Conservative government initiatives: compulsory competitive tendering of housing management (HMCCT) and the Single Regeneration Budget (SRB). These raised the problem of participation in an acute form. The HMCCT process was a complicated one, requiring tenant representatives who were prepared to spend enormous amounts of time being trained, and then attending numerous meetings choosing contractors to go on a tender list, awarding contracts and monitoring them as part of an ongoing process (DoE 1992a, Part 4). They were expected by the government to legitimate a policy which was not of their own choosing and to which the majority of tenant activists had been reportedly hostile or indifferent. There were reports of tenants dropping out of the whole process one by one until only one or two (generally retired) people remained. On the other hand, there were also positive signs that, where tenants did stay the course, involvement in the process had enabled them for the first time to specify what they meant by housing management and what they regarded as important. Their involvement in monitoring contracts was possibly a way in which they could move up the 'ladder' of participation from consultation to real choice about services. Similarly, in the SRB the involvement of local residents is a condition of local partnerships submitting bids, and local authorities in particular are having to find ways of creating structures through which residents can be empowered to take part.

Fifth, the level of participation is important to the implementation of tenants' rights. (For a fuller discussion on the legal context of tenant participation see Chapter 6.) It is not difficult to make the distinction between different types of rights: those referring to individual tenants and their home and collective rights conferred on groups of tenants, rights enshrined in law and those which are granted by a landlord as an accepted part of good practice, and so on (Birchall 1992). Lurking underneath this kind of discussion is another distinction to which it is harder to put a label, between rights which are easily claimed and acted on by tenants and those which, while being on the statute book, are relatively unused. Contrast the succession rights to a council tenancy, which are well known and used, and the 'right to repair' granted in the Housing Act 1980 to tenants dissatisfied with the landlord's performance, which has been very little used. In any attempt to implement consumer rights there has to be an awareness of the conditions which make for the active use of rights: access to information and legal advice, self-confidence, an open attitude among officials, a clear complaints procedure, backup from tenants' associations and so on (Birchall 1992). One basic condition is, of course, the willingness of tenants to participate in the process of claiming their rights.

What does the literature on tenant participation tell us? Scattered throughout the many reports and manuals there are occasional glimpses into the level of participation achieved, and even more occasional attempts to explain this. For instance, a London Housing Unit report says:

> it is clear that different schemes have varying levels of involvement either because they do not have the same structure or because they are at different stages in their growth. (Dickson and Robertson 1993 p.130)

The report provides evidence for what promoters had expected, that there are lower participation rates in estate management boards (EMBs) than in tenant management co-operatives (TMCs), but it also finds that this is not explained simply by the larger size of EMBs. The passage of time is seen as an important factor: other things being equal, participation levels decline over time. However, these tantalizing suggestions remain undeveloped and are not connected up with any theory of what motivates individuals to participate.

Participation manuals tend to give advice based on an implicit understanding of the costs of participating, advising that a crèche should be available, a warm and comfortable room should be chosen for meetings and so on. They acknowledge that participation has to be rewarding or else tenants will cease to participate; their complaints have to be acted on, and the process of participation has to be more than tokenistic. Scattered among these generalizations are theories of human motivation, but these are not made explicit or used in a systematic way. George Homans says, in relation to more general social behaviour, that everyone offers generalizations, maxims and proverbs, but 'each of these . . . while telling an important part of the truth, never tells it all, and nobody tries to put them together' (Homans 1961 p.1).

What is participation?

Before presenting theories of motivation, it is important to understand what we mean by participation. There are at least three types. First, there is taking part in decision-making, involving attendance at general meetings, becoming a committee member and so on. This is thought to be the crucial type because without it decision-making is not democratic, officers are not called to account and tenant-led organizations do not achieve autonomy. But there is also, second, more direct action such as clearing land, picking up rubbish, gardening, running playgroups and so on. Where it can be offered, such direct participation does provide an alternative for those who wish to express their approval for a tenant-led organization, but have a low 'boredom threshold' at formal meetings or feel inhibited by them. Third, there is participation in the social life associated with the organization. This also has the attraction of being accessible to those who find meetings difficult or unattractive, and it releases skills which tenants often already have in organizing fund-raising events, day trips, entertainment for the elderly and children and so on. It has the added attraction of involving those who are at the margins of the formal organization: children, teenagers and the very elderly. The propositions developed by theories of motivation ought to take into account all three of these types of participation.

It is important to bear in mind the limitations on any attempts to improve tenant participation. There is a crucial distinction between participation as an end in itself and as a means to an end (touched on in Chapter 1). Some activities are pleasurable in themselves while others are more instrumental. The mix depends to some extent on the attitude of the individual, but participation in meetings is usually seen as a means to an end and the social side of the tenant organization as an end in itself, while direct activities such as gardening have features of both. It is important to keep participation-as-means down to manageable levels, because it is usually engaged in only insofar as tenants see a payoff for it, and it has easily calculable 'opportunity costs'; participants can weigh up the value to them of spending the time in other, perhaps more productive, ways. In contrast, participation-as-end is inherently enjoyable, and can be expanded to include more people and more time without the participants experiencing strained loyalties. Promoters of all types of tenant-led organization have to make sure that they use meeting time efficiently and cut down on the opportunity costs of participation-as-means.

An individualistic theory of participation

There are two contrasting motivation theories which we might label 'individualist' and 'communitarian'. The individualist approach, developed by Homans in the late 1950s, is a blend of behaviourist psychology and 'elementary economics', adapting generalizations from Skinner's experiments with animals to human interaction (Homans 1961, 1974). The approach assumes that people are motivated by individual rewards and punishments, and provides a set of quite simple generalizations about how they interact. The communitarian approach was developed by a sociologist, Sorokin, who also based his generalizations on a range of psychological experiments, but who interpreted the results very differently. This approach assumes that people can be motivated by collective goals, a sense of community and co-operative values (Sorokin 1954).

Homans assumes that human behaviour is motivated by payoffs – it depends on the amount of reward and punishment it fetches. Amalgamating and adapting the propositions in his first and second edition (which are slightly different), we find seven key propositions. First:

(a) The more often a person's participation is rewarded, the more likely the person is to continue to participate.

People make decisions about the likely rewards from participating because of stimuli in their environment which they have learnt to associate with reward or punishment. Because they learn from past experiences, they do not have to calculate whether or not to participate each time, but rely instead on habits formed in the expectation of receiving rewards or avoiding punishment. It is the repetition of actions based on the similarity between the current situation and previous ones which allows us to predict how people will behave and thus, hopefully, to change the value of the rewards and the type of stimuli so that participation levels can be increased. The second proposition is:

(b) If in the past a certain kind of participation activity has been found rewarding, then the more similar the current activity is to the past one, the more likely people are to participate.

This simply means that rewarding forms of participation build up the expectation of more rewards, so people get into the habit of taking part. This is a powerful counter-weight to another proposition we will encounter in Sorokin's theory, that participation tends to decline over time. Other things being equal, it does decline, but perhaps not as quickly if people are used to taking part. The force of habit is sometimes so ingrained that people admit that they do not really know why they still attend a committee that is recognized as no longer rewarding. It continues to be just something they do without thinking much about it. Third:

(c) The more valuable participation is to a person, the more often he or she will be encouraged to participate.

It is almost impossible to put a value on the rewards which people receive, since their own valuation tends to be a very personal one and rational calculation is mixed up with emotions and expectations. We can at least put rewards in rank order, and say that the higher the value put on participation relative to other activities, the more likely someone is to participate. This explains why it is relatively easy to encourage participation in improvement schemes, where someone's home is at stake, but not to be able to sustain this after the improvement is completed, when the rewards from participation become less valuable. Promoters have to concentrate on other goals which are valued, and these are not always associated with housing; they could be childcare facilities or employment training or crime prevention. Fourth:

(d) The more often a person has received a reward from participation, the less valuable any more of the same kind of reward becomes, and the less he or she will participate.

This is the 'satiation proposition', and it works against proposition (a). It is most obviously true of basic needs such as for food; once we have eaten enough we no longer value further amounts of the same food, and so do not take part in finding it. Supposing a tenants' association is successful in obtaining most of what tenants want – they feel they are being listened to and their views taken into account. Paradoxically, although participation continues to be rewarding, they can begin to take it for granted. Having got most of the improvements needed on an estate, they can ease up on the pressure and have a rest. This can be very hurtful to those who have worked hard to obtain the desired result, but it is understandable, particularly when associated with another proposition we will meet below, that some people make a rational decision to 'freeload' while others do the work. The converse is also interesting: *the more often a person has been deprived of a reward, the more valuable that reward becomes.* So tenants who have never had a chance to make their views known will probably jump at the chance when it is offered. Fifth:

(e)   The more unequally a person sees the rewards being distributed, the more likely he or she is to be angry, and so to experience participation as unrewarding.

So far the propositions have concerned just a simple exchange relationship. What happens when other tenants' groups are competing for a slice of a budget, or are making an SRB bid? Someone has to lose, and in such a situation anger at a lack of distributive justice has an extremely bad effect on the willingness to continue to participate, as unsuccessful local authorities in the first round of SRB found out (Oatley 1995). Further, the withdrawal of an expected reward is experienced as a punishment and, because avoidance of punishment is itself a kind of reward, Homans says that it actually becomes rewarding to avoid participating in the future (Homans 1961). Because the promoters of tenant participation want the relationship to extend over many different exchanges, it is important that they establish some rules of distributive justice quite early on, so that participants can see outcomes as being fair.

Related to this idea of fairness is a sixth proposition which Homans developed later to describe the consequences of disappointment:

(f)   When a person's participation does not receive the reward expected, the result is anger. He/she is more likely then to perform aggressive behaviour, and the results of such behaviour become more valuable.

As participation workers frequently observe, once tenants have been disappointed in the results of their efforts, it becomes much harder to interest them in new initiatives. One failure can have repercussions well into the future.

What happens when there are two or more rewards available? There are, in fact, always alternatives; when people decide not to participate in a meeting, or in voluntary work, or in a social event, they do so usually because they want to do something else at that time. Because they cannot do two things at once, the alternatives not chosen reflect back on the value of what is chosen, experienced as costs. So, a seventh proposition is:

(g)   In choosing between alternative actions, a person will choose that one for which, as perceived by him/her at the time, the value of the result multiplied by the probability of getting the result is greater.

The costs of participation vary depending on what else a person wants to do with the time. We know not to programme a meeting at the same time as a favourite soap opera or a crucial football match on television. Homans says 'for an activity to incur cost, an alternative and rewarding activity must be there to be foregone' (Homans 1961 p.59). Unemployed people will find participation less costly than those with a full-time job. People, often women, who have to look after children will find direct costs in arranging childcare, either in paying a babysitter or indirectly in incurring an obligation to do the same for someone else. More generally, the costs of participating include the degree of interest or boredom felt in a meeting, the degree of discomfort at having to sit for a long time, feelings of inadequacy at not being able to understand what is going on and so on. It is not clear whether in Homans's theory these are costs or punishments, but in either case they will have the effect, other things being equal, of lowering participation in the long run.

Finally, all of this assumes that the kinds of activity offered as participation remain constant. But there can be changes in kind, as the content of meetings changes, or the emphasis shifts from volunteering to paid work, or from formal meetings to more sociable events. The level of participation changes also with the type of participation offered. If the level is falling, notwithstanding the first proposition concerning habit, it is worth offering people something else instead.

There are, of course, severe limitations to Homans's approach. It is reductionist, deriving propositions about human behaviour from experiments on animals and on human subjects in experimental conditions. It is individualist, assuming that if we know about individual behaviour we can generalize about social behaviour, and this does not take into account the effects of belonging to a group. It is heavily dependent on American sources, and other cultures might not value individual rewards so highly (Homans 1961). Most important for our purpose is the fact that, when applied to tenant participation, it only works well where respondents really do have an instrumental view; in a study of six housing co-operatives, for instance, it only illuminated one case study where the co-operative was dominated by an instrumental attitude among members (Birchall 1985).

When participants themselves express more communitarian sentiments, it seems unethical to distort their world view by converting expressions of collective sentiment and purpose into the language of individual reward. We need a theory which can take at face value the views of participants who explain their motivation in communitarian terms. For this we can turn to Sorokin.

A communitarian theory of participation

Sorokin identifies five key independent variables which have direct effects on the levels of participation – duration, extensity, adequacy, intensity and purity – and he treats participation as a dependent variable. Together they make up a quite comprehensive theory which has already been applied successfully to housing and consumer co-operatives (Birchall 1984, 1988b).

First, *duration*. It is tempting to use the analogy of human ageing, and to say that organizations are young, become middle-aged and then grow old. Over time, democracy is likely to turn into oligarchy, and participation declines (Michels 1949) – the greater the age, the lower the participation. This happens because participation becomes routinized, fewer important decisions need to be made or these can be left to trusted leaders, and so oligarchy sets in. In contrast, some housing co-operatives never grow old, but fade out as key members who have worked too hard in the early years experience 'burnout' and others are not available, or prepared, to take their place; in fact, this problem may be a greater one than that of oligarchy in tenant-led organizations. However, these trends are not inevitable, and depend on the attitudes of members (which will be explored further below) and on the more active variables such as intensity, purity and adequacy.

Extensity is the size of an organization and the nature of its geographic base. Other things being equal, the greater the extensity, the lower the participation. There are good reasons for this. First, there is a limit to the amount of urban space with which people identify; studies have shown that this is often restricted to a few streets (Young and Willmott 1957). On the other hand, most tenants do identify with an estate even if it contains over 1000 dwellings, and chopping up an estate into smaller units in order to satisfy arbitrary criteria about, for instance, the optimum size of a TMC may be counter-productive. At Fairbridge TMC in Bridgeton, Glasgow, tenants did not particularly identify with the small corner of a large estate parcelled off by the landlord for an experiment in tenant control (Birchall 1988a); with hindsight we can now see that an EMB for the whole estate might have been more appropriate. It is always worthwhile for promoters first to check what natural boundaries the tenants themselves put on their locality, before deciding to press ahead with an area-based tenant organization. The main difficulty is likely to come if the housing stock is scattered (a problem for housing associations more than for local authorities), when any type of organization is likely to be difficult to organize. More subtly, the layout of an estate may encourage or discourage social interaction, and so a larger estate with streetscapes and adjoining back gardens may be more friendly than a smaller one with flats in point blocks in which tenants do not often pass each other: we might propose that the lower the level of social interaction, the lower the level of participation.

Second, there are limits to effective participatory democracy. These can be seen quite easily in meetings; there are natural limits such as the extent to which a voice will carry, the length of time a meeting would need to take if all wish to be heard and so on (Dahl and Tufte 1973). While these limits can to some extent be circumvented, for instance by installing microphones and limiting the length of time for speeches, meetings change their character above a certain size and become more remote. Important general meetings may attract over 100 people, but day-to-day business will probably never attract more than around 50, whatever the size of the estate. Similarly, management committees change their character if they grow to more than around 15 members, because the business they transact and the trust placed in them as representatives require more interaction between participants than can be fitted into the time.

What this means is that promoters are probably right to see the more tenant-controlled forms of organization as needing to be smaller, while partnership forms can be larger; in the end, both will be subject to the same natural ceilings on the numbers participating. The generalization holds: the larger the organization, the lower the level of participation. The fact that EMBs plan for a lower level of democratic involvement by tenants seems to indicate that they should be formed on large estates, leaving the more compact estates to TMCs. Steps can be taken, however, to counteract this effect of size. For instance, Speirs TMC, with 200 dwellings, has a system of 'close reps', one person for every two walk-up blocks, elected by the people in those blocks. This device binds the different parts of the estate together, but still has a natural limit based on the size to which the committee can grow; Speirs' committee is particularly large. EMBs could (and should) also have area representatives, but on a large estate these areas might themselves be the size of an average TMC. Yet there is no absolute reason that tenant-controlled organizations have to remain small; in Scotland both TMCs and community ownership co-operatives are being formed at around 500 dwellings, and there are plenty of precedents around the world for some very large housing co-operatives – Co-op City in New York has 5000 dwellings. There may even be an advantage in this, as it adds to the pool of possible committee members.

To complicate matters even further, tenant-controlled organizations can be formed which are *too small*. During the late 1970s and early 1980s the orthodoxy among co-operative development agencies was that 'small is beautiful' and co-operatives were formed with as few as 12 dwellings in one street, or even one shared dwelling with cluster flats. The problem here, apart from the hugely expensive promotional and developmental costs, is that there is a very small pool from which to draw active committee members. Of course, at that level, co-operatives can be run by general meeting, but this is expensive on time and effort. The St Andrew's Street Housing Co-op in Beverley was formed to save and renovate one street, but in the early days it was difficult to find enough active members to serve on the committee. With the opening of a sheltered housing scheme for the elderly and the influx of new families into newbuild housing on the street, the democratic side of the co-operative was assured, and the original members could take a well-earned rest (Birchall 1988a).

Adequacy refers to whether an organization is succeeding in its aims – the greater the adequacy, the greater the participation. This is obvious, since people will not take part if they think an organization will fail, and if it succeeds will be encouraged to see their contribution as important. This is a communitarian restatement of Homans's first proposition about reward, although in terms of common goals. The conditions for a successful tenant organization are therefore that a landlord has failed to deliver a satisfactory service, that the tenants care about their homes and estate (and do not expect a quick exit through a transfer out) and that they expect their participation will make a difference. The greater the effectiveness of existing services, the lower the stimulus to tenants to take them over, and so in cases where the landlord is quite effective a lower-level tenant organization might be all that can be achieved; this may be why estate committees have often been more popular than TMOs. On the other hand, if the landlord has been seen to fail and trust has been undermined, the conditions for a TMC or even a transfer of ownership are to hand; the Cloverhall TMC in Rochdale was formed because the tenants emphatically believed that they could not do a worse job than the council.

A complication arises from the dynamic nature of each situation. What may not be feasible now may become so in a year's time, which is why 'stepping-stone' type structures such as informal estate forums, formal joint committees and so on are essential starting points. Saul Alinsky, the American community activist (see Chapter 12), advised that every new community group should be enabled to achieve a victory early on, because in this way its further growth will be guaranteed. For instance, at Glendale, a TMC whose committee were having difficulty in persuading tenant members to support it, an early fight to replace defective boilers which were bursting and flooding the houses was decisive in showing just how effective the co-operative could be (Birchall 1988a). On the other hand, in a situation where the tenants are cynical about the capabilities of the landlord, early results by professional staff themselves may be necessary in order to prove their good faith to the tenants. Last, and paradoxically, if the staff are too successful and the tenants do not want deep-rooted changes, the conditions for partnership may be undermined as the tenants are now more satisfied and have less reason to participate; in such a case, an estate committee may be all that is needed to monitor conventional housing-management structures.

Intensity concerns the sense of community on an estate – the greater the intensity, the greater the participation. This is because if people have emotional ties to each other they will care about each other's welfare, be more committed to their environment, and will put a higher value on improvements to it. It follows that a strong community base can produce a more tenant-controlled form of TMO: a TMC or an ownership co-operative. A weak community base will seriously handicap the promotion of a TMO, although if the tenants have instrumental goals they may not need the sense of community to sustain them. In fact, the sense of community may come after the campaign has been started to improve conditions on the estate (see Birchall 1988a). The only occasion when a tenant organization does not benefit from the strengthening of the sense of community is when the latter is already strong and the organization is seen as purely instrumental; in this case, the strength is gained indirectly, but no direct credit goes to the tenant organization for fostering the sense of community. However, in most cases the proposition holds – the greater the intensity, the greater the participation. It pays a tenants' organization to include in its aims such expressions of practical caring as activities for children and teenagers, and services to elderly people, single parents and people with disabilities. In this way it will enlarge the sense of 'adequacy' as well as fostering 'intensity'. It pays, also, to look to the conditions under which community can be built up: provision of meeting rooms, community centres and other facilities. The tenant-controlled forms of TMO seem to be best at doing this; Cloverhall TMC, for instance, uses its office space to good effect by offering rooms to a playgroup, while Speirs has helped to develop a youth training scheme at a redundant school.

Purity concerns the values underlying the motivation to participate; the greater the purity, the greater the participation. In any organization some members will derive satisfaction from knowing that the organization is working according to certain deeply held principles, and so in Homans's terms they will find it rewarding to participate. When people say they feel an obligation to participate, that is 'purity' at work. The reason that some people feel a sense of duty and others do not is mysterious, but we know that good training (discussed in Chapter 9) and the sense of being part of a social movement (Lowe 1986) can bring it out.

In practice, all these variables are present in varying strengths; they vary over time and in quite complex but reasonably predictable ways. Depending on how they work together, they set up either a virtuous or a vicious cycle; strengths or weaknesses in each independent variable tend to reinforce each other and to have a cumulative impact on levels of participation. Once a virtuous cycle is entrained, the effect is 'synergic', that is, the combined strength of several variables all working in the same direction is greater than if they were working separately. For this reason, interventions to improve the organization's performance in one area will have knock-on effects in others, and so even small improvements in performance, in the sense of community, in the sense of obligation and shared values, ought to be well worth trying.

It is generally thought that (following Michels) duration also varies negatively with purity; over time, we might expect commitment to the organization to decline and oligarchy to set in. One skill which promoters will need in the future is that of knowing when an organization has run its course and needs to be wound up or converted into a different form (Williams 1994). The ability to convert without too much conflict or expense is going to be crucial if such a decline is to be halted and perhaps stabilized at a lower level. On the other hand, it may be that duration works the other way, in that over time habits build up and commitment to the organization and participation in its structures may become habitual and taken for granted. (See Birchall 1995 for the case of tenant co-partnership estates.) Duration varies positively with intensity; the sense of community builds up over time. This seems to be true even if other factors are at work; studies of neighbourhood caring have found that the single most important factor leading to a sense of caring is length of time spent in the neighbourhood (Willmott 1987). But this is only true when the composition of the community remains the same. Attention needs to be paid to the rate of turnover of members; if this is too fast, then there will not be a chance for a sense of community to build up.

Similar points can be made about adequacy and purity. If the turnover is too quick, tenants will not have enough time to learn how to manage tenant-participation structures, whatever form they take. Resources put into training will not pay off, because the pool of trained members will soon be exhausted; in one co-ownership society, where high rents were driving members to leave as soon as they could afford to buy a house, less than two years after the committee had won an important battle for compensation over defects in the buildings nearly all had left, and those remaining were not sufficiently motivated even to form a committee (Birchall 1988a). On the other hand, an influx of new members may revitalize a committee and save it from turning into an oligarchy; it is the *rate* of flow of members in and out of the estate which has to be carefully monitored.

Generally, on estates which are effectively managed the turnover is low, and so the balance between out- and in-migration is about right. But attention still has to be paid to the induction of new members, something that some organizations do not do systematically, especially if the turnover is low. Even more overlooked is the induction of the children of members as they come of age; eventually they may inherit the tenancy and yet their commitment cannot be taken for granted. It follows that, if there is a large proportion of tenants expecting to transfer out of an estate, it would be unwise to embark on an ambitious programme of training with the expectation of forming a high-level self-management organization. However, this may not be the problem it used to be, since during the 1980s the 'residualization' of council housing has made it more and more difficult to guarantee transfers, and tenants are beginning to realize that they are stuck on an estate. Paradoxically, a worsening situation for individual tenants may strengthen the commitment to collective action.

Adequacy has quite a strong relationship with intensity. The greater the sense of community, the greater the value placed on the effective management of an estate (although it does not guarantee the means to do so). Conversely, a well-managed TMO usually leads to a strengthening of community and pride in the estate. Similarly, the sense of commitment to self-managing (purity) produces a drive to succeed, while success reinforces commitment. A sense of community usually produces a felt commitment to the values of democracy and co-operation, and it makes it easier for tenants to agree common goals. Conversely, a joint commitment to the idea of self-management, while it may begin as an intellectual or political commitment because it produces intense social interactions over time, soon becomes reinforced by the sense of community.

In practice, these three variables are so intertwined that it is often difficult to separate them. Certainly, when asked about their motivations tenants will switch from one justification to another, even within the same sentence, without feeling the need to unravel them. Improvements in the organization's performance on one variable should affect the others, and so if improvement in one area is difficult, attention to another where change is easier may be a good strategy. For instance, a TMO which is having difficulty agreeing an agency agreement with the local authority can fill in the time with more social activities and care for children and the elderly. A TMO which is riven with social tensions between tenants in different parts of an estate can concentrate on delivery of a first-class service. A TMO which is stalled by a lack of money for improvements to the estate can make links with other tenants' groups and engage in training in how to run a campaign.

However, it is possible to run a successful tenant organization without much intensity or purity, provided that the tenants really desire improvements to their estate. Such a starting point has produced some strong organizations, notably the Glasgow Community Ownership Co-ops. But for these to succeed over time, intensity and purity have eventually to become significant, otherwise tenants will have achieved their aims and will have no further interest in the organization. The complaint was made at Glendale TMC that once the tenants had 'got their house' they did not want to know (Birchall 1988a). It was expected that, after they had finished their improvement schemes (which were contingent on forming a community ownership co-op), the Glasgow co-operatives would have gone the same way, but the very process of managing their own improvements seems to have produced a demand for ongoing quality of service, an increased sense of community and a commitment to the idea of self-management.

Just because participation is classed as a dependent variable does not mean that it has no effects. There is feedback of a direct kind on the variables analysed above. The quality of the participation experience is important in itself. Tenants may want tangible benefits, have some sense of community and some embryonic commitment to working together, but be put off by the high personal opportunity costs of taking part. This may be because meetings are too long, exhausting, difficult to understand, held in a stuffy or uncomfortable meeting hall, or because the costs in childcare or lost wages are too expensive. If participation is enjoyable, informative and enhances the self-image of the participants, it reacts with the other variables to strengthen and confirm them. Whatever else they do, promoters and committee members must cut down the opportunity costs as much as possible. Here Homans and Sorokin are in agreement.

Attitudes to participation

What do we know about attitudes to participation? In a later edition of his work, Homans provides a fivefold categorization of responses to the demand for participation (Homans 1974). First, there are the *true believers*, who are prepared to participate in order to achieve common goals. Second, there are the *freeloaders*, who want to obtain the benefits without sharing in the opportunity costs of participation. Third, there are the *sceptical conformers*, who do not expect participation to work, do not participate, but otherwise tend not to cause trouble. Fourth, there are the *holdouts*, who refuse to conform but stay in the participation structures and withhold approval, often spreading gossip and misinformation, but always injecting a note of cynicism and suspicion into the proceedings. Last, there are the *escapees*, who are so disenchanted that, given a chance, they will leave the process altogether; in the case of tenant-controlled housing (ownership and management co-operatives) this desire to escape may be literal and involve a move of home.

The consequences of different mixes of these types are quite easy to predict. There are at least three different scenarios. In the first one, there are enough true believers to form a committee, and enough to back them up and provide a 'pool' of supporters from whom replacement committee members can be drawn when current members get tired or 'burn out'. True believers may carp about the freeloaders, even worry that the latter will destabilize the organization, but usually their worries are exaggerated (see Birchall 1988a). In such circumstances, virtually any form of tenant-participation structure will have guaranteed backing, and at the estate level promoters may as well go for a tenant management co-operative. In the second scenario, there is a small pool of true believers and a large majority of freeloaders. Unless some freeloaders can be persuaded to become true believers, disillusion and 'burnout' will occur sooner, and there will be no replenishment of the management committee. The organization will need backup from professional staff and councillors and so non-mutual forms would be preferable to fully mutual ones: an estate committee, EMB or community housing association would be preferable to a TMC or ownership co-operative.

In the third scenario, there are some true believers, some freeloaders, but a substantial minority of sceptics who are suspicious, and a few holdouts who are actively prepared to undermine the organization, given the chance. These holdouts may even be people who previously took an active part in the running of a tenants' association before it was opened up to new members, or superseded by another form such as an EMB. A bad pre-existing landlord–tenant relationship will sour relations within the organization, and so there will be a high level of scepticism to overcome. More particularly, tenant leaders may be habituated to a confrontational style of interaction with the landlord, which becomes inappropriate when a partnership is entered but like all habits is hard to break. Also, when a tenant-led organization is seen to be successful, there is sometimes a 'psychology of failure' to surmount, a tendency for some participants secretly to hope it will fail. This might seem a strange point, but it has often been observed when people who have been used to failure are confronted with success; the problem is to come to terms with past failure, which no longer looks legitimate. The question is raised: 'Why did we not do something like this before?', and it induces guilt and resentment (MacCrystal 1987).

The implications of this third scenario need to be carefully worked out. First, if the scepticism comes from a bad relationship with the landlord, this may be a powerful spur to the forming of a TMC or ownership co-operative, because the sceptics become true believers on their own behalf by distancing themselves from the council; this happened at Speirs TMC in Glasgow and Cloverhall TMC in Rochdale, two outstandingly successful TMCs. Second, if the scepticism is rooted in a confrontational style, the formation of a TMO by promoters may involve the replacement of those tenant leaders with others prepared to switch from a campaigning strategy to one of partnership; something like this is said to have occurred at Bloomsbury EMB in Birmingham. Last, it may be the case that the partnership forms (estate committees, EMBs) may suffer less from the 'psychology of failure' reaction, because tenants can see the achievements of the TMO as being to some extent owing to outside intervention.

It is quite easy to ascertain the current proportions of all of the five types of individual response to a tenant-participation scheme by administering a questionnaire (see Birchall 1985). However, there is one further complication: the proportions of each type can change over time, sometimes quite rapidly. For instance, at Speirs TMC, tenant activists had to battle against scepticism for several years before nearly all the tenants had become members and been converted, if not to true believers, at least to freeloaders. Yet the TMC was, and is, outstandingly successful (Birchall 1988a). The right type of tenant organization cannot be determined by the existing state of mind of tenants, because this can be changed. However, if scepticism persists alongside difficulties in securing a large enough pool of true believers, then a partnership form (estate committee, EMB) would be the wisest course, and also the most humane one; it would put less of a burden on the true believers. If the mix of attitudes changes over time, then a transition to a more pure form of tenant self-management could be effected; measurement of the mix would be one important determinant of whether such a change was advisable.

Conclusions

There is no easy answer to how to improve the level of participation in tenant-led organizations. This discussion has opened up several important lines of enquiry but has not provided simple answers, because there are none. It is hoped that, by careful application of the kinds of theory used here, and of related social psychological and organizational theories, promoters and activists will at least have the tools with which to think deeply and analytically about their own situation and to begin to attempt to predict what might happen if one or another form of tenant organization were promoted and, when things go wrong, how they might begin to put them right.

References

Association of Metropolitan Authorities (AMA) (1990), *Towards Tenant Participation*, London: AMA.

Birchall, J. (1984), 'Why should people participate?', *Journal of Co-operative Studies*, **51**, pp.50–56.

Birchall, J. (1985), 'Housing co-operatives: a study in the theory and practice of user control', DPhil Thesis, York University.

Birchall, J. (1988a), *What Makes People Co-operate? A Strategy for Member Participation in Housing Co-operatives*, Oxford: Headington Press.

Birchall, J. (1988b), *Building Communities: the Co-operative Way*, London: Routledge and Kegan Paul.

Birchall, J. (1992), 'Council tenants: sovereign consumers or pawns in the game?', in Birchall, J. (ed.), *Housing Policy in the 1990s*, London: Routledge, pp.163–189.

Birchall, J. (1995), 'Co-partnership housing and the Garden City Movement', *Planning Perspectives*, **10**, pp.329–358.

Crossley, R. (1992), *The Right to Manage: Proposals for Simplifying Tenant Management of Local Authority Housing*, Manchester: Priority Estates Project.

Dahl, R. and Tufte, E.R. (1973), *Size and Democracy*, Stanford: Stanford University Press.

Department of the Environment (DoE) (n.d.), *The Guide to the Right to Manage*, London: HMSO.

Department of the Environment (DoE) (1992a), *Tenant Involvement and the Right to Manage*, Consultation Paper, London: HMSO.

Department of the Environment (DoE) (1992b), *Competing for Quality in Housing*, London: HMSO.

Dickson, J. and Robertson, I. (1993), *Taking Charge*, London: London Housing Unit.

Fraser, R. and Gibson, M. (1991), *It's a Better Way of Working: Tenant Participation in Housing Associations*, London: National Federation of Housing Associations.

Homans, G. (1961), *Social Behaviour: Its Elementary Forms*, London: Routledge and Kegan Paul.

Homans, G. (1974), *Social Behaviour: Its Elementary Forms*, 2nd Edn, New York: Harcourt Brace Jovanovich.

Lowe, S. (1986), *Urban Social Movements: The City After Castells*, London: Macmillan.

MacCrystal, S. (1987), 'Galliagh Co-operative: a case study', *Journal of Co-operative Studies*, **60**, pp.37–41.

Michels, R. (1949), *Political Parties*, Chicago: Free Press.

Oatley, N. (1995), 'Competitive urban policy and the regeneration game', *Town Planning Review*, **66**(1).

Phillips, S. (1992), *Tenants Together: Tenant Participation and Council Housing*, Manchester: Tenant Participation Advisory Service/Priority Estates Project.

Platt, S., Piepe, R. and Smyth, J. (1987), *Heard or Ignored*, London: National Federation of Housing Associations.

Platt, S., Newton, C. and Willson, M. (1990), *Whose Home? Accountability to Tenants and Communities*, York: Joseph Rowntree Memorial Trust.

Sorokin, P.A. (1954), *The Ways and Power of Love*, Boston: Beacon Press.

Williams, R. (1994), *Controlling Change: A Guide for Tenant Controlled Organizations to Legal Structures and How to Change Them*, Liverpool: Partners in Change.

Willmott, P. (1987), *Friendship Networks and Social Support*, London: Policy Studies Institute.

Young, M. and Willmott, P. (1957), *Family and Kinship in East London*, London: Routledge and Kegan Paul.

9 Training for tenants

Benita Wishart and Robert Furbey

The title of this chapter should not be misunderstood. Tenants are not cast here in a passive role but as active contributors to a vital process for effective involvement in housing and community decision-making. Tenants engaging in participation each bring their own particular knowledge and skills to the task and, as they often point out to housing officers and other professionals, 'we live here twenty-four hours a day; you go home at five!'

Yet, as tenants become involved in particular processes of participation they confront demands for specialized technical or legislative knowledge, or the need for new skills to enable them to run an efficient and effective organization. Access to training, therefore, is a vital resource and, as we shall see below, is seen as such by the great majority of tenants. Organizations which encourage participation, but do not support tenant participation through providing or resourcing training, can fairly be accused of setting up tenants to fail.

The following discussion explores five key issues. First, we assess more fully the relevance of training to participation, placing a particular emphasis on the view of tenants. Next, through the eyes of both tenants and trainers, we review the practice and experience of training. Third, attention is given to the issue of accreditation, as a device to underwrite quality, attract resources and provide avenues of personal progression. The resourcing of training is then given more specific attention, and finally some observations are made regarding ways of strengthening training provision.

The focus here, therefore, is on training for tenants and residents. However, these are not the only stakeholders for whom training is a pressing concern. Housing officers, professionals in other policy sectors, policy-makers, caretakers and wardens can all benefit from training to develop their understanding of policies and practices of participation and increase their ability to work effectively with tenants. We shall see that training for staff and tenants need not be conducted separately and, without training for all these groups, a formal commitment to participation can become empty.

The chapter draws on research at Sheffield Hallam University and the Tenant Participation Advisory Service (England), funded by the Joseph Rowntree Foundation (Furbey *et al.* 1993). The main aim of this research was to explore tenants' views on training, so amplifying their voice in the national debate on training for participation. However, tenants cannot always specify their requirements until they have actually gained some experience of training, or been advised (and perhaps inspired) by other groups and activists. Hence, the insights of trainers were also sought, particularly in relation to good practice in training and the obstacles to effective provision.

The inquiry centred on meetings with 20 tenants' organizations and interviews with providers of training in six case-study localities in England. These localities encompassed both urban and rural areas. The tenant groups were based in both the local authority and the housing association sectors. They included locality-wide federations of tenants' and residents' associations, estate-based associations and tenant management organizations (TMOs). Contributions to the study were obtained from over 50 actual or potential providers of tenant training.

The relevance of tenant training

Tenants' perceptions of training

It may well be assumed by others that tenants engaging in participation require training in order to achieve their aims. However, the notion that they 'need training' could strike tenants themselves as patronizing. How do tenants perceive the idea of 'training'?

In fact, it is clear that training is rarely seen by tenants as a foreign, or academic, idea being foisted on them by professional 'outsiders'. Tenants themselves identify training as a crucial priority. Hence, when asked to rank the ingredients of success for effective participation on a checklist, tenants in our research study identified training as second in importance only to having a place to meet.

Of course, tenants' views of training are diverse. Varying responses were given to the question, *Training – what do you think it means?* Most tenants reacted with positive comments. One, for example, observed that:

> If you've got the right training you don't have to start off with Joe Bloggs and end up with Fred Bloggs. You can go straight to the man.

Others, however, had very little experience and some could not identify immediately how training related to tenant participation. For some, 'training' had negative connotations because of past bad experiences or simply because it reminded them of school. One response was:

> I don't like the word 'training'. It sounds so formal, institutionalized; jogging up and down on the spot.

It appears, therefore, that the term 'training' can be off-putting but, for the great majority, the experience of training is welcomed. The approach of some more seasoned tenants in one group was to invite new members of their association to a 'general discussion' of an issue, but not to describe the event as being 'training'.

Training topics

There is considerable variety within tenants' organizations and each group has a range of aims relating to its specific context and stage of development. Training needs are correspondingly diverse. Nevertheless, it is possible to identify the following broad categories of training which support tenants in:

- developing personal qualities and general skills;
- gaining specialist skills;
- running a successful organization;
- approaching the landlord; and
- acquiring specialist knowledge.

When asked to outline the content of helpful training, tenants and trainers tend to specify similar items. However, our research uncovered some differences. For example, although some of the groups employed workers or managed premises, these responsibilities were not mentioned as training priorities by tenants. By contrast, many trainers regarded these as important matters. Also, some trainers pointed to the importance of skills in conflict resolution, whereas no tenants' group mentioned this even though some organizations had listed this as one of the problems which they were facing. These differences may signal the need for caution in basing training programmes simply on the initial expressed wishes of 'consumers'. This is a context in which 'producers' may have a valuable perspective, to be taken into account in the *negotiation* of training with tenants.

First-stage training

A particular issue in establishing training services for tenant organizations concerns the potentially varying needs of established and newly formed organizations. In fact, although members of new groups are likely to benefit from 'basic' training (such as group organization skills, the management of meetings, and understanding local authority structures and key landlord operating procedures), many members of more established organizations can benefit from such training sessions. New members join longer-established associations, and experienced members can develop bad procedures or require new ideas and techniques to achieve progress. As one federation worker remarked:

> If they're experienced but ineffective, then they need training, because they're wasting their energies.

Conversely, new groups may be bolstered from the start by members who bring with them to the organization confidence, knowledge, skills and qualities from their earlier careers.

Tenants' groups need to encourage the involvement of new members, and their development to positions of responsibility, to enable the organization to benefit from new perspectives and to ensure that long-serving individuals do not form a clique or become 'burnt out'. As one trainer observed, there is a constant need for basic training because:

> If we're talking about democratic organizations with a proper turnover, rather than a self-perpetuating oligarchy, there are going to be people coming on to committees who don't know what they're doing.

Hence, although the content of training may vary according to an organization's collective level of expertise and experience, essentially there should be a 'pool of training' on which groups can draw as necessary, rather than specific 'first-stage' and 'second-stage' provision. This conclusion is given added support by research for the Department of the Environment (DoE) into the training needs of TMOs and the subsequent recommendations for training programmes. While TMOs may have specific training requirements related to this specific form of tenant involvement in housing provision, many basic or generic skills and areas of knowledge were identified by TMO members (DoE 1994). Overall, it appears that the needs of particular organizations depend on several factors, including:

- the aims of the group;
- the skills and knowledge within the group;
- the extent to which these assets are shared;
- the circumstances in which the group is working; and
- the nature of the problems being faced.

How do tenants use training?

The list of training categories presented above indicates that tenant training can encompass a very wide range of topics. Training is also used by tenants in diverse ways. Most groups apply training to the pursuit of particular objectives, yet training can also empower in a wider sense.

Our research indicates that tenants' application of training can be categorized as follows. First, training can be used to acquire specific skills and knowledge. Examples here include skills in the management of meetings or knowledge of 'how the council works' or how to run a credit union. Second, training is used to open up and 'demystify' housing procedures, for example by improving the understanding of jargon or the commonly used acronyms of housing administration, or of specific aspects of estate management (for example, in dealing with rent arrears). Third, training can be a source of new ideas about how to improve the estate or develop the organization. Fourth, training can be a means to new confidence and assertiveness. Women made particular mention of this aspect of training. In the words of one woman:

> The more knowledge you acquire, the more confidence you have to stand up because you know you're right.

Finally, for some tenants training becomes a catalyst for changes in other parts of their lives and a source of wider personal development. Hence, one woman said she had used training to:

> evaluate my life . . . Before I came on this I'd never thought of going to college or university. I am now! I think it's come out of all this. It's made me realize there's a lot more out there for people.

Practice and experience

Who provides training?

Tenant-training services can be provided by a wide range of organizations. Not all of these focus exclusively on housing issues or work solely with tenants. Access varies greatly between localities and in some areas, notably the metropolitan conurbations, tenants have a much greater choice of training provision. Sources of training include the following:

- Landlord organizations.
- Staff employed by tenants' organizations, such as tenants' federation development workers.

- Tenants themselves – some tenants' organizations provide training for other groups while, within associations, tenants may be in a position to use their own knowledge or skills to train others.
- National housing and estate-focused organizations, such as the Priority Estates Project (PEP) and the Tenant Participation Advisory Service (TPAS), working across the country to promote tenant participation.
- Locally based development agents. These are organizations receiving Section 16 or Section 87 funding (from the DoE and the Housing Corporation respectively) for the promotion and development of tenant management.
- Community workers, operating on behalf of a variety of statutory and voluntary organizations.
- Mainstream providers of adult education. Included here are further education colleges which offer a range of vocational and non-vocational educational opportunities for the over-16s; local education authority adult education services which traditionally offer a variety of 'leisure' classes; and 'community schools' which, besides providing education for children, offer opportunities for the neighbourhood's adult population.
- Workers' Educational Association (WEA) courses. This is another institution of adult education, but a voluntary body with branches throughout the country offering classes managed by volunteer members and local tutor organizers. It has a tradition of liberal adult education.
- University extra-mural or continuing education departments.
- Councils for Voluntary Service (CVS), umbrella organizations for the voluntary sector in each locality.
- 'Independent trainers' from both the voluntary and the statutory sectors. Some of these are based in institutions which are concerned predominantly with the provision of training. Others operate within organizations with wider aims. An example of the latter encountered in our research was a training co-ordinator working within a grant-aided resource centre for voluntary groups.
- Specialist organizations which provide occasional training as part of their wider function. Examples here include law centres, community architects and play forums.

The issue of which organizations are best equipped and situated to provide training for tenants is discussed later in the chapter. A first consideration is the quality of training and its effectiveness in meeting tenants' needs.

What is good practice in tenant training?

In our research, both tenants and trainers expressed some firm views on good and bad practice in tenant training. Table 9.1 summarizes the range of opinions held by tenants.

This table indicates some diversity in tenants' views and experience of training practice and there are some clear contradictions. For example, some tenants prefer training to be provided for their organization alone, while others value events shared with tenants from other groups. However, this may reflect simply the experience of specific successful or unsuccessful training events or the confidence of the particular individual. Then, some argue strongly that training events should last a maximum of two hours, while others favour a whole, concentrated weekend.

Nevertheless, despite these differences, many of the points presented in Table 9.1 command widespread assent, such as the pressing need for training to be relevant to the needs of the specific organization and the importance of an interactive style in training sessions.

Trainers vary in their approaches to their task and hold different views on good training practice. Generally, however, their views were similar to those of tenants. One trainer crystallized a common view in suggesting:

> There's no universal thing that doesn't work. It's only wrong if tenants get it at the wrong time or it's imposed on them.

Hence, it was felt that getting to know a group and their expectations helps to ensure relevance. Any assessment of training needs should begin with an audit of the positive aspects of the group and, ideally, training should be 'negotiated' with the tenants. Of course, this is not always possible as tenants often attend 'off-the-peg' events rather than participate in sessions developed specifically for their own organization. In such circumstances it is important to provide adequate prior information about an event's objectives and content to enable tenants to make an informed choice on whether or not to attend.

One particular matter, noted frequently by tenants, is the need for training to be conducted in plain language, with careful attention paid to an explanation of technical terms. Reflecting on an occasion when this did not occur, one tenant remarked:

> I'm not educated, but if they could speak in plain English we could all understand it better . . . I know nothing about architecture and buildings. It fell on my deaf ears. It bored me stiff. They used terminology that went over my head.

However, despite its importance to tenants, none of the trainers with whom we spoke mentioned this issue. Perhaps it is the case that the use of plain language is second nature to the great majority of them. But, less optimistically, it may be the case that many remain unaware of their routine use of complex expressions.

Table 9.1 Good practice in tenant training – tenants' opinions

1. Where and when to hold it?

● *Where?*

— Estate based (especially for tenants lacking experience) *or*
— With other groups – 'talking with other tenants' *or*
— Visits – can see what can be achieved.

● *With whom?*

— Not with other groups if they are too different.

● *Timing?*

— Must suit different needs and levels of confidence.
— Need plenty of time (day/weekend).
— Not 'too long'; small amount of information at once.
— Need breaks.
— Should not bar young people or people with jobs or children.

● *Venue?*

— Comfortable, warm, not crowded, everyone can see and hear.
— Some surroundings might put people off (e.g. Holiday Inn for people with little confidence).
— Transport should be provided.

2. A good trainer

— Good speaker and presenter; good personality; a good chair; speaks clearly and slowly; interesting presentation.
— Trainers with training in presentation skills. It's no good if the trainer has the knowledge but does not know how to present it.
— Does not talk down to participants; not like a teacher.
— Boosts confidence; explains clearly tasks set.
— Admits when doesn't know something, but finds it out.
— Doesn't impose ideas that worked elsewhere.
— Makes everyone feel wanted.
— Makes participants feel comfortable and able to ask questions.
— Has experience of what the group is doing.

3. Making it useful

— Relevant to what the tenants are doing, the problems faced and the type of estate: at the right time; for the right person; gives ideas that can be used; practical – gives a few points to put into practice; interesting subject.
— Aimed at the right level: going through it step by step; trainer does not

assume a level of knowledge, but finds out; at the right pace for the group; at tenants not professionals.
— Trainer checks understanding before moving on to the next point.
— Tenants can negotiate the programme so it meets the group's needs.
— Training is not forced on the group.

4. Type of training/running training

— Fun.
— Role plays; small discussions.
— Using actual examples.
— Follow-up sessions.
— Everyone can participate: not a lecture; able to contribute and share knowledge; practical – e.g. practise chairing meetings; small groups; uses tenants' experiences and knowledge.
— Individual help.
— Provides a safe environment.
— Informal: 'teacher not at front like school'; cups of tea help to break down barriers; food encourages people to come.
— Well organized: on time; right time allowed; not too much information at once; time for questions.

5. Communications

— No jargon, plain English, technical terms explained, no abbreviations.
— Audio-visual: videos used in small groups when everyone can see; videos which groups could use to train themselves; using videos to film participants; good visual aids used.
— Handouts to take away.
— Report relating to subjects discussed sent to participants after the event.
— Information sent out in advance makes it clear what to expect and makes it possible to choose workshops.
— Mixing with other people.

Equality of opportunity

The existence of formal training opportunities is of little use if tenants' actual participation is blocked. There is a range of barriers which must be overcome to ensure that access to training is available to the widest cross-section of people. An initial consideration is the selection of an appropriate venue for training. Cultural sensitivity is important here – for example, the use of pubs, religious buildings or social centres perceived as the preserve of a particular ethnic group can all variously narrow access. The selection of a training venue, therefore, needs to be made with careful reference to the target participants and to the stage of development of trust and mutual acceptance within the group. Beyond this, some tenants may need assistance with transport or transport costs. There may also be a need for crèche facilities and for signing or interpretation. If food is provided, again there is a need for cultural sensitivity.

Within the actual training programme, a prime task for trainers is to ensure that tenants feel comfortable with the setting. Clear strategies need to be established for dealing with discriminatory remarks, ideally enlisting the reinforcement of the wider membership of the group, and all should have an opportunity to contribute. Tenants without good literacy skills can feel ill at ease if required to read or write. Fear of appearing inadequate in these respects can be a powerful disincentive to attend. Trainers with whom we spoke described several strategies for addressing this problem. Several referred to the emphasis which they place on discussions and practical exercises in training sessions. If tenants are asked to write, some trainers preface the activity with the reassurance that 'they're your notes – I won't look at them'. Most fundamentally, perhaps, many trainers stress the importance of creating a 'safe atmosphere' in which participants feel able to be open concerning their needs. Finally, literacy problems can be tackled by forging links between tenant-training programmes and basic adult education provision.

Regarding the explicit approach to equal opportunities issues within training sessions, it is essential that they are introduced and developed in such a way that tenants perceive their relevance. Often, the best method may be to integrate equality issues into all training subjects, rather than singling them out as a 'special' topic. As one trainer remarked:

> The only way equal opportunities training works is if you inject it into every single aspect of the training from the word 'go'. Every single issue has it throughout – not any special add-on. It should always be there.

However, specific training on equal opportunities policies, racial harassment and cultural understanding is both necessary and potentially very successful. One tenant, describing a visit to a mosque, reflected:

> It shows you there's not much between the religions really. It gave you an insight into their beliefs and religion. You started to understand.

But training which is seen as irrelevant or which makes tenants seem defensive can have the opposite effect:

> I thought it was wrong. We went there for the 'environment and planning', and we got 'Chinese culture in London'.

That meeting turned sour for me because he was going to tell me I had a problem [being a racist].

One device used by several trainers to counter such responses was to relate discussion of discrimination to participants' own experience.

Accrediting training

The accreditation debate

The previous discussion has underlined the importance of training for tenants and the ways in which they can gain from well-planned and delivered programmes. But training and the actual operation of a tenants' organization demand many hours of voluntary involvement. Holmes found that one in five of the activists interviewed in her study of suburban estates had devoted over seven hours to their organization in the previous week (Holmes 1992). Should such commitment receive further rewards?

Recent years have brought intense debate concerning the relative virtues of education 'for its own sake' and accredited education for more formal qualifications (Ecclestone 1992). Similarly, tenants also have different views on whether their training should lead to a specific qualification. 'Accreditation' is the formal recognition of learning, often as a qualification for a particular practice. Various benefits are claimed for the accreditation of training. Frequent arguments are that:

- it provides formal recognition of the learner's knowledge and skills;
- it is a source of satisfaction for the learner;
- it can increase the learner's confidence;
- it can increase the learner's employment prospects;
- it can provide access to, or exemption from, other qualifications;
- it can give the learner status in the eyes of professionals and people in the locality;
- accredited courses are generally seen as vocational, and so more likely to attract funding;
- accredited courses are usually subject to external validation, so providing both learners and the wider world with an assurance of quality; and
- formal qualifications are the way in which society increasingly judges and distinguishes between people.

Several of these advantages are captured by this remark by one of the trainers in our study:

I actually think, however much they come along and say, 'I don't want to do an exam', they actually want to have something at the end of it because they've put so much into these courses. By the end of it, they're saying, 'I wish I'd got something to show for it.' They could take it to an employer.

Against these claims for accreditation it is possible to identify some potential disadvantages. Hence:

- people may be deterred from attending training programmes owing to the fear that, because the course is accredited, there may be exams;
- once accreditation becomes widespread there is a danger that the remaining unaccredited provision will be perceived as lacking quality;
- accreditation may draw learners into material which is not considered by them to be relevant, and there may be less flexibility to permit coverage of all the issues which learners *do* perceive as central to their concerns;
- accreditation may lead to the creation of what is perceived as an élite group of 'professional tenants'; and
- accreditation can divert tenants towards the production of coursework or the compilation of portfolios and away from activity focused on their organization's actual objectives.

Despite this general debate on accreditation (see also NIACE/REPLAN 1990), and despite its potential advantage as a means to lever in resources for tenant training, none of the trainers interviewed in our study offered accredited programmes or were aware of the limited existing avenues of accreditation in this specific field. It is to a review of the latter that we now turn.

Current accredited training for tenants

There are three main existing avenues of accredited training for tenants. First, there is the National Certificate in Tenant Participation (NCTP), accredited by the Chartered Institute of Housing. This is the only nationally recognized qualification in Britain which focuses specifically on tenant participation. It is designed for tenants of local authorities and housing associations, members of housing co-operatives and tenant management organizations, and also housing professionals. Course content includes participation in housing management and design, the promotion of participation, and more contextual issues such as social policy. The NCTP is generally delivered on one day a week over a year in colleges and universities, although access across the country is presently limited. From the authors' own experience of developing and delivering this qualification, the course has the merits of bringing tenants together from a range of organizations to gain from each other's experience and of lowering the barriers between tenants and housing workers. On the other hand, this is a course for tenants with some experience and confidence. For others a year-long course can be too demanding, while a nationally validated curriculum carries the risk of inflexibility.

Second, there is the Advanced Diploma in the Organization of Community Groups offered by the Royal Society of Arts (RSA). This is a competence-based qualification developing knowledge and skills relevant to tenants but not focused specifically on housing issues. Among the core requirements are those which require students to show competence in organizing an event, managing an organization's financial resources and managing human resources. However, the breadth of this programme is not necessarily well adjusted to the immediate individual needs of tenant activists, who often have quite specific responsibilities and are not involved directly in all aspects of their organization. Also, critics of this qualification point to the danger of learners becoming submerged in paperwork, to its relative weakness on equal opportunities issues (seen by many community workers as essential) and its inadequate explicit attention to the personal development of community (and tenant) group members. It appears that, currently, few tenants pursue this diploma.

Finally, attention should be drawn to the flexible means of accreditation provided by the Open College Networks (OCNs) which are found across Britain. These networks award credits which can be collected to form a 'study passport' which is nationally transferable. An OCN does not itself offer courses. It works with tutors and colleges to establish accredited provision, monitor quality and award credits. The courses themselves are offered by a range of colleges and other educational and voluntary organizations. Provision through OCNs has some important advantages. They can be quite flexible, offering scope for negotiation of the content by tutors and students. Moreover, a course developed for the specific purposes of a particular group can be accredited. Also, tenants who begin the course need not be required to register with the OCN and to commit themselves to assessment, but they can opt into the framework later if they so choose.

Reflecting on this section, it is clear that accreditation is not appropriate for all tenant training. However, accreditation can be an important means of recognizing and rewarding individual commitment, offering enhanced prospects for employment and attracting resources to tenant training. Yet our discussion has also underlined the very limited extent of existing provision.

Resourcing training

Existing channels

Of the trainers interviewed in our research, 70 per cent identified the local authority as an important source of funding. Other sources mentioned were the DoE, the Housing Corporation, individual housing associations, Training and Enterprise Councils (TECs), central government-financed regeneration schemes, the European Social Fund (ESF) and charitable trusts. Our earlier discussion has also shown the possibility of using accreditation to lever in funds from educational sources, notably the Further Education Funding Councils (FEFCs). However, the present recourse of so many tenant trainers to local authorities for resourcing is likely to present long-term difficulties owing to central spending controls and the capping of municipal revenue expenditure. Indeed, it is clear that the current provision of tenant training in Britain confronts several significant resourcing difficulties. These are now briefly explored.

Problems with resources

Many trainers related problems in funding their activities. For example, the recognition of equal opportunities issues, by adding to costs, often increases financial pressures. In the words of one trainer, there is:

> always a bit of a battle between equal opportunities ideals and the practicalities of the situation.

Many trainers complained of the time consumed by fund-raising, so detracting from the design and delivery of their service. Application to some funding sources, such as the ESF, requires a considerable commitment of time, with great uncertainty surrounding the outcome. Also, many training organizations, notably educational institutions, require minimum numbers to register for a course to secure resources. This can conflict with good training practice. One trainer observed that:

> the government believes that bums on seats equals quality; but, in fact, it tends to reduce the actual educational value of such occasions. Inevitably, there's a clash of interest between maximizing numbers and doing something of educational value.

Another problem is found in the restrictive conditions attached to resources offered by some institutions. In particular, DoE Section 16 funding was criticized by most trainers who had received it for being inflexible and linked inappropriately to a narrow range of management options:

It seems crazy that you can start working with a group, and if you reach the point at which they are clearly not going down those two routes of EMB or TMC then, strictly speaking, we're supposed to say, 'sorry, that's the end of it', and your [the present authors'] title of 'first-stage training for tenant participation' comes to a sudden end, even though it is still issues of tenant participation that are at stake.

A further source of complaint was the attachment, perceived as naïve, of training resources, linked narrowly to housing issues:

> The frustrating side of the work is that estates are much more complex than just housing. A lot of residents I meet are in quite poor health. [And] it would be nice to teach them about mediation for resolving neighbourhood nuisance. The longer you do this work, the more you realize it's narrow and rather impoverished, because of Section 16 – not in its narrowness of vision but in its off-the-shelf solutions. When we're meeting people there are many things you feel you want to tackle.

Such comments remind us that the provision of tenant training is not a straightforwardly neutral and technical enterprise. As Chapter 4 of this book illustrates, tenant training occurs within a political context and resourcing is related to a political agenda, both in housing and education. (The present authors have explored the politics of tenant training elsewhere with reference to competence-based training funded by Section 16 – see Furbey *et al.* 1996.)

Similar constraints can also affect other recipients of central government funding. During the development of the NCTP a conflict occurred between tenant members of the development committee and the DoE as the latter expressed a wish to limit bursary finance to members of tenant management organizations, although this restriction was later lifted.

Many tenant organizations receive some funding from their landlord. However, this is frequently not sufficient to give access to the training which they want. This is often also the case for TMOs where training is funded from a limited estate budget. The amount of training which can be extracted from such finite sources can vary widely, in relation to significant differences in prices. Some organizations offer free training, securing their payment from mainstream public funding. Others levy substantial charges. Clearly, tenants need to be informed on the full range of options.

Strengthening training

Having reviewed the present state of tenant-training opportunities in England, we now examine some means to strengthen future provision.

Discussion here will focus on the issue of access to information on training opportunities; the potential for linking tenant training to education and training in other policy contexts; possibilities for broadening the range of training providers (particularly through drawing on the resources of adult education); fostering better collaboration between trainers; and the facility offered by the National Tenant Resource Centre. This will lead to our concluding section in which we shall consider briefly the development of locality-based 'tenant-training forums' as an institutional means of consolidating and improving tenant training services.

Access to information

Our research revealed that both tenants and trainers are unaware of the full range of actual and potential providers of training for tenant participation. Tenant associations affiliated to established federations of tenants' organizations were best placed here, but for many other groups the channels of information were limited and fragile, especially in rural areas. Moreover, tenants with the least experience and most need of training were often those with the least knowledge on how to access information on training options. It is clear, therefore, that although the issue of resources explored in the previous section remains crucial, any new investment will not produce the best returns unless it is made in the context of a better-informed policy community of consumers and producers of training. In some localities Councils for Voluntary Services and Community Work Forums can be valuable channels of communication, giving guides to local training or directories of training providers. However, this resource is not widely available. Stronger links between the wider voluntary sector and tenants' organizations would offer prospects of much better information on training opportunities for tenant groups.

Links with wider education and training provision

Many of the training topics identified as relevant and important by tenants are not specific to housing. Rather, they include wider skills such as negotiating or running meetings, or the acquisition of knowledge in such broader policy settings as charity law or welfare rights. For training in these areas tenants can draw on the services of trainers outside the sphere of housing. Ideally, tenants should be able to connect with wider structures of citizenship education which address other constituencies such as school governors, health service users and local environmental protection groups.

Another potential linkage is between training for tenants and training for housing professionals. The experience of the NCTP is that both parties can gain greatly from joint programmes. Kirklees Metropolitan District Council in West Yorkshire has developed this process further by opening all its internal training for housing staff to tenants. Of course, such joint events will not be appropriate for all tenants and, indeed, some may find them intimidating. They also raise questions concerning the 'incorporation' of tenants' energy within officially approved agendas. But they can be an effective and low-cost form of training with many indirect benefits.

Tapping new sources

Another consideration is the possible under-utilization of potential sources of tenant training. Here, adult education services emerge as, in the words of one tenant leader, 'the great untapped resource'. Many staff in this sector have particular experience in working with adult learners and helping them to grow in confidence. Colleges and adult education centres are found throughout the country, have staff with a diversity of specialisms, and are reasonably well equipped with information technology and other equipment of value to tenants' organizations. Compared with some other training organizations, training arranged through adult education is also potentially cost-effective, especially if incorporated within colleges' accredited provision. (For a more developed discussion of adult education and accreditation see Furbey *et al.* 1994.)

Within our research localities many potential trainers, currently working in other fields, were unaware of tenant activity or had connections with only one particular tenant association. As training provision is often demand led, this underlines the importance of tenants' organizations having an awareness of the full range of possible providers and to spread awareness of their activities and needs among training institutions.

Encouraging collaboration

For their part, trainers themselves were often not aware of other trainers operating in their locality. Nevertheless, although some trainers simply identified their own organization as being in the best position to offer tenant training, one in five interviewees expressed a commitment to the principle of collaboration with other agencies. As one trainer based in housing practice observed:

> You actually need an organization with some experience in education to marry up the expertise and the way of offering it so people would learn from it.

Examples of such collaboration could be a partnership for specific purposes of federation development workers offering training sessions with financial staff from a housing organization, or adult education tutors working with an experienced outside tenant activist. Of continuing importance here is the matter of tenant choice. In the words of another trainer:

> I think if we had a whole network going, including the university . . . colleges, adult services and the voluntary sector, so that at any given point the tenants' group could tap into the one they most wanted, that would be ideal.

Although, in principle, most trainers can see no barriers to working in collaboration with other agencies, in practice some types of trainer (for example community workers) are much more likely than others (for example landlord organizations) to engage in such activity. In a context in which trainers are often in competition with each other, comments such as the following were the exception:

> We try not to be possessive about our training materials. Anyone in West Yorkshire can come and photocopy it. A lot of people could open things up a bit. We're grant aided. It's very different if you're a freelance. I can understand them wanting to hang on a bit more.

A further advantage of collaboration was seen by some trainers to lie in its potential for an efficient use of resources. Further, such inter-institutional working would provide opportunities for the exchange of information and the dissemination of good practice. Also, tenants' involvement in selecting trainers and negotiating the content of collaborative programmes can increase their sense of ownership over their training. However, practical difficulties remain. There is keen competition among trainers for funding, and collaboration requires extra time and extra resources:

> Everyone's fighting for survival so nobody is secure enough to look out and work together.

The National Tenant Resource Centre

In 1995 the National Tenant Resource Centre opened near Chester. Drawing on the experience of the National Tenant Training Centre in Denmark, this facility offers a residential base for a range of tenant-training courses. A comprehensive library is being developed and the centre will be a focus for sharing experiences, developing models of good practice and, importantly from the standpoint of this chapter, increasing the knowledge of training opportunities elsewhere. Particular innovations include a youth room to encourage activities in participation involving young people, and the use of Walter Segal self-build residential accommodation. The centre is designed to play a leading national role in tenant training.

Conclusions – towards 'tenant-training forums'?

This chapter has shown that training is a vital prerequisite for effective tenant participation. This is recognized clearly by the great majority of tenants. We have seen that tenant training in England is offered by a wide range of organizations, although certain agencies, notably those of adult education, are neglected. In terms of the content of training, there is much good practice and some that is less than satisfactory. But perhaps the key point is that no single training organization has the perspective, skills or knowledge to offer a comprehensive service to tenants.

Resources for training are often restricted and trainers operate in a competitive context. While competition may work to drive up training standards, it may also militate against inter-agency collaboration and the breadth of perspective which tenant training requires. Accreditation is one important instrument by which extra resources may be secured, although we have seen that this is not an unproblematic path to travel.

Finally, we have emphasized the importance of training being *negotiated*, with tenants as active participants in the choice of trainer and programme content and, indeed, involved themselves whenever possible as trainers of others.

In the light of this summary, what institutional innovations might best improve tenant training in England (and perhaps elsewhere), ensuring widely accessible, appropriate, affordable and sustainable provision in the future? The conclusion drawn in the light of our research (see Furbey *et al.* 1993, Section 7) was that the way ahead may lie in the development of local 'tenant-training forums'. A forum would be composed of tenants, landlord organizations and a range of local trainers. Ideally, tenants would be able to bring to the table, through independent funding schemes (Dean 1992), their own resources to empower them as purchasers of services. The forum's brief would be to assess local tenant-training needs, review current provision, identify funding sources, establish priorities and commission the delivery of programmes. Forums could also promote training, assess its quality, disseminate good practice and link local provision to national resources.

At the time of writing, TPAS (England), in partnership with the University of Glasgow, is conducting further research into tenant training involving the development and appraisal of some experimental models of the tenant-training forum concept.

References

Dean, R. (1992), *Independent Funding for Tenants*, Coventry: Chartered Institute of Housing.

Department of the Environment (DoE) (1994), *Training for Tenant Management*, London: HMSO.

Ecclestone, K. (1992), *Understanding Accreditation*, London: UDACE.

Furbey, R., Wishart, B., Hood, M. and Ward, H. (1993), *First-Stage Training for Tenant Participation*, final report on a project funded by the Joseph Rowntree Foundation, Sheffield: School of Urban and Regional Studies, Sheffield Hallam University.

Furbey, R., Wishart, B., Hood, M. and Ward, H. (1994), 'The great untapped resource: adult education, citizenship and tenant participation', *Adults Learning*, **5**(8), April, pp.204–206.

Furbey, R., Wishart, B. and Grayson, J. (1996), 'Training for tenants: "citizens" and the enterprise culture', *Housing Studies*, **11**(2), pp.251–269.

Holmes, A. (1992), *Limbering Up*, Middlesborough: RIPE.

NIACE/REPLAN (1990), *Valuing Volunteers: The Accreditation of Volunteers' Training and Experience*, Leicester: National Institute of Adult and Continuing Education.

10 Tools for empowerment

Charles Ritchie

This chapter gives an outline introduction to what constitutes Operational Research (OR) and its application as a tool for empowerment. The term itself covers a confusing range of activities and the skills and experience of individual OR practitioners vary dramatically. OR as a science is often located within mathematics, although it has also been located alongside a range of other disciplines, such as management theory, aimed at improving decision-making in organizations. This chapter will only focus on a fraction of what is practised under the banner of OR, the intention being not to explain OR but rather to show how a discipline developed in one sector (mainly that of large-scale production and services in commerce and government) can be adapted to serve the needs of tenants wishing to become involved in housing management.

OR's official history locates its beginnings in the Second World War when inter-disciplinary groups of scientists worked on a wide variety of logistical and operational problems related to the war effort. After the war, OR as an aid to project management was taken up by the newly nationalized industries and, in subsequent years, by a wider range of industrial, commercial and service organizations. The aim was to apply the 'scientific method' to solving a new range of problems and to increase output, improve efficiency and maximize profit. The early successes of OR tended to be related to large-scale problems, often with a significant technical element (such as planning and running large capital programmes and development projects, stock control, or maintenance and replacement decisions). OR provided the means by which management could squeeze out a few extra percentage points of production from the same labour and resources, or shave a few per cent off production costs.

The acceptance and use of OR approaches continued to expand throughout the post-war period until, by the 1970s, most large commercial, industrial and service organizations in the public, private and government sectors contained some function similar to OR. The term OR is not that well known since it often comes under the wider heading of management services, project management, business planning, resource planning or stock control.

Processes, not techniques

All of this seems a long way from concepts of empowerment and the active involvement of local communities in housing management and decision-making. However, while OR was developing a range of (often mathematical) approaches to tackling operational problems, many in OR were working in a wide variety of organizations on issues of strategic planning and assisting decision-makers in situations which were characterized by uncertainty and complexity. OR practitioners began to talk about 'messy' or 'unstructured' problems, where the role of the OR worker was to help organizations to understand situations and to explore possible strategies with greater confidence. Much of this type of work led to the development of a range of problem-structuring methods (often referred to as 'soft' methods), many of which were specifically designed for working with groups (Rosenhead 1989).

Throughout these developments of OR as a discipline, most front-line OR practitioners continued to draw on a wide range of fairly basic analytic approaches – simple statistical analyses or computer spreadsheet models. In fact, most practitioners recognized that the application of these techniques was of less significance than the *process* of involvement itself. The process of involvement in OR, from initial project negotiation through to final disengagement, was paramount and was *the* crucial factor in ensuring success. Many OR practitioners in the 1970s began to distinguish themselves from other forms of technical support, such as statisticians or computer experts, by the attention they gave to involving 'clients' in the problem-solving process. Although the term was not used at the time, this emphasis on the process of OR could be seen as an attempt at achieving 'empowerment'.

OR approaches, however, are not intrinsically empowering or disempowering. The process of any involvement is the overriding factor in determining to what extent tenants and residents are empowered. We will consider below involvement based around repairs and maintenance planning. This is a highly technical issue, requiring substantial and far from straightforward analyses. Certain technical examination was necessary and could not have been avoided, but discussions at the end of the study showed that the tenants involved had gained a great deal – in terms of technical knowledge, confidence and skills – because of the attention paid to the *process* of involvement (an important element in radical community work – see Chapter 1).

Understandably, there has been considerable resistance from those working in the community and voluntary sector to taking on management techniques developed in the commercial sector. There are too many examples where techniques and approaches which have proved successful in a commercial or business setting have failed badly in the community or voluntary sector because they have been transferred without due attention to the culture and needs of the new environment. It is only more recently that a literature has emerged which attempts to address some of these issues (Handy 1988, Hudson 1995).

Community Operational Research

As noted above, the development and expansion of OR after the war occurred largely in industrial and commercial settings. However, many OR practitioners believed that it could be used to benefit a wider cross-section of society and actively pursued this goal (Rosenhead and Thunhurst 1982, Rosenhead 1986). Yet, before the mid-1980s, very little OR had been used with groups and organizations in the community and voluntary sector. In 1986 the OR Society agreed to establish and fund a research unit, based at the Northern College for Residential Adult Education near Barnsley, to investigate the usefulness of OR approaches in the community sector. Since that time there has been a considerable amount of OR activity with community and voluntary organizations (Ritchie *et al.* 1994). The Community OR Unit opened in 1988, since when community housing has been one of its main areas of activity. The housing work of the unit was initially founded on long-term involvement with two recently established community housing groups facing very different situations, but both placing a very high priority on the empowerment of tenants through involvement in housing-management decision-making. These two case studies will be explored in some depth.

The first group we will examine is the Thurnscoe Tenants Housing Co-operative (TTHC), founded by former British Coal tenants in 1988 to prevent their homes being sold at auction to private landlords (see Chapter 2). The Unit worked with the co-operative for nearly five years. In the beginning it helped TTHC to develop its long-term strategy during its early months of existence. Later, it went on to assist the co-operative with detailed financial planning, developing a house sales policy, running structured street meetings, undertaking a survey of the membership and reviewing its allocations policy (Thunhurst *et al.* 1992, Thunhurst and Ritchie 1992). Although the co-operative employed the Yorkshire Metropolitan Housing Association (YMHA) to undertake the day-to-day management of the housing stock, it did not have any further resources to assist with the range of other 'development' activities which were necessary for it to survive. Therefore, the Unit also had considerable involvement in many of the day-to-day issues of running the organization and providing advice and assistance.

The second group we look at came from Belle Isle, a council-owned estate in South Leeds which, at the time of the Unit's initial involvement, was in the process of establishing an Estate Management Board (EMB) (Percy-Smith *et al.* 1990). The style of the Unit's involvement was different to that at Thurnscoe. Since the board was supported by a number of full-time staff, the Unit's role was more akin to that of external consultant working on defined areas of project work. The main focus of the Unit's work was around repairs, maintenance and major capital improvements, although within these areas the actual work ranged from detailed financial and technical work through to public consultation.

Despite these very different settings a close and friendly working relationship developed with both groups, and the Unit was able to under-take both formal and informal evaluations of its involvement with them.

Thurnscoe Tenants Housing Co-operative

Thurnscoe is a mining village in South Yorkshire, located in the Dearne Valley which sits at the intersection of the boroughs of Barnsley, Rotherham and Doncaster. The local pit had closed two years before the Unit's involvement in the area. Progressively, since the 1960s, British Coal had been divesting itself of its housing stock. In January 1987, the tenants of Thurnscoe discovered, by accident, that their homes were to be auctioned at a hotel in London. The tenants managed to have the sale stopped and, following considerable activity and protracted negotiations, they formed themselves into a co-operative and bought their 361 homes with a mortgage of £1.75 million. A condition of the mortgage was that housing management should be carried out by an established housing association for at least the first three years.

During its establishment TTHC had been able to draw on the assistance of a small number of individuals and organizations, in particular a co-operative development worker with Barnsley MBC and the regional officer from Shelter. However, while the group was passionately committed to maintaining the integrity and cohesion of housing in their area, none of its members had any experience of running a large financial undertaking. The group was able to use the facilities of Northern College to help to develop some of the basic groupworking and committee skills and confidence to continue what it had started.

The co-operative's introduction to the Unit came as a natural progression of this involvement with the wider college. The close working relationship which developed with staff from the Unit was to last for over five years and informal contacts still remain. Over that period the Unit worked on a wide variety of issues, ranging from *ad hoc* advice or assistance at events to in-depth strategic- and financial-planning exercises. Only three of these areas of involvement will be described in this chapter. However, it is worth emphasizing the value of the various developments in the relationship and trust which underpinned the success of the work.

Strategic planning

The first involvement focused on the information needs of TTHC and whether it needed a computerized database for holding information about members of the co-operative and the housing stock. A brief study indicated that this was not an early priority and that a card-based system would suffice. The first significant piece of work was to help the members of the co-operative's committee consider how they should move forward as the new owners and managers of the largest stock of rented housing in the area. While there was real elation at their success in taking over the stock, no one really knew what they could achieve in the longer term and how they should start. Therefore, a strategic-planning workshop was organized. The workshop was structured using an OR method known as *Strategic Choice* (Friend and Hickling 1987).

Strategic Choice is a well-established method which has been developed over a number of years. It has been used widely, particularly in complex public planning exercises. In outline, the approach is made up of four activity stages (Shaping, Designing, Comparing and Choosing). These are used, not in a strictly linear fashion, to help a group work through its current situation by highlighting areas where decisions need to be made and clarifying the links between decisions. This method is also very useful for explicitly handling and tackling the different types of uncertainty that arise in any situation. During the course of the workshop (which can run over several days) the group moves towards developing *Strategic Options* and criteria by which the success of the different options should be judged. The final output of the workshop is a *Commitment Package*, which is essentially a list of tasks to be undertaken now and later – some of these will include further investigations which may help the group reduce some of the areas of uncertainty.

In the case of TTHC, an immediate concern was the maintenance and repair of the housing stock. Flip-charts and 'post-it' notes were used for an initial brainstorming of the issues and uncertainties related to this. By the end of one morning it had been agreed to focus on three key areas of decision-making in relation to taking over the maintenance work: the choice between putting work out to tender or building up a direct works force; deciding priorities; and undertaking the administrative work. The next stage in the process was to compare two contrasting strategies, one involving a 'crash programme' of training and early take-over of the repair service by the co-operative, the other involving a 'slow but steady' take-over. It was clear that members of the committee were ideologically in favour of the former strategy. Subsequently, the facilitators found themselves testing whether the 'slow but steady' approach had any countervailing advantages, before then drawing out the areas of uncertainty that seemed to get in the way of following the 'crash programme'.

The following figures are intended to give some indication about the content and outputs from a Strategic Choice workshop. Figure 10.1 shows

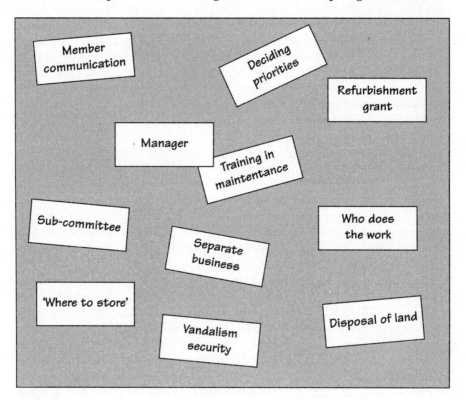

Figure 10.1 Issues

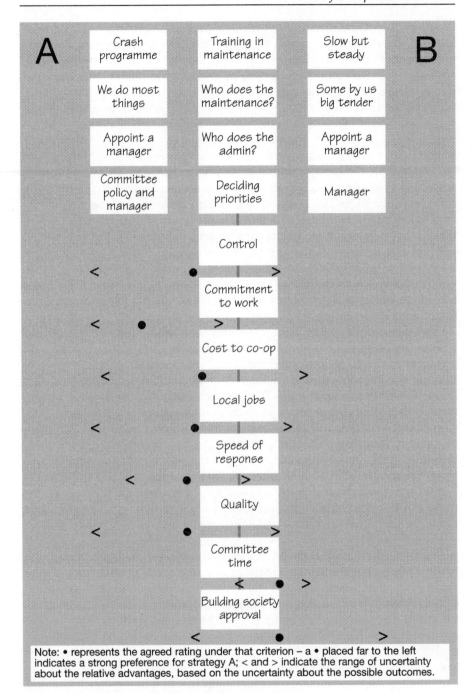

Note: • represents the agreed rating under that criterion – a • placed far to the left indicates a strong preference for strategy A; < and > indicate the range of uncertainty about the relative advantages, based on the uncertainty about the possible outcomes.

Figure 10.2 Comparison of contrasting strategies

the clustering of issues arising out of the initial brainstorming and discussion sessions. The closer to the centre, the higher the priority attached by members of the group to that issue. Figure 10.2 (see p.227) shows the comparison sheet on which the two contrasting strategies ('crash programme' and 'slow but steady') were rated against the various criteria derived.

Out of the discussion of uncertainties came a number of practical actions that could be considered to reduce these and the skeleton of an outline action plan, or Commitment Package, emerged. It was clear that many investigations needed to be made and that the co-operation of YMHA would be vital for the 'crash programme' to have any chance of success. A second workshop was arranged, to take place over one-and-a-half days, involving staff from YMHA. This second workshop focused on comparing the establishment of a community business to undertake repair work (an option which was finding increasing favour among members of the committee) with the status quo of continuing to employ outside contractors. Flip-charts were used to build up a systematic record of the assumptions relating to the various stakeholder groups that appeared to support each strategy. As at the end of the previous workshop, a list of actions to be followed through was drawn up.

Over the course of the Unit's involvement with TTHC it ran several further workshops, based around elements of Strategic Choice, with members of the co-operative's committee – on one occasion using a newly developed computer-assisted package. Members of the committee said they found the approach clear and understandable and that they felt it helped them both to ensure that they had carried out a full investigation and to be clear about why they had made particular decisions. From the Unit's point of view, it was clear that the Strategic Choice exercise was beneficial in introducing rigour and completeness into the process of Strategic Review. However, it did not in itself encourage a creative exploration of the options. Therefore, it was found more practical to use Strategic Choice as the framework within which to include other approaches which facilitate creativity (in particular, drama and action methods).

The success of these early sessions provided the platform for a long and productive relationship between the co-operative and the Unit. In addition to the Strategic Review sessions referred to above, the Unit undertook a wide variety of other work across a spectrum of topics ranging from 'hard' technical issues (such as financial planning) to 'softer' issues (such as trying to assess the wider membership's long-term aspirations for the co-operative). The 'hard' issues provided the opportunity to test the utility of traditional, classical OR methods to a different social context. In contrast, the 'soft' issues required a greater amount of innovation and the need to combine OR approaches with techniques from other disciplines. However, in both situations there was a very clear message that techniques themselves (whether OR or others) are not intrinsically appropriate or empowering. The overriding factor, as we have already suggested, is the process.

One of the 'hard' issues tackled was the serious financial problems that TTHC faced. Work in this area also meant that the co-operative had to confront two apparently conflicting objectives: the need for financial viability against the expressed wish to retain affordable rented housing in the area. Although TTHC had bought the 361 houses at an average price of around £5000 each, the vast majority of the stock was in extremely poor condition. While British Coal had undertaken minor repair works to the properties, no major modernization work had been carried out during the previous 30 years or more. As such, most properties needed substantial works, such as new roofs, windows and damp-proof courses, to maintain the basic fabric of the properties. In addition, virtually all the houses needed substantial internal modernization to bring them up to an acceptable standard for the 1980s.

The true state of some properties was only revealed to members of the co-operative committee when, with the assistance of the Unit, they carried out a complete house-to-house members' survey (Booker 1990). The survey contained questions on the condition of the housing stock, but even more revealing to the committee was just visiting some of the houses of older co-operative members. They were not only shocked by the conditions in which some people were living, but also by the fact that some tenants had accepted that such a low level of housing facility was all they could (and should) expect. It was estimated that the houses needed a total expenditure of between £5 million and £7 million to bring them up to a reasonable standard.

Preliminary investigations held before TTHC was established had indicated that the co-operative might be eligible for a range of grants from local and central government, and from Europe. However, it gradually became apparent that no such funding would be available and that the co-operative had to be 'self-sufficient'. The only sources of finance would be through rental income or sale of assets (that is, the houses themselves). It was clear that in order to determine an agreed strategic direction the co-operative would need, first, to have a detailed understanding of the scale of the financial problem and options available and, second, to know what balance to strike between the financial and social aspirations of the membership. The Unit was able to assist in both areas.

The financial work drew on well-established OR-type approaches involving the development of a relatively simple model of the co-operative's finances on a computer spreadsheet. The concept of computer spreadsheet modelling is fairly straightforward. It can be thought of as a computerized 'ledger sheet' – that is, a sheet of paper ruled into rows and columns. Each 'cell' (that is, the intersection of a row and column) can then be programmed as a number or a formula defining the relationship between other cells.

Therefore, using only the most simple arithmetic, it is possible to build a model of a housing organization's finances which incorporates elements such as the number of houses, sales and selling prices, rent levels, loans, interest rates, inflation, voids, repairs and maintenance, and so forth. Then, by changing any of these figures, it is possible to investigate the impact and the inter-relationship between the different elements through a series of 'what if?' questions. Once the model has been developed, any number of investigations can be conducted rapidly.

However, the process of developing and using the model was crucial to its acceptance and use by the committee. It was important that the model could be used with confidence directly by members of the committee to answer their queries rather than the Unit using it to produce and present plans and options for consideration by the committee. Therefore, the development of the model needed to be a learning process, particularly since members of the committee had had no previous experience of financial planning or management. In this way, they would build up their confidence to use the model and to analyse the figures involved without the need to depend on the presence of staff from the Unit.

One of the most important features of the model was that the overall finances of TTHC were simultaneously displayed as 'per house per week' figures. This was a simple but clear aid to understanding, in that numbers with several zeros at the end were 'translated' into figures that had more meaning and practical relevance for individual members. Furthermore, after substantial use of the model, members of the committee began to develop a clear understanding of the relationships between key variables and, in particular, appreciate the co-operative's vulnerability to changes in interest rates. This led to the development of a number of 'key facts and figures', such as (say) 'a £1 rise in rents could pay for the modernization of 50 houses'. A few of these key relationships were written on to flip-charts and permanently displayed in the committee's meeting room. These permanent reminders aided the process of assimilating complex financial data into the committee's everyday discussions. These early spreadsheet modelling exercises convinced the committee that any substantial improvements to the housing stock could only be achieved through a policy of selling houses as they became vacant. The number of houses which should be sold, and how bad the condition of a house should be before it was sold, were items for further discussion and approval by the wider membership.

The approach taken to using spreadsheet models had helped the committee to develop its basic understanding of financial issues. It had also proved popular with members of the committee. In later years, when the co-operative was considering re-financing and becoming a registered housing association, new spreadsheet models were developed to underpin the committee's deliberations.

A wide range of other finance-based work was also undertaken, including developing options for the annual rent rise and investigating the economics of an individual house. Throughout these activities the same message was becoming abundantly clear – that it *is* possible to make a complex and difficult subject understandable and accessible through the development of simple modelling techniques and by paying attention to the process of involvement.

Public consultation

A second and contrasting activity with the co-operative focused on the process of *public consultation*. As noted above, it was important for members of the committee to understand and handle complex technical information. However, it was equally important for them to be able to communicate with the wider membership and to gather their views and opinions on a wide range of issues. Of course, the co-operative used many of the traditional methods of doing this – such as newsletters, public meetings, and just talking to people – but there were occasions when they felt that a more detailed and structured consultation was necessary.

TTHC had been formed out of necessity rather than as a conscious and informed decision by all involved. The situation they had faced required them to either establish the co-operative or risk their homes being sold to an unknown, and possibly distant, landlord. People were voting against the landlord option rather than being committed to co-operative principles. Therefore, once TTHC was established, it was only those on the committee and a few other interested individuals who had the slightest idea of what they were letting themselves in for. Few knew the potential or the pitfalls and few wanted to be actively involved in management or decision-making. There was a real risk that the committee would become perceived as the 'new landlord' and, furthermore, that they might start to take on that role. So it was important that a two-way communication was established as soon as possible.

The Unit had assisted the co-operative in undertaking a survey of all the membership to gather necessary information about the members themselves and the condition of the housing stock. However, it was agreed that a different form of consultation was required to allow members a chance not only to learn more about the workings of the co-operative and the problems it faced, but also to find out their views about its future. With these aims in mind, a series of 'street meetings' was organized. The intention was to invite no more than 30 people to each meeting to allow in-depth discussion and exploration of the issues. It was agreed that it would be helpful to have some structure to the meetings to give focus to the discussions. However, the purpose of the meetings was also to allow the wider membership to decide what the key issues were!

It was decided that the structure of the meetings should be based around Nominal Group Technique (NGT) (Delbecq and Van de Ven 1971). This is a sort of 'upwards cascade', in which people start by working on their own or in pairs, move on to work in small groups, and then finally come together in a plenary session. In the case of TTHC, people working in pairs were asked to think about and write down what they thought were the three biggest problems facing the co-operative. Having spent five minutes discussing these with their partner, they were then asked to move into groups of six. Each group was 'facilitated' by a committee member and each created a list of problems. Of course, some problems had been highlighted by more than one pair and this fact was noted. Subsequently, each group moved on to agree which were the most important problems and which were the most immediate. Finally, each group was asked to discuss two or three of the problems in some depth to see if they could agree any ways forward. The facilitator made notes and contributed factual information where necessary, but tried not to enter into the details of the discussion too much.

After each group had worked together for about an hour, with a break for refreshments, everyone was brought together to share their discussions. As each group reported back their ordered list was displayed and notes were made about the potential solutions or other issues that had arisen in their discussions. The wider meeting was then invited to contribute ideas and notes were made of the points raised. Finally, members at the meeting were asked to vote for (or against) any of the issues or solutions which they felt were important (or not) or which they supported (or opposed).

During the evaluation of the meeting, it was agreed that the structured approach had been more successful than everyone had expected. A few of the members of the co-operative had not expected to be involved in such a process, but very few reacted negatively. None of the meetings managed to attract more than 20 people and some had to be cancelled. However, at the end of the process the committee had gathered a significant amount of information about the views of the wider membership which contributed to their own subsequent discussions and decision-making. While they had picked up a great deal of information through informal discussions at the meetings, the committee agreed that the outputs of the structured process should carry most weight (with information from the informal discussions remaining largely complementary).

TTHC successfully used a similar process at one of its annual rent-setting meetings. However, on other occasions it was felt that a more traditional style of public meeting was appropriate. It was also agreed that the NGT-type meeting was most successful when the question that people were being asked to address was fairly concrete. The more speculative or abstract the question, the more time was spent discussing what the question meant and how it could be interpreted.

A range of other approaches were also used to assist the consultation process. Some of the most interesting, from the Unit's point of view, were those which were able to use the creativity generated through 'action' methods with the structuring strengths of OR approaches.

The Unit's involvement with TTHC continued over a number of years and only ended, by mutual agreement, when some members of the committee felt that they needed a period of consolidation rather than strategic planning and development. Many of the policies developed in the early years of TTHC still form the basis of the strategic direction of the co-operative, such as vacant houses requiring more than a specified level of work being sold to pay for a programme of enveloping houses. Lower interest rates in the 1990s also eased TTHC's financial problems considerably, but the co-operative still faces many years of hard work before it can consider the job finished.

Belle Isle North Estate Management Board

The Belle Isle North Estate Management Board (BINEMB) emerged from a Priority Estate Project (PEP) established by Leeds City Council (unconnected with the national PEP body) in March 1985. It was initially a three-year project funded through the Urban Programme, later extended through mainstream funding by the City Council. At the time the Unit first established contact with Board members, substantial progress towards negotiating the management agreement with the City Council had already been made. Although Board members had undertaken a variety of training, there were many issues which members were still trying to come to grips with – particularly in respect to some of the more technical issues relating to repairs, maintenance and housing finance. Major modernization works had also been undertaken, through Estate Action funding, on some areas of the estate, but the greater part remained untouched.

Initial contact was established through a tenant member of the Board attending a short course at Northern College. A brief presentation on the Unit's work in Thurnscoe convinced her that the Board was facing similar issues. A meeting was arranged with workers seconded to the Board. Coincidentally, one of these workers had been on a Master's course in OR some years earlier, and this had not left him with a great deal of confidence when he heard that someone was coming from Northern College to talk about 'community OR'. From his experience of doing the course, 'community' was the last thing that he would have expected to see prefixing 'OR'! It was apparent that he perceived OR as a highly mathematical and academic tool which would only have a role to play in relation to the more technical aspects of housing management.

At the initial meeting with BINEMB it was agreed that the Unit should become involved in helping the Board to devise and submit a bid for capital funding for a major modernization programme still outstanding on the estate. The Whole House Improvement (WHI) scheme which had already started on the estate was experiencing increasing delays, largely because of funding problems. There was also a general feeling that, while the WHI scheme had initially been the ideal solution for the estate's problems, when finance was limited other approaches spreading expenditure around the estate might be more desirable. However, this could also be seen as lowering expectations and 'admitting defeat'.

Capital spending

The Unit's work with BINEMB started with the production of a report on the systems and information that would be required to put together a bid for capital funding. Clearly, this was a fairly technical piece of work, but it was undertaken by the Board with the help of staff from the Unit and relevant council officers. The report contained information flow diagrams and identified the relevant data needed in relation to the condition of the housing stock, costs of different types of work, current plans and, perhaps most importantly for the EMB in its first year, tenants' wishes. It also highlighted the problem of obtaining historical information about the estate (such as what expenditure had already been incurred). The council had seen no need to isolate spending on individual estates. This fact was to prove both a problem and an opportunity over the next few years.

In addition, a 'cartwheel' calendar was designed to illustrate the timescales for different key activities and deadlines. Showing the year in a circular way rather than in the traditional linear format helped to demonstrate how activities recur each year and that it is not always helpful to think of the year as having a beginning and an end.

This preparatory work helped the Board to undertake the capital-bidding exercise for that year (Ritchie 1991). While it was possible to set in motion efforts to gather some of the technical and financial information, it was recognized that one of the main problems of finding out what tenants think is important invariably invites the answer 'my house'. BINEMB needed to find out the underlying criteria by which any modernization scheme could be judged. It was agreed to hold an 'away-day' at Northern College to help the Board to focus on its own priorities and to plan how it should consult the wider membership.

The day began with a short role play to establish the likely attitudes of councillors, council officers and the DoE to any modernization plans. A modified version of an OR/Systems approach, known as Strategic Assumption Surfacing and Testing (SAST – a grand title for an approach which is, in essence, quite simple), was used. Board members were asked to work in three separate groups to consider three very distinct approaches to modernization: the current WHI approach; dividing money equally across all houses each year and letting individual tenants choose the work to be done on their own house; and annual 'focused' schemes with a different focus each year (such as works on old people's houses, security schemes or a roofing scheme). Each group then had to 'sell' its particular approach (regardless of how good the members actually thought it was) to the others. The other groups then criticized the presented approach, particularly taking the view of a tenant who would not benefit from the scheme. In this way people's initial ideas were explored and developed, leading to the formulation of new ideas and a broader understanding of the wider issues.

Meanwhile, the main points raised were being recorded on flip-charts so that, at the end of all three presentations, there were charts showing the advantages and disadvantages of each. By working through these charts, it was possible to see that these advantages and disadvantages could be clustered to give the underlying criteria by which people were judging schemes. This was done with the agreement of all participants, leaving 11 measurements for judging the success of a modernization scheme. It was clear that some of these criteria were more important than others, so everyone was given four coloured stickers (red for most important, blue for the next and so on) and were allowed to 'vote' for the ones they most favoured. This gave a final ordered list of the criteria for BINEMB to judge approaches to modernization.

The full version of SAST extends beyond this simplified account and offers a mechanism for looking at what actions are necessary in order to develop *any* strategy. In this way, the process is able to highlight the steps which are common to different approaches in strategic decision-making and which may be undertaken regardless of the nature of the problem to be addressed (see Mason and Mitroff 1981).

In the case of BINEMB, the SAST approach was felt to have been effective and fun, so it was decided that a similar (but simplified) approach should be used in public meetings to gather people's views. For these meetings a variation on the NGT approach employed in Thurnscoe was used. The public meetings opened with a quiz which was constructed to give useful information, generate discussion and be entertaining. Some of the meetings suffered from the usual attendance problems, but by the end of the process the Board was able to say that it had taken into account the views of the wider membership and become clearer about its own ideas.

Crucially, the exercise with BINEMB had shown that the main criteria for any capital-funding bid were that the money should be directed towards the houses in the greatest need of repair *and* that spending should be spread as widely as possible. It also highlighted the need to develop feasible plans and to stick to them. People were prepared to wait for home improvements, so long as they had a definite date for when these would start in which they could place some trust.

Repairs and maintenance: budgeting and monitoring

A final area of work with BINEMB that will be covered in this chapter is related to its long-term involvement in repairs and maintenance. The success of the Unit's earlier involvement had led to an invitation from the Board to attend meetings of its property sub-group which was responsible for overseeing the maintenance and improvement of the houses. This gave the Unit a good overview of the activities of the EMB and the opportunity to see the way in which tenant Board members were presented with information and how effectively this was interpreted and handled.

Staff from the Unit attended a training day on repairs and maintenance with Board members. It was an interesting day and included a presentation illustrating the spending profile on repair works required during the lifetime of a property. The theory behind this presentation was that, given the age, repair history and condition of the housing stock, it should be possible to devise a repairs and maintenance budget. Other issues were highlighted, such as the advantages of planned or programmed repairs over random or responsive repairs, and the need for budgeting and monitoring spending on repairs. These ideas were not new. In fact, repairs and maintenance planning is one of the main areas of traditional OR and there are many OR practitioners who work on nothing else. However, it was reassuring to have reinforced some of the recommendations about the need for a housing condition survey and historical information on capital and revenue spending, contained in our earlier report!

Following this event the Unit was asked to run a training day based on monitoring repairs and maintenance expenditure. It was agreed that it would be more interesting and informative if the session was based on actual spending on the Belle Isle estate over recent years. The only way to obtain the necessary figures was to analyse a stack of computer printouts detailing individual orders which had been paid each month. A considerable amount of analysis later, and only ready the day before the training event, a breakdown of repairs by trade and cost for each of the previous 16 months had been produced. Many hours of hard work had boiled down into just a few diagrams which did not even demonstrate the degree of seasonality in repair trends that had been expected. However, the figures seemed to demonstrate that the budget allocation for repairs was inadequate. This was clearly a significant concern. Also, further analysis revealed considerable delays between commissioning, completing and paying for works, which meant that the figures provided to the Board, which showed works paid for each month, were unreliable for monitoring purposes.

The focus of the training day moved from a general examination of repairs and maintenance budgeting and monitoring towards a specific consideration of the situation faced by BINEMB. Board members were shown a number of different ways of presenting information on repairs and maintenance, all based on simple graphs and bar charts. It was agreed that a combination of these diagrams would provide an adequate set of tools for monitoring spending.

Clearly, the budget shortfall was an important issue for the EMB. However, there remained considerable doubts about the adequacy of the information available – particularly that it was incomplete. The general consensus of those involved was that this deficiency was because of inadequate data-recording and reporting systems. There was no reason to expect any deliberate error, but it was felt that the council was unable to isolate spending on the Belle Isle estate and that the budget had probably been based on city-wide figures. Nevertheless, whatever the reason, challenging the budget figure needed to be handled sensitively.

After some considerable time and delicate negotiations, a new budget was eventually produced which gave the Board the flexibility to programme some minor works if they were able effectively to monitor and control their repairs and maintenance budget. This led to a programme of work which provided a strong link between the Unit and BINEMB for a considerable time. The Unit facilitated a quarterly meeting of all Board members to review spending on maintenance and repairs. These meetings became the central element of the decision-making process for repairs spending. It is perhaps useful to consider briefly the process and tools used during these meetings, since they seemed to provide a valuable means of monitoring the actual spending on repairs and future projections against the budget in a way that could be quickly and readily communicated.

At the first meeting of the financial year, after BINEMB had received its budget allocation, the Board would devise and agree its repair expenditure policy. This policy would usually be based on the recommendations of the Board's surveyor and a review of the previous year's spending. Furthermore, the Board would also propose a number of additional improvement schemes, based on its own knowledge of the estate, which could be undertaken if the funds became available. The Board was experienced enough to know that there would usually be a call in February each year for small capital projects and so it was advisable to have a number of schemes ready 'on the shelf'.

At the start of each quarterly meeting, summaries showing spending to date against the budget were presented and discussed for clarification (see Figures 10.3 and 10.4). The main points highlighted by the figures usually related to the monthly variability and the position of current spending against budget. The next issue to be discussed would be the projected figure

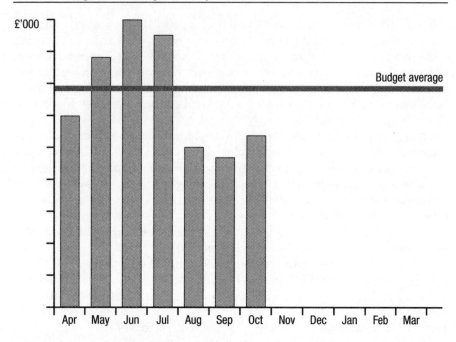

Figure 10.3 Monthly spending profile

for total annual spending. Two estimates of this figure were always produced, one by the Board's surveyor and one by the Unit, using a standard mathematical forecasting model. It was helpful to discuss the possible reasons for these forecasts differing and to look at the way in which they had changed since the previous quarter. Through these discussions Board members would develop a very good 'feel' for the likely level of under- or overspend, as well as the possible actions necessary either to limit and control spending or to sanction expenditure on one of the improvement schemes identified at the start of the year.

These types of meeting have continued beyond the involvement of the Unit. It has been possible to hold a number of one-day workshops to help the Board review its progress or to consider specific issues. Budgeting, and monitoring repairs and maintenance expenditure, have remained important topics, and it is noticeable that Board members retain a sophisticated understanding of the issues involved.

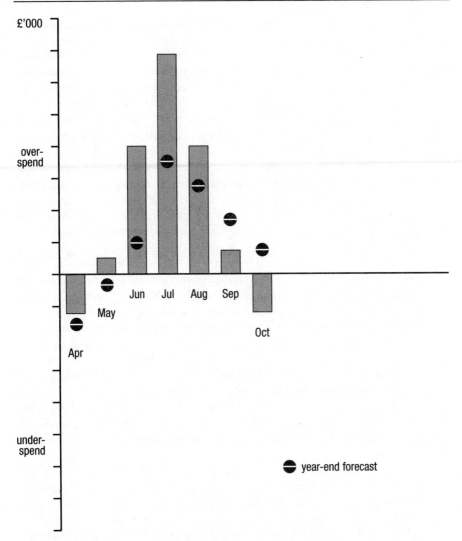

Figure 10.4 Cumulative under/overspend and forecast year-end figure

Housing management training game – 'Managing the Estate'

The experiences of the Unit's work with Thurnscoe, Belle Isle and a wide range of other community housing organizations, as well as its involvement on a range of housing courses delivered at Northern College, confirmed (unsurprisingly) that most tenants and tenant organizations face similar issues and problems in becoming involved in housing management. However, these experiences also showed that community OR was able to offer a range of contributions beyond the invaluable assistance that was also being given by tenant participation and community-development workers.

The key areas where community OR appeared to offer valuable assistance seemed to be around the facilitation of tenant participation in technical issues such as repairs, maintenance and financial planning. Involvement with Thurnscoe in particular had highlighted the value of simple computer-based financial spreadsheet models in allowing tenants to develop a real 'feel' for finance by being able to ask a series of 'what-if?' questions, effectively playing with some key variables until they achieved a 'solution' which satisfied their need. Subsequently, the Unit decided to develop a housing management 'game', to be called 'Managing the Estate'. A central element of this game would be a computer spreadsheet representation of a housing estate and its finances. The intention was to develop the game as a suite of connectable modules, each focusing on different elements of housing management. The first module to be completed, 'Setting the rent', focuses on housing finance, repairs and maintenance, and capital programme planning. An allocations module has also been developed (Bhargava 1995).

The aims of the game are to introduce participants to the complexities of running a large housing organization and to give them the opportunity of developing and testing strategic plans for such an organization. In addition, it was felt that it was important for tenants to gain a better understanding of the different roles, objectives and perspectives of different groups involved in housing management; to appreciate the relationships between long-term planning decisions and day-to-day activities; and to consider the trade-off between financial and non-financial factors when developing and assessing strategic plans.

Management games have been a significant and important area of work for OR practitioners working in 'traditional' organizations. A recent example is the game called 'HOME', developed by Hoskyns Consulting for use by local authorities facing compulsory competitive tendering for housing-management services. The common features of most of these games are the element of role-playing and the existence of a computer-based model to undertake all calculations resulting from the decisions made by the different role-players. 'Managing the Estate' includes both these features. However, the game draws less on traditional role-playing approaches, where people tend to take on a single role throughout, but allows tenants to explore different viewpoints through other action methods.

Tenants are introduced to Allfield, an imaginary housing estate (either local authority or housing association), which has undergone some modernization over recent years. Unfortunately, finances have run out before all of the work has been completed. Participants then explore the key issues on the estate through playing the part of a variety of individual or group interests (for example, tenants in modernized, partially modernized and unmodernized properties, housing managers, tenant associations and so on), drawing on their own experiences. Each time the game has been used participants have generated their own unique and fascinating issues and problems.

Having uncovered the key issues and problems, the next stage is to come up with proposals for change. Working in small groups of housing-management staff, they develop a strategy for the estate. Subsequently, each group has to work through a series of decisions about major modernization works, repairs and, finally, rent-setting. Inevitably, the groups go through a number of iterations as they realize that their original development plans for the estate result in unacceptably high rent increases. The final element of the game involves the housing-management teams having to present their proposals to 'tenants', and suffering the consequent barrage of questions and protest.

The game has proved to be an extremely useful vehicle for allowing tenants to gain a good understanding of housing finance issues. It also acts as an excellent introduction to a much deeper discussion of legislation and other constraints surrounding financial decision-making in the area of housing.

Conclusions

As noted at the beginning, the intention of this chapter was not only to communicate something of the scope of OR approaches and their value in involving tenants, but also to illustrate how techniques developed in one sphere can make a contribution in another totally different context. It is perhaps worth recapping on some of the common areas of work with tenants where OR approaches have proved to be valuable:

- *Links between decisions*: it is important that problems and decisions are not considered in isolation. Although it will be necessary to focus on key problem areas, it is important to recognize that a decision made in one area can restrict options in another. Strategic Choice, in particular, is explicit about identifying these links.
- *Identifying and handling different types of uncertainty*: most situations involve a whole variety of unknowns, including people's views and aspirations, market conditions, what other organizations are planning to do and so on. Successful management can be thought of as the ability to develop strategies to cope with uncertainty, retaining flexibility and

undertaking activities to reduce the unknown. Also, any analysis should explicitly acknowledge what is unknown, so that it may be necessary to investigate a number of different scenarios.

● *Stakeholder analysis*: it is always useful to be clear about who is involved in any decisions, who will be affected by them, and what their views and reactions are likely to be.

● *Problem structuring, not problem solving*: it is often helpful to approach problems with a view to making sense of the situation rather than believing that it is possible to develop a 'final solution'. The external environment will usually react and adapt to any solution to create a different problem.

● *Handling both qualitative and quantitative data*: there is the temptation with quantitative data either to ignore it, because it is 'too difficult to handle or understand', or to let it dominate thinking to the exclusion of all other factors, particularly when dealing with financial information. Inevitably, both quantitative and qualitative types of information are important and this needs to be recognized.

● *Structured and rigorous analysis*: perhaps above all else, OR provides a structured approach to strategic analysis. Without some form of underlying structure it is easy for analysis and decision-making to become side-tracked and focused on 'the easy' rather than 'the important'.

However, experience has also highlighted some of the weaknesses of OR. In particular, most OR approaches do not in themselves inspire creativity. Indeed, some people find that the rigour of some OR approaches can stifle creative thinking and exploration. This may certainly be the case in approaches involving numbers. Therefore, careful attention needs to be paid to the process of application, perhaps sacrificing some of the rigour to allow space for creative investigation. As the experience of the Unit has shown, it is possible to be creative by combining techniques from different disciplines, such as drama, role play and action methods, with OR.

It is vital that OR methods are made accessible. Some are simple and straightforward to explain (for instance, the SWOT analysis – Strengths, Weaknesses, Opportunities and Threats), while others can appear daunting. Sometimes, this is because the words and titles themselves are unwieldy (for example, Strategic Assumption Surfacing and Testing is hardly 'user friendly'). In other cases, a written description of a multi-stage technique can disguise the simple and clear logic of the approach, while a textbook on Strategic Choice can be intimidating. However, the groups with which we have worked using these approaches to strategic decision-making have commented on how much the process is based on 'common sense'. Consequently, we would argue that management and organizational theory can learn, for instance, from the experience of architects who have been prepared to abandon the use of detailed scale drawings and precise models in favour of less precise planning techniques based on rougher models made of cardboard and polystyrene so that people can get involved in experimenting with ideas.

It is impossible to overemphasize the importance of the process of applying OR and similar approaches. Very few, if any, techniques for strategic planning are inherently empowering. A straightforward process of voting can be manipulative and intimidating. However, there are few approaches which cannot be made participative or empowering. The Unit's location in Northern College, a residential adult education college, has meant that skill transference and capacity-building in communities has always been high on the agenda, and it is very rare that this has not been possible. Careful attention needs to be paid to building relationships, ensuring that planning sessions and activities are inclusive, and that the timing and pace of any involvement are closely monitored. There is no reason that the use of any particular set of techniques and approaches should prevent the development of the mutual trust and respect which are necessary for any successful engagement.

Finally, it is important to recognize the limitations of the approaches used. The application of OR does not remove the need for good community-development work and the wide range of additional support and resources needed to help groups to develop and flourish. Without doubt, the most successful work of the Unit has taken place when there has been a variety of other support services available and it has been possible to combine the strengths and resources of each. OR does not replace the role of community-development workers, tenant-participation officers or housing-management staff. It can, however, provide a way of making the work of these groups and individuals more productive and more rewarding for all concerned.

References

Bhargava, S. (1995), 'Managing the Estate', *ACORN: The Newsletter of the Community OR Unit*, **11**, pp.1–2.

Booker, P. (1990), 'A co-operative survey', *ACORN: The Newsletter of the Community OR Unit*, **4**, p.1.

Delbecq, A. and Van de Ven, A. (1971), 'A group process model for problem identification and programme planning', *Journal of Applied Behavioural Science*, **7**, pp.446–492.

Friend, J. and Hickling, A. (1987), *Planning Under Pressure*, Oxford: Pergamon.

Handy, C. (1988), *Understanding Voluntary Organizations*, Harmondsworth: Penguin.

Hudson, M. (1995), *Managing Without Profit*, Harmondsworth: Penguin.

Mason, R. and Mitroff, I. (1981), *Challenging Strategic Planning Assumptions*, New York: Wiley.

Percy-Smith, J., Sheehan, B. and Hawtin, M. (1990), *Belle Isle North Estate Management Board: Monitoring and Evaluation Interim Report*, Leeds: Policy Research Unit, Leeds Metropolitan University.

Ritchie, C. (1991), 'Belle Isle North Estate Management Board', *ACORN: The Newsletter of the Community OR Unit*, 5, p.3.

Ritchie, C., Taket, A. and Bryant, J.W. (eds) (1994), *Community Works: 26 Case Studies Showing Community Operational Research in Action*, Sheffield: PAVIC Publications.

Rosenhead, J.V. (1986), 'Custom and practice', *Journal of the Operational Research Society*, 37, pp.335–345.

Rosenhead, J.V. (ed.) (1989), *Rational Analysis for a Problematic World*, Chichester: Wiley.

Rosenhead, J.V. and Thunhurst, C. (1982), 'A materialist analysis of operational research', *Journal of the Operational Research Society*, 33, pp.111–122.

Thunhurst, C. and Ritchie, C. (1992), 'Housing in the Dearne Valley: doing community OR with the Thurnscoe Tenants Housing Co-operative: Part 2 – an evaluation', *Journal of the Operational Research Society*, 43(7), pp.677–690.

Thunhurst, C., Ritchie, C., Friend, J. and Booker, P. (1992), 'Housing in the Dearne Valley: doing community OR with the Thurnscoe Tenants Housing Co-operative: Part 1 – the involvement of the Community OR Unit', *Journal of the Operational Research Society*, 43(2), pp.81–94.

11 Community involvement, housing and equal opportunities

Charlie Cooper and Murray Hawtin

Up until the late 1970s community studies largely fluctuated between empirical approaches, based mainly on participant observation (such as Bell and Newby 1971), and theoretical structuralist accounts (such as the Community Development Projects established in the early 1970s). The former tended to be largely descriptive, non-generalizable accounts of kinship networks and other voluntary associations, while the latter tended to romanticize the notion of 'community' as an ideological base around which 'social forces may be mobilized with great effect' (Crow and Allan 1994 p.21) thereby obscuring inequalities existing *within* communities. During the 1970s, however, sociological attention increasingly focused on the dynamics of unequal access, discrimination, oppression and the fragmentation of communities. The 'community' began to be seen as either inclusive or exclusive, liberating or constraining, depending on the perceptions and identities of the members. If community-led regeneration strategies are to have any success, they need to be founded not only on a clear conceptual understanding of the ideological aims and policy objectives of community involvement, as discussed in Chapter 4, but also on an appreciation of the experiences and needs of a diverse range of community interests. This understanding is particularly crucial if community-development strategies are to achieve the wider aims of promoting social justice and greater equality of opportunity.

This chapter examines how social inequalities in British communities have been structured and reinforced. It explores the contribution of discourses relating to gender, 'race' and disability to the development of more efficacious community-development strategies in housing, particularly in respect of promoting greater opportunity for all. Other 'differences' may also serve to exclude people from fully participating in societal processes, including sexual preference and age. However, we have chosen to focus on

245

gender, 'race' and disability partly to illustrate important processes of exclusion and inequality, and partly because these have received most attention within social policy research. Our debate begins with an examination of gender inequalities.

Community involvement, housing and gender

John Grayson has shown in Chapter 2 that women have been at the forefront of community campaigns throughout history. 'Stated bluntly, working-class women living in areas such as Glasgow's tenements *"had* to learn to co-operate"' (Crow and Allen 1994 p.41, quoting Damer 1990 – original emphasis). However, these activities have mostly gone unrecognized and certainly unpaid. It can be argued that women's activities in the community are shaped to a significant extent by women's predetermined gender role as 'carers'. For women:

> organizing in the community often revolves around family life and entails: stretching scarce resources to their limit through self-help networks; providing day-care facilities; getting access to decent, affordable housing; preventing school closures; securing rights to minimum incomes; and a host of other issues linked to women's caring roles. (Dominelli 1995 p.134)

Despite the fundamental importance of childcare, housing, education, sustenance and so on, such activities have traditionally been accorded a secondary status (made almost invisible and confined to the private realm) compared with traditional 'men's work' in the so-called mainstream economy.

This section focuses on the contribution of the feminist critique of social policy, drawing on different theoretical and strategic strands within feminist thinking. What unites the threads of the feminist perspective is the shared belief that 'the personal is political' and the attention given to the areas of reproduction and, specifically, social reproduction (that is, not simply women's child-bearing role, but also the physical, emotional and material processes involved in caring for and sustaining other people). Key questions addressed by feminists are: why should women play such a central role in protecting and nurturing others? And why is this role generally performed voluntarily without payment? Is this the natural law? If not, how can it be changed? In tackling these questions six dominant approaches in feminist writing will be discussed: libertarian/New Right feminism; liberal feminism; welfare feminism; radical feminism; socialist feminism; and black feminism. Each approach has attempted to explain women's oppression and set out a different vision on how society should be organized. (For a comprehensive overview of these positions see Williams 1989.)

Libertarian/New Right feminism is largely founded on the ideology of neo-liberalism, emphasizing individualism, liberty, the market and minimal state intervention. Its analysis concludes that state intervention has prevented women from achieving equality in society, for instance through protective employment legislation which has dissuaded employers from recruiting women. This leads to the resolution that discrimination can best be removed by encouraging free competition and reducing state interference. There is an acceptance of the traditional neo-liberal assumption that with the expansion of capitalism will come the benefits of freedom and democracy for all (see Fukuyama 1989). Socialist feminists have argued that this view is clearly 'class blind' and favours white professional women with the means to pay for domiciliary support.

Liberal feminists agree that women should be allowed to compete freely with men in the market place, but that this right must be protected by the state through legislation. Mary Wollstonecraft, in *A Vindication of the Rights of Women* (1792), argued that women have the same reasoning powers as men and should be granted equal rights to the vote, to educational opportunities and to employment opportunities. More recently, liberal feminists have focused on gender inequalities caused by sex discrimination and have campaigned for legislation to address this, such as the Sex Discrimination Act 1975. Unlike libertarian feminists, liberal feminists are not opposed to state intervention. However, the liberal feminist position tends to reduce the causes of women's inequality to solely discriminatory *attitudes*, assuming that if these are removed then equal access to opportunity will readily follow. Socialist feminists have again argued that this position ignores class bias, while black feminists have pointed to the added dimension of racism.

Welfare feminism was identified in Olive Banks's *Faces of Feminism* (1981) as a distinct strand of feminist thinking because it focused less on women's opportunities in the public arena and more on the private sphere. Welfare feminism characterizes women's campaigns between 1900 and 1945 for state-provided maternity benefits, infant health centres, ante-natal clinics, birth control and family allowances – measures that would help women perform their domestic role more effectively. The focus is on helping women perform their 'biologically determined' role in the family and local community, thereby reinforcing the very conditions which cause women's dependency in the first place – that is, the sexual division of labour in the family.

Radical feminism focuses on men's power over women, exercised through the state. It highlights the degree of male domination in all areas of the state apparatus – the civil service, parliament, the judiciary and the upper echelons of welfare institutions. Women's oppression, in other words, is the result of *patriarchy* institutionalized throughout society. Patriarchy represents the exercise of male control over women's biology (for example, the medical profession exercising control over women's reproductive powers through fertilization programmes and family-planning techniques) and through physical power over women. This analysis has been translated into such campaigns as the 'Reclaim the Night' marches (protests against street violence and rape), Greenham Common Women's Peace Movement and anti-pornography (including the firebombing of a bookshop in Leeds). Radical feminists argue that gender divisions in society are largely the product of socially constructed 'realities' in a male-dominated world, including representations of the 'aggressive macho male' and the 'submissive, nurturing female' as underpinnings of gendered role expectations. Men become fathers and breadwinners, women become mothers and housewives. Consequently, some radical feminists advocate 'separatism' as a means of combating patriarchy. If patriarchy lies within the nature of men, embedded in male violence and aggression, then women need to campaign and organize separately. Firestone (1971) argued that women's liberation from male domination hinged on the development of new reproductive technologies which would remove the need for women to bear children within their bodies. Again, however, differences between women, structured around race and class, are overlooked in the radical feminist analysis and women are assumed to share common interests. Additionally, men were 'angered by the way it presented the whole male sex as an oppressing group; they called for an appreciation of the complex subtleties of power between the sexes' (Bradley 1996 p.89). In contrast, other radical feminists have attempted to shift the focus away from the notion of 'women as victims' of male power to one that celebrates women's unique human qualities – as co-operative, sharing, tender, caring people. This focus has underpinned campaigns for alternative forms of welfare provision built on the feminist value of co-operation – for example, women's refuges, well-woman clinics and rape crisis centres.

Socialist feminism emerged as an alternative perspective in the 1960s, drawing largely on feminist interpretations of Fabianism and Marxism. This position gives greater attention to the wider social and economic structures and processes shaping societal relationships, although it criticizes traditional male socialist and Marxist accounts for giving insufficient attention to the dimension of women's oppression. Throughout the history of the British socialist movement women's concerns have largely been ignored. For example, the ideas of Sylvia Pankhurst, the suffragette who campaigned to make women's demands central to any socialist manifesto in the early part of the twentieth century, were rejected by other socialists as irrelevant to the needs of what was mainly a male-dominated labour movement. Additionally, by the middle of the century women's issues in the socialist movement were largely overshadowed by the fight against Fascism or

Stalinism. However, in the 1960s women's concerns re-emerged as central to the struggle for socialism.

While socialist feminism shares welfare feminism's confidence in state welfare provision as a means of enhancing opportunities for women, it has also campaigned to change the character of welfare agencies. This included challenging the rigid hierarchical model of traditional welfare bureaucracies with demands to put in place more democratic forms of provision which allow for extensive user participation. Through promoting greater democracy and equality, socialist feminists believe that sexism in welfare organizations can be rooted out. This approach was central to the New Left agenda of a number of Labour metropolitan authorities in the 1980s, influencing the development of a number of initiatives, including equal opportunities units and women's committees. These policy developments targeted local issues specific to women, embracing childcare provision, cheap and safe public transport, safety on the streets and on housing estates, protection against domestic violence, and greater employment opportunities. Some local authorities provided subsidies to assist local women's groups to set up and run support projects specifically for women. Segal suggests that the most important achievement of the socialist feminist movement is that, like radical feminism, it made the private realm of women a 'public' issue – but more so because of its involvement in mainstream local politics. Feminist involvement brought the question of domestic and private experience into the public world of social and economic planning (Segal 1987).

Some Marxist feminists, however, criticized such approaches of the New Left for being reformist and piecemeal. For example, Weir and Wilson argued that feminist campaigns which aim to redistribute wealth and opportunity from men to women *before* achieving a redistribution from rich to poor are futile. They suggest that women's liberation lies in a class-based attack on the capitalist system and emphasize the need to change society's structures and patterns of wealth distribution, as opposed simply to reforming existing social arrangements (Weir and Wilson 1984). The issue is seen to be not just about institutionalized power relationships between men and women, but also about class exploitation through waged labour and unpaid domestic labour. Furthermore, the history of housing and welfare provision has been one of middle-class control exerted over the working class, including middle-class professional women controlling their working-class sisters through the imposition of value judgements about what it means to be a 'good' housewife and mother. This was the housing-management style of Octavia Hill and her 'lady' rent-collectors who went into the homes of working-class families to teach the art of good housekeeping. It also continued in many of the housing-management practices throughout the twentieth century. This emphasis on class and the capitalist mode of production in socialist feminism has been seen as one of its main weaknesses. For instance, it fails to explain gender divisions in non-capitalist or agrarian societies. This criticism led some socialist feminists to reformulate their position by combining their account of capitalism with an analysis of patriarchy. Gender divisions were to be explained by a 'unified systems theory, discerning a single complex structure of capitalist patriarchy or patriarchal capitalism' (Bradley 1996 pp.87–88), where Marxist explanations of production relationships were incorporated into notions of social reproduction and gender divisions of labour in the home and at work.

In the 1980s black feminists widened the focus of the gender debate by introducing the dimension of 'race', so often ignored in earlier feminist writing. Black women's simultaneous experience of sexism and racism both compounds and reconstitutes their oppression. Williams (1989) refers to the example of a black mother who is characterized not simply in terms of a 'negative' (that is, black) and a 'positive' (that is, mother) but as a 'double negative' (someone reproducing more black people). Consequently, during the abortion campaign of the 1970s the 'right to choose' rally of white feminists was not considered appropriate to the needs of black women. White women's fertility was taken for granted, while fertility rights for black women were in question because of a national concern about the numbers of black people already living in Britain. It is largely due to this concern that a number of women originally involved in the abortion campaign decided to split and form the reproductive rights campaign committed to defending the rights of black women against unwarranted abortions and sterilization. Moreover, black feminists challenged the white feminist assumption that the family was a site for patriarchal domination, arguing that for many black women 'the family was a source of solidarity and support against the racism and subordination they experienced in white-dominated society' (Bradley 1996 p.97).

On 18 March 1979, nearly 300 black women attended the National Black Women's Conference in Brixton, marking an important stage in the development of an autonomous black women's movement in Britain. The occasion was described by *Spare Rib* as 'historic', bringing together for the first time Asian, Afro- and Indo-Caribbean, African and black women born in Britain. The ultimate ambition of the conference was to establish an umbrella organization for groups and individuals active in anti-racist, feminist and community campaigns, a purpose built on the conviction that if the voice of black women in Britain was to be heard then black women themselves must lead the struggle against the specific type of oppression they faced:

> For too long the fact that as Black women we suffer triple oppression has been ignored – by male dominated Black groups; by white dominated women's groups;

and by middle-class dominated left groups. This continual lack of interest in the situation of Black women created a vicious circle, so that many of us who wanted to speak out were reluctant to do so. But by contacting each other, and working together, we have now broken this circle. (*Spare Rib* October 1979 No. 87 p.42)

Black feminists have pointed to the omission of specific black women's issues in welfare campaigns. In the USA, for instance, the Black Power movement, while recognizing that 'race' issues were at the heart of the historical development of power relationships in American society, failed to deal with 'women's race' as an important factor in determining life chances. Equally, the white-oriented women's movement tended to underplay the 'race' factor in black women's oppression:

The notion of 'sisterhood' among women was thus exposed as a myth. Indeed, some claimed that in its assumptions of common experience, white feminism could itself be seen as racist . . . [and] argued that the gains of feminist politics were often at the expense of black and working class women. The freedom gained by white middle-class women to pursue careers or achieve economic equality with men depended on the exploitation of low-paid black or working-class women acting as servants or childminders. The feminist movement minimized the contributions of black women and failed to study or prioritize their needs. (Bradley 1996 p.97)

Black feminists have disputed, for instance, the conceptual use of 'patriarchy', claiming that this obscures differences of power *between* women. Black women do *not* have the same access to dominant white power structures as white women. They have to face white women racists or racist state policies.

A further concern for black feminism is the characterization of women's welfare work as a continuation of women's domestic role as cook, cleaner, carer and nurturer. Carby queries the applicability of this representation to black women, suggesting that, in the case of their domestic, nursing and cleaning roles, it is the racist image of the black woman as 'servant' or 'slave' that prevails (see Carby 1982, 1987).

While there has been a tendency within feminism to construct a 'hierarchy of oppression' (Bradley 1996 p.98), with different perspectives seeking to depict their own unique situation as most worthy of attention, there is little doubt that feminist writing illuminates the diversity of women's experience within communities and the connections between gender and other dimensions of social inequality – particularly 'race' and class. In addition, feminist thinking has highlighted the need to place 'women' at the centre of any agenda for social change. More specifically for our purpose, the principles of egalitarianism, co-operation and democracy held by socialist and black feminism must be at the heart of any community-development strategy if it is to achieve that strategy's broad aims of economic justice and social inclusion. In attempting to explain how these principles could operate in practice, Dominelli (1995) draws on the lessons of the Greenham Common Women's Peace Movement. Her analysis highlights eight key feminist principles that could be applied to community work practice more generally. These are:

- the adoption of non-violent forms of confrontation;
- the rejection of hierarchies and formal leaders in favour of democratic collective working;
- the use of groupwork discussions to explore people's fears, expectations, willingness to take risks, skill and knowledge development needs, tactics and new ways of social organizing;
- the development of networks throughout the country to broaden the campaign's support base and resources;
- the need to redefine social problems, focusing on their social and personal nature and thereby raising individual consciousness;
- the need to redefine the role of professionals to focus on their *servicing* activities rather than their *controlling* activities, thus enabling a more equal power relationship to emerge;
- the use of joyous symbols (such as flowers and coloured ribbons) to challenge the vacuous values of society (such as greed and destruction); and
- allowing participants only to become involved to the degree with which they feel most comfortable.

These principles alone, however, cannot address the broader structural factors shaping women's life chances. In particular, black feminists have stressed that greater attention needs to be given to the autonomy of racism and its distinctive historical role in safeguarding the dynamics of capitalism. This concern is explored more fully in the next section.

Community involvement, housing and race

Studies dating back to the 1960s point to entrenched patterns of ethnic minority group disadvantage in the British housing system, measured in terms of place of residence, housing standards, mobility and access (Rex and Moore 1967, Pahl 1975, Brown 1984). Rex and Moore contributed significantly to the sociological understanding of competitive urban processes and social exclusion in housing. They demonstrated that, while white middle-class households could generally gain access to home-ownership in desirable suburbs and white working-class people could ordinarily secure access to council housing, a marginalized sector of the population (including a high proportion of black immigrants) usually found themselves restricted to inner-city zones of transition.

Although a more recent analysis of urban trends suggests that the black Caribbean population is more integrated in Britain than in the USA (Office for National Statistics 1996), the evidence suggests that 'ethnic minorities generally fare markedly worse than the white population on grounds of unemployment, pay, housing, or as victims of crime' ('Blacks and Asians still at social disadvantage', *The Guardian* 8 August 1996). In tenant-participation schemes, while there are many factors which may prevent people of all racial and cultural backgrounds taking part, some factors act specifically against black communities:

> Sometimes these factors are culturally based, sometimes they may be connected with racism – or they may be organizational. Often they are a mixture of race and culture, and how the organization relates to these issues. (Clarke 1994 p.15)

Research conducted by the Federation of Black Housing Organizations (FBHO) suggests that the lack of participation by black people is:

> not a result of apathy amongst the black tenants but due mainly to the exclusion of black households from participation. Exclusion takes the form of blatant refusal to allow black tenants to use communal facilities or to gain access to other available resources such as funding, the non-existence of black workers on tenants federations, activities organized from the perception of white tenants which had little appeal to black tenants, and the absence of issues of importance to black households on tenant associations' agendas. (see Cooper 1991 p.4)

Explanations of racial disadvantage have been structured around what Sarre (1986) called the dualism of *choice*, which stresses that it is the wish of ethnic minorities to live together so as to derive social and cultural benefits (see Dahya 1974), and *constraint*, which emphasizes the externalities that force ethnic minorities to live in the least desirable areas. Within the 'constraint' explanations there is a further dualism between Marxist approaches, which stress both the economic causes and the role of social class and colonialism in structuring racial disadvantage (see Castles and Kosack 1973), and Weberian approaches, which emphasize the existence of exclusionary allocation processes in both the public and private housing sectors which serve to disadvantage black people (see Rex and Moore 1967).

People from ethnic minorities are over-represented among the poorly paid and unemployed, putting them at an economic disadvantage alongside poor white people. However, people from ethnic minorities suffer an additional disadvantage by virtue of their racial status – reinforced through institutional racism, direct discrimination and racial harassment. Recent debates have attempted to locate 'racism', and the process of 'racial differentiation', in their historical context. British culture has traditionally classified and stigmatized all 'new settlers': in the nineteenth century Irish slum-dwellers were associated with 'backwardness', 'alien social habits', a 'threat to social order', and their 'disgusting domestic companion, the pig' (see, for example, Burnett 1986 p.58). Such images were then used to rationalize the 'social alienation' of Irish people in the least desirable areas. These interpretations of cultural and racial differences were firmly entrenched in Social Darwinism and deterministic biological arguments which sought to justify the 'purity of race', the 'survival of the fittest species' and the subordination of biologically inferior groups. As Williams shows, this social imperialism was deployed by both Liberals and Labourite parties from the late nineteenth century to subdue the organized working class who in turn recognized 'an *apparent* material as well as ideological basis . . . to believe in imperialism and racial supremacy' as well as retaining 'a principled belief in entitlement to welfare benefits *by nationality*' (Williams 1996 p.64 – original emphasis). Nationalistic fervour has underpinned immigration-control policies throughout the twentieth century and served to deny black people equal access to welfare provision. At the time 'Homes for Heroes' was pledged after demobilization from the First World War, black workers and their families were being attacked by gangs of white thugs in South Tyneside, Liverpool and Cardiff (Williams 1996). Furthermore, 'by 1925 both the Board and the editorial columns of the *Jewish Chronicle* were attacking the LCC [London County Council] for proposing that aliens be excluded from all municipal housing' (Cohen 1996 p.41). And again, after the Second World War:

> Black people had to organize for themselves, for example, in Liverpool in 1948 the Colonial People's Defence Committee organized for the welfare of Black seamen who were denied benefits when unemployed even when many were war veterans. (Williams 1996 p.65)

While the atrocities committed in the name of National Socialism in Germany in the late 1930s did much to discredit Social Darwinism, racism has persisted in new and acceptable forms, usually to protect the 'national interest' in times of economic crisis rather than protect the purity of the species (Mulgan 1991). Jacobs argues that the role of black immigrants in the post-war welfare state was to maintain low social expenditure. Low-waged black workers were acceptable in the welfare state but they were not expected to use it: 'they could build council houses but were not expected to live in them' (Jacobs 1985 p.13). The National Health Service has continued to rely on this type of labour (from countries including India, Ireland, Malaysia, southern Europe and the Caribbean). In a study of one London hospital, 84 per cent of domestics and 82 per cent of catering workers were identified as coming from abroad (Doyal *et al.* 1981). In this way, female immigrant workers particularly have been used to keep down the cost of welfare provision. Meanwhile, black people have been depicted as 'scroungers' on the welfare state. The process by which racial disadvantage has to be explained in relation to national and international socio-economic processes has been termed 'structural racism' (Ginsburg 1992). An understanding of the position of black people in Britain, and black women in particular, requires an internationalist framework of analysis featuring imperialism, the role of workers from developing countries in the international division of labour, and the role of the state in controlling labour mobility through immigration controls.

Since the economic crisis of the 1970s the dynamics of racism changed again, exemplified in New Right ideological thinking on the 'enemy within' where 'the threat to national unity comes from the cultural differences of the Black communities and their resistance to assimilating into British culture' (Williams 1996 p.50). Images were constructed, for instance, which characterized black youth as a threat to law and order (Hall *et al.* 1978). Such thinking underpins what Ginsburg terms 'subjective racism'; that is, overt and irrational racial prejudice and discrimination by key individuals in society (Ginsburg 1992). As a consequence, 'black tenants are more likely to find themselves on more heavily controlled and policed estates. The 1981 riots crystallized a rationalization of such policies for the right' (Williams 1996 p.69).

From the 1970s a number of housing studies focused on 'institutional racism', a process originally identified by the Black Power movement in the USA. Stokely Carmichael and Charles Hamilton defined this as a less overt and far more subtle form of racism and therefore less identifiable and consequently less likely to be condemned by the public (Ginsburg 1992). In the context of British housing, for instance, a study of Nottingham Housing Department in the mid-1970s highlighted that council housebuilding programmes failed to provide the larger units required by some black households. A Commission for Racial Equality (CRE) study of housing allocations in Hackney between 1978 and 1979 identified institutionalized managerial assumptions about the area preferences of black applicants (Morris and Winn 1990). Studies of Greater London Council's (GLC) allocation policies in Tower Hamlets identified similar assumptions about black households' area preferences, which led to the ghettoization of Bengalis in unpopular deck-access blocks of flats in Spitalfields and their exclusion from new GLC developments (Phillips 1986, Forman 1989). Henderson and Karn's study of allocations in Birmingham in the 1970s identified that residential qualifications and the exclusion of owner-occupiers and extended families from applying for council housing disproportionately disadvantaged African-Caribbean and Asian applicants (Henderson and Karn 1987). Similar processes have been identified in studies of the private housing sector where, for example, finance institutions have applied more stringent criteria for assessing the status of black people applying for loans. In another case, an estate agent in Oldham would only recommend houses in 'white areas' to prospective white purchasers and houses in 'Asian areas' to prospective Asian purchasers (Ginsburg 1992). Habeebullah and Slater's investigation in Rochdale identified a number of factors deterring Asians from accepting rehousing on council estates, despite their experience of poor housing conditions and overcrowding – the most significant deterrent being the fear of leaving a supportive community environment for one perceived as insecure and isolated:

> When looking for support or help at difficult times, if it is not forthcoming from neighbours, there are few other possibilities on estates. Very few tenants had had help or support from their local tenants' association. (Habeebullah and Slater 1990 p.48)

Consequently, in searching for the causes of persistent racial disadvantage in the British housing system, it is clear that explanations of choice cannot be divorced from an understanding of the constraints within which those choices are made. As Harrison states, there are:

> severe limits over the extent to which community or locality level empowerment for marginalized groups could occur in UK cities . . . [owing to] the dominance of economic liberalism; economic decline allied with public expenditure constraints; the centralizing and paternalistic traditions of governmental social policy; the reluctance to accept diversity of aspirations, needs and cultures; and the reluctance to acknowledge the distributional impact of those public policies that were not focussed on marginalized groups. (Harrison 1995 p.129)

It is in this context of economic disadvantage and processes of structural and institutional racism that the 'participation strategies' of ethnic minority communities in urban policy in Britain have had to develop. Furthermore, it is precisely those urban policies that are designed to promote community development in urban regeneration that appear to be exacerbating racial tensions:

> There now appears to be sufficient evidence to suggest that one of the unintended consequences of the many funding strategies targeted at community organizations through Urban Programme and other channels in the 1980s was the exacerbation of tensions and conflicts both within a given minority ethnic community, between

such communities and between these communities and local majority communities. (Harrison *et al.* 1995 p.146)

Harrison *et al.*'s study of community action in three multi-racial localities in Bristol, Leicester and Tower Hamlets focuses on the dynamic of competition between community interests over scarce urban resources. The question of who represents these communities' interests was highly problematic and contentious. Four types of representation were identified: constitutional (such as elected councillors); religious (for example Anglican and Muslim leaders); 'grass-roots' (such as local residents); and professional (such as community workers). Key issues to be addressed were politicized racial divisions, gate-keeping and élitism. Within different racial groups, interests were sometimes divided by political allegiance (particularly between Labour and Liberals). Key gate-keepers, including community workers and tenant representatives, were in a powerful position to offer or withhold 'participation' opportunities to other interest groups. Where gate-keepers attempted to target the involvement of ethnic minority representatives, such as religious leaders, there was a concern that such representation might be élitist (such as established elderly males representing newly arrived Bangladeshi women). To address these concerns Harrison *et al.* identify a number of possible strategies, including:

- reserving places on committees for under-represented groups;
- holding new members' meetings to provide induction training for under-represented groups;
- employing black community-development workers to signal that an initiative is open to black people;
- targeting community-development support at under-represented groups;
- adopting meeting styles that do not inhibit participation – for instance, styles that avoid complicated jargon, formalized procedures or culturally bound ways of personal interaction;
- holding meetings in accessible and safe environments such as locations which are within easy reach of home, free from racial harassment and culturally inviting;
- planning activities which reflect the broader community's needs;
- setting targets based on the community's identification of priorities and establishing appropriate monitoring arrangements for measuring the degree of community integration; and
- establishing strategies for containing conflicts and facilitating dialogue between competing interests.

Harrison *et al.* acknowledge that the employment of black community workers could be perceived as a regressive move, and that 'it is often damaging for black community workers to only work with black groups as it colludes with wider social and institutional processes which tend to channel and marginalize black professionals into work on race-exclusive issues' (Harrison *et al.* 1995 p.149). However, Harrison also acknowledges that separatism, a feature of some black-run housing organizations in Britain, can have an important strategic role in empowering black communities by facilitating anti-racist practices and reflecting 'neglected community needs and voices' (Harrison 1995 p.103). This is supported by Williams, who suggests that welfare strategies 'must be informed and regenerated by the needs articulated by Black people themselves' (Williams 1996 p.63). Recently, a survey of 600 black people in London, Birmingham, Manchester, Liverpool and Nottingham found that 40 per cent thought that a separate black political party or organization would benefit them (*The Guardian* 20 September 1996). This reflects a significant dissatisfaction among black people in Britain for the political representation provided by the mainstream parties.

Harrison *et al.* stress that there is no one paradigm for community-development practice and that each situation will have its own specific dynamic requiring different forms of community organizing. However, they suggest that some attention will need to be given to the development of arbitration and conflict-resolution skills, together with a greater emphasis on understanding racialized inter-group dynamics in community-work education and training. Only then will community-development strategies become more effective in constructively confronting racism. This tactic was fundamental to the success of tenant opposition to the government's initial plans for Housing Action Trusts (HATs), where strategies of resistance included a constant process of negotiation to find common ground among tenants 'in an attempt to produce a cohesive movement that will then be able to achieve its goals' (Woodward 1991 p.54). In the case of tenants in Tower Hamlets this involved maintaining unity between tenants perceived as divided on ethnic lines. A similar if perhaps more far-reaching strategy for community development is advocated by Habeebullah and Slater who, in relation to the needs of Asians in Rochdale, found:

> There is clearly a strongly-felt need for a source of advice and information which is in tune with the community's point of view and needs, which can bridge the gap between the urgent need for housing, and the anxiety or distrust of council estates as an unknown quantity. Equally, there is a view that at present Asian tenants, who experience problems once rehoused on estates, do not have an agency or organization to which they can turn with confidence for a supportive response. (Habeebullah and Slater 1990 p.52)

The inadequacy of attempts to address the housing needs of Asians in Rochdale at the time, and indeed in other local authority areas, can be ascribed to the 'failure to give sufficient weight to the closely-related issues of neighbourhood, community and cultural identity' (Habeebullah and Slater 1990 p.58). The issue moves beyond housing and requires comprehensive solutions involving an authority-wide response. Habeebullah and Slater's strategy embraces a number of areas recommended in Harrison *et al.*'s findings, including the need for:

- updated information on Asian households' own needs and preferences;
- more comprehensive information and education on the housing options available;
- a counselling service to assist applicants to make more informed judgements about their housing choices;
- consideration of 'group allocations' of Asian households to estates;
- close collaboration with Asian agencies;
- an inter-agency approach to tackling racial harassment; and
- a comprehensive community-development strategy.

The comprehensive community-development strategy proposed would involve three key phases. The first would seek to build confidence among Asian households that council estates offered attractive options for rehousing. The second would seek to develop the minimum conditions of 'liveability' on estates once Asian households had moved (that is, freedom from harassment and access to cultural and religious facilities). The third would seek to develop a sustainable, supportive environment similar to that currently provided in Asian neighbourhoods. All these phases would require the involvement of new community forums, with direct links to tenants' federations, whereby Asian and white residents could meet to discuss issues of common interest and to advance better mutual understanding (Habeebullah and Slater 1990). The process of mutual understanding is particularly crucial if racist assumptions in the tenants' movement are to be challenged.

Although it is unlawful under the Race Relations Act 1976 to discriminate on grounds of race, colour, nationality or ethnic origin, a CRE research report (based on replies from 84 local authorities and 100 housing associations) showed that only 37 per cent of councils and 33 per cent of housing associations required tenants' associations to meet equal opportunity conditions. This led to the production of an action plan for tenants' associations covering the need to:

- demonstrate a 'commitment' to equal opportunities through a policy statement;

- attract 'new' tenants on to tenants' associations;
- include ethnic minorities in campaigns;
- confront racists at meetings;
- set targets to be monitored (for example, on recruitment of ethnic minorities);
- encourage ethnic minorities to stand for election and to volunteer for delegations to the landlord or at conferences;
- co-operate with the landlord and other agencies on racial harassment procedures;
- translate newsletters, posters and other publicity material;
- organize activities that attract ethnic minorities; and
- organize training sessions on equal opportunities.

Alongside these recommendations a plan of action for landlords is also proposed, covering the need to:

- demonstrate a public commitment to racial equality;
- work only with tenants' associations who adopt an equal opportunities policy;
- include the promotion of equal opportunities in job descriptions of all staff responsible for tenant-participation initiatives;
- brief support agencies responsible for developing tenants' associations on equal opportunity policies;
- demonstrate a comprehensive and widely publicized policy commitment to equal opportunities with procedures for dealing with harassment, and encourage tenants' associations to co-operate with this statement; and
- introduce performance indicators for monitoring how far tenants' associations reflect the ethnic population in the area.

The CRE report also includes guidelines on training and advice on running meetings that do not deter ethnic minorities from attending, and the need for the local authority to offer support, information and advice for tenants' associations (covering local census data, translating material, ethnic monitoring systems, ethnicity questionnaire surveys to establish any correlation between needs/satisfaction and race, specialist staff and facilitating equal opportunities training). The report also includes a model constitution for tenants' associations which includes clauses on equal opportunities (CRE 1993).

These guidelines, policies, practices and strategies alone, however, remain insufficient if racism is to be challenged at the level of central state institutions. Black feminists have stressed that anti-racist struggles necessitate a broader internationalist approach – one that challenges cultural imperialism, racist immigration controls, the institutionalized deprivation of welfare provision to black people and the internationalized exploitation of cheap immigrant labour (Williams 1989, 1996). These wider structural representations of 'racism' underpin the more extensive practices of social exclusion which are historically specific to the needs of capitalism. Until these are removed, alongside the development of 'new' social movements at the grass-roots level of tenants' organizing, then the genuine incorporation of black people into housing policy-making remains a distant possibility.

Community involvement, housing and disability

There is substantial research evidence to show that people with disabilities experience significantly poorer standards of living than people without disabilities (Barnes 1991), and also that the principal reason for this is less to do with the physical impairment of the individuals themselves but more to do with the *disabling environment* in which people with disabilities live (Oliver 1990). In exploring the nature of housing disadvantage of people with disabilities, this section will show how social attitudes to, and representations of, 'disability' have contrived to exclude people with disabilities from participation in mainstream society. This exclusion has been exacerbated by social policy responses which have served to reinforce the dependency of people with disabilities. These issues of social exclusion and dependency have led to the emergence of new social movements organized around a redefinition of 'disability' and calls for more egalitarian solutions to address the disadvantage of people with disabilities.

The social exclusion of people with disabilities, while largely founded on exclusionary practices in the labour market, has been exacerbated in Britain since industrialization through control mechanisms that have incarcerated people with impairments in segregated institutions. Even where more sympathetic approaches have been adopted, people with disabilities have tended to remain subjected to the decisions and practices of able-bodied professionals. As Lewis, writing in 1992 from a disablement perspective, argues:

> More than a decade of sympathetic able-bodied professionals and able-bodied run organizations for people with disabilities practising the art of persuasion, has done little to advance disabled people's position in society. As everyone is aware, or should be, we still experience blatant institutionalized discrimination in all areas of social life. The 'caring and administering' ethos is deeply ingrained and still re-inforces negative attitudes in society towards people with disabilities. (Lewis 1992 p.15)

Institutionalization was still the norm, particularly for many people with mental disabilities, until the 1980s when New Right ideology gave added impetus to care-in-the-community policies. Earlier care-in-the-community policies had been largely based on a sociological critique of the 'asylum' (Goffman 1961, Townsend 1962, Illich 1976). Prior to this debate 'non disabled "normality" became the necessary prerequisite for community participation' (Barnes and Mercer 1995 p.33). People with disabilities have largely been treated as incapable of making their own decisions, a process founded on the traditional 'medical model' of disability where the dominant discourse is about 'treatment' to restore 'normality'. Discrimination against people with disabilities is institutionalized throughout all areas of society, exercised through 'disablist imagery and language which keeps the traditional fears and prejudices which surround impairment alive' (Barnes 1996 p.97). Reactions to disability have varied over time, from superstition (Luther advocated murdering all children with disabilities at birth because they were possessed) to distrust, mockery and compassion (see Thomas 1982). These emotions have collectively conspired to marginalize people with disabilities from the rest of society.

The post-war settlement in Britain acknowledged the rights of people with disabilities to receive integrated services. Indeed, 'Britain was one of the first western nations to establish the notion of rights for people with disabilities in law with the setting up of the welfare state in the 1940s' (Barnes 1996 p.103). Since then, however, there has been a retreat from this position and a 'gradual but intensifying drift from rights-based to needs-based policies' (Barnes 1996 p.103). Housing policies in particular have contributed to the social exclusion of people with disabilities. While it is estimated that there are 4.25 million people with mobility problems in Britain, there are only around 80 000 accessible homes (Barnes 1996). According to Andrew Rowe, most mainstream dwellings are designed for people who are 'male, fit and aged between 18 and 40'. What little provision has been made for people with disabilities has usually been designed under the label 'special needs housing', marginalized and ghettoized (see Cooper and Walton 1995 p.1). The problem is exacerbated by a lack of accessible transport facilities, a lack of accessibility to other buildings (shops, public houses, meeting halls and so forth), and a lack of 'visitability' to the homes of friends and relatives without disabilities, factors which severely limit opportunities for social interaction and participation.

People with disabilities rely more on the public rented housing sector than people without disabilities. An estimated 50 per cent of households with people with disabilities live in the public rented sector, largely because local authorities have had a statutory responsibility since the Chronically Sick and Disabled Persons Act 1970 for the special needs of people with disabilities (Morris 1990). Consequently, the privatization of public rented housing and cutbacks in housing investment programmes since the late 1970s have had a disproportionate impact on the housing opportunities of people with disabilities. The 'right-to-buy' provisions have resulted in more houses than flats being sold, therefore the public rented sector now manages an increasing proportion of flats which are the least adaptable or desirable properties. Increasing dependency on the housing association movement is unlikely to see the situation improve because associations have traditionally had a much poorer record of providing homes for people with disabilities – largely because they have had no statutory responsibility to do so. Since the Housing Act 1988 and its subsequent guidelines and directives, mixed funding and the need for associations to work within the market discipline have led to a reduction in space standards and increasing difficulties for special needs associations to raise the necessary private finance. This situation was exacerbated by the Conservative government's desire to restrict the allocation of social housing grant to a smaller number of 'cost-efficient' housing associations (Cooper and Walton 1995).

Such processes of exclusion have not been tolerated passively by people with disabilities and disablement campaigns have become increasingly militant since the 1980s. The roots of the disablement movement can be located in the radical politics of civil rights campaigns in the 1960s. This movement has challenged the traditional medical model of disability as a sickness or impairment that stigmatizes people and attempted to introduce an alternative 'social model' couched in the language of 'individual limitation' and 'socially imposed restriction' (Barnes and Mercer 1995 p.34). The focus is on the social constraints imposed on people with impairments by a discriminatory society. Three principal assumptions underpin the values held by this movement: consumer sovereignty, self-reliance, and political and economic rights.

The growth of the Independent Living Movement (ILM) in the USA in the late 1960s highlighted the fact that the main obstacles to the individual and collective empowerment of people with disabilities were 'hostile physical and social environments, and the operation of medical and rehabilitation services' (Barnes and Mercer 1995 p.35). One of the ILM's primary aims was to create alternative forms of provision controlled and managed by people with disabilities themselves. The first Centre for Independent Living (CIL) was established in Berkeley, California, in 1972 by students with disabilities. Today there are hundreds of such schemes throughout the USA providing a range of services, including peer counselling, advice, advocacy and accessible housing. In Britain, CILs developed in a different guise because the paternalistic state-welfare system was more firmly entrenched. British CILs focused more on providing advice services rather than direct provision. In 1981 the British Council of Organizations of People with Disabilities (BCODP) was formed to act as a co-ordinating body for groups working with people with disabilities. The BCODP represents around 82 organizations acting on behalf of over 250 000 people with disabilities (Barnes 1996). It has promoted a number of initiatives aimed at allowing people with disabilities to achieve greater autonomy through more active and direct forms of political participation. One of the more successful examples of such an approach is the Derbyshire Coalition of People with Disabilities (DCDP) which aimed to achieve independent and integrated living for all people with disabilities by ensuring that they participated fully in the social, economic and political life of their community. In achieving its objective the DCDP identified seven basic needs which had to be met:

- *Information* – accessible specialist information dealing comprehensively and clearly with every aspect of independent and integrated living is essential if people with disabilities are to make rational choices about where and how they want to live.
- *Counselling and advocacy* – people with disabilities who have lived in secure but overprotective institutions may have become passive recipients of care and might lose the will or ability to think and act for themselves. This can result in low expectations and aspirations and therefore they may need peer-group support and advocacy from other people with disabilities experienced in practising independent living to motivate them to start believing in themselves again.
- *Accessible housing* – the key to physical integration is well-designed housing. All housing should be accessible and adaptable to ensure the widest possible choice and to permit the integration of people with disabilities naturally into the community.
- *Technical aids* – there are over 13 000 types of aids for people with disabilities to choose from and so there is a need to develop a fully comprehensive database system to allow people with disabilities the opportunity to discover suitable aids and to test these out.
- *Personal assistance* – there may well be cases where people with disabilities require domiciliary support. A range of services should be made available and, in view of the intimacy of some of these areas of support, individuals should be given some degree of choice over by whom, when and how these tasks are performed.
- *Transport* – a range of transport types are needed, from wheelchairs through to accessible taxis and forms of public transport.
- *Access to the built environment* – full mobility and freedom to participate in society are only possible if the built environment is fully accessible. This includes housing, workplaces, recreation and leisure centres, educational establishments, welfare organizations and health services.

The DCDP's involvement with Derbyshire Council achieved a number of important concessions. These included a *Statement of Intent*, agreed in 1981, which pledged seven objectives in respect of the rights of people with disabilities in the county. These were:

● the active involvement of people with disabilities in decision-making processes;
● the promotion of an accessible, barrier-free built environment;
● the promotion of integrated independent living opportunities;
● the promotion of accessible public transport facilities;
● the promotion of integrated education;
● the development of integrated employment opportunities; and
● the dissemination of information, advice and advocacy.

Following this pledge a Joint Working Party of the DCDP and Derbyshire Social Services Department began examining proposals for a Derbyshire Centre for Integrated Living (DCIL) which was established by the mid-1980s. Throughout the 1980s the membership of DCDP increased to include all kinds of impairments and it became recognized as one of the largest democratically organized and informed voices of people with disabilities in the country. The DCIL provided a means of enhancing choice and control in the lives of people with disabilities through the provision of specialist services such as peer-group counselling, an employment agency, a planning and design consultancy, a comprehensive information bureau and the promotion of local access groups. It was jointly funded by the local authority, health authorities, the European Social Fund and its own fund-raising. However, in the 1990s the DCIL and DCDP both suffered massive funding cuts, resulting in staff redundancies and threatening their long-term viability.

There has been a growing awareness of institutional discrimination against people with disabilities in British state-sponsored welfare programmes in the 1980s. For example:

> most British schools, colleges and universities are not prepared to accommodate students with impairments in a mainstream setting . . . In 1989 Local Education Authorities (LEAs) in England and Wales spent £820 million on special education; most of it went on segregated schooling rather than integration. (Barnes 1996 pp.97–98)

Furthermore, many professionals have been reluctant to engage in meaningful participatory practices with people with disabilities. For instance:

> While the introduction of the 1986 Disabled Persons (Services, Consultation and

Representation) Act promised meaningful collaboration between service users and providers, there is a widespread disregard for the law by local authorities. For example, Section 10 of the Act required local authorities to consult with organizations of disabled people when planning services. Government research shows that most have chosen to speak to voluntary organizations for disabled people and charities; many simply do not bother – only one London borough can boast 'a positive stance' toward disability organizations. (Barnes 1996 p.104)

The issues of institutional discrimination and resistance to purposeful participation practices, combined with the retrenchment of welfare spending, have forced disablement movements to adopt increasingly militant campaigns in the 1980s and 1990s. Since the 'Rights not Charity' march of July 1988 there have been:

a growing number of demonstrations and civil disobedience campaigns by disabled people and their supporters up and down the country on a range of issues . . . In order to focus the public's attention on . . . injustices disabled people are now prepared to risk public ridicule, arrest and even imprisonment . . . What disabled people and their organizations are demanding is the introduction of comprehensive anti-discrimination legislation which, first, establishes a suitable framework for the enforcement of policies which would ensure the meaningful integration of disabled people into the mainstream economic and social life of the community . . . and, second, provide[s] public confirmation that discrimination against disabled people for whatever reason and in whatever form is no longer acceptable. In other words, legislation which emphasizes social rights rather than individual needs and focuses on the disabling society in which we live, and not on individual disabled people. (Barnes 1996 p.107)

The Disability Discrimination Act 1995, the provisions of which come into force over the next few years, is considered by many activists in the disablement movement to be a poor substitute for effective civil-rights legislation. There is no plan to establish a national enforcement body, such as the Equal Opportunities Commission or the Commission for Racial Equality. Consequently, people with disabilities will have to turn to an already depleted legal aid system if they feel that they have been discriminated against. As Heddell argues, 'If the Disability Discrimination Act cannot be enforced or used easily by those who need it most, what value is it to society?' (Heddell 1996 p.9).

As Barnes points out, anti-discrimination legislation alone has not addressed racism and sexism in Britain, largely because the semi-autonomous status of the Commission for Racial Equality and the Equal Opportunities Commission has allowed them to 'be subdued through government control of funds and appointments' (Barnes 1996 p.108). A national enforcement agency for disabled equality is therefore unlikely to fare better. Consequently, while anti-discrimination legislation is important, there is also a need for a more comprehensive strategic framework integrating *autonomous* organizational structures with access to resources.

Conclusions

The key argument presented in this chapter is that any strategy seeking to incorporate communities into urban regeneration and housing initiatives must demonstrate an understanding of how social exclusion is constructed along the lines of gender, 'race' and disability. While the feminist critique of the welfare state is diverse and complex, it offers a broader understanding of social processes and new ways of exploring social policy. In particular, liberal and welfare feminists have highlighted the potential role of the state in ameliorating gender inequalities through expanding welfare programmes. Radical feminists have added those elements of women's 'personal lives' which require 'political attention'. Socialist feminists have pointed to the way in which women's oppression is underpinned by 'patriarchal capitalism' (or 'capitalistic patriarchy', depending on the emphasis). Finally, black feminists have shown how some women are treated differently to others and that life chances are not solely dependent on gender or class relationships but also on 'race'. What ties the strands of the feminist discourse together, however, is the unequivocal conclusion that the outcomes of societal processes are inextricably linked not only to gender differences, but also to 'race' and class.

In formulating emancipation strategies, feminists have aimed to make it possible for women to gain a greater degree of control over their lives. These strategies have included experiments in 'utopian communities' involving collective service provision covering canteens, home helps, childcare, laundries, nurseries, health care, cinemas and shops. The assumption was that such forms of provision would free women to participate more in the democratic processes of government, although feminists have highlighted that democracy means much more than merely voting and that democratic control has to be extended to all aspects of people's lives. In proposing alternative futures, Rowbotham highlights a number of possibilities for liberation with the aid of communal kitchens, communal washing machines and communal neighbourhood dormitories – forms of domestic organizing that would help to develop the concept that cooking, washing and childcare are the responsibility of the community and not just of women (Rowbotham 1986).

Contemporary discourses on 'race' and society have broadened the perspective on notions of community and democracy by identifying the ways in which minorities are excluded on racial and ethnic criteria. While there are different views about how best to deal with these concerns there seems little doubt, as Solomos and Back observe, that civil-rights movements have had at best only 'a partial impact on established patterns of racial inequality and have not stopped the development of new patterns of exclusion and segregation' (Solomos and Back 1996 p.218). Attempts at developing anti-racist strategies have proved problematic for a number of reasons:

> At a conceptual level there has been a notable lack of clear conceptualizations of the political and social objectives of anti-racist movements or their limitations. At the level of policy and practice there has been both confusion and hostility to the attempt to institutionalize a bureaucratic framework for the implementation of anti-racist policies, in relation to such areas as education, social welfare, adoption and training. (Solomos and Back 1996 pp.117–118)

The problem with conceptualizing anti-racist strategies can partly be explained by the changing dynamic of racism. This chapter has shown that racism has manifested itself in different ways at different periods, most recently in terms that claim to represent the national interest. However, underpinning these different manifestations is the categorization of human groups based on political geography, thereby permitting the assertion that specific races do not belong because of their cultural and social characteristics (Solomos and Back 1996). This racism compounds the general difficulties that face ethnic minorities in feeling connected to the democratic process. The challenge for community development is to confront those discourses that seek to construct meanings of 'race' and racism in popular culture by offering an analysis of contemporary racist notions and practices and developing alternative models of democracy and participation that give voice to marginalized interests.

Finally, since the International Year of the Disabled Person in 1981, a new focus for community participation has emerged around the concept of 'normalization' and social integration for people with disabilities. This followed the development of the social model of disability that stressed that people's impairment is largely constructed by social factors: 'what disables people is their inability to function in an able-body oriented world which denies or does not take account of their rights and needs' (Croft and Beresford 1996 p.185). The disablement perspective has challenged the intentions of participatory techniques that have merely served to maintain control over people with disabilities rather than allowing them to take control over their own lives. (For a discussion of 'self-advocacy' for people with learning difficulties see Dowson 1990.) This has led to a view of participation advocating that communities should only become involved in initiatives where they have genuine control. Once autonomous social movements have been established, alliances with agencies from other sectors can, and should, be forged.

References

Banks, O. (1981), *Faces of Feminism*, Oxford: Martin Robertson.

Barnes, C. (1991), *People with Disabilities in Britain and Discrimination: A Case for Anti-Discrimination Legislation*, London: Hurst & Co./British Council of Organizations of People with Disabilities.

Barnes, C. (1996), 'Institutional discrimination against people with disabilities and the campaign for anti-discrimination legislation' in Taylor, D. (ed.), *Critical Social Policy: A Reader*, London: Sage, pp.95–112.

Barnes, C. and Mercer, G. (1995), 'Disability: emancipation, community participation and people with disabilities' in Craig, G. and Mayo, M. (eds), *Community Empowerment: A Reader in Participation and Development*, London: Zed Books, pp.33–45.

Bell, H. and Newby, C. (1971), *Community Studies*, London: George Allen and Unwin.

Bradley, H. (1996), *Fractured Identities: Changing Patterns of Inequality*, Cambridge: Polity Press.

Brown, C. (1984), *Black and White Britain: The Third PSI Survey*, London: Heinemann.

Burnett, J. (1986), *A Social History of Housing 1815–1985*, 2nd edn, London: Methuen.

Carby, H. (1982), 'White woman listen! Black feminism and the boundaries of sisterhood' in CCCS, *The Empire Strikes Back: Race and Racism in 70s Britain*, London: Hutchinson, pp.212–235.

Carby, H. (1987), *Reconstructing Womanhood*, New York: Oxford University Press.

Castles, S. and Kosack, C. (1973), *Immigrant Workers and Class Structure in Western Europe*, Oxford: IRR/Oxford University Press.

Clarke, V. (1994), *Getting Black Tenants Involved: A Good Practice Guide for Housing Associations and Co-operatives*, London: CATCH.

Cohen, S. (1996), 'Anti-semitism, immigration controls and the welfare state' in Taylor, D. (ed.), *Critical Social Policy: A Reader*, London: Sage, pp.27–47.

Commission for Racial Equality (CRE) (1993), *Room for All: Tenant Associations and Racial Equality*, London: CRE.

Cooper, C. (1991), 'Tenant participation in the 1990's', *Black Housing*, **7**(11), pp.4–5.

Cooper, C. and Walton, M. (1995), *Once in a Lifetime: An Evaluation of Lifetime Homes in Hull*, Occasional Paper No. 3, Hull: Policy Studies Research Centre, University of Lincolnshire & Humberside/DesignAge.

Croft, S. and Beresford, P. (1996), 'The politics of participation', in Taylor, D. (ed.), *Critical Social Policy: A Reader*, London: Sage, pp.175–198.

Crow, G. and Allan, G. (1994), *Community Life: An Introduction to Local Social Relations*, New York: Harvester Wheatsheaf.

Dahya, B. (1974), 'The nature of Pakistani ethnicity in industrial cities in Britain' in Cohen, A. (ed.), *Urban Ethnicity*, London: Tavistock.

Dominelli, L. (1995), 'Women in the community: feminist principles and organizing in community work', *Community Development Journal*, **30**(2), April, pp.133–143.

Dowson, S. (1990), *Keeping it Safe: Self-advocacy by People with Learning Difficulties and the Professional Response*, London: Values Into Action.

Doyal, L., Hunt, G. and Mellor, J. (1981), 'Your life in their hands: migrant workers in the National Health Service', *Critical Social Policy*, **1**(2), pp.54–71.

Firestone, S. (1971), *The Dialectic of Sex*, London: Jonathan Cape.

Forman, C. (1989), *Spitalfields: A Battle for Land*, London: Hilary Shipman.

Fukuyama, F. (1989), 'The end of history?', *The National Interest*, **16**, pp.3–18.

Ginsburg, N. (1992), 'Racism and housing: concepts and reality' in Braham, P., Rattansi, A. and Skellington, R., *Racism and Antiracism: Inequalities, Opportunities and Policies*, London: Open University/Sage, pp.109–132.

Goffman, E. (1961), *Asylums*, Chicago: Aldine Publishing Company.

Habeebullah, M. and Slater, D. (1990), *Equal Access: Asian Access to Council Housing in Rochdale*, London: Community Development Foundation.

Hall, S., Critcher, C., Jefferson, T., Clarke, J. and Roberts, B. (1978), *Policing the Crisis*, London: Macmillan.

Harrison, L., Hoggett, P. and Jeffers, S. (1995), 'Race, ethnicity and community development', *Community Development Journal*, **30**(2), April, pp.144–157.

Harrison, M.L. (1995), *Housing, 'Race', Social Policy and Empowerment*, Aldershot: Avebury.

Heddell, F. (1996), 'Change it from the top', *Guardian Society*, September 25.

Henderson, J. and Karn, V. (1987), *Race, Class and State Housing*, Aldershot: Gower.

Illich, I. (1976), *Limits to Medicine – Medical Nemesis: The Expropriation of Health*, London: Marion Boyars.

Jacobs, S. (1985), 'Race, empire and the welfare state: council housing and racism', *Critical Social Policy*, **5**(1), pp.6–28.

Lewis, B. (1992), *Access for Life: A Case for Adaptable, Accessible Homes in a Barrier-free Environment*, Clay Cross: Derbyshire Coalition of People with Disabilities.

Morris, J. (1990), *Our Homes, Our Rights: Housing, Independent Living and Disabled People*, London: Shelter.

Morris, J. and Winn, M. (1990), *Housing and Social Inequality*, London: Hilary Shipman.

Mulgan, G. (1991), 'The spectre of 90s fascism: Nazi business', *Marxism Today*, November, p.5.

Office for National Statistics (1996), *Ethnicity in the 1991 Census*, London: HMSO.

Oliver, M. (1990), *The Politics of Disablement*, London: Macmillan.

Pahl, R.E. (1975), *Whose City? And Further Essays on Urban Society*, Harmondsworth: Penguin.

Phillips, D. (1986), *What Price Equality?*, London: GLC Housing Research and Policy Report No. 9.

Rex, J. and Moore, R. (1967), *Race, Community and Conflict: A Study of Sparkbrook*, Oxford: Oxford University Press.

Rowbotham, S. (1986), 'Feminism and democracy' in Held, D. and Pollitt, C. (eds), *New Forms of Democracy*, London: Sage, pp.78–109.

Sarre, P. (1986), 'Choice and constraint in ethnic minority housing – a structurationist view', *Housing Studies*, **1**(2), pp.71–86.

Segal, L. (1987), *Is the Future Female? Troubled Thoughts on Contemporary Feminism*, London: Virago.

Solomos, J. and Back, L. (1996), *Racism and Society*, Basingstoke: Macmillan.

Thomas, D. (1982), *The Experience of Handicap*, London: Methuen.

Townsend, P. (1962), *The Last Refuge: A Survey of Residential Institutions and Homes for the Aged in England and Wales*, London: Routledge and Kegan Paul.

Weir, A. and Wilson, E. (1984), 'The British Women's Movement', *New Left Review*, **148**, pp.74–103.

Williams, F. (1989), *Social Policy – A Critical Introduction*, Cambridge: Polity Press.

Williams, F. (1996), 'Racism and the discipline of social policy: a critique of welfare theory' in Taylor, D. (ed.), *Critical Social Policy: A Reader*, London: Sage, pp.48–76.

Wollstonecraft, M. (1792/1975), *A Vindication of the Rights of Women*, New York: Norton.

Woodward, R. (1991), 'Mobilizing opposition: the campaign against Housing Action Trusts in Tower Hamlets', *Housing Studies*, 6(1), pp.44–56.

12 Understanding community involvement in housing

Charlie Cooper and Murray Hawtin

This final chapter will pull together the threads of the various contributions set out in the preceding chapters to construct a framework for understanding community-involvement policies and practices in housing in a range of contexts. As contributors to this book have shown, the prospects for community involvement in housing provision are improving as we approach the next millennium. Locally, nationally and internationally there have been notable expressions of institutional support for community involvement in various social and economic development projects. In Britain, there is a growing belief in the potential of tenant participation to assist in the physical, social and economic renewal of run-down housing estates.

Linked with these developments in Britain has been a growing public concern with the traditional mechanisms of democracy and accountability, a concern that has spawned various committees and commissions – such as the Nolan Committee on standards in public life, the Local Government Commission for England (LGCE) on the structure of local government in the shires, the Commission for Local Democracy (CLD) and the Labour Party policy review on local democracy. These delegations have raised a number of general principles on which concepts of democratic accountability should be based – such as openness (Nolan Committee 1995), building on the 'identities and interests of local communities' (LGCE 1995 p.25), ensuring that 'good government' is 'democratic' rather than 'efficient' (CLD 1995 p.3), and promoting the active involvement of citizens in the design of public policy performance standards (Labour Party 1995).

Notwithstanding this resurgence of interest in public accountability, recent policy initiatives at the national level would appear to offer few proposals for innovative democratic practice. Furthermore, as Burton and Duncan demonstrate, the recommendations of the various reviews of governance in Britain have so far fallen short of making proposals that would create genuine opportunities for people to participate more fully in the regulation of those state and quasi-state institutions responsible for the decisions affecting their lives. For instance, the LGCE says little 'about the type of assistance that might help councillors perform their representative roles and responsibilities more effectively' (Burton and Duncan 1996 p.8), while:

> the Labour Party has found it as difficult as anyone to reconcile a commitment to the primacy of elected representatives who 'remain the bedrock of local democracy'... with a desire to involve a wider range of local residents in decisions which affect their lives. (Burton and Duncan 1996 p.10)

Moreover, 'New Labour' has been behind two of the most draconian measures yet pioneered to monitor and control how local residents behave on council estates – the community safety order (CSO) and probationary tenancies. The idea of CSOs, included in Labour's consultation document *A Quiet Life* (June 1995), would permit the police and local authorities to determine what constitutes anti-social behaviour and to seek a civic injunction based on evidence given by proxy. Probationary tenancies, pioneered by Labour-controlled Manchester City Council and included in the Conservatives' Housing Act 1996, allow local authorities to monitor the behaviour of new tenants and, at the end of the probationary period, decide whether or not to grant a secure tenancy. Repossession can be gained without having to prove any of the grounds normally applying to a secure tenancy and without having to rely on the discretion of a court. While neighbour nuisance is, no doubt, a problem for those having to live close to anti-social behaviour, the new system of housing management and tenant 'control' that is emerging in Britain, as suggested by Jerry Smith in Chapter 7, is not contributing to the enhancement of tenants' rights but is, instead, giving greater discretion to landlords and law enforcers. Furthermore, there appears to be a shift in the nature of the housing debate, with the provision of affordable housing becoming of less concern than controlling 'neighbours from hell'. These trends can be seen to be a reflection of:

> a highly atomized, fragmented society ... [where] people tend to experience their problems in an individuated way rather than as the product of a social system. So, for example, the underlying problem of inadequate housing is an invisible issue. But the immediate nuisance of a neighbour's pounding stereo looms large. To most people in such circumstances, new measures against neighbour nuisance seem like common sense, while the demand for decent housing for all appears far removed from reality. Neighbour nuisance has also been made to seem more important by the fragmentation of communities and the breakdown of informal channels of communication between people. There is a greater propensity to feel

unnerved by the close proximity of others, especially now that neighbours are less likely to form part of a network of acquaintances. The sound of a neighbour's television set is more likely to be disturbing if you have never met the person watching it. It will sound louder still if you think your neighbour is unapproachable and incapable of compromise. (Calcutt 1995 pp.3–4)

We would argue that the problems of urban disintegration – be they structural problems associated with economic and social inequality, or neighbourhood tensions caused by intra-community conflicts – need to be addressed through mechanisms and processes open to the direct involvement of the wider community's interests in decision-making. However, contemporary policy statements and practices, while proclaiming the advantages of community involvement, appear inconsistent and ambiguous – reflecting different and usually conflicting concepts about the aims of community participation.

Furthermore, although there is an abundance of literature on various aspects of tenant involvement and accountability, there have been few systematic attempts at bringing together the various notions about the community-development process and concepts of 'power' into a more generalizable model of understanding. There have been many 'how-to-do-it' manuals, describing the key aims, objectives and stages of the tenant-participation process, or suggesting key ingredients of successful tenant-participation practices. However, too often these focus on short-term, area-based projects, involving little more than cosmetic consultation exercises, with issues of democracy, empowerment and social justice tagged on almost apologetically. Additionally, evaluations of tenant-participation practice are usually confined to housing-management performance indicators or measurements of tenant satisfaction. The wider social, political, economic and environmental concerns of tenants and their landlords – particularly, but not exclusively, local authority landlords – are generally ignored. Limiting the scope of tenant participation in this way is arbitrary and generally unhelpful.

As Somerville and Steele (1995) have argued, making sense of tenant participation requires an analysis of the concept within its broader theoretical, social and political context. They argue that tenant-participation arrangements need to be evaluated in terms of effective involvement, representativeness and balance of power – realized through creating the right blend of external support, democratic selection and civic education. While this approach offers a valuable contribution to the debate, it remains, as we have argued in Chapter 4, too narrowly focused – being restricted to tenant-participation arrangements at the local 'micro level'.

Our model (see Figure 12.1) aims to offer a framework for developing a broader understanding of the implementation of community involvement in

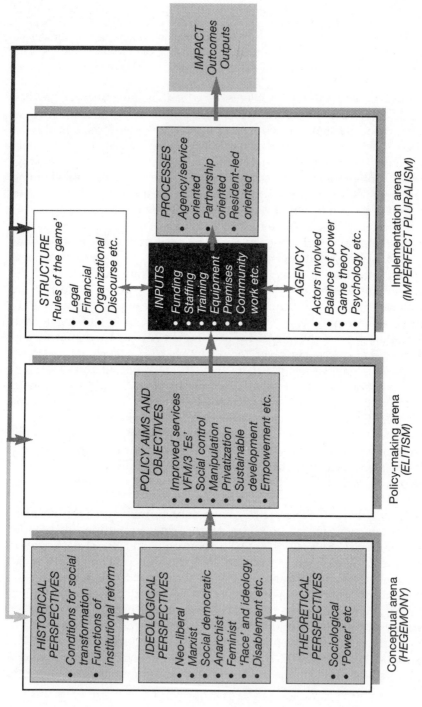

Figure 12.1 A framework for understanding tenant participation/community involvement in housing

STRUCTURE
'Rules of the game'
- Legal
- Financial
- Organizational
- Discourse etc.

PROCESSES
- Agency/service oriented
- Partnership oriented
- Resident-led oriented

INPUTS
- Funding
- Staffing
- Training
- Equipment
- Premises
- Community work etc.

AGENCY
- Actors involved
- Balance of power
- Game theory
- Psychology etc.

Implementation arena
(IMPERFECT PLURALISM)

IMPACT
Outcomes
Outputs

POLICY AIMS AND OBJECTIVES
- Improved services
- VFM/3 'Es'
- Social control
- Manipulation
- Privatization
- Sustainable development
- Empowerment etc.

Policy-making arena
(ELITISM)

HISTORICAL PERSPECTIVES
- Conditions for social transformation
- Functions of institutional reform

IDEOLOGICAL PERSPECTIVES
- Neo-liberal
- Marxist
- Social democratic
- Anarchist
- Feminist
- 'Race' and ideology
- Disablement etc.

THEORETICAL PERSPECTIVES
- Sociological
- 'Power' etc

Conceptual arena
(HEGEMONY)

housing by integrating the institutional arrangements for participation at the 'micro level' – including the effects of *inputs* (funding, training, skills development, external support, competence and so on) and *processes* (that is, 'top-down', 'bottom-up' and 'partnership' approaches) – with the wider *structures* and *policy aims and objectives* determined at the 'macro level'. The arrows in the figure indicate the direction of influence on the flows of the tenant-participation process.

We would argue that our framework offers a wider lens through which the concept of tenant participation can be more scrupulously examined. Tenant-participation research to date has been largely grounded on models that only apply to the 'implementation arena', with the focus of enquiry too narrowly defined on structures, inputs, processes and outputs. It has largely ignored the 'policy-making arena' and the 'conceptual arena'. As a consequence, it fails to offer a clear analytical understanding of the full dimensions of tenant participation.

For an understanding of tenant participation to be complete it must include a historical perspective of social development. History reveals 'some clear tendencies that suggest the operation of consistent forces' (Mayer 1994 p.25). As John Grayson has shown in Chapter 2, tenant involvement in Britain emerged out of the wider struggle over wages and rents between the capitalist class and the working class, in evidence throughout much of the social history of housing since the mid-nineteenth century, with tenants organizing within autonomous social movements. Tenants have played a significant role in the history of class struggle which, in turn, has been the driving force of social transformation. This historical understanding is important for two key reasons.

First, it illustrates 'when revolutionary transformations are possible and how they should be conducted' (Mayer 1994 p.26). Without this historical understanding tenant campaigns aimed at transforming societal processes will have little prospect of success. Today, council tenants have largely lost two of the key 'weapons' to which they once had recourse in bringing their demands to bear – the rent strike and withholding labour. The majority of council tenants are now on housing benefit, being unemployed or in non-unionized, low-waged, service-sector employment. This factor clearly limits the potential for contemporary tenant movements to instigate radical social change. However, as Grayson argues, tenants need to be aware of their history and to rediscover it.

Second, a trail through the history of capitalism depicts how social institutions adapt themselves to maintain the status quo. Power-holders will recognize the benefits of entering into new functional relationships and, as a consequence, new ways of social organizing will emerge (Cohen 1988). As Grayson has shown, the direction of tenant participation changed following the social conflicts of the late 1960s. Throughout the 1970s and 1980s tenant participation changed incrementally to become a highly professionalized practice. This shift can be seen to have been part of a wider project involving the manipulation of 'recalcitrant' communities to co-operate with government plans. In the 1990s, these plans became more closely related to the privatization of what was left of the public housing sector – through stock transfers to housing associations and local housing companies, or through housing management compulsory competitive tendering (HMCCT) – or improving service provision. As Paul Lusk and Jerry Smith have shown in Chapters 3 and 7 respectively, recent state-sponsored community-involvement strategies have been concerned with applying market solutions and the principles of 'value for money' and 'consumer choice' to such problems as physical decay, crime, neighbourhood nuisance and economic degeneration. This is not to dispute that some tenant-participation initiatives have achieved significant benefits and improvements in people's living conditions. But such improvements do not mean that the same people have gained genuine control over their lives, or that there has been a sufficient devolution of power to local communities to decide on issues affecting their future prosperity. We therefore need to understand the functional purpose of these arrangements for preserving the interests of the dominant power-holders.

How tenant participation's history is interpreted will be strongly influenced by the ideological and/or theoretical stance of the historian. Additionally, interpretations of the history of tenant participation will influence the development of ideological and theoretical thinking. In turn, the ideological position taken by the key actors involved in policy-making will strongly influence the policy aims and objectives for tenant participation. Policies will largely dictate the discourse (reflecting ideology) and the legal, financial and organizational 'structures' (namely, the 'rules of the game') in which tenant-participation activities will be discussed and subsequently implemented. Furthermore, the 'rules of the game' will largely determine the key 'actors' to be involved and the balance of power between them, as well as the availability of 'inputs' and permissible processes of involvement. While the 'rules of the game' for tenant participation are clearly crucial, the effect of 'human agency' also needs to be considered. Some individuals and groups may strive to achieve ends which are inconsistent with those sought by policy-makers.

The impact of tenant participation, measured in terms of quantitative outputs (such as value for money, the 3 'Es', housing-management performance indicators, indices of tenant satisfaction and so forth) and qualitative outcomes (in particular, who gains and who loses), will strongly affect how tenant participation is approached (indicated in Figure 12.1 by the darker shading on the feedback line). The way in which the 'actors' involved play the 'game' may change in response to the outcomes of previous games played. To a lesser extent, impact will also feed into policy evaluation, judged against the original aims and objectives, and, to an even lesser extent (indicated in Figure 12.1 by the lighter shading on the feedback line), into a reconsideration of theoretical perspectives.

The aims and objectives of tenant participation are rarely explicit or clear, largely because of the possibility of underlying conflicts between the participants. Primarily, the aims and objectives of tenant-participation policies, and the range of choices given to tenants and communities, will reflect the values held by the key power-holders in policy-making and to what extent these subscribe to the 'market', 'social democratic' or 'collective' model of provision (discussed in Chapter 4). For instance, is community involvement about promoting individual freedom and market efficiency, or is it about collective rights and social equality? Are tenants perceived as 'customers', 'consumers' or 'citizens'? And to what degree should communities be allowed to get involved? Should community involvement be representative or participatory? Is community involvement about manipulating or empowering people?

The development of tenant participation since the late 1970s largely coincided with the ascendancy of neo-liberal political economy and changing central–local relationships. Prior to this shift, local government was largely concerned with the general welfare of its citizens and community work attended to wider holistic concerns such as social inequality and poverty – as exemplified in the Community Development Project (CDP) approach (see below). Under the Conservatives and in the face of CCT and other centrally imposed reforms, the focus of local government concern was on the improvement of service provision to customers. Consequently, outputs (performance indicators) and value for money were of greater importance than notions of citizenship or outcomes measured in terms of greater social equality. Tenant-participation practice in Britain has therefore become a fragmented version of previous community-development approaches. It has become service oriented and concerned primarily with customer satisfaction and improving the housing service. Empowerment now means little more than tenants or communities having a say over *parts* of service delivery, which itself has become fragmented through privatization, while basic social relationships and inequalities remain unchallenged.

Calculating the impact of any policy will not only include an assessment of its tangible outputs (through a cost–benefit analysis of immediate and longer-term effects) but also its symbolic impact (that is, people's perceptions of and attitudes to the policy). This latter appraisal may be entirely unrelated to the tangible outputs of a policy. For example, investment in community participation in housing may not address the real problems faced by poor communities, but it may reassure society as a whole that the government does care about the poor (that is, achieve 'legitimation'). This symbolic value may be seen as equally important to decision-makers as other more discernible outcomes.

As Bo Bengtsson and David Clapham have indicated in Chapter 5, tenant involvement is not confined to the housing estate or neighbourhood, nor to the organizational levels of landlord–tenant interaction. Tenants and landlords may also be active more widely in civil society, either as members of political parties, pressure groups and/or professional associations in the political/state arena (at local and national levels), or as consumers and providers of goods and services in the market arena. Therefore, investigating tenant participation requires attention to how participants engage in different 'arenas of activity'. Our model, however, suggests three significant arenas (in contrast to Bengtsson and Clapham's four) in which the tenant participation 'game' is played: the *conceptual arena* (in which ideas about tenant involvement are formed); the *policy-making arena* (in which policy aims and objectives are negotiated); and the *implementation arena* (in which tenant-participation practices are implemented).

Running throughout the core of the three arenas is the notion of power, discussed in Chapter 4. In the conceptual arena, interpretations of history and theoretical perspectives of power will inform ideology. In turn, ideology will influence the degree to which policy aims and objectives address notions of empowerment. These notions will subsequently largely determine the balance of power operating in the implementation arena. Clearly, the conceptual arena is the dominant level at which the rules for tenant participation are sustained. It is where the 'common sense' for tenant-participation activity is formulated and refined, as defined in its broadest sense in terms of values, customs, language and ways of behaving. It is where the moral and political leadership dominating the discourse shaping the tenant-participation process is constructed. Discourse is central to an understanding of how power is exerted over tenants. As Purvis and Hunt explain:

> discourses impose frameworks which limit what can be experienced or the meaning that experience can encompass, and thereby influence what can be said and done. Each discourse allows certain things to be said and impedes or prevents other things from being said. Discourses thus provide specific and distinguishable mediums through which communicative action takes place. (Purvis and Hunt 1993 p.485)

From the conceptual level, power is diffused through the medium of language throughout the social order in a subtle, 'naturalized' way. This action is particularly apparent when we consider the discursive devices that have played such an important part in housing policy and practice in Britain (see Chapter 4). The conceptual level can therefore be characterized as the seedbed of 'hegemony'.

Negotiations within the 'policy-making arena' will be strongly influenced by key political and economic interest groupings. As Bengtsson and Clapham have shown, the representation of the British tenants' movement has been weak at the level of national policy decision-making. In contrast, within a different political arrangement, the Swedish tenants' movement achieved a stronger position in the policy-making arena. This has allowed tenants in Sweden to collectively influence the 'rules of the game' played out at the estate level. Others have demonstrated that such an arrangement has contributed to the achievement of economic, social and political efficiencies largely absent from the British experience (see Barlow and Duncan 1994). In Britain, policy discussions largely mirror the interests of élitist bodies seeking to enforce their common concerns. Tenant-participation policy-making in Britain can therefore be conceived of as 'élitist'.

At the implementation stage, tenant-participation activities are opened up to a wider range of 'actors' and interest groupings, negotiating at the level of the local state, in local 'markets', within and between organizations, on housing estates and in neighbourhoods. The implementation arena can therefore be characterized as 'pluralist' or, more accurately, 'imperfect pluralism' because of the differential access to the participation process discussed in Chapter 11.

Inputs to the implementation of tenant participation will include any available state or private sources of funding and service agency support. They will also include a range of tools and techniques, based largely on social psychology and organization/management theory (as Johnston Birchall and Charles Ritchie demonstrate in Chapters 8 and 10 respectively), and options for skills development, education and training (outlined by Benita Wishart and Rob Furbey in Chapter 9). Techniques have been designed to enable promoters and activists to conduct a systematic assessment of the motivations and attitudes within communities, thereby allowing appropriate institutional participation arrangements to be designed to suit the local context. In addition, the use of operational research systems allows local groups to, *inter alia*, identify which stakeholders should be involved in decision-making; undertake strategic analyses and make strategic choices; and design management information systems and performance controls.

There have also been recent developments in the use of new information technology (IT) as a mechanism for sharing ideas on democracy, civic politics, community empowerment and community enterprise. Two major experiments in 1995, the Labour Party Conference and the United Nations' Fourth World Conference on Women in Beijing, offered the opportunity for people to access policy discussions through the Internet. Additionally, a number of women's groups have used the Internet for networking and exchanging ideas (*Virtual Democracy* BBC2 15 November 1996). Some commentators are already referring to 'cybernets as the basis for a community . . . and . . . for civic democracy' (McBeath and Webb 1997 p.249).

One Web site established to facilitate dialogue between community organizations is 'Hive', described as a 'civic forum/community enablement on-line' allowing 'thousands of civic organizations from all sectors to feed into decision making at Westminster' ('Hive' 30 October 1996 www.gn.apc.org/hive/ p.1). Operating alongside Hive is INSINC, the National Working Party on Social Inclusion in the Information Society, established by IBM and the Community Development Foundation in 1995. Its aim is to examine the impact of new IT on local communities, and to assess the potential for a socially inclusive information society. INSINC defines a socially inclusive information society as:

> a society characterized by a high level of information intensity in the everyday life of most citizens and in most workplaces; and by the use of common or compatible technology to generate, store, manipulate and transfer information, for a wide range of personal, social, educational and business activities. A socially-inclusive information society . . . will have ready, easy-to-use public and individual access to the communication channels without heavy dependence on private or public agencies as intermediaries[;] will ensure that the kinds of information which are essential for day-to-day life, for full participation in society, and for support in times of need, are easily available at no cost or at very low cost[;] will invest heavily in the information handling and communication skills of its citizens, raising their levels of information awareness, competence in discriminating when faced with large quantities of information, and ability to exploit information. (Hive News 30 October 1996 www.gn.apc.org/hive/news.html p.2)

Investment in discrimination skills is particularly important, as techniques and information are never value free and may be used to propagate more effectively the aims of those using them – whether or not those aims are explicit. Aims may merely be to maintain the status quo where tenant-participation tools are used to channel or suppress dissension or conflict. Communities do need to be able to evaluate critically different information sources and techniques in order to exploit those inputs that best serve their needs.

Understanding community involvement also requires attention to the way in which policy aims and objectives are achieved – that is, the 'process' – which touches on issues of democracy and empowerment considered in Chapter 4 and touched on by Smith in Chapter 7. Analysing tenant participation needs to include an examination of the 'actors' involved, the relative 'power' each brings to the process and the 'structures' within which they operate. It also requires an understanding of the structural inequalities and barriers to involvement outlined in Chapter 11. Who is permitted to be involved in the process and who is excluded? Geographic areas are not socially homogeneous and are cross-cut by different interest communities. Tenant participation therefore needs to be concerned with a set of values which emphasizes equal opportunities for all sections of the community if it is to have real meaning.

The inputs, processes and structures for tenant involvement remain largely defined and set by those participants with comparatively greater power. Principally, as Stuart Lowe demonstrates in Chapter 6, the centrally constructed framework for tenant participation is highly circumscribed and prescribed in terms of scope. Most tenant-participation arrangements are ordered in hierarchical 'top-down' forums, from authority-wide committee level to estate-based groups whose constitution is narrowly defined by set criteria. Issues typically focus centrally on housing-management factors and service delivery. These approaches can be described as *agency* or *service oriented*.

At the other extreme are 'bottom-up', often spontaneous, *ad hoc* activities, involving groups of residents concerned with one or more local issues which may or may not be of principal concern to the housing authority. Again, there may be considerable external pressure placed on these groups to conform to the landlord's notion of 'suitability', exerted through funding criteria, training and/or ability to participate. A number of community-work studies in the 1970s focused on this notion of 'acceptable' groups. For instance, Cockburn's study of Lambeth showed how senior officers and councillors soon moved to withdraw the legitimacy of local community neighbourhood councils after some had become involved in open conflict with the council (Cockburn 1977). Despite this, as Lowe has suggested in this book and in his own work on urban social movements (Lowe 1986), out of these prescribed activities may emerge 'social movements' which, with community-work support, can achieve both personal and collective development through awareness raising, confidence building, effective campaigning and attempts at power transference. The case of Walterton and Elgin in London, described by Lusk in Chapter 3, where tenants campaigned to defeat the local authority's plans to privatize their homes and subsequently establish their own tenants' company, conforms to the notion of a successful social movement. These approaches can be described as *resident-led oriented*, aided by community development.

An alternative to the 'top-down' and 'bottom-up' approaches is a third framework – *the partnership approach* – such as Tenant Management Organizations (TMOs). Originally, many TMOs started as localized 'bottom-up' campaigns – such as the Belle Isle North estate discussed by Ritchie in Chapter 10 – although the crusade may often be taken on by, if not incorporated into, the landlord body through a 'partnership'. While the agenda may become tightly prescribed by the local authority (working within the constraints set by central government), as Smith has shown in Chapter 7 such partnership approaches do offer wider possibilities for achieving community influence and sustainable redevelopment – particularly with the injection of a radical community work ethos.

Figure 12.2 offers a typology of these three models for tenant participation. Our typology is similar to the institutional arrangements for tenant participation offered by Somerville and Steele – that is, marketized arrangements, tenant-controlled management and partnerships (Somerville and Steele 1995). Our point of departure is to emphasize the agency/service orientation of their 'marketized arrangements'. We also suggest that the three models are not intended to be seen as independent of each other but may, and ideally should, overlap and co-exist (as demonstrated in the figure). Applying this typology to the 'processes' box of the 'implementation arena' of our framework, it can be seen that the diagram (Figure 12.1) can be depicted three times, each substituting very different histories, ideologies, theories, policy aims and objectives, structures, inputs, actors and, especially, the impact (which also corresponds with the three spheres set out in Figure 12.2).

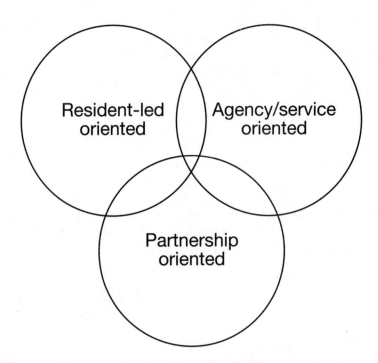

Figure 12.2 A typology of approaches to tenant participation

Most approaches to tenant participation emphasize the agency/service orientation, largely aimed at meeting the needs of the service provider rather than those of the user. There may be some overlap with the other two approaches – particularly with some claim to 'partnership' or 'community development' – but this is largely tokenistic. In contrast, although predominantly 'bottom-up' approaches can be seen to be essentially organic responses to local problems and needs, removed from a political or categorical strait-jacket, they are invariably potentially marginalized from mainstream decision-making. Consequently, it may be preferable if both 'top-down' and 'bottom-up' approaches can operate together. Tenant participation is not easy, and there is a fine line to tread between what has been described as 'in' and 'against' the state: 'in' has its inherent dangers of co-option and manipulation, while 'against' might lead to a social movement becoming marginalized and perceived as 'unreasonable' or 'unrepresentative'. Tenants therefore do need to work in partnership with state institutions and other support agencies – but they also need to keep their independence and avoid a cosy co-operative cabal. There needs to be an element of tuition on conflict which, contrary to some belief and as demonstrated from past experience by Grayson in Chapter 2, *can* be constructive.

Such radical approaches to community politics have traditionally been stronger in the USA, exemplified in the ideas and work of Saul Alinsky (1970). Alinsky ran a community-development foundation offering community-work support to assist in the development of politically active and sustainable communities:

> In order to do this the organizer needs to weld the community together in a series of campaigns which are capable of mobilizing the people on the basis of real, achievable demands directed against clearly identified enemies. For Alinsky, the specific aims of these campaigns become almost secondary. Clearly it is important to win them, but it is the mobilization itself and the new organizational structures that arise from them which matter most. If all goes well they will become self-sustaining, and the previously unorganized and marginalized will be able to make their voices heard. (Cochrane 1986 p.54)

Once community groups become self-sustaining they will be able to formulate and campaign on their own aims and objectives.

Alinsky's approach influenced some community workers involved in the CDPs set up in Britain in 1969. The CDPs adopted a *'structural conflict* model to understand the situation of inner city residents in terms of social and economic inequality' (Blackman 1995 p.162 – original emphasis). The CDPs' prescribed solution to the inner-city problem lay in the redistribution of wealth and power, achieved through the politicization of working-class communities and through broader social, political and economic restructuring. This is also the perspective of the Association of Community Workers (ACW), which sees the need to address the problems of powerlessness and inequality in the inner city through the redistribution of resources and power (Harris 1994). Merely expecting local communities to mobilize around partnerships with statutory agencies to address the problem of multiple deprivation is, by itself, insufficient. As Mayer suggests, 'How individual motivation is translated into collective outcome depends almost entirely upon the social structure within which the interaction takes place' (Mayer 1994 p.31). While this perhaps overstates the influence of social structure at the expense of 'agency', a more even distribution of the 'balance of power' within partnership approaches is surely needed for effective community involvement to happen.

The British government's reaction to the CDP analysis was to close down the projects in 1979, since which time the radical community-development approach has largely been absent from tenant-participation practice. We would argue that there is a need to reincorporate such an approach into all tenant-participation initiatives and to link the development of community politics at the neighbourhood level to the broader national political framework.

To enable communities to achieve these wider community-development objectives will require effective training and support – as highlighted by Benita Wishart and Rob Furbey, and Charles Ritchie, in Chapters 9 and 10 respectively. Here, however, we identify the ultimate paradox in that the government ostensibly sought to give more 'power' to service users at a time when it was doing all it could to reduce the power base of local authorities. Although not noted for empowering tenants in the past, local government offers at least a greater possibility of democratic and participatory control and the potential for communities to have some influence.

What is needed is a more visionary concept of tenant participation, one that includes the values of radical community action. These have been described in some detail in Chapter 1, but it might be useful to summarize here how the key principles of the community work approach could feed into future tenant-participation strategies:

- First, tenant participation needs to be founded on a more coherent understanding of the way in which societal processes structure social inequality, oppression and the related problems of powerlessness and alienation.
- Second, the aims and objectives of tenant participation need to give greater emphasis to the development of self-determination and awareness through the promotion of: equality of resources; social and political education; expertise and skills; access to information; unity

around issues of common concern; mutual respect; sustainable structures for active involvement; and the growth of alliances to influence decision-making.

● Third, in achieving these aims and objectives, tenant-participation workers should work in ways which: confront issues of belief and ideology; allow communities to identify and articulate the issues and problems for themselves; assist communities to design their own constitutions; respect all people's contributions and oppose power relationships; avoid imposing their own or their employing agencies' values or ways of working (see Harris 1994).

Confronting power relationships, as we have already suggested above, requires an understanding of how power retains its hold. We have also seen, however, that power is omnipresent, running through the entire social body as popular 'discourse', 'hegemony' or 'common sense'. This leads to the dilemma of:

> how resistance is possible given the ever more pervasive grip of disciplinary society. The problem is: if we view common sense as providing the taken-for-granted medium of lived experience, how is any alternative possible? How can we escape from the bleak scenario in which dominant discourses so construct us that resistance seems impossible? Where can resistance, 'good sense' or opposition come from? (Purvis and Hunt 1993 p.495)

But discourses can be contested. There is always the possibility of constructing an alternative 'common sense' that both undermines previously dominant discourses and unites marginalized groups into cohesive popular movements (see Chapter 4). Michel Foucault's notion of 'genealogy' as a form of resistance offers a strategic insight into how this might occur. Genealogy as resistance involves:

> using history to give voice to the marginal and submerged voices which lie 'a little beneath history' – the voices of the mad, the delinquent, the abnormal, the disempowered. It locates many discontinuous and regional struggles against power both in the past and present. These voices are the sources of resistance, the creative subjects of history. (Sawicki 1991 p.28)

Marginalized communities need to develop an understanding (and suspicion) of those disciplines and discourses which, while staking their claim to offering universal 'truths', serve to 'individualize' and oppress. In this way, disempowered groups can begin to make sense of the discursive forces that produce them and, subsequently, to distance themselves from them – thereby transforming their relationship to them. In short, people need to resist the 'identity' established by institutions interested in regulating and controlling it. Communities can adapt language to their own ends and, consequently, 'dis-identify' with the discourse (Sawicki 1991). This emancipatory project can be aided by the strategic intervention of a community-development approach based on the three key principles outlined above. The way in which community development can act as a *liberating progressive force* is addressed by Keith Popple in his attempt to construct what he calls a 'progressive community work praxis' (Popple 1994). In developing his thesis Popple draws heavily on the ideas of Antonio Gramsci and Paulo Freire.

Gramsci argued that oppressed groups do not necessarily have the conceptual tools to fully understand their 'situation', nor the means to formulate effective alternative strategies to counter hegemony. Therefore, if change is to take place, he suggested 'that "external agents" in the guise of intellectuals, organizers and leaders are required' (Popple 1994 p.29). The question is, are community workers in a position to assist subordinate groups to develop a counter-hegemony? Popple suggests that they are. Although most community workers are employed by the state, they are also in a contradictory position *vis-à-vis* the state system through encouraging communities to be self-determining. Furthermore, hegemony is never completely secure because people's 'common-sense' knowledge, formed out of everyday experiences within communities, may be in conflict with the views offered by the prevailing dominant ideology. Therefore, community workers have the potential to engage in:

> assisting in the making and remaking of the conditions necessary for radical social changes . . . We can say therefore that the work of community workers in facilitating the response of the non-élite means they have a strategic place within the changing social milieu . . . Community workers are situated in a pivotal position within the civil society for although they are employees of the state and are required to play a part in maintaining the social system, they are not necessarily in agreement with its ideology. Progressive community workers therefore have opportunities to work alongside members of communities as they articulate their contradictory understanding of the world and their situation within it. Progressive community work is also concerned with moving between the terrain of ideas and discussion and into transforming action to change people's material situation. (Popple 1994 pp.30–31)

Here we see the need for community politics in housing to engage with debates within the 'conceptual arena' of our model and thereby gain greater influence over the policy-making and implementation stages of tenant participation.

In considering how progressive community work might operate in practice, Popple draws on Freire's concept of 'conscientization'. Before communities can develop a strategy for change they must first comprehend their present situation. However:

> the nature of ideological domination means that the oppressed accept, and frequently collude with, the reproduction of a society's inequalities and the explanations and justifications offered for the status, power and privilege of their oppressors. Overcoming this false ideology means overcoming people's pessimistic and fatalistic thinking. (Popple 1994 p.32)

Freire, while acknowledging the enormity of this task, believes that educators can help oppressed communities to gain a 'critical consciousness' of their experiences and problems through reflecting on their cultural and historical reality (Freire 1976). As Popple goes on to argue:

> progressive community work is not a mediating process between the oppressed and oppressors but is a liberating force that recognises the inherent contradictions in capitalism while providing a practice that centres on developing a critical dialogue and increasing a political consciousness. (Popple 1994 p.33)

Conclusions

As we have seen from the contributions to this book, tenant participation can be viewed as a 'conflictual' model of power, represented by a 'ladder' depicting different levels of landlord–tenant interaction representing different degrees of empowerment. This model, however, fails to account for the wider social structures and discursive practices shaping the tenant-participation process, as well as the possible involvement of other actors. An alternative view emphasizes collaboration and pluralism, where it is assumed that all parties involved in tenant-participation 'partnerships' have equal access to the decision-making process. Such pluralist explanations have ignored, however, the existence of an élite who set and control the agenda, or the power of hegemony in determining the consciousness of the participants.

While community participation may be a process of climbing the ladder, it is also a question of overcoming the barriers, playing a game, collectively seeking to put pressure on decision-makers to expand the agenda, and broadening people's consciousness to enable personal and/or collective cognizance. However, as it has emerged in Britain, tenant participation remains largely confined to improving service delivery and social planning. This largely reflects the concerns of policy-makers and practitioners, who use tenant participation as a tool to maintain the status quo while the critical issue of social alienation remains unresolved. In contrast, the radical community-development ethos is about conflict and challenging existing power relationships. The radical community-work approach uses the tools of participation with this ethos in mind and seeks to build a *genuine* partnership between local people and state agencies. It adopts a holistic perspective that recognizes the need to develop long-term, localized tactics, founded on popularist issues articulated by a broader-based, skilled, politically aware, educated citizenry. Tenant-participation approaches must take on the *values* of radical community development (not just the tools) if they are successfully to tackle the root causes of social exclusion. Such approaches were not acceptable to the former Conservative administrations. But will such a form of tenant participation prosper under another regime?

References

Alinsky, S. (1970), *The Professional Radical*, New York: Harper and Row.
Barlow, J. and Duncan, S. (1994), *Success and Failure in Housing Provision: European Systems Compared*, Oxford: Pergamon.
Blackman, T. (1995), *Urban Policy in Practice*, London: Routledge.
Burton, P. and Duncan, S. (1996), 'Democracy and accountability in public bodies: new agendas in British governance', *Policy and Politics*, **24**(1), pp.5–16.
Calcutt, A. (1995), 'Neighbour watch', reproduced from *Living Marxism*, **82**, September, on www.junius.co.uk/LM/LM82/LM82_Housing.html.
Cochrane, A. (1986), 'Community politics and democracy' in Held, D. and Pollitt, C. (eds), *New Forms of Democracy*, London: Sage, pp.57–77.
Cockburn, C. (1977), *The Local State: The Management of Cities and People*, London: Pluto Press.
Cohen, G.A. (1988), *History, Labour and Freedom: Themes from Marx*, Oxford: Oxford University Press.
Commission for Local Democracy (CLD) (1995), *Taking Charge: The Rebirth of Local Democracy*, London: Municipal Journal.
Freire, P. (1976), *Education: The Practices of Freedom*, London: Writers and Readers Publishing Co-operative.
Harris, V. (ed.) (1994), *Community Work Skills Manual*, Newcastle: Association of Community Workers.
Labour Party (1995), *Renewing Democracy, Rebuilding Communities*, London: Labour Party.
Local Government Commission for England (LGCE) (1995), *Renewing Local Government in the English Shires: A Report on the 1992–95 Structural Review*, London: HMSO.
Lowe, S. (1986), *Urban Social Movements: The City After Castells*, London: Macmillan.
Mayer, T. (1994), *Analytical Marxism*, London: Sage.
McBeath, G.B. and Webb, S.A. (1997), 'Cities, subjectivity and cyberspace' in Westwood, S. and Williams, J. (eds), *Imagining Cities: Scripts, Signs, Memory*, London: Routledge, pp.249–260.
(Nolan Committee) Committee on Standards in Public Life (1995), *Standards in Public Life: First Report of the Committee*, London: HMSO.
Popple, K. (1994), 'Towards a progressive community work praxis' in Jacobs, S. and Popple, K. (eds), *Community Work in the 1990s*, Nottingham: Spokesman, 24–36.
Purvis, T. and Hunt, A. (1993), 'Discourse, ideology, discourse, ideology, discourse,

ideology . . .', *British Journal of Sociology*, **44**(3), pp.473–499.

Sawicki, J. (1991), *Disciplining Foucault: Feminism, Power, and the Body*, London: Routledge.

Somerville, P. and Steele, A. (1995), 'Making sense of tenant participation', *Netherlands Journal of Housing and the Built Environment*, **10**(3), pp.259–281.

Index